T0320532

# C++ Template Metaprogramming in Practice
## in Practice

# C++ Template Metaprogramming in Practice

# A Deep Learning Framework

By Li Wei

CRC Press
Taylor & Francis Group
Boca Raton London New York

CRC Press is an imprint of the
Taylor & Francis Group, an **informa** business

AN AUERBACH BOOK

First edition published 2020
by CRC Press
6000 Broken Sound Parkway NW, Suite 300, Boca Raton, FL 33487-2742

and by CRC Press
2 Park Square, Milton Park, Abingdon, Oxon, OX14 4RN
Published with arrangement with the original publisher, Posts & Telecom Press.

© 2021 Taylor & Francis Group, LLC
CRC Press is an imprint of Taylor & Francis Group, LLC

---

**Library of Congress Cataloging-in-Publication Data**

---

Names: Wei, Li, author.
Title: C++ template metaprogramming in practice : a deep learning framework / Li Wei.
Description: First edition. | Boca Raton, FL : CRC Press, 2021. | Includes bibliographical references and index. | Summary: "Using the implementation of a deep learning framework as an example, C++ Template Metaprogramming in Practice: A Deep Learning Framework explains the application of metaprogramming in a relatively large project and emphasizes ways to optimize systems performance. The book is suitable for developers with a basic knowledge of C++. Developers familiar with mainstream deep learning frameworks can also refer to this book to compare the differences between the deep learning framework implemented with metaprogramming and compile-time computing with deep learning frameworks using object-oriented methods. Consisting of eight chapters, the book starts with two chapters discussing basic techniques of metaprogramming and compile-time computing. The rest of the book's chapters focus on the practical application of metaprogramming in a deep learning framework. It examines rich types and t systems, expression templates, and writing complex meta-functions, as well as such topics as: Heterogeneous dictionaries and policy templates, an introduction to deep learning, type system and basic data types, operations and expression templates, basic layers composite and recurrent layers, and evaluation and its optimization. Metaprogramming can construct flexible and efficient code for C++ developers who are familiar with object-oriented programming; the main difficulty in learning and mastering C++ metaprogramming is establishing the thinking mode of functional programming. The meta-programming approach involved at compile time is functional, which means that the intermediate results of the construction cannot be changed, and the impact may be greater than expected. This book enables C++ programmers to develop a functional mindset and metaprogramming skills. The book also discusses the development cost and use cost of metaprogramming and provides workarounds for minimizing these costs"—Provided by publisher.
Identifiers: LCCN 2020024624 | ISBN 9780367609566 (hardback) | ISBN 9781003102311 (ebook)
Subjects: LCSH: C++ (Computer program language) | Neural networks (Computer science) | Software patterns.
Classification: LCC QA76.73.C153 W437 2021 | DDC 005.13/3--dc23
LC record available at https://lccn.loc.gov/2020024624

---

ISBN: 978-0-367-60956-6 (hbk)
ISBN: 978-1-003-10231-1 (ebk)

Typeset in Adobe Garamond Pro
by KnowledgeWorks Global Ltd.

# Contents

## PART II  THE DEEP LEARNING FRAMEWORK

# Preface

Please note that although the title of this book contains C++ and deep learning, it is not suitable for readers who know nothing about C++ or who want to in-depth learning from this book. This book is for programmers who have experience in C++ programming. We will take the implementation of a deep learning framework as an example, to discuss how to integrate metaprogramming technologies in a relatively large project, and provide more possibilities for runtime optimization through compile-time computation.

C++ is a widely used programming language. Most C++ developers write code in an object-oriented way—the C++ projects in our daily life are basically organized in this style; almost every C++ tutorial uses most of its space to talk about object-oriented programming; every programmer with years of experiences in C++ development will have his or her own views in object-oriented programming. Object-oriented programming has become such mainstream in C++ development that some people think C++ is just an object-oriented dialect, similar to many programming languages.

But in fact, C++ supports more than just object-oriented programming. It also supports another programming paradigm: generic programming, from which a set of programming methods are derived, namely compile-time computation and metaprogramming.

Some readers may not have heard of generics and metaprogramming, but almost every developer has been engaged with them, maybe not be aware of that. The C++ standard template library (STL) we use in daily life is a typical generic class library, which also contains metaprogramming codes, such as the algorithm selection logic based on iterator tags. In fact, we are so used to STL that it has become an indispensable part of C++ for many people. On the other hand, many programmers hardly ever use the STL-like paradigm to develop their own libraries. While writing code, the first thing we think about is usually "introducing base classes, then deriving from them…". That's the way we're familiar with, and the easiest way to think of. But is that really the most appropriate way?

Whether it is appropriate or not, different people have different views. The author of this book considers that we should first think about why we choose C++ to develop program before answer the question.

Some people use C++ because it is popular with relatively perfect standard support. Yes, that's the advantage of C++, but it's also not easy to get started and hard to master C++. TIBOE[1] shows that Java is more popular to C++. It's not hard to understand: Java is easier to learn and use than C++; Java developers hardly need to worry about problems like wild pointers, and can execute same packages across different platforms. Many problems that can be dealt with C++ can also be solved with Java or other programming languages. By contrast, the cost of learning and using C++ is much higher. So why do we insist on using C++ to develop?

---

[1] http://www.tiobe.com/index.php/content/paperinfo/tpci/index.html

One of the main reasons is that C++ is more efficient than Java and other languages, and its grammar is easier to learn and maintain than assembly language and other low-level languages. C++ programs do not support binary porting and developers need to handle pointers manually to ensure that there is no memory leak. All this effort in return is the execution speed comparable to assembly-language program. In the author's opinion, if we don't demand to run programs quickly and efficiently, it is absolutely unnecessary to choose C++.

So on the one hand, when using C++, we should take advantage of its speed and ensure that programs can run as fast as possible; on the other hand, we should keep the grammar as concise as possible, so that the developed module can be easily used. C++ programs have natural advantages in running speed. But even so, there is still something to do to make programs run faster. For example, when frequently invoking the *push_back* operation in *std::vector*, it's better to call the *reserve* interface to reserve memory in advance; when calling functions, we can use constant reference to transfer complex parameters, and so on. These techniques are well known to all. Besides, there is another technique not widely used: compile-time computing.

## Compile-time Computing and Metaprogramming

As mentioned earlier, C++ programs pursue efficiency and ease of use. So what does that have to do with compile-time computations? The author believes that, compared with pure runtime computation, proper use of compile-time computation can make better use of the information in the operation itself and improve system performance.

Let's take an example to show "information of the operation itself" and how it can be used to improve the performance of the system.

Now assume that our program needs to model the concept of "matrix." Matrix can be considered as a two-dimensional array, in which each element is a numerical value. You can specify the row and column IDs to get the value of the corresponding element.

A relatively complex system may involve different types of matrices. For example, in some cases we may need to introduce a data type to represent a matrix with "all elements zero." In another case, we may need to introduce an additional data type to represent the unit matrix, in which elements are all zero except that the elements on the principal diagonal are one.

If we adopt the object-oriented method, we can easily introduce a base class to represent the abstract matrix type, and on this basis derive some concrete matrix classes. For example:

```
1   class AbstractMatrix
2   {
3   public:
4       virtual int Value(int row, int column) = 0;
5   };
6   class Matrix      : public AbstractMatrix;
7   class ZeroMatrix : public AbstractMatrix;
8   class UnitMatrix : public AbstractMatrix;
```

The *AbstractMatrix* class defines the base class of a matrix, where the *Value* method returns the corresponding element (assuming it is an int value) when the row and column IDs are passed in. After that, we introduce several derived classes, using *Matrix* to represent general matrices and

*ZeroMatrix* to represent matrices with all elements are zero, and *UnitMatrix* to represent unit matrices.

All concrete matrix classes derived from *AbstractMatrix* must implement the *Value* method. For example, for *ZeroMatrix*, its *Value* method should return a value of 0. For *UnitMatrix*, if the row ID and column ID passed to the *Value* method are the same, it should return 1, otherwise it should return 0.

Now consider how to write a function that inputs two matrices and calculates the sum of them. Based on the classes defined earlier, the matrix addition function can be declared as follows:

```
1   Matrix Add(const AbstractMatrix * mat1, const AbstractMatrix * mat2);
```

Since each matrix implements the interface defined by *AbstractMatrix*, we can traverse the elements of the two matrices separately in this function, sum the corresponding elements, save results in the result matrix and return.

Obviously, this is a relatively general implementation, which can solve most problems, but for some special cases, its performance is poor. For example, there may be the following scenarios of performance optimization:

■ When adding a *Matrix* object with a *ZeroMatrix* object, we can simply return the *Matrix* operand as the result.
■ If a *Matrix* object is added to a *UnitMatrix* object, most elements in the result matrix are the same as those in the *Matrix* object, and the value of the element on the main diagonal is the value of the element in the corresponding position in the *Matrix* object plus 1.

In order to increase the computing efficiency in such special cases, we can introduce dynamic cast in *Add* and try to obtain the actual data types corresponding to the parameters.

```
1   Matrix Add(const AbstractMatrix * mat1, const AbstractMatrix * mat2)
2   {
3       if (auto ptr = dynamic_cast <const ZeroMatrix *>(mat1))
4           // take corresponding treatment
5       else if (...)
6           // other cases
7   }
```

There are two problems in the above design: firstly, a large number of if branches will make the function complex and difficult to maintain. Secondly, when calling *Add*, the expression inside if needs to be judged. This is a runtime behavior involving runtime computing. Introducing too many judgments may even slow down the running speed of the function.

There is a classic solution to this kind of problem: function overloading. For example, we can introduce the following functions:

```
1   Matrix Add(const AbstractMatrix * mat1, const AbstractMatrix * mat2);
2   Matrix Add(const ZeroMatrix * mat1, const AbstractMatrix * mat2);
3   ...
```

```
4   ZeroMatrix m1;
5   Matrix m2;
6   Add(&m1, &m2);  // calling the second optimization algorithm
```

The first version corresponds to the general case, while the other versions provide optimization for some special cases.

This approach is so common that we may not realize that we are already using compile-time computations. In fact, this is a typical compile-time computation. The compiler needs to select the appropriate function to match the user's call and the selection process itself is a computational process. In this compile-time computation process, we use the information that "the matrix type involved in addition calculation is a *ZeroMatrix*," and therefore improves the system's performance.

Function overloading is a very simple compile-time computation. Although it can solve some problems, its use scenarios are relatively narrow. What this book will discuss is more complex compile-time computation methods: we will use templates to construct several components, which explicitly contain the logic that needs to be processed by the compiler. The compiler uses the values (or types) derived from these templates to optimize the system. These templates for compile-time computation are called metafunctions, and the corresponding computation methods are called metaprogramming or C++ template metaprogramming.

## Metaprogramming and Large-scale System Design

Metaprogramming is not a new concept. In fact, as early as 1994, Erwin Unruh showed a program that can use compile-time computations to output prime numbers. However, due to various reasons, the research on C++ template metaprogramming has been in a state of tepidity. Although several metaprogramming libraries (such as Boost::MPL, Boost::Hana, etc.) had been developed, there are relatively few cases of applying these libraries to solve practical problems. Even if occasionally used, these metaprogramming libraries and technologies are often in an auxiliary position, assisting object-oriented methods to construct programs.

With the development of C++ standard, we are pleased to find that a large number of grammars and tools have been introduced into the new standard, which makes metaprogramming easier. This also makes it possible for us to use metaprogramming to construct relatively complex programs.

This book will construct a relatively complex system: a framework for deep learning. Metaprogramming is no longer a subsidiary role, but the leading role of the whole system. Previously, we mentioned that one of the advantages of metaprogramming and compile-time computing is to make better use of the information of the operation itself to improve system's performance. Here is an overview of how this can be achieved in large-scale systems.

A large-scale system often contains a number of concepts and each concept may correspond to a variety of implementations with their own advantages. With metaprogramming, we can organize different implementations corresponding to a same **concept** into loose structures. Furthermore, concepts can be classified with tag, so as to maintain existing concepts, introduce new concepts, or introduce new implementations of existing concepts.

Concepts can be combined. A typical example is that the addition of two matrices will construct a new matrix. We will discuss a very useful technique in metaprogramming: expression templates. It is used to combine existing types and form new ones. The new type will retain all the information in the original type(s) and can be optimized at compile time.

Metaprogramming computations are performed at compile time. With deeper use of metaprogramming technology, one of the following problems is the interaction between compile time and runtime. Generally speaking, in order to achieve a balance between efficiency and maintainability, we must consider which computations can be completed at compile time, which are best placed at runtime, and how to transition between them. In the implementation of the Deep Learning Framework, we will see a large number of examples of compile-time and runtime interactions.

Compile-time computation is not a purpose, but a means. We hope to improve runtime performance through compile-time computations. In the last chapter of this book, we will see how to optimize the performance of the deep learning framework based on existing compile-time computations.

## Target Readers and Reading Suggestions

This book will leverage compile-time computing and metaprogramming to build a deep learning framework. Deep learning is a hot-spot field of current researches. With Artificial Neural Network (ANN) as the core, it includes a large number of technical and academic achievements. We mainly use it here to discuss the methods of programming and compile-time computing, not to make a large and comprehensive toolkit. However, the deep learning framework we construct is extensible, and through further development, we can fully realize most functions that the mainstream deep learning frameworks can achieve.

Even if the above limitations are introduced into the scope of the discussion, the book, after all, covers both metaprogramming and deep learning. Without background knowledge, it is difficult to complete the discussion. Therefore, we assume readers to have a certain understanding of advanced mathematics, linear algebra, and C++, specifically including the following:

- Readers need to have a certain understanding of C++ object-oriented development technology and templates. This book is not a C++ 101 book. If readers want to acquire introductory knowledge and related contents of the new standard of C++, they can refer to relevant introductory books.
- Readers need to understand basic concepts of linear algebra, such as matrix, vector, matrix multiplication, and so on. Many operations of ANN can be abstracted into matrix operations, so basic knowledge of linear algebra is indispensable.
- Readers need to have a basic understanding of concepts of calculus and derivatives. Gradient is a basic concept in calculus, which plays a very important role in the training process of deep learning modules. A large part of the operation of deep learning is calculation and propagation of gradients. Although this book will not mention advanced knowledge in calculus, readers are required to understand at least some basic concepts such as partial derivatives.

## Usage Cost of Metaprogramming

Metaprogramming can construct flexible and efficient code, but it also has its corresponding costs. This book will focus on metaprogramming. But before that, it is necessary to clarify the cost of metaprogramming, so as to let readers have a more comprehensive understanding of this technology.

The cost of metaprogramming mainly consists of two aspects: development cost and use cost.

## Development Cost

Essentially, the development cost of metaprogramming does not come from the technology itself, but from the cost of programmers changing their coding habits. Although this book is about a programming technology in C++, the technology is quite different from object-oriented C++ development methods. In a sense, metaprogramming is more like a new language seamlessly connected with object-oriented C++. Even a C++ master still takes some effort to master and use it well.

For C++ developers familiar with object-oriented programming, the main difficulty in learning and mastering this new programming method is to establish the mode of thinking in functional programming. The metaprogramming approach at compile time is functional, which means that the intermediate results of the construction cannot be changed and the impact may be greater than expected. This book will help readers gradually establish such a mode of thinking through a large number of examples. We believe that after reading this book, readers will have a relatively in-depth understanding of it.

The second problem with metaprogramming is the difficulty of debugging. The reason is simple: most C++ programmers focus on runtime programming and most tools are optimized for runtime debugging. Accordingly, compilers perform much worse in outputting debugging information for metaprograms. In some cases, the error information of metaprogram output by compilers is more like a short article, and it is difficult to locate problems at a glance. There is no particularly good solution to this problem. Do more experiments and look at output information of compilers and you'll soon find the hang of it.

The last problem is that there are fewer metaprogramming developers than object-oriented C++ developers. That makes it difficult to use metaprogramming when many developers collaborate: if others can't understand your codes, the cost of learning and maintenance will be higher. The author often encounters such problems in work, which in fact indirectly led to the publication of this book. If you want to convince your collaborators to use metaprogramming in developing C++ programs, you can recommend this book: this can also be a small advertisement.

## Usage Cost

The development cost of metaprogramming is mainly subjective, which can be reduced by improving programmers' skills; but in contrast, the usage cost of metaprogramming is mainly objective and more difficult to deal with.

Usually, if we want to develop a package and deliver it to others, the package often contains header files and compiled static or dynamic libraries, where the main logic of the program is located. It has two advantages. First, the package provider won't worry about leaking the main logic in the static or dynamic library. Users cannot see the source code. To obtain the main logic in the library, one needs to use means like reverse engineering, which costs relatively high. Secondly, users of packages can compile and link their own programs faster: since the static or dynamic libraries in packages are already compiled. When we use them, we only need to link them, unnecessary to compile them again.

But if we develop a meta-library and deliver it to others, those two benefits are usually not available. Metaprogram logic is often implemented by templates. Currently, the compilation mode supported by mainstream compilers is to put templates in header files. It leads that the main logic of metaprograms is in header files, which will be provided to users with release of packages. The cost for users to understand and copy the corresponding logic is therefore greatly reduced.

Secondly, the program calling metafunctions needs to compile the corresponding logic in the header file in each compilation process, which will prolong time of compilation.[2]

If we can't afford the described costs introduced by metaprogramming, we need to consider compromise solutions. A typical way is logic splitting, which is: formalizing what consumes much compile time and those we want to keep secret into static or dynamic libraries; organizing what takes a short time to compile and can be shown to end-users into metafunctions and providing them in the form of header files, so as to ensure to take advantages of metaprogram. The way of division depends on specific circumstances of projects.

## Contents of This Book

The book consists of two parts. The first part (Chapters 1 and 2) discusses the basic techniques commonly used in metaprogramming; these techniques will be used in the second part (Chapters 3-8) to construct a deep learning framework.

- **Chapter 1: Basic Tips**. This chapter discusses basic concepts of metafunctions and the possibility of using templates as containers. Based on this, we'll also discuss the basic writing rules of sequences, branches, and looping code. Those methods constitute the core of the whole metaprogramming system. After that, we will discuss some classic techniques, including the Curiously Recurring Template Pattern (CRTP), which will be used later.

- **Chapter 2: Heterogeneous Dictionaries and Policy Templates**. This chapter will use the knowledge of Chapter 1 to construct two components. The first component is a container that holds different types of data objects. The second component maintains a policy system. Both components will be used in the subsequent development of the deep learning framework. Although this chapter has focused on the application of technologies introduced in Chapter 1, the author still classifies it as the basic technology of metaprogramming. It is because these two components are relatively basic and can be applied to other projects as components. These two components do not involve deep learning, but we will use them as auxiliary components when we develop the deep learning framework in the future.

- **Chapter 3: A Brief Introduction of Deep Learning.** Beginning with this chapter, we will construct a deep learning framework. This chapter outlines the background knowledge of the deep learning framework. Readers who have not been exposed to deep learning before can have a general understanding of the field from this chapter, so as to clarify main functions of the framework we want to develop.

- **Chapter 4: Type System and Basic Data Types**. This chapter discusses the data involved in the deep learning framework. To maximize the advantage of compile-time computing, the deep learning framework is designed as a framework with rich data types: it supports many specific data types. As the number of supported types increases, how to organize these types effectively becomes an important issue. This chapter discusses the tag-based type organization, which is a common method of classification in metaprogramming.

- **Chapter 5: Operations and Expression Templates**. This chapter discusses the design of operators in the deep learning framework. Artificial neural networks involve many operators, including matrix multiplication, matrix addition, element-wise logs, and more complex

---

[2] It should be noted that there are ways to avoid putting implementation code of template classes in the header file. However, those methods are quite limited, so this book will not discuss them.

operations. In order to optimize a large number of computations involved in the system as a whole, an expression template is used here to represent the results. This chapter discusses the implementation details of expression templates.

- **Chapter 6: Basic Layers**. On the basis of operators, we introduce the concept of layer. A layer associates related operators in the deep learning framework and provides forward and backward propagation interfaces for users. This chapter discusses the basic layers and describes how to simplify the interface and design of them with the heterogeneous dictionary and policy template constructed in Chapter 2.

- **Chapter 7: Composite and Recurrent Layers.** Based on Chapter 6, we can construct various layers and use them to build artificial neural networks. But there is a problem with this approach: the layers in artificial neural networks are ever-changing. If we write code by hand for every layer that has not appeared before, then the workload will be relatively large, which is not what we want to see. In this chapter, we will construct a special layer: composite layer, which is used to combine other layers to produce new layers. One complex part of the composite layer is automatic gradient calculation, which is an important concept in the training process of artificial neural network. If automatic gradient calculation cannot be realized, the significance of the composite layer will be greatly reduced. This chapter discusses an implementation of automatic gradient computation, which will be the most complex metafunction implemented in this book. Based on that, this chapter also gives a typical implementation of the recurrent layer based on the composite layer.

- **Chapter 8: Evaluation and Its Optimization**. Deep learning system is computationally intensive, both for training and prediction. There are many ways to speed up the calculation. Typically, batch computing can be used to process multiple sets of data at the same time to maximize the processing power of the computer. On the other hand, we can simplify and merge multiple computational processes mathematically so as to improve the computational speed. This chapter discusses those related topics.

## Source Code and Compiling Environments

This book is a practical book in metaprogramming, and many theories are illustrated by examples. Inevitably, it involves a lot of code. The author tries to avoid listing a lot of code in the book (which is equivalent to wasting the reader's time and money), so that only the core code and logic that need to be discussed are quoted in the book. The complete code is given in the source code attached with this book.

Readers can download the source code in this book at https://github.com/liwei-cpp/MetaNN/tree/book. The source code contains two folders: MetaNN and Test. The former includes all the logic in the deep learning framework, while the latter is a test program to verify the correctness of the framework logic. The contents discussed in this book can be found in the MetaNN folder. When reading this book, it is important to have a reference source code at hand so that it can be consulted at any time. This book devotes much space to elaborating relevant designing ideas and lists only core codes. Therefore, the author strongly recommends reading the book with referring to the source code, so as to have a deeper understanding of what is discussed in the book.

For most technical points implemented in MetaNN, the Test folder includes corresponding test cases. Therefore, readers can read the test cases after understanding implementation details of a technical point in order to further grasp the use of the corresponding technology.

The contents of the MetaNN folder are all header files, while the Test folder contains some CPP files that can be compiled into an executable program. However, the C++ metaprogramming discussed in this book is relatively uncommon and some techniques in it adopt the new C++ 17 standard. Therefore, not all mainstream compilers can compile files in the Test folder. The experimental environments in which the author tried to compile and succeed are listed below.

### Requirements of Hardware and Operating System

In order to compile the program in the Test folder, you need a 64-bit computer, which is recommended to contain at least 4GBytes of memory. Meanwhile, a 64-bit operating system needs to run on the computer. The author has compiled the Test code on Windows and Ubuntu.

### Compiling the Test Programs with Ubuntu and GCC

GCC is a common compiler component on Linux. The author's first compilation environment is based on Ubuntu 17.10 and GCC. We use the g++ compiler in GCC to compile the test program.

- First, make sure that GCC 7.1 or later is installed on the system, along with **make**, **git** commands.[3] We can use **g++ –version** in a terminal to check whether the compiler meets the requirements.
- Download the source code of this book.
- Open a terminal.
- Execute **cd MetaNN/Test** to enter the directory where the code resides.
- Execute **make -f Makefile.GCC** to compile the code. If the compiler's version is too low, the system will give a warning message. A compiler with a low version may cause compilation failure.
- After compiling, a **bin** directory has been created; containing an executable file **Test**. Run this file and it will show the execution results of each test case.

### Compiling the Test Programs with Ubuntu and Clang

In addition to GCC, Clang is another common compiler in Linux. Based on Ubuntu and Clang, the **Test** program in source code can also be compiled.

Many Linux distributions come with Clang compilers. However, the versions of these compilers may be relatively low and may not fully support the C++ 17 standard. It requires installing a higher version of the Clang compiler. The author installed Clang 6.0. This book will not discuss how to install the compiler. Readers can search for installation methods on the Internet.

- First, make sure that Clang 6.0 or a later version is installed on the system, along with make, git commands. We can use clang++ **–version** in a terminal to check whether the compiler meets the requirements.
- Download the source code of this book.
- Open a terminal.
- Execute **cd MetaNN/Test** to enter the directory where the code resides.

---

[3] Readers can search the Internet for the installation methods of these tools.

- Execute **make -f Makefile.clang** to compile the code. If the compiler's version is too low, the system will give a warning message. A compiler with a low version may cause compilation failure.
- After compiling, a **bin** directory has been created; containing an executable file **Test**. Run this file and it will show the execution results of each test case.

### *Compiling the Test Programs with Windows and MinGW-w64*

Many readers are using the Windows operating system. Here's a brief introduction to how to compile the source code of the book in Windows.

The most common compiler in Windows is Microsoft Visual Studio. But when the author tried to compile the test program with its VC++ compiler, the system prompted "compiler is out of space." This means that the memory required to compile the test code exceeds the upper limit of the VC++ compiler. Therefore, here we introduce the use of MinGW-w64 as a compiler to compile test programs in Windows[4]:

- Download and install the latest MinGW-w64 on SourceForge's official website. During installation, the Architecture should be chosen as x86_64.
- Find the subdirectory contains g++ and mingw32-make in the installation directory of MinGW-w64 and add it to the system environment variables. Make sure you can run these two commands directly on the console.
- Download the source code of this book.
- Open a Windows console.
- Execute **cd MetaNN/Test** to enter the directory where the code resides.
- Execute **make -f Makefile.MinGW** to compile the code.
- After compiling, a **bin** directory has been created; containing an executable file **Test**. Run this file and it will show the execution status of each test case.

## Code Format of the Book

The author avoids listing a lot of non-core codes when discussing technical details. At the same time, for the sake of discussion, a line number is usually included in front of each line of a code segment: in subsequent analysis of the code segment, sometimes line numbers are used to refer to specific lines and illustrate the functions that the line implements.

The line number is only for the convenience of subsequent code analysis and does not indicate the location of the code segment in the source code file. A typical case is that when the core code segment to be analyzed is relatively long, the display and analysis of the code segment are alternating. At this point, each segment is counted from line number 1, even if there is a relationship between the current segment and the previous segment. If readers want to read the complete code and make clear the relationship of the code segments, please refer to the source code attached to the book.

---

[4] When the book's Chinese edition was released, the latest Visual Studio compiler was the 2017 version, which seems not to support compiling this code. However, based on feedback from a reader (Dafei Zhao), this code can be compiled in Visual Studio 2019 Preview. In order to ensure consistency with the Chinese edition, we will not discuss compiling the code with Visual Studio 2019 here.

## About the Exercises

Except Chapter 3, each chapter gives a number of exercises at the end to help readers consolidate the knowledge in each chapter. These questions are not simple and some have no standard answers. Therefore, if readers encounter difficulties in some practices, please do not lose your heart. You can choose to skip them and continue to read the following chapters. Having mastered some of the techniques described in this book, we may be able to solve the previous exercises when reviewing them. Note again, some questions are open-ended and have no standard answers. Don't be discouraged if you can't give an answer or if your answer is different from others'.

## Feedback

Because the author's level is limited and metaprogramming is a complex and challenging field, this book will inevitably have shortcomings. Readers are kindly requested to make corrections. The email address of the author is liwei.cpp@gmail.com. Please use this email address to report any issues pertaining to this book.

MATAB® is a registered trademark of The Math Works, Inc. For product information, please contact:
The Math Works, Inc.
3 Apple Hill Drive
Natick, MA 01760-2098
Tel: 508-647-7000
Fax: 508-647-7001
E-mail: info@mathworks.com
Web: http://www.mathworks.com

# Acknowledgment

First of all, I would like to thank my family for their "indulgence" and support. I have the habit of reading and programming every day, but my family did not know that I was writing books and knew little about my field of study. However, they still gave me the greatest support. As the father of two children, I don't have much time to accompany them. It's my family members that have shared my obligations so that I could have time to do what I wanted to do. Here, I would like to thank you from the bottom of my heart.

Secondly, I would like to thank my former colleagues in Baidu's Natural Language Processing Department, for their encouragement and support when I had a plan to write a book and hesitated for fear that I could not do it well. Special thanks to Zhang Jun, who carefully read many chapters of the book, put forward pertinent amendments, and contributed some of the contents of Chapter 3 of this book. I had hoped to add his name to the author's column of the book, but was dismissed, so I had to thank him here.

Thirdly, I must offer my thanks to Chen Zihan, Liu Weipeng, Gao Bo, and Rong Yao. As experts in the field of C++, they spent their precious time in reviewing the book, putting forward pertinent opinions and suggestions, and writing recommendations for this book. Dr. Rong Yao also gave me his treasured books, which did not only affirm what I have done, but also strengthened my confidence to continue researches.

Finally, I would like to thank the editors of People's Posts and Telecommunications Publishing House, especially Mr. Fu Daokun. In the process of editing the complete book, Mr. Fu devoted a lot of efforts to make the whole publishing process go smoothly. It can be said that without the hard work of him and his colleagues, this book would not have come out. Thank you for their great support!

## Recommendation I

In the middle of the night, I suddenly received a WeChat message from Mr. Chen Jikang. He hopes that I can write a recommendation for the book C++ *Template Metaprogramming Practice*. I have a keen interest in C++ template metaprogramming, but have known just a little about deep learning and have never learned it systematically, so I want to take this chance to broaden my horizons and have accepted Mr. Chen's invitation gladly. Then there is the following text.

Learning programming is a long-term process. If you want to improve yourself quickly, you need to get out of your "comfort zone." Only by constantly finding a lot of difficult tasks (but not too difficult to solve) and taking time to achieve them one by one can your programming skills be improved most quickly. The module of the "deep learning framework" created in this book is perfect for readers to try to develop and implement by themselves. Although the book will provide source code, I advise readers not to look at the source code first, but to follow the book and implement MetaNN by yourself. Look up the author's code after your own success or giving up; I believe readers will have a deeper understanding of it.

In the process of reading this book, I spent most of my time in the first two chapters. These two chapters introduce the skills of C++ template metaprogramming, and the author writes very well. Chapter 1 begins with an introduction to how readers should understand template metaprogramming. I think when I was reading the book *C++ Template Metaprogramming*, I went through many detours—because its explanation was not easy to understand, coupled with the lack of experience at that time, it was through learning *Haskell* language that I finally understood C++ template metaprogramming thoroughly. If I had read the first chapter of this book, I believe it would save a lot of time.

Starting from Chapter 2, the author has already arranged "big assignments." Starting from Chapter 4, this book formally introduces the process of using C++ template metaprogramming techniques to implement MetaNN, a simple framework for deep learning. If the reader does not understand the first two chapters well, it will be very difficult to start with Chapter 4. Of course, this is not a bad thing; at least this can illustrate two points: their own technical level is indeed inadequate; the book does have real material, you can learn a lot from it.

I should figure it out that the technical difficulty of this book is quite great. Readers should have a certain knowledge of C++ templates, and also need to understand some basic contents of C++ 11 and C++ 14, so as not to constantly query relevant information and interrupt their thinking while reading this book. However, even if you have learned template metaprogramming, you need to think hard when reading and practicing the content of the book, so as to improve your programming skills.

Finally, I would like to say that the code in this book is quite well written. Perhaps the author has taken a lot of best practices of C++ as his own instincts in the long-term coding work, so he has not spent a lot of ink to fully introduce the details of all aspects of the code. As you read the book, you can try to think about why the author wrote it this way (rather than in other ways), and what the codes in the book have in common with the best practices described in other C++ books. It is also a process of learning.

Learning without thought is bewildered, thought without learning is slack. I wish you all a pleasant and rewarding reading.

**Chen Zihan (vczh)**

# Recommendation II

Template Metaprogramming (TMP) has always been regarded as a terrible area in C++ programming by most people. Type design is a kind of work that needs a lot of experience. One important reason why C++ language is powerful is that it has strong typed characteristics. With this feature, developers can implement a wide variety of static checks at compile time, so that many potential software defects can be exposed as soon as possible, preventing them from reaching link time or even running time. Conversely, any flaw in type design will bring the original sin to all objects of the type, even all objects of the derived types. Moreover, once the software is online and distributed to users, it is not easy to modify. Therefore, type design, especially basic type design in large-scale software, has become a challenge for engineers. Template metaprogramming, on the basis of this, goes a step further. It can be said that: for engineers responsible for type design, their products are the **objects** and their operation; then, for engineers responsible for template metaprogramming, their products are the **types** and their operation, that is, the upstream of the former. For the vast majority of C++ developers, it is not easy to use objects with ease. Therefore, one can imagine the difficulty of designing types, being free to produce and tailor types as needed, and providing this ability as a service for other engineers to use. So, although there are plenty of books about C++ language, there are few explaining template metaprogramming. Even books on this subject are so basic, which inevitably causes the reader to question: template metaprogramming is really great, but what does it have to do with my daily work? Shouldn't this be a toy for experts on the C++ Standards Committee who have sparse hair?

So the last word of the title of this book, *C++ Template Metaprogramming Practice*, has caught my eyes immediately. Template metaprogramming, deep learning framework, and Practice, these key words all have a fatal appeal.

As a senior C++ enthusiast, I can clearly feel the quality and weight of this book. Starting with the first line of code, this book adopts the modern C++ standard. It can be said that the author is a new generation engineer who learns and masters C++ directly from modern C++ and seldom comes from the stale atmosphere of "C++ Ancient Age." Many grammatical problems that are still entangled in C++ community are not problems at all in this book—C++ is modern C++. Of course, constexpr should be used, of course; Of course, you should use auto; and of course, you should use alias declarations.

With a clear and detailed style, this book focuses on demonstrating the necessary skills of template metaprogramming in modern C++. Modern C++ provides engineers with many necessary tools to enable template metaprogramming to express generation type algorithms in a more direct and clear way. The first chapter of this book provides guidelines on how to use these tools efficiently. But the book is far from being there, because the focus of the book is on the word "Practice."

By constructing a fully functional and powerful deep learning framework, MetaNN, the author shows how template metaprogramming can design specific data and operations involved in deep learning on the type level. The design is hierarchically progressive: first, basic customizable data structure templates and strategies are introduced; then algorithm templates based on these data templates are designed; at last, according to the template-based data and algorithm, the business logic of deep learning is constructed. Although this part of the content is large, it is not tiring to read, because each knowledge point of the explanation is the response and deepening of the language points that have already been systematically explained. It is very valuable that these contents give readers the information that template metaprogramming is really useful in practice and irreplaceable. Each chapter of the book is followed by a number of exercises to inspire readers to think further. Some exercises will enable readers to consider how to further utilize the high-level usage of template metaprogramming from many aspects, expand the deep learning business from other dimensions; and some exercises will remind readers that certain language characteristics can be applied in other industries.

Nowadays, both modern C++ and deep learning are fairly popular. It is a kind of happiness for readers to have such an excellent work written by a real frontline expert. The book does not require much of readers' pre-knowledge, because it is sufficiently detailed. As long as there is a willingness to learn, you will be able to master both modern C++ and deep learning, which can bring you tremendous technological advantages.

I would like to solemnly recommend this book "C++ Template Metaprogramming Practice" to you!

Gao Bo, translator of "C++ Gotchas: Avoiding Common Problems in Coding and Design" and Chinese Edition of "Effective Modern C++"

**Tanjong Pagar**

# Recommendation III

The essence of C++ template metaprogramming is compile-time calculation. The discovery of this programming paradigm is an accident, and its programming style is very strange to ordinary C++ programmers. Programmers accustomed to runtime programming thinking are difficult to understand and adapt to this programming paradigm—template metaprogramming code is like a sealed book written in a language other than C++.

The relationship between C++ template metaprogramming and template programming is a bit like the relationship between deep learning and machine learning. The former is a subdomain of the latter. Difference is that C++ template metaprogramming is much rarer than deep learning, especially in the field of template metaprogramming, for the domestic C++ community, it is quite a rare field.

So far, there are three books that are seriously involved in the field of template metaprogramming, namely, "C++ Template Metaprogramming," "C++ Templates," and "Generative Programming," all of which are written by foreign C++ experts. Therefore, "C++ Template Metaprogramming Practice" written by Mr. Li Wei is the first book in China about template metaprogramming. This is valuable even in the entire C++ community.

The book contains two topics that are very attractive. For me personally, template metaprogramming has long been a point of interest, while deep learning is part of my professional curriculum. I'm honored to be one of the first readers of this book. I've benefited greatly from reading this book.

The author first reimplements some basic metaprogramming techniques using the new language features after C++ 11, and then introduces MetaNN, a scalable deep learning framework based on template metaprogramming techniques. The overall structure of this book is simple and reasonable with in-depth and clear discussion, which is not only due to the author's educational background and research and development experience, but also his enthusiasm for template programming and template metaprogramming technology beyond ordinary people, as well as strong abilities of logical thinking.

This book is bound to be a must-read for C++ enthusiasts. It can also let other C++ programmers understand that, in addition to the familiar C++ programming, there is a parallel world of C++ template metaprogramming and the practices in that field are more exciting.

Have a nice read!

**Dr. Rong Yao**

# Recommendation IV

As Artificial Intelligence emerges from being a buzzword to an "underlying technology" that quietly drives society behind the scenes; the industry is paying more attention to the performance of AI infrastructures. It's really easy to understand—when the development of a technology moves from the exploration phase to large-scale applications, costs, and benefits will become significant. How to train and use modules more efficiently is aimed at more efficient and perfect use of computing resources. Today, C++ is still one of the most mainstream languages that can combine high-level abstraction and ultimate performance, while metaprogramming is recognized as a technology important for custom-type systems and the field in which compile time is in exchange for running time. As a first-line senior engineer at Microsoft, Li Wei combines metaprogramming with deep learning. His dedication to improving performance is worth attention.

**Liu Weipeng, author of Dark Time,**
*Microsoft Senior Engineer*

# INTRODUCTION

1

# Chapter 1

# Basic Tips

This chapter discusses the basic methods involved in metaprogramming and compile-time computing. We'll start with metafunctions and introduce the similarities and differences of functions used at compile time and runtime through some simple examples. We'll also discuss the basic writing rules of sequences, branches, and looping codes. Finally, we'll introduce a classic technique—the Curiously Recurring Template Pattern (CRTP).

The aforementioned content can be regarded as the basic metaprogramming technologies. Subsequent chapters of this book will also be considered as applications of these technologies. Mastering the techniques, as discussed in this chapter, is a prerequisite for skilled use of C++ template metaprogramming and compile-time calculation.

## 1.1 Metafunction and *type_traits*

### 1.1.1 Introduction to Metafunctions

C++ metaprogramming is typically functional programming in which functions have a pivotal figure in the entire programming system. The functions here are different from those defined and used in general C++ programs and are closer to functions in the mathematical sense—mapping or transformation without side effects: with the same input, the results remain the same no matter how many times the function is called.

If there are side effects in a function, it is usually caused by the presence of certain variables that maintain the state of the system. Each time a function is called, even if the input is the same, the difference in the state of the system will lead the output to be different; such a function is called a function with side effects. Metafunctions are called and executed at compile time. During the compilation phase, the compiler can only construct constants as intermediate results, unable to construct and maintain variables that can record the state of the system and change it hereafter, so functions (which are metafunctions) used at compile time can only be functions without side effects.

The following code snippet defines a function that meets the limitations of no side effects and can be used as a metafunction.

```
1  constexpr int fun(int a) { return a + 1; }
```

*constexpr* is a keyword in C++ 11, indicating that the function can be called at compile time and is a metafunction. If this keyword is removed, the function *fun* will only be used at runtime. Although it has no side effects, it cannot be called at compile time.

Consider the following procedure as a counter-example:

```
1    static int call_count = 3;
2    constexpr int fun2(int a)
3    {
4        return a + (call_count++);
5    }
```

This code snippet cannot be compiled—it is wrong. The reason is that the function loses the "no side effects" property—the same input produces different outputs, while the keyword "*constexpr*" attempts to maintain the function's "no side effects" property, which leads to conflict. Compiling it will result in a corresponding compilation error. If the keyword *constexpr* declared in the function is removed, the program can be compiled. But *fun2* cannot be called at compile time because it is no longer a metafunction.

Hopefully, the previous example gives a basic impression of metafunctions. In C++, we use the keyword *constexpr* to represent numeric metafunctions, which is a kind of metafunction involved in C++, but far from all. In fact, type metafunctions are more common in C++, which are metafunctions using types as input and/or output.

### 1.1.2 Type Metafunction

From a mathematical point of view, functions can usually be written in the following form:

$$y = f(x)$$

The three symbols represent input (*x*), output (*y*), and mapping (*f*), respectively.[1] Generally speaking, the input and output of a function are numeric values. But we don't have to limit it; in probability theory, for example, there is a function map from event to probability value, where the corresponding input is the description of an event, not necessarily expressed as a numeric value.

Back to the discussion of metaprogramming, the core of metaprogramming is metafunctions. The input and output of metafunctions can also be of various forms: numeric value is just one kind of them. The metafunction in which the input and output are numeric values is the numeric metafunction mentioned in the previous section. Data types in C++ can also be the input and output of functions. Consider the following scenario: we want to map an integer type to the appropriate unsigned type. For example, when type *int* is the input, the mapping result is *unsigned int*; when *unsigned long* is the input, we want the result of the mapping to be the same as the input. This mapping can also be considered as a function, except that the input of the function is a type like *int*, *unsigned long*, etc., and the output is another type.

---

[1] Functions in C++ can be considered an extension of the above definition, allowing input or output to be empty.

The following code snippet can implement the metafunction as described earlier:

```
1   template <typename T>
2   struct Fun_{ using type = T; };
3
4   template <>
5   struct Fun_<int> { using type = unsigned int; };
6
7   template <>
8   struct Fun_<long> { using type = unsigned long; };
9
10  Fun_<int>::type h = 3;
```

Where is the definition of the function? Programmers who are getting to know metafunctions tend to ask such a question. In fact, lines 1–8 of the code snippet already define a function *Fun_*, and line 10 uses *Fun_<int>::type* to return *unsigned int*, so line 10 is equivalent to defining an unsigned integer variable *h* and initialized with 3.

*Fun_* looks completely different from C++ functions in the general sense, but according to the previous definition of a function, it is not difficult to find that *Fun_* has all the properties required for a metafunction:

■ The input is the information of a type *T* and passes to the *Fun_* template as a template parameter;
■ The output is an internal type of the *Fun_* template, which is *Fun_<T>:: type*;
■ The mapping is embodied in the transformation logic implemented by the template through specialization: if the input type is *int*, the output type is *unsigned int,* and so on.

Before the release of C++ 11, there were already some works discussing C++ metafunctions. In "C++ Template Metaprogramming,"[2] the author considers *Fun_* declared in lines 1–8 in the preceding segment as a metafunction: when the function input is *X*, the output is *Fun_<X>:: type*. At the same time, that book specifies that the input and output of metafunctions discussed should be types. There is nothing wrong with defining a class template that contains a *type* declaration a metafunction: it fully satisfies the requirement that metafunctions have no side effects. But, the author of this book thinks its definition is too narrow. Of course, introducing restrictions like this would be equivalent to unifying the interface to some extent, which would lead to some convenience for programming. But, the author argues that the convenience comes at the expense of the flexibility of code writing and is too costly. Therefore, the definition of metafunctions in this book is not limited to the described forms. Specifically:

[2] Abrahams, David, and Aleksey Gurtovoy. C++ Template Metaprogramming: Concepts, Tools, and Techniques from Boost and Beyond (C++ in Depth Series). Addison-Wesley Professional, 2004.

- The representation of mappings are not limited—functions that begin with *constexpr* as defined earlier, as well as templates that provide an inline *type* declaration discussed in this section, and even other forms of "functions" discussed later, as long as they have no side effects and can be called at compile time, are considered metafunctions in this book;
- The forms of input and output are not limited—the input and output can be types, numeric values, or even templates.

On the premise of decreasing the limitation in the definition of metafunction, we can introduce another definition on the basis of *Fun_*, so as to construct another metafunction *Fun*[3]:

```
1   template <typename T>
2   using Fun = typename Fun_<T>::type;
3
4   Fun<int> h = 3;
```

Is *Fun* a metafunction? As defined in the book *C++ Template Metaprogramming*, it is not at least a standard metafunction because it does not have an inline *type* declaration. However, according to the discussion at the beginning of this chapter, it is a metafunction because it has input *(T)*, output *(Fun<T>)*, and clearly defines the mapping rules. So, we consider it a metafunction.

In fact, the form discussed earlier is also a common way to define a metafunction in the C++ Standard Library. For example, the metafunction *std::enable_if* is defined in C++ 11, while the definition *std::enable_if_t*[4] is introduced in C++ 14. The former (like *Fun_*) is a metafunction with an inline *type* declaration; while the latter (like *Fun*) is based on a definition given by the former and aimed to simplify use.

### 1.1.3 Various Metafunctions

Several methods of writing metafunctions were shown in the preceding section. Unlike the general function, the metafunction itself was not originally introduced at the beginning when C++ language is designed, so the language itself does not give the corresponding provisions to specific forms of this structure. In general, as long as it's ensured that a mapping has "no side effects" and can be called at compile time to have an impact on program behaviors at compile time and even runtime, the corresponding mapping can be called a metafunction. Specific forms of mapping can be ever-changing, and there are no definite rules.

In fact, a template is a metafunction. The following code snippet defines a metafunction that receives the parameter *T* as input and the output is *Fun<T>*:

```
1   template <typename T>
2   struct Fun {};
```

---

[3] Note "*typename*" in line 2 indicates *Fun_<T>:: type* is a type, not static data, which is a writing requirement followed by the C++ standard.
[4] These two metafunctions are discussed in section 1.3.2.

The input of a function can be empty, and accordingly, we can also establish a parameterless metafunction:

```
1   struct Fun
2   {
3       using type = int;
4   };
5
6   constexpr int fun()
7   {
8       return 10;
9   }
```

Two parameterless metafunctions are defined here. The former returns type *int* and the latter returns a value of 10.

Based on the extension of *constexpr* in C++ 14, we can redefine the metafunctions introduced in section 1.1.1 in the following form:

```
1   template <int a>
2   constexpr int fun = a + 1;
```

It looks far from a function and even loses the braces functions should have. But it's really a metafunction. The only thing to note is that the method for calling this function now is different from that in section 1.1.1. For the function in the same section, it is *fun (3)* to call it, and for this function, the corresponding method of invocation becomes *fun<3>*. Except this point, there is no significant difference between the two functions from the point of view of compile-time computing.

The metafunctions discussed earlier all have only one return value. One benefit of metafunctions is that they can have multiple return values. Consider the following code snippet:

```
1   template <>
2   struct Fun_<int>
3   {
4       using reference_type = int&;
5       using const_reference_type = const int&;
6       using value_type = int;
7   };
```

Is this a metafunction? Hope you answer "yes." From the point of view of function, it has input *(int)* and contains multiple outputs: *Fun_<int>::reference_type*, *Fun_<int>::const_reference_type*, and *Fun_<int>::value_type*.

Some scholars object to the metafunction in the said form, arguing that it will increase logical coupling, which can have a negative effect on the program design (see *C++ Template*

*Metaprogramming)*. In a sense, this view is correct, but that does not necessarily mean that this type of function cannot be used at all. We should not avoid using it anywhere just because of the disadvantage. It should be admitted that in some cases, this form of metafunction still has its rationality. Just choose the appropriate form of functions according to actual conditions.

### 1.1.4 type_traits

When it comes to metafunctions, we can't help but mention a metafunction library: *type_traits*. *type_traits* was introduced by *Boost* and included by C++ 11. The corresponding functionality can be introduced through a header file *type_traits*. The library provides transformation, comparison, judgment, and other functions for types.

Consider the following code snippet:

```
1   std::remove_reference<int&>::type h1 = 3;
2   std::remove_reference_t<int&> h2 = 3;
```

Line 1 calls the metafunction *std::remove_reference* to transform *int&* into *int* and declares a variable; line 2 uses *std::remove_reference_t* to do the same thing. *std::remove_reference* and *std::remove_reference_t* are metafunctions defined in *type_traits*. Their relation is similar to *Fun_* and *Fun* that we discussed in section 1.1.2.

In general, writing generic codes often requires this library for type transformations. Our deep learning framework is no exception. This book will use some of these metafunctions and describe its functionality the first time when the function is used. Readers can refer to "C++ Standard Template Library"[5] and other books to understand the library systematically.

### 1.1.5 Metafunctions and Macros

According to the definition of functions discussed earlier, macros can also be considered as a class of metafunctions. In general, however, when people discuss C++ metafunctions, they usually limit the discussion to the *constexpr* function and functions constructed using templates, except macros.[6] It is because macros are parsed by the preprocessor rather than the compiler, which results in that many features which can be exploited at compile time cannot be reached for macros.

Typically, we can use namespaces to wrap *constexpr* functions and function templates to ensure that they do not have name conflicts with other codes. But when using macros as carriers of metafunctions, that advantage will be lost. It is also why the author believes that macros should be avoided in codes as much as possible.

But in a given situation, macros still have their own advantages. In fact, when constructing a deep learning framework, this book will use macros as a supplement to template metafunctions. However, it still requires attention when using macros. Basically, the author believes that the end users of the deep learning framework should be avoided to have access to the macros defined

---

[5] Josuttis, Nicolai M. The C++ Standard Library: A Tutorial and Reference. Addison-Wesley, 2012.
[6] The book Advanced Metaprogramming in Classic C++ has a more in-depth discussion of using macros with templates to construct metafunctions.

within the framework, while it is ensured that macros should be undefined when they are no longer in use.

## 1.1.6 The Nominating Method of Metafunctions in This Book

Metafunctions are in a variety of forms and we can use it quite flexibly. In this book (and the deep learning framework constructed in following chapters), we will use various types of metafunctions. The way that functions are named here will be defined thus to ensure that the style of programs is unified to some extent.

In this book, metafunctions are named differently depending on the form of return values for metafunctions: if the return value of a metafunction is represented by a dependent name, the function will be named the form of *xxx_* (an underscore as the suffix); if the return value of a metafunction is represented directly with a non-dependent name, the name of the metafunction will not contain a suffix in the form of an underscore. The following is a typical example:

```
1   template <int a, int b>
2   struct Add_ {
3       constexpr static int value = a + b;
4   };
5
6   template <int a, int b>
7   constexpr int Add = a + b;
8
9   constexpr int x1 = Add_<2, 3>::value;
10  constexpr int x2 = Add<2, 3>;
```

Lines 1–4 define the metafunction *Add_*; lines 6 and 7 define the metafunction *Add*. They have the same functionality but are called in different ways: lines 9 and 10 call two metafunctions respectively, to assign *x1* and *x2* with the calling result. What line 9 gets is a dependent result (a value depends on the presence of *Add_*), and accordingly, the dependent name uses an underscore as the suffix: *Add_*. Line 10 does not use a dependent formulation when obtaining the result, so there is no underscore suffix in the function name. This form of writing is not mandatory and the book chooses this form only for the sake of style unification.

## 1.2 Template Template Parameters and Container Templates

After going through the previous section, the author believes that readers will have to establish the following understanding: metafunctions can manipulate types and values. For metafunctions, there is no essential difference between types and values: they can be considered as a kind of "data" and used as input and output of metafunctions.

In fact, the data that C++ metafunctions can manipulate consists of three categories: numeric values, types, and templates, which are uniformly referred to as "metadata" to indicate a difference from the "data" manipulated at runtime. The previous section mentioned the first two categories, and this section begins with a brief discussion of the template metadata.

### 1.2.1 Templates as the Input of Metafunctions

Templates can be used as input parameters for metafunctions. Consider the following code snippet:

```
1   template <template <typename> class T1, typename T2>
2   struct Fun_ {
3       using type = typename T1<T2>::type;
4   };
5
6   template <template <typename> class T1, typename T2>
7   using Fun = typename Fun_<T1, T2>::type;
8
9   Fun<std::remove_reference, int&> h = 3;
```

Lines 1–7 define a metafunction *Fun*, which receives two input parameters: a template and a type. It applies the type parameter to the template parameter and returns the applying result as the invoking result. Line 9 uses this metafunction and passes *std::remove_reference* and *int&* as arguments. According to the invoking rule, this function will return *int*, that is, line 9 declares a variable *h* of type *int* and assigns 3 to it.

From the point of view of functional programming, the function *Fun* defined earlier is a typical high-order function, which is a function with another function as the input parameter. It can be summed up as a mathematical expression as follows (in the following formula, the function begins with an uppercase letter and the pure value begins with a lowercase letter in order to describe the relationship between a function and a numeric value more clearly):

$$\text{Fun}(T_1, t_2) = T_1(t_2)$$

### 1.2.2 Templates as the Output of Metafunctions

Similar to numeric values and types, templates can also be used as the output of metafunctions in addition to the input of metafunctions, but it is relatively complex to write.

Consider the following code snippet:

```
1    template <bool AddOrRemoveRef> struct Fun_;
2
3    template <>
4    struct Fun_<true> {
5        template <typename T>
6        using type = std::add_lvalue_reference<T>;
7    };
8
9    template <>
10   struct Fun_<false> {
11       template <typename T>
```

```
12       using type = std::remove_reference<T>;
13  };
14
15  template <typename T>
16  using Res_ = Fun_<false>::template type<T>;
17
18  Res_<int&>::type h = 3;
```

Lines 1–13 define the metafunction *Fun_*:

- When the input is true, its output *Fun_<true>::type* is the function template *add_lvalue_reference*, which can add a lvalue reference to the type;
- When the input is false, its output *Fun_<false>::type* is the function template *remove_reference*, which can remove references from the type.

Lines 15 and 16 are the expression of applying the metafunction *Fun_*: the input is false and the output is saved in *Res_*. Please note that *Res_* is also a function template at this point, which actually corresponds to *std:removal_reference*—this metafunction is used to remove references from the type. Line 18 uses this function template (invoking of metafunction) to declare the object *h* of type *int*.

If readers are confused about this writing and feel it is difficult to grasp, it doesn't matter, because there are relatively few practical applications for templates as the output of metafunctions. However, if readers encounter similar problems in subsequent learning or work, the content of this section can be used as a reference.

Similar to the previous section, the entire process is represented here as a mathematical expression, as follows:

$$Fun(addOrRemove) = T$$

*addOrRemove* is a value of type bool, while *T* is the output of *Fun_* and *T* is also a metafunction.

## 1.2.3 Container Templates

At the beginning of learning a programming language, we often start with the basic data types supported by the language, such as *int* for a signed integer in C++. On this basis, we'll make a natural extension of basic data types and discuss how to use arrays. Similarly, if regarding numeric values, types, and templates as operands of metafunctions, most metafunctions discussed previously are metafunctions with single element as input. In this section, we'll discuss the "array" representation of metadata: the "element" in the array can be numeric values, types, or templates.

There are many ways to represent arrays or even more complex structures. The book *C++ Template Metaprogramming* discusses MPL (Boost C++ Template Metaprogramming Library). It implements STL-like functionality that provides a good representation of complex data structures (such as arrays, collections, mappings, etc.) at compile time.

However, this book will not use MPL. The main reason is that MPL encapsulates some of the underlying details that are important for metaprogramming learning. Simply using MPL will somewhat lead to the loss of the opportunity to learn metaprogramming techniques. On the other hand, learning MPL with knowledge of basic metaprogramming methods will help with a deeper understanding and easier use of MPL. It's just like that we usually start by discussing arrays like *int a[10]* and using them to derive important concepts such as pointers when learning C++. On this basis, we'll grasp a deeper understanding when discussing *vector<int>*. This book will talk about the core techniques of metaprogramming rather than the way some metaprogramming libraries are used. We'll only use some simple custom structures to represent arrays, which are as easy to use as *int\**.

Essentially, what we need is not a representation of an array, but a container: to hold each element of the array. Elements can be numeric values, types, or templates. You can regard these three kinds of data as different categories of operands. Just like that *int* and *float* in C++ are different types, in metafunctions we can simply think that "numeric values" and "types" belong to different categories. A typical array in C++ (whether *int\** or *vector<int>*) can hold only one type of data—the reason for this design is that it's simple to realize and it meets most requirements. Similarly, our containers can hold only one category of operands. For example, a container that can hold only numeric values, a container that can only hold types, or a container that can only hold templates. This kind of containers can already meet the vast majority of needs.

The variadic template has been introduced in C++ 11 to make it easy to implement containers we need[7]:

```
1   template <int... Vals> struct IntContainer;
2   template <bool... Vals> struct BoolContainer;
3
4   template <typename...Types> struct TypeContainer;
5
6   template <template <typename> class...T> struct TemplateCont;
7   template <template <typename...> class...T> struct TemplateCont2;
```

The code snippet declares five containers (equivalent to five arrays defined). The first two containers can hold variables of types *int* and *bool*. The third container can hold types. The fourth container can hold templates as its element and each template element can receive one type as a parameter. The fifth container can also take templates as its element, but each template can hold zero or more type parameters.[8]

Careful readers may find that the discussed five statements are actually declarations rather than definitions (each statement is not followed by a brace, so it is just a declaration). It's also a feature of C++ metaprogramming. In fact, we can add a brace at the end of each statement to introduce a definition. But think about it, do we need to define it? No, we don't. The declaration already contains all the information that the compiler needs, so why do we introduce a definition?

---

[7] Note lines 6 and 7: before C++ 17, in a declaration like *template <typename>class*, *class* could not be replaced with *typename*. The limitation is a bit decreased in C++ 17. But this book follows the writing conventions before C++ 17, which is using *class* instead of *typename* to represent templates.

[8] Containers like *template <auto... Vals> struct Cont* is supported for storing different types of numeric values in C++ 17. This book will not use such kind of containers, so they will not be discussed in detail.

In fact, it is almost an idiom in metaprogramming—the definition is introduced only when necessary, otherwise we can use declarations directly. In the following sections, we'll see a lot of similar declarations and take concrete examples to see how they are used.

In fact, we've almost finished the discussion of data structures so far—we almost only use these data structures when constructing a deep learning framework. If you're not familiar with these structures, it's okay. We'll keep using these data structures in the process of constructing the deep learning framework and you'll be familiar with them.

The data structures are only half the story, and a complete program contains algorithms in addition to data structures. An algorithm is composed of the most basic sequences, branches, and looping logic. In the next section, we'll discuss how to write the appropriate sequences, branches, and looping logic when it comes to metafunctions.

## 1.3 Writing of Sequences, Branches, and Looping Codes

The author believes that readers of this book can skillfully write sequences, branches, and looping codes of runtime. However, this book still carves out a section to discuss this issue. It is because once metafunctions are involved, the corresponding method of code writing will change as well.

### 1.3.1 Codes Executed in Sequence Order

Codes executed in sequence order are more intuitive to write. Consider the following code snippet:

```
1   template <typename T>
2   struct RemoveReferenceConst_ {
3   private:
4       using inter_type = typename std::remove_reference<T>::type;
5   public:
6       using type = typename std::remove_const<inter_type>::type;
7   };
8
9   template <typename T>
10  using RemoveReferenceConst
11      = typename RemoveReferenceConst_<T>::type;
12
13  RemoveReferenceConst<const int&> h = 3;
```

The key point of this code snippet is lines 2–7, which encapsulate the metafunction *RemoveReferenceConst_*. The metafunction contains two statements executed in sequence:

1. Line 4 calculates *inter_type* according to *T*;
2. Line 6 calculates *type* according to *inter_type*.

At the same time, *inter_type* in the code snippet is declared as *private* to ensure that users of the function will not misuse the intermediate result *inter_type* as the return value of the function.

Codes executed in order like this code snippet can be easily understood. The only thing to be reminded is that all declarations in structures now have to be seen as executing statements and their order cannot be swapped at will. Consider the following code snippet:

```
1   struct RunTimeExample {
2       static void fun1() { fun2(); }
3       static void fun2() { cerr << "hello" << endl; }
4   };
```

This code snippet is correct and the order of definitions of *fun1* and *fun2* can be swapped without changing their behaviors. But, if we adjust the order of the code lines in the discussed metaprogramming example:

```
1   template <typename T>
2   struct RemoveReferenceConst_ {
3       using type = typename std::remove_const<inter_type>::type;
4       using inter_type = typename std::remove_reference<T>::type;
5   };
```

That the program won't be compiled. It's not hard to understand: the compiler scans the code in the structure twice at compile time in which the compiler processes the declaration the first time and goes deep into the definition of the methods the second time. Because of this, *RunTimeExample* is correct. In the first scan, the compiler only learns that *RunTimeExample* contains two member functions *fun1* and *fun2*. In the following scan, the compiler learns that *fun2* is invoked in *fun1*. Although the call statement of *fun2* appears before its declaration, it is because of the two scanning processes that the compiler does not report an error such as that *fun2* can't be found.

But in the modified *RemoveReferenceConst*, the compiler will find that *type* relies on an undefined *inter_type* when it first scans the program from top to bottom. It will not continue to scan subsequent lines but instead gives an error message directly. In many cases, we place the metafunctions' calling statements in structures or classes, and thus we should make sure that the statements are in the correct order.

## 1.3.2 Codes Executed in Branches

We can also introduce logic of branches at compile time. Unlike codes executed in order at compile time, the logic of branches at compile time can be represented either as a pure metafunction or in combination with the execution logic at runtime. For the latter, the branches at compile time are often used for the selection of runtime logic. We will see examples of these two scenarios in this section.

In fact, we have implemented codes executed in branches in the previous discussion. For example, in section 1.2.2, we implement a metafunction *Fun_* and use a Boolean parameter to determine the behavior (return value) of the function. This is a typical branching behavior. In fact, using specialization or partial specialization of templates to implement branches is a very common way to implement branches, as in that example. Of course, there are other implementations of branches, each of which has its own advantages and disadvantages. Several of them have been discussed in this section.

### 1.3.2.1 *Implementing Branches Using* std::conditional *and* std::conditional_t

*conditional* and *conditional_t* are two metafunctions provided in *type_traits*, defined as follows[9]:

```
1   namespace std
2   {
3     template <bool B, typename T, typename F>
4     struct conditional {
5         using type = T;
6     };
7
8     template <typename T, typename F>
9     struct conditional<false, T, F> {
10        using type = F;
11    };
12
13    template <bool B, typename T, typename F>
14    using conditional_t = typename conditional<B, T, F>::type;
15  }
```

Its logic is that if *B* is true, the function returns *T*, otherwise *F* is returned. It is typically used in the following way:

```
1   std::conditional<true, int, float>::type x = 3;
2   std::conditional_t<false, int, float> y = 1.0f;
```

The variable *x* of type *int* and the variable *y* of type *float* are defined, respectively.

The advantage of *conditional* and *conditional_t* is that they are relatively simple to use, but the disadvantage is that they are not very expressive—it can only implement binary branches (true and false branches) and it behaves more like a conditional operator expression at runtime: *x = B? T:F;*. Support for multiple branches (a feature similar to switch) is more difficult. Accordingly, the use of *conditional* and *conditional_t* is relatively narrow. Thus, these two metafunctions are not recommended unless there are particularly simple cases of branches.

### 1.3.2.2 *Implementing Branches with (Partial) Specialization*

In the previous discussion, we implement branches using specialization. (Partial) specialization is naturally used to introduce differences, so it is natural to implement branches by this way. Consider the following code snippet:

```
1   struct A; struct B;
2
```

---

[9] Here is just one possible implementation. Different compilers may adopt different implementations, but their logic is equivalent.

```
3    template <typename T>
4    struct Fun_ {
5        constexpr static size_t value = 0;
6    };
7
8    template <>
9    struct Fun_<A> {
10       constexpr static size_t value = 1;
11   };
12
13   template <>
14   struct Fun_<B> {
15       constexpr static size_t value = 2;
16   };
17
18   constexpr size_t h = Fun_<B>::value;
```

Line 18 of the code snippet gives a value to *h* depending on the input parameters of the meta-function *Fun_*, which is a typical branch. The metafunction *Fun_* actually introduces three branches, each with input arguments as *A, B*, and the default. It is natural and easy to understand and use specialization to introduce branches, but the code is generally longer than written in other ways.

In addition to the above method of specialization, there is another way to specialize in C++ 14. Considering the following code snippet:

```
1    struct A; struct B;
2
3    template <typename T>
4    constexpr size_t Fun = 0;
5
6    template <>
7    constexpr size_t Fun<A> = 1;
8
9    template <>
10   constexpr size_t Fun<B> = 2;
11
12   constexpr size_t h = Fun<B>;
```

This code snippet implements the same functionality as the previous code snippet (the only difference is that when a metafunction is called, the former needs to give a dependent name *::value*, while the latter does not), but the implementation is simpler. You can pursue this approach if you want the result returned by the branch to be a single numeric value.

When using specialization to implement branches, one thing to note is that it is illegal to introduce fully specialized branches into a non-fully specialized class template. Consider the following code snippet:

```
1   template <typename TW>
2   struct Wrapper {
3       template <typename T>
4       struct Fun_ {
5           constexpr static size_t value = 0;
6       };
7
8       template <>
9       struct Fun_<int> {
10          constexpr static size_t value = 1;
11      };
12  };
```

This is illegal. The reason is that *Wrapper* is a non-fully specialized class template, but it contains a fully specialized template within it (*Fun_<int>*), which is not allowed by C++ standard and will cause compilation errors.

To solve this problem, we can use partial specialization instead of full specialization and the discussed code snippet can be modified as follows:

```
1   template <typename TW>
2   struct Wrapper {
3       template <typename T, typename TDummy = void>
4       struct Fun_ {
5           constexpr static size_t value = 0;
6       };
7
8       template <typename TDummy>
9       struct Fun_<int, TDummy> {
10          constexpr static size_t value = 1;
11      };
12  };
```

A pseudo-parameter *TDummy* is introduced here, which is used to reform the original full specialization to partial specialization. This parameter has a default value of *void*, so that the metafunction can be called directly in the form of *Fun_<int>* without providing an argument to the pseudo-parameter.

## 1.3.2.3 *Implementing Branches Using* std::enable_if *and* std::enable_if_t

The definitions of *enable_if* and *enable_if_t* are as follows:

```
1   namespace std
2   {
3       template<bool B, typename T = void>
4       struct enable_if {};
5
6       template<class T>
7       struct enable_if<true, T> { using type = T; };
8
9       template< bool B, class T = void >
10      using enable_if_t = typename enable_if<B, T>::type;
11  }
```

There is not particularly important for the implementation of the branch. It is important that when *B* is true, the metafunction *enable_if* can return the result *type*. Branches can be implemented based on this structure. Considering the following code snippet:

```
1   template <bool IsFeedbackOut, typename T,
2            std::enable_if_t<IsFeedbackOut>* = nullptr>
3   auto FeedbackOut_(T&&) { /* ... */ }
4
5   template <bool IsFeedbackOut, typename T,
6            std::enable_if_t<!IsFeedbackOut>* = nullptr>
7   auto FeedbackOut_(T&&) { /* ... */ }
```

A branch is introduced here. When *IsFeedbackOut* is true, *std::enable_if_t<IsFeedbackOut>* makes sense, which makes the first function substitution successfully and correspondingly the second function substitution fail. Conversely, when *IsFeedbackOut* is False, *std::enable_if_t<!IsFeedbackOut>* makes sense, which makes the second function substitution successfully and the first function substitution fail.

There is a feature called SFINAE (Substitution Failure Is Not An Error) in C++. For the discussed procedure, when one function substitution fails and the other function substitution succeeds, the compiler will select the function whose substitution succeeds without reporting the error. The implementation of branches here also takes advantage of this feature.

In general, *enable_if* and *enable_if_t* are used in functions as useful additions to overloads—overloads distinguish among functions with the same name by different types of parameters. But in some cases, we want to introduce functions with the same name, but we can't distinguish among them by parameter type.[10] Thus, we can solve the corresponding overload problem to a certain extent through *enable_if* and *enable_if_t*.

---

[10] We'll see examples like this in the deep learning framework.

It should be noted that *enable_if* and *enable_if_t* can be used in a variety of forms and are not limited to the way described earlier, in which they are used as template parameters. In fact, *enable_if* or *enable_if_t* can be introduced anywhere SFINAE is supported. Interested readers can refer to the instructions in C++ Reference.[11]

*enable_if* or *enable_if_t* also has drawbacks—they are not as intuitive as template specialization and the codes written with them are relatively difficult to read (the author believes that programmers who understand the mechanism of template specialization are more than programmers who know SFINAE).

It should be stated that the example given here based on *enable_if* is a typical way of using a combination of compile time and runtime. *FeedbackOut_* contains the logic of runtime and choosing the right version of *FeedbackOut_* is implemented through the branch at compile time. By introducing a branching method for compile time, we can create more flexible functions.

## 1.3.2.4 Compile-time Branches with Different Return Types

Branching statements at compile time look a bit more complex but more flexible than runtime branches. Consider the following code snippet:

```
1   auto wrap1(bool Check)
2   {
3       if (Check) return (int)0;
4       else return (double)0;
5   }
```

This is a runtime code snippet. First we'd like to briefly explain line 1—in C++ 14, it is not necessary to provide return types explicitly in declarations of functions. The compiler can automatically derive its return type from the *return* statement in the function body, but it is required that all *return* statements in the function body return the same type. For the described code snippet, line 3 does not return the same type as line 4, which can cause a compilation error. In fact, each runtime function's return type is determined at compile time. No matter what form is used to write the function, its return type cannot be changed at runtime.

But at compile time, we can break this limitation in some way:

```
1   template <bool Check, std::enable_if_t<Check>* = nullptr>
2   auto fun() {
3       return (int)0;
4   }
5
6   template <bool Check, std::enable_if_t<!Check>* = nullptr>
7   auto fun() {
8       return (double)0;
9   }
```

---

[11] http://en.cppreference.com/w/cpp/types/enable_if

```
10
11   template <bool Check>
12   auto wrap2() {
13       return fun<Check>();
14   }
15
16   int main() {
17       std::cerr << wrap2<true>() << std::endl;
18   }
```

What is the return type of *wrap2*? In fact, it is determined by the value of the template parameter *Check*. Through this new feature in C++ and the computational power of compile time, we implement a function that can return data of different types at compile time. Of course, in order to execute this function, we still need to specify arguments of template parameters at compile time, thus making the function return data of different types at compile time degenerate into a function that returns a single type at runtime. But, in any case, with the described techniques, compile-time functions will have more powerful features, which is useful for metaprogramming.

The discussed code is also an example of compile-time branches combined with runtime functions. In fact, it is a relatively common programming method to choose the correct runtime function by metafunction at compile time, so a new syntax *if constexpr* is specifically introduced in C++ 17 to simplify the writing of codes.

### 1.3.2.5 *Simplify Codes with* if constexpr

For the code snippet as discussed, it can be simplified in C++ 17 as follows:

```
1    template <bool Check>
2    auto fun()
3    {
4        if constexpr (Check)
5        {
6            return (int)0;
7        }
8        else
9        {
10           return (double)0;
11       }
12   }
13
14   int main() {
15       std::cerr << fun<true>() << std::endl;
16   }
```

Here, *if constexpr* must receive a constant expression, namely, the compile-time constant. When the compiler parses the invocation of a function containing *if constexpr*, it will automatically select the statement body where the *if constexpr* expression is true and ignore other statement bodies. For example, when the compiler parses a function call in line 15, a function will be automatically constructed as follows:

```
1    // template <bool Check>
2    auto fun()
3    {
4    //    if constexpr (Check)
5    //    {
6             return (int)0;
7    //    }
8    //    else
9    //    {
10   //        return (double)0;
11   //    }
12   }
```

The code written with *if constexpr* is more like branching codes at runtime. At the same time, it has an extra benefit that it can reduce the generation of instances. Using the code snippets in the previous section, the compiler needs to construct two instances (*wrap2* and *fun*) when instantiating. But using the code snippets in this section, the compiler produces only one instance of the function *fun* when instantiating. Although good compilers can merge constructed instances with inline or other ways, we cannot guarantee that compilers will do such kind of optimization definitely. In turn, using *if constexpr* can ensure the number of instances constructed by compilers to be reduced, which means reducing resources required for compilation to some extent, as well as the size of compilation results.

However, *if constexpr* also has drawbacks, first of all, if we forget to declare *constexpr* in the code, then some functions can also be compiled. But the choice of branches will transfer from compile time to runtime—at this point, we will still introduce the corresponding selection of branches at runtime and cannot optimize it at compile time. Second, the usage scenario of *if constexpr* is relatively narrow—it can only be placed inside functions in the general sense to select the runtime logic at compile time. If we want to construct metafunctions and return different types as results through branches, then *if constexpr* is powerless. The circumstances under which *if constexpr* should be used also require specific analysis for specific issues.

## 1.3.3 Codes Executed in Loops

In general, we don't organize looping codes in metafunctions with statements like *while* or *for* because they operate on variables. But, at compile time, we deal more with constants, types, and templates.[12] In order to be able to manipulate metadata effectively, we tend to use recursive forms to implement loops.

---

[12] It is allowed to use variables in the *constexpr* function in C++ 14 standard, but with limited support.

Let's take a look at an example. Given an unsigned integer, find the number of 1s in the binary representation of the integer. At runtime, we can use a simple loop to implement. At compile time, we need to use recursion to implement:

```
1   template <size_t Input>
2   constexpr size_t OnesCount = (Input % 2) + OnesCount<(Input / 2)>;
3
4   template <> constexpr size_t OnesCount<0> = 0;
5
6   constexpr size_t res = OnesCount<45>;
```

Lines 1–4 define a metafunction *OnesCount*, and line 6 uses this metafunction to calculate the number of 1s contained in the corresponding binary form of 45.

It may take a while for you to adapt to this programming style. The whole program is not logically complex, which uses the features in C++ 14. The amount of code is similar to writing a runtime *while* loop. The core of the code is *OnesCount<(Input / 2)>* at line 2, which is essentially a recursive call. Readers can think about the behavior of line 2 in the code snippet when *Input* is 45 or any other value.

In general, in a metaprogram that uses recursion to implement loops, a branch needs to be introduced to end the loop. Line 4 in the discussed procedure implements a branch like this—when the input is reduced to 0, the procedure switches to this branch and ends the loop.

A more common scenario of loops is the processing of elements in an array. We discussed the representation of arrays in the previous section and here we give an example of working with arrays:

```
1   template <size_t...Inputs>
2   constexpr size_t Accumulate = 0;
3
4   template <size_t CurInput, size_t...Inputs>
5   constexpr size_t Accumulate<CurInput, Inputs...>
6       = CurInput + Accumulate<Inputs...>;
7
8   constexpr size_t res = Accumulate<1, 2, 3, 4, 5>;
```

Lines 1–6 define a metafunction: *Accumulate*, which receives an array of type *size_t*, sums the elements in the array and takes the result as the output of the metafunction. Line 8 shows the usage of this metafunction: calculates the value of adding from 1 to 5 and assigns the result to *res*.

As mentioned earlier, introducing a branch to terminate the loop is very important for the looping logic in metafunctions. Line 2 of the code snippet is the branch to terminate the loop—when the input array is empty, it will match the template parameters of the function *<size_t... Inputs>*, at which point *Accumulate* returns 0. Lines 4–6, on the other hand, make up another branch—if the array contains one or more elements, it will match this template specialization, which takes out the first element, sums the remaining elements, and adds the result to the first element.

In fact, in this case alone, there is a simpler way to write in C++ 17—that is, using the *fold expression* technique it provides the following:

```
1    template <size_t... values>
2    constexpr size_t fun()
3    {
4        return (0 + ... + values);
5    }
6
7    constexpr size_t res = fun<1, 2, 3, 4, 5>();
```

The *fold expression* is also essentially a simplified writing of loops, with limitations for usage. This book will not focus much on it.

Loops at compile time is essentially control recursive codes through branches. As a result, many writing methods of branches discussed in the previous section can also be derived and used to write corresponding looping codes. Typically, you can write a loop using *if constexpr*, which is left to readers for practice.

### 1.3.4 Caution: Instantiation Explosion and Compilation Crash

Review the previous code:

```
1    template <size_t Input>
2    constexpr size_t OnesCount = (Input % 2) + OnesCount<(Input / 2)>;
3
4    template <> constexpr size_t OnesCount<0> = 0;
5
6    constexpr size_t x1 = OnesCount<7>;
7    constexpr size_t x1 = OnesCount<15>;
```

Consider how many instances the compiler will produce when compiling this code snippet.

When line 6 takes 7 as a template argument, the compiler will use 7, 3, 1, and 0 to instantiate *OnesCount* and construct four instances. Next line 7 passes 15 as the argument to the template and the compiler needs to instantiate the *OnesCount* with 15, 7, 3, 1, and 0. Typically, the compiler will retain the code instantiated with 7, 3, 1, and 0 before, so that if the same instance is required later in the compilation process, the previously saved instances can be reused. For a general C++ program, this way can greatly improve the speed of compilation, but for metaprogramming, it can be a disaster.

Consider the following code snippet:

```
1    template <size_t A>
2    struct Wrap_ {
3        template <size_t ID, typename TDummy = void>
```

```
 4        struct imp {
 5            constexpr static size_t value = ID + imp<ID - 1>::value;
 6        };
 7
 8        template <typename TDummy>
 9        struct imp<0, TDummy> {
10            constexpr static size_t value = 0;
11        };
12
13        template <size_t ID>
14        constexpr static size_t value = imp<A + ID>::value;
15    };
16
17    int main() {
18        std::cerr << Wrap_<3>::value<2> << std::endl;
19        std::cerr << Wrap_<10>::value<2> << std::endl;
20    }
```

This code combines the branching and looping techniques as discussed earlier to construct a class template *Wrap_*, which is a metafunction that receives parameter *A* to return another metafunction. The latter receives the parameter *ID* and calculates $\sum_{i=1}^{A+ID} i$.

When compiling line 18, the compiler will produce a series of instances of *Wrap_<3>::imp*. Unfortunately, when compiling line 19, the compiler cannot reuse these instances because it needed a series of instances of *Wrap_<10>::imp*, which is not the same as the series of *Wrap_<3>::imp*. Therefore, we can't use instances that the compiler has already compiled to speed up compilation.

The reality could be even worse, and the compiler is likely to keep a series of instances of *Wrap_<3>::imp*, as it assumes that there may be a situation in which the instances may be required again in the future. In the previous example, *Wrap_* contains a loop and all instances produced by the loop are saved in the compiler's memory. If our metafunction contains nested loops, the resulting instances will grow exponentially as the number of loop layers increases—all of which are saved inside the compiler memory!

Unfortunately, compilers are often designed to meet the general compilation tasks, and there is relatively little optimization for metaprogramming, a technique currently not widely used. So, compiler developers may not consider the problem of too many instances saved in memory during compilation (this may not be a big problem in the case of non-metaprogramming). On the other hand, if a large number of instances are saved during compilation, it can cause the memory of the compiler to exceed the limit, resulting in compilation failures or even crashes!

It is not alarmism. In fact, when the author writes the deep learning framework, there is a situation where the problem is not paid enough attention to, resulting in too much usage of compilation memory and eventually compilation failures. After carefully modifying the codes, the amount of memory required for compilation is more than 50% less than before, and the compilation no longer crashes.

So, how to solve this problem? It's simple—splitting the loops. For the described code, we can modify it as follows:

```
1   template <size_t ID>
2   struct imp {
3       constexpr static size_t value = ID + imp<ID - 1>::value;
4   };
5
6   template <>
7   struct imp<0> {
8       constexpr static size_t value = 0;
9   };
10
11  template <size_t A>
12  struct Wrap_ {
13      template <size_t ID>
14      constexpr static size_t value = imp<A + ID>::value;
15  };
```

When instantiating *Wrap_<3>::value<2>*, the compiler constructs *imp* with 5, 4, 3, 2, 1, and 0 as arguments. In the subsequent instantiation of *Wrap_<10>::value<2>*, what was previously constructed can be reused and the number of new instantiations will be reduced.

However, there are still shortcomings in this modification. In the previous code, *imp* was placed inside the *Wrap_*, which indicates a close connection between the two. From the point of view of namespace pollution, it will not allow *imp* to pollute the namespace containing *Wrap_*. In the latter implementation, however, *imp* will pollute the namespace—in the same namespace, we can no longer introduce another construct named *imp* for other metafunction to call.

How to solve this problem? It is actually a trade-off: if the logic of the metafunction is simple and will not produce a large number of instances, retaining the previous (worse for the compiler) form may not have too many negative effects on the compiler, while making the code better cohesive. Conversely, if the metafunction logic is more complex (typically nested multi-loops) and may produce many instances, we can choose the latter approach to save compilation resources.

Even if we choose the latter way, we should try our best to avoid namespace pollution. To solve this problem, we will introduce a dedicated namespace to store auxiliary codes such as *imp* when creating the deep learning framework.

## 1.3.5 Branch Selection and Short Circuit Logic

Another important technique to reduce the instantiation at compile time is to introduce short-circuit logic. Consider the following code snippet:

```
1   template <size_t N>
2   constexpr bool is_odd = ((N % 2) == 1);
3
4   template <size_t N>
```

```
5    struct AllOdd_ {
6        constexpr static bool is_cur_odd = is_odd<N>;
7        constexpr static bool is_pre_odd = AllOdd_<N - 1>::value;
8        constexpr static bool value = is_cur_odd && is_pre_odd;
9    };
10
11   template <>
12   struct AllOdd_<0> {
13       constexpr static bool value = is_odd<0>;
14   };
```

The logic of this code snippet is not complicated. Lines 1 and 2 introduce a metafunction *is_odd* to determine whether a number is odd. On this basis, *AllOdd_* is used for a given number *N* to determine whether each number in the sequence of 0–N is odd.

Although the logic is simple, it is sufficient to discuss the issues in this section. Consider how many instances the compiler has instantiated in order to make a judgment in the described code. In line 7 of the code snippet, the system instantiates the recursive template. Given N as the input of the *AllOdd_*, the system will instantiate N + 1 structures.

The core of judgment in the described code is line 8: a logical operation *AND*. For *AND*, it is time to return false as long as one operand is not true. However, short circuit logic like this is not well utilized in the discussed metaprogram—no matter what the value of *is_cur_odd*, *AllOdd_* will evaluate *is_pre_odd*, which will indirectly produce a number of instantiated results, although these instantiations may be of little use for the final evaluation of the system.

The following is an improved version of the program (only the modified sections are listed here):

```
1    template <bool cur, typename TNext>
2    constexpr static bool AndValue = false;
3
4    template <typename TNext>
5    constexpr static bool AndValue<true, TNext> = TNext::value;
6
7    template <size_t N>
8    struct AllOdd_ {
9        constexpr static bool is_cur_odd = is_odd<N>;
10       constexpr static bool value = AndValue<is_cur_odd,
11                             AllOdd_<N - 1>>;
12   };
```

An auxiliary metafunction *AndValue* is introduced here. It will instantiate the second operand only if the first operand of the metafunction is *true*[13]; otherwise, *false* will be returned directly.

---

[13] Typically, the corresponding elements are instantiated only when specific elements inside the template are accessed in C++. Therefore, lines 1 and 2 in this example will not lead the internal element of the second template parameter *TNext* to be instantiated.

Lines 10 and 11 of the code snippet use *AndValue* to reduce the number of instantiations, while also reducing the compilation cost.

## 1.4 Curiously Recurring Template Pattern (CRTP)

Much of what is discussed in this chapter does not involve newly introduced technologies in C++, but is based on some of the usage methods derived from existing technologies. These methods may not be common when writing runtime programs, but they are often used in metaprogramming. These methods can also be considered as idioms in metaprogramming.

If metafunctions are graded, then metafunctions that make basic transformations (such as the input is a type and it returns the corresponding pointer type) are the lowest, above which is the metafunction that contains sequences, branches, and looping logic. With these tools in hand, we can then learn some of the more advanced metaprogramming methods, one of which is CRTP.

CRTP is a way of declaring a derived class and what is "curious" is that the derived class passes itself as a template parameter to its base class. Consider the following code snippet:

```
1  template <typename D> class Base { /*...*/ };
2
3  class Derived : public Base<Derived> { /*...*/ };
```

Line 3 defines the class *Derived*, derived from *Base<Derived>*—the base class takes the name of the derived class as the template parameter. At first glance it seems to be suspected of a circular definition, but it is indeed legal. It just looks a little "curious."

CRTP can be applied in many scenarios and simulating virtual functions is one of its typical applications. Readers accustomed to object-oriented programming are no stranger to virtual functions—we can declare a virtual function in the base class (which actually declares an interface) and implement the interface in different ways in each derived class, providing different functions. It is a classic way to implement polymorphism using inheritance in object-oriented programming. Choosing the correct virtual function to execute requires the corresponding mechanism at runtime to support it. In some cases, the functions we use cannot be declared as virtual functions, such as the following example:

```
1   template <typename D>
2   struct Base
3   {
4       template <typename TI>
5       void Fun(const TI& input) {
6           D* ptr = static_cast<D*>(this);
7           ptr->Imp(input);
8       }
9   };
10
```

```
11   struct Derive : public Base<Derive>
12   {
13       template <typename TI>
14       void Imp(const TI& input) {
15           cout << input << endl;
16       }
17   };
18
19   int main() {
20       Derive d;
21       d.Fun("Implementation from derive class");
22   }
```

In this code snippet, the base class *Base<D>* assumes that the derived class implements an interface *Imp*, which will be called in its function *Fun*. If we use object-oriented programming methods, we need to introduce the virtual function *Imp*. But *Imp* is a function template and cannot be declared as a virtual function, so the CRTP technology is introduced here to implement the similar functionality of virtual functions. In addition to the function template, static functions of classes cannot be declared as virtual functions neither. Introducing CRTP can achieve the similar effect of virtual functions:

```
1    template <typename D>
2    struct Base
3    {
4        static void Fun() {
5            D::Imp();
6        }
7    };
8
9    struct Derive : public Base<Derive>
10   {
11       static void Imp() {
12           cout << "Implementation from derive class" << endl;
13       }
14   };
15
16   int main() {
17       Derive::Fun();
18   }
```

Most functions involved in metaprogramming are related to templates or are often static functions in classes. In this case, if you want to implement a polymorphic feature similar to that of runtime, you can consider using CRTP.

## 1.5 Summary

This chapter discusses some basic techniques that can be used in metaprogramming, from the way metafunctions are defined and the writing of sequences, branches, and looping codes to CRTP. Some of these techniques are specifically designed to write metafunctions, while others need to be combined with metaprogramming to play a greater role. Some technologies seem to be very different from the common runtime programming methods at first glance, and beginners will inevitably feel unaccustomed. But, if practicing over and over again, readers will be able to write metaprograms and achieve most computing functions at compile time after adapting to these techniques.

This chapter only selects relatively basic and representative techniques to introduce and omits many advanced metaprogramming techniques, such as using default parameters to implement branches; implementing loops based on pack expansion, fold expression, and so on. Compared with object-oriented programming techniques, C++ template metaprogramming is a relatively new field, and new techniques have been emerging endlessly. The length of a chapter is difficult to enumerate them all. Interested readers can search for relevant resources to learn.

Even if just using techniques discussed in this chapter, we can perform complex compile-time calculations. Subsequent chapters of this book will use these techniques to construct a deep learning framework. In fact, much of the discussion in subsequent chapters can be seen as a walkthrough in which the techniques discussed in this chapter will be used to solve practical problems. Therefore, readers can fully regard the subsequent contents of this book as exercises for the techniques discussed in this chapter. The process of exercising is also the process of leading readers to become familiar with the knowledge points in this chapter. The author believes that readers will have a more mature understanding of metaprogramming after reading this book.

In addition to using the techniques discussed in this chapter directly, we can also implement specific operations through a number of metaprogramming libraries. For example, using Boost::MPL or Boost::Hana libraries to implement arrays and collections. The interfaces that these libraries provide look very different from the processing methods of arrays discussed in this chapter, but the functionality they implement is similar. Using the processing methods of arrays described in this book is like using basic arrays in C++ at runtime while using metaprogramming libraries such as MPL is more like using *vector* at runtime. This book will not discuss these metaprogramming libraries because the authors believe that it is difficult to use *vector* well enough if the basic arrays are not used well. What this book wants to convey to readers is basic techniques of metaprogramming. The author believes that it will not be difficult for readers to use other advanced class libraries in metaprogramming after laying the corresponding foundations.

## 1.6 Exercises

1. For metafunctions, there is no particularly obvious difference between numeric values and types—the input of metafunctions can be numeric values or types and the corresponding transformation can be conducted between numeric values and types. For example, you can construct a metafunction in which the input is a type and the output is the size of the space occupied by the type variable. This is a typical metafunction, which transforms types into numeric values. Try to construct the function and test it.

2. As a further extension, a metafunction can use both numerical values and types as its input parameters. Try to construct a metafunction with the input parameter as a type and an integer that returns *true* if the size of the type is equal to the integer, otherwise *false* is returned.
3. This chapter describes several form of metafunctions, can you figure out other forms?
4. This chapter discusses class templates as the output of metafunctions. Try to construct a metafunction that returns a metafunction when it receives the input. The latter one returns a metafunction after receiving its input. This is just an exercise and don't have to worry too much about its application scenarios.
5. Construct a metafunction using SFINAE: enter a type *T* and it returns *true* when *T* has subtype *type*; otherwise *false* is returned.
6. Using the wring method of looping codes learned in this chapter, construct a metafunction: enter an array of types, the output is an array of unsigned integers, and each element in the output array represents the size of the corresponding type in the input array.
7. Use short-circuit logic of branches to implement a metafunction. Given an integer sequence, it will determine whether there is an element equals to 1. If there is, it returns *true*; otherwise *false* is returned.

# Chapter 2

# Heterogeneous Dictionaries and Policy Templates

Since its advent, C++ has been criticized frequently for many reasons. Proponents of the C and assembly languages argue that there is too much "flashy" stuff in C++,[1] while programmers who are accustomed with Java and Python are disappointed that C++ is lack of some "natural" features.[2] Weakness lends wings to rumors. As developers of C++, we should admit that there does exist something unsatisfactory while enjoying the convenience of this language. There is nothing perfect in the world, and so are programming languages. As programmers, all we can do is to improve the unsatisfactory aspects and make our programming life a little more comfortable with techniques.

It is from this point of view that this chapter designs and implements two data structures: heterogeneous dictionaries and policy templates. They can all be treated as containers and we can query corresponding values by keys. But unlike runtime containers (such as *std::map*) we often use, keys in these two data structures are compile-time metadata.

These two data structures have their own pros and cons compared to runtime containers. Different data structures have different characteristics and application scenarios. Let's start with the topic of "named arguments" to discuss their application scenarios and characteristics, respectively.

## 2.1 Introduction to Named Arguments

Many programming languages support the use of named arguments when functions are called. The biggest advantage of named arguments is that they provide more information for function calls. Consider the following C++ function, which implements interpolation:

```
1   float fun(float a, float b, float weight)
```

---

[1] Typical statements include, "You invariably start using the 'nice' library features of the language like STL and Boost, and other total and utter crap…"

[2] Typical statements include, "Writing C or C++ is like using a chainsaw with all the safety guards removed."

```
2  {
3      return a * weight + b * (1 - weight);
4  }
```

When calling this function, we will get a completely wrong result if we misplace the order of the three arguments. But, because the three parameters of the function are of the same type, the compiler can't find such an error.

Using named arguments to make function calls can alleviate the above errors to some extent. Consider the following code snippet:

```
1  fun(1.3f, 2.4f, 0.1f);
2  fun(weight = 0.1f, a = 1.3f, b = 2.4f);
```

Line 2 calls with named arguments. Obviously, it's more readable and less prone to error than line 1.

Unfortunately, the C++ language itself does not directly support calling functions with named arguments so far, so the discussed code can't be compiled. One way to use named arguments in C++ is through mapping structures like *std::map*.[3]

```
1  float fun(const std::map<std::string, float>& params) {
2      auto a_it = params.find("a");
3      auto b_it = params.find("b");
4      auto weight_it = params.find("weight");
5
6      return (a_it->second) * (weight_it->second) +
7             (b_it->second) * (1 - (weight_it->second));
8  }
9
10 int main() {
11     std::map<std::string, float> params;
12     params["a"] = 1.3f; params["b"] = 2.4f;
13     params["weight"] = 0.1f;
14
15     std::cerr << fun(params); // calling the function
16 }
```

This code snippet is not complicated: before calling the function, we use *params* to build a parameter mapping, which is equivalent to the process of naming the arguments. Inside the function body, we get corresponding arguments by accessing the key of type string in *params*. Access to each argument involves explicit calls of the correspond argument's name, so such code is much less likely to encounter errors than the version of code given at the beginning of this chapter.

Using containers such as *std::map* reduce the likelihood of errors during the process of delivering arguments. But this approach also has its drawbacks: the storage and acquisition of arguments involves queries of keys, and the process of queries is done at runtime, which requires the

---

[3] For sake of brevity, this code snippet omits the check of the legitimacy of the iterator.

corresponding cost at runtime. Take the previous code snippet as an example: lines 2–4 obtain arguments and lines 6 and 7 dereference the iterator, which all need runtime calculation. Although the corresponding time of calculation may not be long, the acquisition of argument still accounts for a large proportion compared with the main logic of the entire function (floating-point operation). If the function *fun* is called multiple times, then the cost of keys' association with values becomes an unignorable part.

After carefully analyzing the process of using named arguments, it reveals that part of this process can be completed at compile time. The essence of named arguments is to establish a key-to-value mapping. For a determined function, the key (i.e., argument name) required is also determined. Therefore, operations of keys can be executed at compile time and operations of argument values can be executed at runtime.

Another problem with *std::map* is that the type of values must be the same. In the previous example, the delivered parameters are floating point numbers, where you can use *std::map* for key-value mapping. However, if types of parameters a function receives are different, it is much more difficult to use *std::map*—it is often necessary to introduce a base class, wrap different types with class derived from the based class, and then save pointers of base classes in *std::map*. This further increases the expenses at runtime and makes it inconvenient to maintain.

Parameter resolution is a quite basic function in advanced programming languages. This chapter will describe two structures to improve the solution for the pure runtime situation above—to introduce named operations while minimizing the resulting expenses at runtime and better matching metaprogramming. Both structures are used as auxiliary modules in the subsequent deep learning framework.

## 2.2 Heterogeneous Dictionaries

The first module to be introduced is the heterogeneous dictionary *VarTypeDict*. It is a container that holds data and indexes according to key-value pairs. Here, "heterogeneous" means that types of values stored in the container can be different. For example, you can save an object of type *double* and a string of type *std::string* in the container. At the same time, the keys used to index objects in the container are specified at compile time, and the key-based indexing work is mainly finished at compile time.

### 2.2.1 How to Use the Module

Before starting to construct any module, we need to anticipate how to use the module: how can users call the module to implement the corresponding functionality? This is something we need to consider first before coding. So, before discussing the specific implementation, let's look into the interface of the module first.

The example of calling this module is as follows:

```
1    // Declare a heterogeneous dictionary FParams
2    struct FParams : public VarTypeDict<A, B, Weight> {};
3
4    template <typename TIn>
5    float fun(const TIn& in) {
```

```
6          auto a = in.template Get<A>();
7          auto b = in.template Get<B>();
8          auto weight = in.template Get<Weight>();
9
10         return a * weight + b * (1 - weight);
11   }
12
13   int main() {
14       std::cerr << fun(FParams::Create()
15                           .Set<A>(1.3f)
16                           .Set<B>(2.4f)
17                           .Set<Weight>(0.1f));
18   }
```

This is almost a complete example. Line 2 defines the structure *FParams*, which is inherited from *VarTypeDict* and contains the set of arguments required by the function *fun*. *VarTypeDict* is the module to be implemented in this section. The definition of this line means that *FParams* contains three parameters named *A*, *B*, and *Weight* (*A*, *B*, and *Weight* are metadata, of which a specific definition will be given afterwards).

The parameters received by the function *fun* are instances of heterogeneous dictionary containers, similar to *std::map* in the previous section, from which the corresponding argument values can be obtained. On this basis, line 10 calls the core logic of the function and returns the result. It should be noted that the parameter type *TIn* received by the function is not *FParams*, but a type related to *FParams*. Users of heterogeneous dictionaries do not need to care about the specific input type of the function *fun* and just need to know that the appropriate values can be obtained through this argument's method *Get*.

In the *main* function in lines 14–17, we call the function *fun* and print out the corresponding return value. A syntax called "closure"[4] is used here, which may seem a little different from the general writing of programming, but is not difficult to understand. Lines 14–17 are to construct a container to hold the data (*Create*), put in the value of *1.3f* corresponding to *A*, put in the value of *2.4f* corresponding to *B*, and put in the value of *0.1f* corresponding to *Weight*.

One advantage of named arguments is that the order of parameters can be exchanged without affecting the execution results of the program. Consider the following code snippet:

```
1   std::cerr << fun(FParams::Create()
2                       .Set<B>(2.4f)
3                       .Set<A>(1.3f)
4                       .Set<Weight>(0.1f));
```

It will produce exactly the same result as the above invocation.

Previously we defined *FParams* by derivation. In fact, this line can be simplified:

```
1   using FParams = VarTypeDict<A, B, Weight>;
```

---

[4] Detailed explanations can be found in Domain-Specific Languages. Martin Fowler. Addison-Wesley Professional, 2010.

Here, *FParams* is just an alias for *VarTypeDict<A, B, Weight>*. Whether using derivation or introducing type aliases through *using*, *FParams* can perform the function of the heterogeneous dictionary described earlier.

In principle, the previous code snippet is similar to using *std::map*, which is to pack and deliver arguments to the function and unpack them by the function. But there are fundamental differences between the two. Firstly, *VarTypeDict* uses metaprogramming and accordingly, lines 6–8 of the example, which get argument values, are mainly executed at compile time. It only introduces a diminutive expense at runtime.

Secondly, if we forget to assign a key the corresponding value:

```
1   std::cerr << fun(FParams::Create()
2                       .Set<B>(2.4f)
3                       .Set<A>(1.3f);
```

Then the program will encounter a compilation error.

Consider what happens when using *std::map* as a carrier of named arguments and omitting one parameter? At this point, there will be no compilation error but a runtime error. It's always better to have a compilation error than a runtime error. The earlier the error is discovered, the easier it will be to resolve.

Finally, we can place different types of data in the container, such as a simple rewrite of the program to achieve another function:

```
1    struct FParams : public VarTypeDict<A, B, C> {};
2
3    template <typename TIn>
4    float fun(const TIn& in) {
5        auto a = in.template Get<A>();
6        auto b = in.template Get<B>();
7        auto c = in.template Get<C>();
8
9        return a ? b : c;
10   }
11
12   fun(FParams::Create().Set<A>(true).Set<B>(2.4f).Set<C>(0.1f));
```

In this code snippet, *fun* determines to return *B* or *C* based on the Boolean value of the incoming parameter *A*. The types of parameters *fun* receives are no longer the same. If you use a structure like *std::map*, you must introduce a base class as the basic type of value stored in the container. But with *VarTypeDict*, it will be unnecessary to resort to inherence—*VarTypeDict* inherently supports heterogeneous types.

The core of the previous code snippet is *VarTypeDict* and we would like to implement a class that provides all the above features. The essence of *VarTypeDict* is a container of several key-value mappings, which is quite similar to *std:map* at runtime, except that its keys are constants of the compile time. Therefore, before discussing the specific implementation of *VarTypeDict*, it is indispensable to consider what to use to represent the information of keys.

## 2.2.2 *The Representation of the Keys*

Keys in *VarTypeDict* are compile-time constants. For the definition:

```
1  struct FParams : public VarTypeDict<A, B, Weight> {};
```

We need to introduce compile-time constants to represent *A*, *B*, and *Weight*. So, what should be used as carriers? We have a lot of options, and integer constants (such as *int* values) are the most typical choice. For example, we can define:

```
1  constexpr int A = 0;
```

The definitions of *B* and *Weight* are similar to this. But here's a problem of numerical conflict. For example, we may define *A=0* in some place and *B=0* somewhere else. Now, we want to use both *A* and *B* in one function. So when *Set* (or *Get*) is called, the compiler will not know which of them to be Set (or Get) if *A* (i.e., a numeric value of 0) is passed in. To prevent this situation, we need a mechanism to avoid defining keys with the same value. This mechanism itself increases the maintenance expenses of codes. For example, when multiple people are developing at the same time, it may be necessary to assign key value ranges to everyone in order to avoid conflicts; while maintaining codes, it may be required to record which key values have already been used and which values have not been occupied yet; after a period of development, you might need to adjust the key values already in use, such as making key values with similar meanings adjacent, which may lead to adjustments of many keys. With the amount of code increasing and modules becoming more complex, the maintenance expenses of this mapping will multiply.

The problem with integers is that they are poorly descriptive—we can't understand meanings of corresponding keys from their literal values. To solve this problem, it's natural for us to consider using strings. Strings are well descriptive—their meanings are clear from a literal point of view. It is also easier to ensure that strings do not conflict than to ensure that integers do not conflict. For different parameters, we can always introduce qualifiers to manifest their meanings as accurately as possible and describe their differences from other parameters. This kind of qualified information can be easily added to strings to avoid conflicts. So, how about using strings as keys?

Unfortunately, the support for strings is not good enough at compile time for the time being. Using strings as template parameters for *VarTypeDict* is not a good alternative.

In fact, the use of strings as template parameters is indeed supported in C++, but the types of strings that can be used as template parameters are limited. Data types such as *std::string* can't be used as template parameters. In general, if we want to use a string as a template parameter, we will use a string literal such as "Hello."

String literals can be used as non-type template arguments. Non-type template arguments can be declared in two ways, by reference or by value. If a string is declared by reference, the length of the string will be considered as part of its type information. At this point, "Hello" and "C++" are considered to belong to different types because of their different lengths.

If declared by value, the type of the string literal will be transformed into the corresponding pointer type; therefore, "Hello" and "C++" will be considered as *const char\**. We can introduce a template that receives *const char\** as a parameter type and pass in a string to it:

```
1  template <const char* info>
2  struct Temp;
```

```
3
4    constexpr char a[] = "Hello";
5    using Res = Temp<a>;
```

At this point, the template parameter for the instance *Temp* is not a string, but a pointer to the string. It will lead to a problem—we may construct two strings with the same content pointing to different addresses and the instances *Temp* constructed from this may be different:

```
1    template <const char* info>
2    struct Temp;
3
4    constexpr char a[] = "Hello";
5    constexpr char a2[] = "Hello";
6    using Res = Temp<a>;
7    using Res2 = Temp<a2>;
```

Is the type of *Res* the same as the type of Res2 in the described code snippet? Not necessarily. It depends on whether the compiler makes *a* and *a2* point to the same address. If the compiler finds that the content of *a* is the same as that of *a2*, then it may introduce optimization, which makes *a* and *a2* point to the same address and results in *Res* and *Res2* of the same type. Otherwise, if *a* and *a2* point to different addresses in the compilation result, *Res* and *Res2* will be of different types.

If we want to use strings as keys in *VarTypeDict*, we need to define the literal values of these strings uniformly somewhere (e.g., using a single CPP file to store all constants, such as *a* and *a2*) and then use such constants as template parameters when instantiating templates. Similar to using integers, it will also increase the complexity of template definitions and is not conducive to extension.

These problems with strings make it unsuitable for strings to be keys in *VarTypeDict*. As mentioned earlier, it is relatively difficult to compare different strings at compile time and their types might be different. These characteristics make it relatively cumbersome to handle strings. So, in general, we try to avoid using strings and string-related operations at compile time.

So, what should be used as a key? In fact, the key here only needs to support the "equal" judgment in order to be able to index the corresponding value based on its index. There is a quite natural thing that can support the judgment—the name of the class (or structure). Here the name of the structure is used as the key. In the earlier example, the declarations for *A*, *B*, and *Weight* are as follows:

```
1    struct A; struct B; struct Weight;
2
3    struct FParams : public VarTypeDict<A, B, Weight> {};
```

*A*, *B*, and *Weight* are just used as keys and their definitions are not necessary in the program, so there's no need to introduce definitions – it's enough just to provide declarations.

*A*, *B*, and *Weight* appear twice in lines 1 and 3 of the preceding code snippet. We can further simplify it and combine the two:

```
1    // struct A; struct B; struct Weight; to leave out this line
```

```
2    struct FParams : public VarTypeDict<struct A,
3                                        struct B,
4                                        struct Weight> {};
```

It can further simplify the program.

### 2.2.3 Implementation of Heterogeneous Dictionaries

*VarTypeDict* contains the core logic of heterogeneous dictionaries, and this section will analyze its implementation.

#### 2.2.3.1 External Framework

The external framework code of *VarTypeDict* is as follows:

```
1    template <typename...TParameters>
2    struct VarTypeDict
3    {
4        template <typename...TTypes>
5        struct Values {
6        public:
7            template <typename TTag, typename TVal>
8            auto Set(TVal&& val) && ;
9
10           template <typename TTag>
11           const auto& Get() const;
12       };
13
14   public:
15       static auto Create() {
16           using namespace NSVarTypeDict;
17           using type = typename Create_<sizeof...(TParameters),
18                                          Values>::type;
19           return type{};
20       }
21   };
```

*VarTypeDict* is a class template that contains a static function *Create*, which constructs the *type* based on the template parameters passed into *VarTypeDict*, and then returns the object corresponding to that type.

The object returned by *Create* is actually an instance of *Values<TTypes...>*, which is a template located inside *VarTypeDict* that provides functions *Set* and *Get*. So, for the previous code snippet:

```
1    std::cerr << fun(FParams::Create()
2                         .Set<B>(2.4f)
```

```
3              .Set<A>(1.3f)
4              .Set<Weight>(0.1f));
```

*Create* in line 1 is equivalent to constructing a variable of type *Values<TTypes...>* and the next few *Sets* are equivalent to passing data into *Values<TTypes...>*.

    *Values* is defined inside *VarTypeDict* and has its own template parameter *TTypes*. *TTypes* is a variadic template like *TParameters*. In fact, they all hold type information inside themselves. Keys are saved in TParameters while the corresponding numeric types are saved in *TTypes*. For example, for the following code snippet:

```
1   VarTypeDict<A, B, C>::Create()
2               .Set<A>(true).Set<B>(2.4f).Set<C>(0.1f);
```

The objects constructed after execution are: *VarTypeDict<A, B, C>::Values<bool, float, float>*.

    Let's first look at the specific implementation of the function *Create*.

## 2.2.3.2 Implementation of the Function Create

The function *Create* is the first external interface in the entire module, but there is a problem with this interface when it is implemented. Consider the following code snippet:

```
1   VarTypeDict<A, B>::Create()
2               .Set<A>(true).Set<B>(2.4f);
```

*Create* returns an instance of *Value<TTypes...>*. This instance needs to contain the specific data types of each value in the container ultimately. Ideally for this code snippet, it returns an instance of type *Value<bool,float>* after the function *Create* is called. The subsequent *Set* will set data based on the information. But programs are executed statement by statement. When *Create* is executed, the system can't know what numeric type (i.e., *bool, float*) will be set. How can it assign the type information to *TTypes*?

    There are several approaches to solve this problem. For example, we can adjust the interface design to bring forward this part of information so as to provide it before *Create* was called. However, in this case, the caller of the module needs to explicitly provide this part of information. For example, to call the interface code snippet as follows:

```
1   VarTypeDict<A, B, bool, float>::Create()
2               .Set<A>(true).Set<B>(2.4f);
```

It will intensify the burden on the caller and increase the likelihood of a program error (consider what would happen if the caller writes the wrong value type in *VarTypeDict*): it is not a good solution.

    A better way to handle this is to introduce a "placeholder type":

```
1   struct NullParameter;
```

At the beginning of calling the function *Create*, we can fill *TTypes* with this placeholder type, and modify the type to the actual type in the later *Set*. Take the previous code snippet as an example (where the corresponding return type is given after each call):

```
1   VarTypeDict<A, B>
2       ::Create()       // Values<NullParameter, NullParameter>
3         .Set<A>(true)  // Values<bool, NullParameter>
4         .Set<B>(2.4f); // Values<bool, float>
```

Based on this idea, the function *Create* is implemented as follows:

```
1   namespace NSVarTypeDict
2   {
3   template <size_t N, template<typename...> class TCont,
    typename...T>
4   struct Create_ {
5       using type = typename Create_<N - 1, TCont,
6                                 NullParameter, T...>::type;
7   };
8
9   template <template<typename...> class TCont, typename...T>
10  struct Create_<0, TCont, T...> {
11      using type = TCont<T...>;
12  };
13  }
14
15  template <typename...TParameters>
16  struct VarTypeDict {
17      // ...
18
19      static auto Create() {
20          using namespace NSVarTypeDict;
21          using type = typename Create_<sizeof...(TParameters),
22                                      Values>::type;
23          return type{};
24      }
25  };
```

The main logic of the function is actually located in *Create_* inside the namespace *NSVarTypeDict*.[5] The metafunction *Create_* is called inside *Create*, which passes in the parameter, obtains its return result (type), employs that type to construct an object, and returns it.

　　*Create_* itself implements a loop, which contains two parts. The former (lines 3–7) is the primary template, which receives the following three parameters:

---

[5] *NS* is a shorthand for namespace. *NSVarTypeDict* indicates it includes the core logic for *VarTypeDict*. As described in Chapter 1, the introduction of namespace here to locate some common logic can reduce the number of instantiations in the compilation and improve the efficiency of compilation. It is also one of the styles of the entire library.

1. *N* represents the number of elements to be constructed;
2. *TCont* is a container type that stores the final result (array of types);
3. *T* is a sequence of types that have already been generated.

Inside it, it constructs a type of *NullParameter* and places it in an array of types. With *N* minus 1, it proceeds with the next iteration.

Another specialization of *Create_* (lines 9–12) represents the case of *N=0*, which is the case of ending the loop. At this point, the system returns the array of types *TCont<T...>* directly.

*Create_* is called inside *Create*, which passes in the size of *TParameter*[6] and the array container *Values* to hold the results of the type calculation. There are two points to note here. Firstly, *Values* and *Create* are both defined inside *VarTypeDict*, so it's unnecessary to specify its outer class *VarTypeDict* when accessing *Values* in *Create*. Secondly, only two template parameters are provided when *Create* calls *Create_*. At that time *T...* in *Create_* will correspond to an empty sequence, which is allowed by the C++ standard.

*Create* is used to construct the initial array of types, using the previous code snippet as an example:

```
1   VarTypeDict<A, B, C>::Create();
```

It will construct *Values<NullParameter, NullParameter, NullParameter>* and this newly constructed type will provide the interfaces *Set* and *Get*.

### 2.2.3.3 The Main Frame of Values

The main logic of *Values* is as follows[7]:

```
1    template <typename...TParameters>
2    struct VarTypeDict
3    {
4        template <typename...TTypes>
5        struct Values
6        {
7            Values() = default;
8
9            Values(std::shared_ptr<void>(&&input)[sizeof...(TTypes)])
10           {
11               for (size_t i = 0; i < sizeof...(TTypes); ++i)
12               {
13                   m_tuple[i] = std::move(input[i]);
14               }
```

---

[6] It is obtained with the keyword *sizeof...*, which is a keyword in C++ 11.

[7] The function *Set* adds *&&* at the end of its function signature, which indicates that the function can only be used for rvalue. In the program, *std:move* and *std:forward* are used for lvalue-to-rvalue conversion and perfect forwarding. These are the features in C++ 11 and readers can refer to the books about C++11 or search the web for "ref-qualifiers," "rvalue reference," "perfect forwarding." The author won't elaborate them any further.

```
15              }
16
17      public:
18          template <typename TTag, typename TVal>
19          auto Set(TVal&& val) &&
20          {
21              using namespace NSMultiTypeDict;
22          constexpr static size_t TagPos = Tag2ID<TTag, TParameters...>;
23
24              using rawVal = std::decay_t<TVal>;
25              rawVal* tmp = new rawVal(std::forward<TVal>(val));
26              m_tuple[TagPos] = std::shared_ptr<void>(tmp,
27                  [](void* ptr) {
28                  rawVal* nptr = static_cast<rawVal*>(ptr);
29                  delete nptr;
30              });
31
32      using new_type = NewTupleType<rawVal, TagPos, Values<>, TTypes...>;
33              return new_type(std::move(m_tuple));
34          }
35
36          template <typename TTag>
37          auto& Get() const;
38
39      private:
40          std::shared_ptr<void> m_tuple[sizeof...(TTypes)];
41      };
42  };
```

The logic of *Set* is also listed here and will be analyzed. In addition to *Set*, *Values* also provides a *Get* interface. But this interface is relatively simple, so the analysis is left to readers.

*Values* is a class defined inside *VarTypeDict*, so the template parameters of *VarTypeDict* are also visible to *Values*. In other words, within *Values*, there are two sets of parameters that can be used: *TParameters* and *TTypes*. These two sets of parameters are two arrays of the same length, the former representing keys and the latter representing types of values.

The data storage area at the inner core of *Values* is a smart pointer array *m_tuple* (line 40). Each of its elements is a *void* smart pointer. These pointers of type *void* can be converted to a pointer of any other type, so they are used to store argument addresses here.

The default constructor of *Values* contains no operation. Another constructor receives a smart pointer array as input and copies it to *m_tuple*. The *Set* method will use this constructor to implement its logic.

*Values::Set* is a function template and it receives two template parameters that represent the key (*TTag*) and type of value that will be set (*TVal*). *TVal* is the second template parameter. According to the automatic derivation rules, when the function template is called, only the first template parameter of *TTag* needs to be provided, the compiler can derive the type information of the second parameter automatically. That is, assuming that *x* is an object of type *Values*, then:

```
1  x.Set<A>(true);
```

When called, *TTag* will be *A*, and *TVal* will automatically be deduced as type *bool*.

*Values:: Set* also calls several metafunctions in *NSVarTypeDict* to implement its internal logic. The incoming parameter will be processed as follows:

1. *NSVarTypeDict::Tag2ID* is called to obtain the position of *TTag* in *TParameters* and save the calling result in *TagPos* (line 22).
2. *std::decay* is called to process *TVal*. It removes qualifiers like *const*, references, etc. contained in *TVal*. The result type is then used to construct a copy of the input parameter in the heap and place the address of the copy at the appropriate location of *m_tuple* (lines 24–30).
3. Because new parameters are passed in, the array of types *Values<TType…>* needs to be modified accordingly. *NSVarTypeDict::NewTupleType* is called to obtain the new type, use it to construct a new object and return the result (lines 32 and 33).

### 2.2.3.4 *Logic Analysis of* NewTupleType

Due to limited space, only *NewTupleType* is analyzed here, while the logic of *Tag2ID* is left for readers to analyze.

Suppose that when *Set* is called for *Values<X1, X2, X3>*, the second value in the array is updated. The type of the newly incoming data is *Y*, so we need to construct a new type *Values<X1, Y, X3>* in order to record the information. It is essentially a process of scanning and replacement—to scan the original array of types, find the location to replace and replace with the new type. *NewTupleType* implements the corresponding function.

*NewTupleType* calls *NewTupleType_* to implement its logic. The declaration of *NewTupleType_* is as follows (similar to *Create_*, this function processes each element of the array in turn):

```
1  template <typename TVal, size_t N, size_t M,
2           typename TProcessedTypes,
3           typename... TRemainTypes>
4  struct NewTupleType_;
```

*TVal* is the target data type for replacement; *N* indicates the location of the target type in the array of types; *TProcessedTypes* is an array container that contains the scanned part; *TRemainTypes* contains the part to be scanned and replaced; and *M* is an auxiliary variable, which represents the number of types that have been scanned.

In addition to the discussed declarations, *NewTupleType_* provides two specialized versions that together form a loop. The first specialized version scans the first half of the array, as follows:

```
1  template <typename TVal, size_t N, size_t M,
2           template <typename...> class TCont,
```

```
3                    typename...TModifiedTypes,
4                    typename TCurType,
5                    typename... TRemainTypes>
6    struct NewTupleType_<TVal, N, M, TCont<TModifiedTypes...>,
7                          TCurType, TRemainTypes...>
8    {
9        using type =
10           typename NewTupleType_<TVal, N, M + 1,
11                           TCont<TModifiedTypes..., TCurType>,
12                           TRemainTypes...>::type;
13   };
```

It corresponds to the case of *N!=M*. The specialization uses *TCont<TModifiedTypes...>* to represent the types of which the replacement scanning has been completed; *TCurType*, together with *TRemainTypes*, represents the types of which the replacement scanning has not been completed (where *TCurType* represents the type processed currently). Because *N!=M*, *TCurType* is simply put into the *TCont* container and the next type is to be processed.

The compiler will take the next specialization if *N==M*:

```
1    template <typename TVal, size_t N,
2              template <typename...> class TCont,
3              typename...TModifiedTypes,
4              typename TCurType,
5              typename... TRemainTypes>
6    struct NewTupleType_<TVal, N, N, TCont<TModifiedTypes...>,
7                          TCurType, TRemainTypes...>
8    {
9        using type = TCont<TModifiedTypes..., TVal, TRemainTypes...>;
10   };
```

Now that the element to be replaced has been found, all the system has to do is to replace *TCurType* with *TVal*, and concatenate the *TRemainTypes* on the back of the sequence and then return.

*NewTupleType* is essentially just a shell for *NewTupleType*, it calls *NewTupleType_* to implement its logic:

```
1    template <typename TVal, size_t TagPos,
2              typename TCont, typename... TRemainTypes>
3    using NewTupleType
4        = typename NewTupleType_<TVal, TagPos, 0, TCont,
5                          TRemainTypes...>::type;
```

The analysis of the core code of *VarTypeDict* is as described. Although the entire module may seem complex, in essence, it does not break away from the sequences, branches, and loops as discussed in Chapter 1. As long as carefully analyzed, the logic therein is not difficult to understand.

Due to limited space, not all the metafunctions and logic involved in *VarTypeDict* are listed and analyzed here. Some similar analyses are left in the exercises for readers. It is suggested that readers should complete the rest of the program analysis carefully. Only through continuous practice can we better grasp the writing method of metafunctions.

## 2.2.4 A Brief Analysis of VarTypeDict's Performance

From the analysis discussed, it is obvious that *VarTypeDict* maintains a mapping that maps the keys at compile time to the runtime values in essence. From this point of view alone, it is not much different from the feature *std::map* mentioned at the beginning of this chapter. However, *std::map* and similar runtime constructs inevitably incur excessive runtime expenses in the process of using them. For example, when we insert an element into it, *std::map* requires to compare the keys to determine the location to insert. The process of comparison takes up the amount of computation at runtime. The *Set* function implemented by *VarTypeDict* class also requires similar work of looking up, but the corresponding code is:

```
1  constexpr static size_t TagPos = Tag2ID<TTag, TParameters...>;
```

It is done at compile time and does not take up the cost at runtime. And if the compilation system is smart enough, the intermediate *TagPos* will be optimized away—it won't take up any memory. These advantages are incomparable to the equivalents of runtime containers.

Similarly, the *Get* function can also benefit from compile-time calculation.

## 2.2.5 std::tuple as the Cache

Everything will look like a nail in the eyes of a man who has a hammer. It is true of many people and programmers can't avoid it. For beginners of metaprogramming, when we realize the benefits of metaprogramming, we may want to use metaprogramming techniques to implement every part of the code, which is euphemistically called to reduce runtime operation expenses with compile-time calculations.

A typical construct that consumes runtime costs is the pointer, which requires extra space to save the address and needs to be dereferenced to obtain the actual value when used. In *VarTypeDict*, we used an array of *void* pointers to hold the values. A straightforward idea is to get rid of it and use compile-time calculations to further reduce costs.

In fact, the array of pointers in *VarTypeDict* also has its replacements at compile time, of which a typical one is *std::tuple*. For the declaration in the original program:

```
1  std::shared_ptr<void> m_tuple[sizeof...(TTypes)];
```

It can be modified to:

```
1  std::tuple<TType...> m_tuple;
```

It seems to shrink operations of memory allocation and recycling in the pointer implementation and speed up the program. But in fact, it is not a good idea.

The main reason to avoid using *std::tuple* is the update logic in *Set*. According to the previous analysis, *TType...* maintains the current value type and every time *Set* is called, the corresponding

*TType...* is going to change. If we use *std::tuple<TType...>* as the type of *m_tuple*, the type of *m_tuple* changes every time it is updated.

Simply changing the type doesn't make much difficulty, but the problem is that beside type modification, we also need to copy the data from the original tuple to the new tuple. The two *tuples* are of different types, so each element in the *tuple* needs to be copied or moved one by one in the assignment. If *VarTypeDict* contains *N* elements, then the *N* elements in the *tuple* need to be copied or moved each time *Set* are called. In order to set all the parameter values, the entire system needs to call *N(N–1)* copies or moves. These operations are done at runtime and the costs introduced may be greater than runtime costs of using pointers. Meanwhile, we also need to introduce some logic at compile time in order to support such moves. Therefore, it is not cost-effective to use *std::tuple* as the storage space of values in any way.

## 2.3 Policy Templates

Heterogeneous dictionaries can be regarded as containers that use keys to index-related values. The keys are constants at compile time, and the values can be objects at runtime. This characteristic of heterogeneous dictionary allows it to be applied in many scenarios. Typically, we can construct objects of heterogeneous dictionaries as argument containers of functions.

Also, it is precisely because values of heterogeneous dictionaries are runtime objects that they can't be applied in certain scenarios. Compared with functions, templates can also receive arguments, but arguments received by templates are constants at compile time. Meanwhile, template parameters can be types or templates in addition to numeric objects—these can't be processed by heterogeneous dictionaries themselves. In this section, we will consider another construct, policy templates, to simplify the input of template parameters.

### 2.3.1 Introduction to Policies

Considering the following scenario: we want to implement a class that encapsulates the concept of "accumulation." A typical cumulative strategy includes addition and multiplication. These strategies' behaviors are different, but their calling interfaces are similar. To maximize code reuse, we consider introducing a class template to encapsulate different behaviors:

```
1   template <typename TAccuType> struct Accumulator { /* ... */ };
```

In this definition, *TAccuType* represents the "cumulative" strategy adopted. Inside *Accumulator*, you can choose the appropriate processing logic based on the value of this parameter.

In fact, there may be other options for cumulative classes too. For example, we might want this class to accumulate and also average the cumulative results. Further, we would like to be able to control whether the class carries out the average operation. Also, we hope to control the types of values used in the calculation, and so on. Based on the discussed considerations, the previously defined template *Accumulator* is extended as follows:

```
1   template <typename TAccuType, bool DoAve, typename ValueType>
2   struct Accumulator { /* ... */ };
```

The template contains three parameters called policies,[8] which act on templates and control their behaviors. Each policy is represented as a key-value pair, where the key and value are compile-time constants. Each policy has its own set of values. For example, for the described example, the value set of *TAccuType* includes "addition," "multiplication," and so on; the value set of *DoAve* includes *true* and *false*; for *ValueType*, it could be *float*, *double*, and so on.

In general, to facilitate the use of templates, we assign default values to each of them, corresponding to common usages, such as:

```
1   template <typename TAccuType = Add, bool DoAve = false,
2               typename ValueType = float>
3   struct Accumulator { /* ... */ };
```

It means that *Accumulator* accumulates with addition by default and does not average, with *float* as its return type. Users of the class can use the default behavior of *Accumulator* as follows:

```
1   Accumulator<> ...
```

This form of invocation can meet demands in the general sense, but in some cases we need to alter the default behavior. For example, if we want to change the calculation type to *double*, we should use the following declaration:

```
1   Accumulator<Add, false, double> ...
```

It means that the value type alters from the default *float* to *double*, and other policies remain unchanged.

There are two problems with this setup. Firstly, *Add* and *false* before *double* can't be left out, even if they are equal to the default values—otherwise the compiler will match *TAccuType* with *double*, which can produce unpredictable results (usually compilation errors). Secondly, considering the discussed statement alone, it may be difficult for people unfamiliar with *Accumulator* to grasp the meaning of these parameters.

It would be much better if we could explicitly name each argument value when setting template parameters. For example, if it is written as follows:

```
1   Accumulator<ResType = double> ...
```

Then the meaning of the settings will be clarified. But in fact, named template arguments are not directly supported in C++. The discussed statement does not meet C++ standards and will result in a compilation error.

Although we can't write it as "key-value" as discussed, we can adjust it to a form accepted by C++ standard. This form is referred to in this book as the "policy object."

---

[8] In fact, there is a similar concept: *trait*. Usually *traits* are used to describe attributes, while policies are used to describe behaviors. But traits and policies are not always clearly separated. Interested readers can read the book "C++ Templates: The Complete Guide." This book will use the name "policy" uniformly.

### 2.3.1.1 Policy Objects

Each policy object belongs to a policy and their relationships are like that between objects and classes in C++. Policy objects are compile-time constants that contain all the information about keys and values and are easy to read. A typical policy object is as follows:

```
1  PMulAccu // To accumulate by multiplication
2  PAve     // To average
```

The policy objects defined in this book begin with a capital letter *P*. Depending on its name, users can clearly grasp the meaning of the policy described by the object at a glance. For templates that support policy objects, it is quite simple to alter their default behaviors. For example, assuming that the class template *Accumulator* discussed earlier supports policy objects, we can write as follows:

```
1  Accumulator<PDoubleValueType>
2  Accumulator<PDoubleValueType, PAve>
3  Accumulator<PAve, PDoubleValueType>
```

Line 1 indicates that the default behavior is modified to use *double* as the type of values. Lines 2 and 3 represent using *double* as the type of values and averaging. It is not difficult to see from the declaration that when assigning a policy object to a template, the order is arbitrary. With policy objects, we can obtain all benefits of named arguments.

### 2.3.1.2 Policy Object Templates

The construction and use of policy objects are separate. We need to first construct a policy object (such as *PAve*) and then use that object when declaring instances of *Accumulator* later (such as *Accumulator<PAve>*).

It introduces a problem that, the policy designer needs to declare all possible policy values in advance in order to enable policy users to use the policy object effectively. For example, *PAve* and *PNoAve* can be constructed to represent averages and non-averages, respectively—which is equivalent to enumerating options for whether to average. In some cases, this enumeration is relatively simple—for example, it only takes two cases to enumerate the question of whether to average. But in other cases it is unrealistic to enumerate all possible values to construct a collection of objects. For example, we defined *PDoubleValueType* previously to represent the return value of accumulation as type *double*. But, if we want to support other return value types, we need to introduce more policy objects, such as *PFloatValueType*, *PIntValueType*, and so on. And it is often unrealistic to cite all the cases. To solve this problem, we introduced the policy object template, which is a metafunction that can pass in template parameters to construct a policy object. For example, we can construct a policy object template to represent the type that holds the results of calculation:

```
1  PValueTypeIs<typename T>
```

Users can use the template as follows:

```
1  // Equivalent to Accumulator<PDoubleValueType>
```

```
2    Accumulator<PValueTypeIs<double>>

3

4    // Equivalent to Accumulator<PDoubleValueType, PAve>
5    Accumulator<PValueTypeIs<double>, PAve>
```

Using the policy object template, we delay the timing of constructing the policy object until the policy is used. It eliminates the need to prepare a large number of policy objects in advance for the use of policy.

Once there is a policy object, the function template and class template that use the object are called policy templates[9]. Chapter 16 of the book "C++ Templates: The Complete Guide"[10] gives a way to construct policy objects and policy templates. Interested readers can refer to it. But, for the policy templates in that book, there is a strict limit on the number of template parameters—if we want to change the maximum number of policy objects it can receive, the entire construct needs to be adjusted accordingly from the bottom layer. This section builds a more flexible structure based on it, and we will analyze its implementation principles later. But before diving into the details, let's take a look at how to use the framework provided in this book to introduce policy objects such as *PValueTypeIs* and *PAve*.

## 2.3.2 Defining Policies and Policy Objects (Templates)

### 2.3.2.1 Policy Grouping

An actual system might contain many templates like *Accumulator*: each template uses policy objects and some templates might share policy objects. Therefore, simply declaring and using policy objects are not enough for complex systems. A better idea is to divide these objects into different groups according to their functionality. Each template can use one or more groups of policy objects.

There is mutual exclusion among policy objects with different value, which belongs to the same policy. For example, it can be defined that *PAddAccu* and *PMulAccu* represent the accumulation by addition and multiplication, respectively. When instantiating cumulative objects, we can only choose one from the two and can't introduce both policy objects at the same time—in other words, the following code snippet is meaningless:

```
1    Accumulator<PAddAccu, PMulAccu>
```

To describe the groups to which a policy object belongs and mutual exclusions, we introduced two properties for each policy object: the major class and the minor class. The major class represents the group to which it belongs and the minor class describes the information about mutual exclusion. If two policy objects belong to the same major class and the same minor class, then they are mutually exclusive and can't be used at the same time.

There are many approaches to depict groups in C++. For example, we can put each group in a separate namespace or place different groups of policy objects in different arrays—but these two are not good choices. It is because policy objects will participate in the calculation of the metafunction

---

[9] Note the difference between a policy template and a policy object template: the former represents a template that uses policy objects, and the latter represents a template that constructs policy objects.

[10] Josuttis, N. M., & Gregor, D. (2003). C++ Templates: The Complete Guide (Vol. 338). Boston: Addison-Wesley Professional.

and the metaprogramming method of operating the namespace in C++ is not mature. It is also not appropriate to use arrays: as discussed in the section of heterogeneous dictionaries, it may take a lot of effort to maintain the relationship between array indexes and keys when using arrays.

Our approach is to use a class (or structure) as the carrier of a group, where the policy information contained therein is defined internally. Each policy is a key-value pair and both the key and the value are compile-time constants. Similar to heterogeneous dictionaries, we also use type declarations to represent keys, but introduce few limitations for values—it can be types, values, or even templates. The only thing to note is that, as discussed earlier, each policy has a default value. Here's an example of a simple policy group:

```
1    struct AccPolicy
2    {
3        struct AccuTypeCate
4        {
5            struct Add;
6            struct Mul;
7        };
8        using Accu = AccuTypeCate::Add;
9
10       struct IsAveValueCate;
11       static constexpr bool IsAve = false;
12
13       struct ValueTypeCate;
14       using Value = float;
15   };
```

This policy group is named *AccPolicy*: as the name suggests, it contains policies that *Accumulator* needs. The group contains three policies, which correspond to exactly three common types of policy.

1. Accumulation policy: it could be enumerated and its possible values compose an enumerable set. Lines 3–7 define all possible enumeration values for this policy (*Add* and *Mul* for addition and multiplication). Line 3 also defines the minor class of the object of the policy as *AccuTypeCate*. Line 8 defines the key of the policy as *Accu* and the default value is *AccuTypeCate::Add*.
2. Whether-to-average policy: we can also set it as an enumerable policy, but to show the diversity of policy, here we choose another way—numerical policy. Line 11 defines a policy with the key as *IsAve* and the default value of *false*, which means no average. The object to which this policy belongs also has its minor class, which is defined as *IsAveValueCate* in line 10.
3. Value-type policy: line 14 defines this policy with the key as *Value* and the default value of *float* and the minor class of the object is *ValueTypeCate*.

In fact, in addition to the discussed policies, we can define other types of policies, such as the policy with a template as its value. But these three types of policies are the most common policy types that are used.

In the described code snippet, although we introduced some definitions, we did not logically associate the policy key with its minor class. At the same time, readers may have noticed that there is a name correlation between the key of the policy and its minor class. In fact, this correlation is intentional. In this book, we agree:

- For a type policy, its minor class is the key name with *TypeCate* as a suffix;
- For a numeric policy, its minor class is the key name with *ValueCate* as a suffix.

## 2.3.2.2 Declarations of Macros and Policy Objects (Templates)

On the basis of defining policies, we can further introduce policy objects (templates). This book provides several macro definitions to easily define a policy object (template)[11]:

```
1   TypePolicyObj(PAddAccu, AccPolicy, Accu, Add);
2   TypePolicyObj(PMulAccu, AccPolicy, Accu, Mul);
3   ValuePolicyObj(PAve, AccPolicy, IsAve, true);
4   ValuePolicyObj(PNoAve, AccPolicy, IsAve, false);
5   TypePolicyTemplate(PValueTypeIs, AccPolicy, Value);
6   ValuePolicyTemplate(PAvePolicyIs, AccPolicy, IsAve);
```

This book introduces four macros:

1. *TypePolicyObj* is used to define type policy objects;
2. *ValuePolicyObj* is used to define numeric policy objects;
3. *TypePolicyTemplate* is used to define type policy object templates;
4. *ValuePolicyTemplate* is used to define numeric policy object templates.

In the preceding code snippet, we define four policy objects and two policy object templates with these four macros. Take line 2 as an example: it defines a compile-time constant *PMulAccu* (where *P* represents policy and this book will use this form to define policy objects) and its corresponding major class and minor class are *AccPolicy* and *AccuTypeCate*, respectively, with the value of *AccuTypeCate::Mul*.[12] Line 5 defines a type policy object template, *PValueTypeIs*, and its major class and minor class are *AccPolicy* and *ValueTypeCate*, respectively. Readers can understand the rest of the definitions in the same way.

Here are a few points to note.

Firstly, it is not necessary to define a policy object (template) in a macro, which is just a shorthand. We'll give the implementation details of the macros later. Macros can be completely avoided but they can greatly simplify the definition of objects.

Secondly, several definitions of the six objects mentioned earlier actually describe the default values of policies again. These objects are introduced only for convenience. Users can use the default value without introducing a policy object when using a policy template or can introduce an object to explicitly specify the value of the policy—even if the value explicitly specified is the same as the default value, it is also legal.

---

[11] In fact, this is the only place in this book where macros are used. The author is quite wary of using macros and readers can refer to Chapter 1 of this book to obtain related statements.

[12] Macros automatically expand *Accu* and *Mul* inside, thus constructing *AccuTypeCate* and *AccuTypeCate::Mul*.

Finally, policy objects do not conflict with policy object templates—we can define both the policy object and the policy object template for the same policy. For example, in the previous code snippet, we define both *PAve* and *PAvePolicyIs*, which are compatible.

### 2.3.3 Using Policies

Once a policy is defined, we're ready to use it. Consider the following example[13]:

```
1   template <typename...TPolicies>
2   struct Accumulator
3   {
4       using TPoliCont = PolicyContainer<TPolicies...>;
5       using TPolicyRes = PolicySelect<AccPolicy, TPoliCont>;
6
7       using ValueType = typename TPolicyRes::Value;
8       static constexpr bool is_ave = TPolicyRes::IsAve;
9       using AccuType = typename TPolicyRes::Accu;
10
11  public:
12      template <typename TIn>
13      static auto Eval(const TIn& in)
14      {
15          if constexpr(std::is_same<AccuType,
16                          AccPolicy::AccuTypeCate::Add>::value)
17          {
18              ValueType count = 0;
19              ValueType res = 0;
20              for (const auto& x : in)
21              {
22                  res += x;
23                  count += 1;
24              }
25
26              if constexpr (is_ave)
27                  return res / count;
28              else
29                  return res;
30          }
31          else if constexpr (std::is_same<AccuType,
```

---

[13] The selection logic at compile time is implemented here using *if constexpr*. *DependencyFalse<AccuType>* in the code snippet is a metafunction with a value of false, which indicates logic that shouldn't be triggered. We can't use *static_assert (false)* directly, but we can use code like this to mark logic that shouldn't be triggered.

```
32                                      AccPolicy::AccuTypeCate::Mul>::value)
33            {
34                ValueType res = 1;
35                ValueType count = 0;
36                for (const auto& x : in)
37                {
38                    res *= x;
39                    count += 1;
40                }
41                if constexpr (is_ave)
42                    return pow(res, 1.0 / count);
43                else
44                    return res;
45            }
46            else
47            {
48                static_assert(DependencyFalse<AccuType>);
49            }
50        }
51   };
52
53   int main() {
54       int a[] = { 1, 2, 3, 4, 5 };
55       cerr << Accumulator<>::Eval(a) << endl;
56       cerr << Accumulator<PMulAccu>::Eval(a) << endl;
57       cerr << Accumulator<PMulAccu, PAve>::Eval(a) << endl;
58       cerr << Accumulator<PAve, PMulAccu>::Eval(a) << endl;
59       //  cerr << Accumulator<PMulAccu, PAddAccu>::Eval(a) << endl;
60       cerr << Accumulator<PAve, PMulAccu,
61                       PValueTypeIs<double>>::Eval(a) << endl;
62     cerr << Accumulator<PAve, PMulAccu, PDoubleValue>::Eval(a) << endl;
63   }
```

*Accumulator* is a class template that receives policies, which provides a static function *Eval* to calculate the cumulative results. Several examples of calls are given in lines 55–62. Line 55 uses the default policy: add-cumulative, non-average, and returning floats—because there is no specific policy object specified in the *Accumulator* declaration, *Accumulator* will use the default value of the policy specified at the time of policy definition when obtaining policy-related parameters. Lines 56 and 57, on the other hand, introduce non-default policy objects for calculation—to implement the accumulation of non-average and average by multiplying, respectively. The output of line 58 is exactly the same as that of line 57: the order in which policies are set is swappable. If the code in line 59 is enabled, the compilation will fail and the system will prompt "Minor class set conflict!"—meaning that two conflicting policy objects can't be set at the same time.

Lines 60 and 61 of the preceding code snippet use the previously defined template *PValueTypeIs* and pass in *double* as an argument, which indicates *double* is used as the type to hold results. Its behavior is consistent with line 62.

It should be noted that although the output of line 57 is exactly the same as that of line 58, the specific types in calculation are different. That is, the types of *Accumulator<PMulAccu, PAve>*, and *Accumulator<PAve, PMulAccu>* are different. It is different from the heterogeneous dictionary discussed in the previous section. For them, we can change the order of *Set*'s invocation, with the type of the resulting dictionary container remain unchanged. However, if the order of the policy objects is changed, the type of the template instantiation will vary.

How does a policy object change the default behavior of a template? We need to dive deeply into the details of the implementation to understand it. Before that, let's start with some background knowledge—only by understanding it can we proceed to discuss details of the implementation.

### 2.3.4 Background Knowledge: Dominance and Virtual Inheritance

Before we discuss the specific implementation of policy templates, let's start by understanding some background knowledge to clarify how it works. Consider the following code snippet:

```
1   struct A { void fun(); };
2   struct B : A { void fun(); };
3
4   struct C : B {
5       void wrapper() {
6           fun();
7       }
8   };
```

So, which function *fun* (*A::fun* or *B::fun*) will be called when the function *C::wrapper* is called?

It is not a difficult question to answer. According to the rules of inheritance in C++, if the definition of *fun* is not found in *C*, the compiler will look for its base class, base class of the base class, and so on, that is, along the derived relationship of *C*. Until a function named *fun* is found. In this example, *B::fun* will be called.

The inheritance relationships of the discussed three classes are shown in Figure 2.1.

Here, a solid arrow is used to represent an inheritance relationship, pointing in the direction to the base class. In the figure, *B* inherits from *A* and the two define functions with the same name. At this point, we call *B::fun* dominates *A::fun*. When searching, the compiler will select a dominant function.

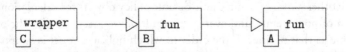

**Figure 2.1  A simple single-inheritance relationship.**

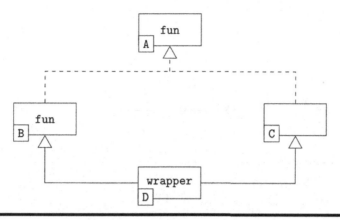

**Figure 2.2 Dominant relationship in multiple inheritance.**

Another typical dominant relationship occurs in the case of multiple inheritance, as shown in Figure 2.2.

The dotted arrow here represents the relationship of virtual inheritance, that is,

```
1   struct B : virtual A;
2   struct C : virtual A;
```

We assume that *D::wrapper* will call the function *fun*. In this figure, *C* inherits the function *fun* in *A*, while *B* redefines *fun*. Accordingly, the newly defined function in *B* is more dominant. So, *D* will select *B::fun* when calling.

Note that in the case of multiple inheritance, the previous discussion is valid only if virtual inheritance is used. Otherwise, the compiler will report resolution ambiguity. In addition, for Figure 2.2, if the function *fun* is also defined in *C*, the compiler will report resolution ambiguity even with virtual inheritance—because there are two dominant functions, and there is no dominant relationship between them, which makes the compiler unable to choose.

The dominant relationship between functions is discussed earlier. In fact, dominant relationships exist not only between functions. There is a similar dominant relationship in terms of type and constant definitions.

## 2.3.5 Policy Objects and Policy Dominance Structures

Having understood the relationship of domination and inheritance, we can consider the construction of policy objects. The reason why a policy object can "change" the default policy value is actually that it inherits the defined policy class and changes the original policy value in its own definition, which forms a dominant relationship.

For example, on the basis of a given *AccPolicy*, *PMulAccu* can be defined as follows:

```
1   struct AccPolicy {
2       struct AccuTypeCate { struct Add; struct Mul; };
3       using Accu = AccuTypeCate::Add;
4       // ...
```

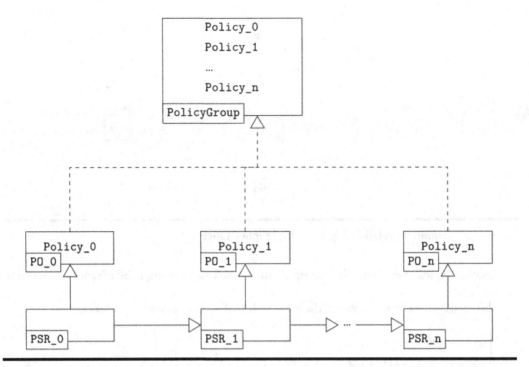

**Figure 2.3   Policy Dominance Structure.**

```
5    };
6
7    struct PMulAccu : virtual public AccPolicy {
8        using MajorClass = AccPolicy;
9        using MinorClass = AccPolicy::AccuTypeCate;
10       using Accu = AccuTypeCate::Mul;
11   }
```

Here is a complete definition of *PMulAccu*. Lines 8 and 9 define the major and minor class of *PMulAccu*. The metafunctions that operate on them will be discussed later and it is not necessary to be concerned with them for the time being. We only need to focus on line 10, which redefines the value of *Accu*. According to the dominant relationship, if a class *X* is inherited from *PMulAccu*, when searching for *Accu* information in class *X*, the compiler will return *AccuEnum::Mul* instead of *AccuEnum::Add*, the default value defined in *AccPolicy*.

A policy template can receive multiple policy objects and the behavior of a policy template is determined by these policy objects. Based on the policy objects received by the policy template, a dominance hierarchy structure of the policy can be constructed through metaprogramming, as shown in Figure 2.3.

*PO_0~PO_n* represents policy objects that can be used as template parameters and belongs to the same group. They are virtually inherited from the same policy class, *PolicyGroup*. On this basis, we have introduced several peripheral classes, *PSR_0~PSR_n*.[14] Each peripheral class has

---

[14] PSR is an abbreviation for Policy Selection Results.

two base classes, except *PSR_n*, which has only one base class. If *PO_0~PO_n* are compatible, that is, the minor classes of any two policy objects are distinct, then starting from *PSR_0* and searching, we must find a definition of no ambiguity in dominance for any policy belonging to the group. This definition comes either from the class *PolicyGroup* (corresponding to the default value of policy) or from a policy object (corresponding to a non-default value).

After defining this structure, the following main task is to introduce metafunctions and construct the structure based on the policy objects.

## 2.3.6 Policy Selection Metafunction

### 2.3.6.1 Main Frame

The external interface of the entire policy template is the policy selection metafunction: *PolicySelect*. Review how this metafunction is used:

```
1   template <typename...TPolicies>
2   struct Accumulator {
3       using TPoliCont = PolicyContainer<TPolicies...>;
4       using TPolicyRes = PolicySelect<AccPolicy, TPoliCont>;
5
6       using ValueType = typename TPolicyRes::Value;
7       static constexpr bool is_ave = TPolicyRes::IsAve;
8       using AccuType = typename TPolicyRes::Accu;
9
10      // ...
11  }
```

Line 4 calls *PolicySelect*, the policy selection metafunction, with arguments *AccPolicy*, the policy group information we are concerned about, and *TPoliCont*, an array of policies consisting of policy objects received by the template. *TPolicyRes* returned by the metafunction is the policy dominance structure shown in Figure 2.3. On this basis, lines 6–8 use this structure to obtain the corresponding policy parameter values.

*PolicyContainer* is an array container of policies and its declaration is almost the same as the declaration of a compile-time array we saw earlier:

```
1   template <typename...TPolicies>
2   struct PolicyContainer;
```

*std::tuple* or other containers can be used as a substitute for it. However, with this container declaration, the functionality of the array can be easily identified from its name.

*PolicySelect* is simply the encapsulation of the metafunction *NSPolicySelect::Selector_*:

```
1   template <typename TMajorClass, typename TPolicyContainer>
2   using PolicySelect
3       = typename NSPolicySelect::Selector_<TMajorClass,
4                                     TPolicyContainer>::type;
```

It passes the parameters to *NSPolicySelect::Selector_*, which implements the core computational logic. *NSPolicySelect::Selector_* is defined as follows:

```
1   template <typename TMajorClass, typename TPolicyContainer>
2   struct Selector_;
3
4   template <typename TMajorClass, typename... TPolicies>
5   struct Selector_<TMajorClass, PolicyContainer<TPolicies...>> {
6       using TMF = typename MajorFilter_<PolicyContainer<>,
7                                         TMajorClass,
8                                         TPolicies...>::type;
9
10      static_assert(MinorCheck_<TMF>::value,
11                    "Minor class set conflict!");
12
13      using type = std::conditional_t<IsArrayEmpty<TMF>,
14                                      TMajorClass,
15                                      PolicySelRes<TMF>>;
16  };
```

By introducing template specialization, *Select_* limits its second parameter to a container of type *PolicyContainer*. It does three tasks internally.

1. To call the metafunction *MajorFilter_* to filter the array and create a new *PolicyContainer* array—ensuring that the major class of all the elements in the array is *TMajorClass* (lines 6–8).
2. To call the metafunction *MinorCheck_* to check the array generated in the previous step, ensuring that the elements in it do not conflict—that is, there are no policy objects with a same minor class (lines 10 and 11).
3. To construct the final return type (lines 13–15).

In these three steps, the first step is essentially a linear search, which is relatively simple. The corresponding analysis is left to readers. Let's look directly at the logic of the second step.

### 2.3.6.2 The Metafunction MinorCheck_

As already emphasized, the minor classes of policy objects as parameters of a single template can't be the same. Otherwise, it is illogical and the compiler will therefore encounter a situation in which parsing is ambiguous, giving a compilation error. But, since the compiler can already prompt an error message, why do we introduce this metafunction to check here again? In fact, the error message given by the compiler is "resolution ambiguity" and does not clearly indicate the cause of this ambiguity—the policy objects conflict. Therefore, it is necessary to introduce an additional check here to give a clearer message.

Lines 10 and 11 of the previous code snippet finish this check. It calls the function *MinorCheck_*, passes in an array of policy objects and gets the return value of the function (a compile-time constant of type Boolean). It uses *static_assert* introduced in C++11 to check. *static_assert* is a static assertion that receives two parameters: when the first argument is false, a compilation error is generated and an error message provided by the second argument will be output.

The metafunction *MinorCheck_* is to detect the input array of policy objects (each element in this array belongs to the same policy group) and determine whether any two elements in it have the same minor class. If not, it returns *true*, otherwise *false* is returned.

Consider how to implement the logic at runtime. The corresponding algorithm is not complex and a nested loop can solve it:

```
1  for (i = 0; i < VecSize; ++i) {
2      for (j = i + 1; j < VecSize; ++j) {
3          if (Vec[i] and Vec[j] have same minor class)
4          {
5              return false;
6          }
7      }
8  }
9  return true;
```

The discussed code illustrate the solution algorithm: in the outer loop, we process each element in the array in turn, compare them with the elements behind it through the inner loop. As soon as we find there are policy objects with the same minor class, it will return *false*. If the whole comparison is complete and no such situation is found, then *true* is returned.

The implementation logic of metafunctions is almost the same in nature—just introducing a similar nested loop. There are merely some differences between compile-time and runtime loops, which make it look a bit complicated.

```
1  template <typename TPolicyCont>
2  struct MinorCheck_ {
3      static constexpr bool value = true;
4  };
5
6  template <typename TCurPolicy, typename... TP>
7  struct MinorCheck_<PolicyContainer<TCurPolicy, TP...>> {
8      static constexpr bool cur_check
9          = MinorDedup_<typename TCurPolicy::MinorClass,
10                     TP...>::value;
11
12     static constexpr bool value
13         = AndValue<cur_check,
14                MinorCheck_<PolicyContainer<TP...>>>;
15 };
```

*MinorCheck_* receives an array of policy objects called *TPolicyCont*, which forms an outer loop through specialization.

Let's start with the specialized version. The input parameter for this version is *PolicyContainer<TCurPolicy, TP...>*, which indicates that it receives an array with *PolicyContainer* as a container containing one or more elements. The first element is *TCurPolicy* and the remaining elements are represented as *TP....*

On this basis, the program first obtains the minor class corresponding to the policy object (line 9), then calls *MinorDedup_* to pass in the obtained value and compare it with all subsequent elements (i.e., inner loop), and return the result of the comparison to a compile-time constant *cur_check*.

If the return value is true, indicating that the minor class of each subsequent element is not *TCurPolicy*, then the system could execute the next detection, which is done by the recursive call of *MinorCheck_* in line 14. Here, we use *AndValue*, a custom metafunction, to implement the short-circuit logic of judgment—if the current detection returns *cur_check* as *false*, then the program will return *false* directly with no further detection. The metafunction returns *true* only if the current result is *true* and the subsequent result (i.e., the result corresponding to line 14) is *true*.

The termination logic for the outer loop is defined in the primary template of *MinorCheck_*. When all elements in the input array of policy objects are processed and the recursive call is executed again, the arguments passed in to the metafunction will be *PolicyContainer<>*. It is not possible to match the specialized version of the template (the specialization version requires at least one element in the array). The compiler will then match the primary version of the template (lines 1–4). For this definition, it simply returns *true* and thus terminates the loop.

The inner loop logic is defined in the metafunction *MinorDedup_*:

```
1    template <typename TMinorClass, typename... TP>
2    struct MinorDedup_ {
3        static constexpr bool value = true;
4    };
5
6    template <typename TMinorClass, typename TCurPolicy, typename... TP>
7    struct MinorDedup_<TMinorClass, TCurPolicy, TP...> {
8        using TCurMirror = typename TCurPolicy::MinorClass;
9
10       constexpr static bool cur_check
11           = !(std::is_same<TMinorClass, TCurMirror>::value);
12
13       constexpr static bool value
14           = AndValue<cur_check,
15                   MinorDedup_<TMinorClass, TP...>>;
16   };
```

This metafunction also has an primary template and a specialized version, which implements the termination and iteration of the loop, respectively. It receives a sequence of parameters, the first of which is the class minor type to be compared. The subsequent parameters are the policy objects to be compared with. The specialized version of the template is the body of the loop: to obtain the *MinorClass* of the currently processed policy object (*TCurPolicy*) at line 8 and call *std::is_same* to compare it with *TMinorClass* at lines 10 and 11. *std::is_same* is a metafunction in the

C++ standard library, receiving two type parameters and returning *true* when they are the same, otherwise *false* is returned.

Lines 13–15 implement a loop similar to *MinorCheck_*: if the current checking result is true, then it continues the loop and perform the next detection, otherwise returns *false* directly.

Similar to *MinorCheck_*, *MinorDedup_* implements the termination logic of the loop in its primary template: to return *true*.

### 2.3.6.3 Construct the Final Return Type

After "filtering policy objects based on group names" and "checking the minor classes of policy objects in the same group," the final step of the policy selection metafunction is to construct the final return type, the policy dominance structure.

There is a small branch to deal with: in some cases, the input of this step is an empty array, *PolicyContainer<>*. There are two reasons for encountering empty arrays: one is that the user does not introduce a policy object to adjust the default behavior of the template when using it; the other is that the adjusted policy object belongs to other groups. Thus, in the first step of policy selection, an empty array of policies is generated by filtering.

The policy dominance structure shown in Figure 2.3 requires at least one policy object in the input array. Therefore, if there are no objects in the array, then it needs to be processed separately. It is simple to deal with: if the array does not contain objects, the default policy definition can be returned directly.

```
1   template <typename TMajorClass, typename... TPolicies>
2   struct Select_<TMajorClass, PolicyContainer<TPolicies...>> {
3       ...
4       using type = std::conditional_t<IsArrayEmpty<TMF>,
5                                        TMajorClass,
6                                        PolicySelRes<TMF>>;
7   };
```

*TMF* is the array of policy objects generated in the first step; *IsArrayEmpty* is used to determine whether the array is empty. If the array is indeed empty, then *TMajorClass* is returned directly. The default values for each policy in that group are defined in *TMajorClass*.

If *TMF* is not empty, then it can be used to construct the policy dominance structure. This dominance structure is represented here as *PolicySelRes <TMF>*:

```
1    template <typename TPolicyCont>
2    struct PolicySelRes;
3
4    template <typename TPolicy>
5    struct PolicySelRes<PolicyContainer<TPolicy>> : public TPolicy {};
6
7    template <typename TCurPolicy, typename... TOtherPolicies>
8    struct PolicySelRes<PolicyContainer<TCurPolicy, TOtherPolicies...>>
9        : public TCurPolicy,
10         public PolicySelRes<PolicyContainer<TOtherPolicies...>> {};
```

Based on Figure 2.3, this code snippet is straightforward to understand. *PolicySelRes* implements the whole logic with two specializations. The input of this metafunction is an array of *PolicyContainer*. If the array contains two or more elements, the compiler will selects the second specialization (lines 7–10), which is derived from two classes.

1. *TCurPolicy*: the current policy object, which is the vertical connection from *PSR_x* to *PO_x* in Figure 2.3 ($x \in [0, n-1]$).
2. *PolicySelRes<PolicyContainer<TOtherPolicies...>>*: corresponding to horizontal connection from *PSR_x* to *PSR_(x+1)*($x \in [0, n-1]$).

If there is only one element in the array, the compiler will select the first specialization (lines 4 and 5), which is derived from only one class, corresponding to the vertical connection in Figure 2.3 from *PSR_n* to *PO_n*.

## 2.3.7 Simplifying Declarations of Policy Objects with Macros

So far, we have basically completed the main logic of policy templates. In order to use policy templates, we need to:

1. Declare a class that represents a policy group and contains default values of policies in the group;
2. Declare a policy object or policy object template and associate it with the policy group;
3. Use *PolicySelect* in the policy template to obtain policy information for a specific group.

The second step requires the introduction of a class for each policy object or policy object template. Here are four macros introduced to simplify this step:

```
1    #define TypePolicyObj(PolicyName, Ma, Mi, Val) \
2    struct PolicyName : virtual public Ma\
3    { \
4        using MajorClass = Ma; \
5        using MinorClass = Ma::Mi##TypeCate; \
6        using Mi = Ma::Mi##TypeCate::Val; \
7    }
8
9    #define ValuePolicyObj(PolicyName, Ma, Mi, Val) ...
10   #define TypePolicyTemplate(PolicyName, Ma, Mi) ...
11   #define ValuePolicyTemplate(PolicyName, Ma, Mi) ...
```

Due to limited space, only the definition of *TypePolicyObj* is listed here. It is not difficult to figure out that its essence is to construct a class virtually inherited from the policy group, while setting the value of the major class, minor class, and policy.

Here's a trick to simplify the code. In order to declare the group to which the policy object belongs, we need to introduce statements like "*using MajorClass = Ma;*" for each policy object. Such a statement needs to be added to all policy objects (templates) derived from *Ma*. We can simplify it with introducing this declaration in the definition of the policy. For example, for *AccPolicy* defined earlier, we can write as follows:

```
1   struct AccPolicy
2   {
3       using MajorClass = AccPolicy;
4       // ...
5   }
```

It simplifies the definition of the discussed macros and removes the statements of *MajorClass*:

```
1   #define TypePolicyObj(PolicyName, Ma, Mi, Val) \
2   struct PolicyName : virtual public Ma\
3   { \
4       using MinorClass = Ma::Mi##TypeCate; \
5       using Mi = Ma::Mi##TypeCate::Val; \
6   }
```

Readers can analyze the implementation of the other three macros.

It should be noted that macros are introduced only to simplify the declarations of policy objects. We can also declare such objects without macros. The power of macros is limited. For some policy objects that we can't use these macro to declare, we may consider using a generic (template) class for declaration.

## 2.4 Summary

In this chapter, we discussed the implementation of heterogeneous dictionaries and policy templates.

Both modules are essentially containers, which access values in containers by key. For heterogeneous dictionaries, the keys are compile-time constants, and the values are objects at runtime; for policy templates, the keys and values are both compile-time constants. Due to the different features of compile time and runtime, the details of their implementations are also quite distinct.

Although the discussion in this chapter is based on named arguments, constructs such as heterogeneous dictionaries can also be applied in scenarios other than delivering function arguments. For example, they can be used as simple containers like *std::map*. Compared with *std::map*, the heterogeneous dictionaries can index faster and have the advantage of storing different data types.

Each data structure has its pros and cons. Although heterogeneous dictionaries have the above advantages compared to *std::map*, it also has its own disadvantages. Precisely to support the storage of different data types as well as indexes that can be processed at compile time, the number of elements contained in a heterogeneous dictionary is fixed, not like *std::map* in which elements can be added and deleted at runtime.

But conversely, while it is not possible to add new elements to a heterogeneous dictionary at runtime, we can add or remove elements to a heterogeneous dictionary through metafunctions at compile time. This part is left to readers for practice.

Compared to heterogeneous dictionaries, the values of policy templates are also compile-time constants, where information other than values, such as types and templates, can be saved accordingly. This chapter discusses only a preliminary implementation of policy templates. In Chapter 7, we'll further extend policy templates discussed in this chapter to introduce hierarchical relationships that allow it to handle more complex situations.

This chapter did not introduce any new metaprogramming knowledge in fact (the discussion of domination is not related to metaprogramming, but the basic knowledge related to C++ inheritance, which falls into the object-oriented field). We've just determined the interface of the two modules and implemented them with metaprogramming. The basic techniques we use are the programming methods of sequences, branches, and loops as discussed in Chapter 1. However, compared to Chapter 1, it is not difficult to recognize that the procedures of sequences, branches, and loops written in this chapter are more complex and more flexible. To truly master programming techniques like this, readers need to continue experiencing and practicing.

The modules constructed in this chapter will be used in the deep learning framework as basic components. Starting from Chapter 3, we'll discuss the implementation of the deep learning framework.

## 2.5 Exercises

1. *NSVarTypeDict::Create_* uses a linear method to construct elements. That is, constructing elements one by one. Thus, the number of loop executions at compile time and the number of instantiations is $O(N)$. Can you modify its logic so that the number of loop executions and instantiations at compile time is $O(log(N))$?

2. Read and analyze the implementation logic of *NSVarTypeDict::Tag2ID*.

3. This chapter analyzes the implementation logic of *NSVarTypeDict::NewTupleType_*. This metafunction contains a declaration with two specializations. In fact, its definition can be simplified: specialization 1 ($N!=M$) and specialization 2 ($N==M$) are actually branches, which can be combined using *std::conditional_t*. Rewrite the implementation of this metafunction according to the above idea. Think about the pros and cons of the original and modified implementation.

4. Read and analyze the implementation logic of *VarTypeDict::Values::Get*.

5. *VarTypeDict::Values::Set* adds *&&* at the end of its signature indicating that the function can only be used for rvalue. Define a *Set* that can be used for lvalue and think about what advantages and disadvantages this new function has compared with the old one.

6. One constructor of *Values* that receives the array is to be called by the function *Values::Set*. *Set* is also a function defined in *Values*. So, can we modify the access qualifier to the constructor from *public* to *private* or *protected*? Give reasons and try to modify the access qualifier and compile it to see if it meets your expectations.

7. Replace the array of pointers in *VarTypeDict::Values* with *std::tuple*, and implement the version of *VarTypeDict* that does not require explicit allocation and release of memory. Analyze the complexity of the new version.

8. In section 2.3, we give a class for cumulative computation and use it to demonstrate the concept of the policy and policy object. In fact, we can use policies in function templates in addition to class templates. Rewrite the example provided in this section, using a function template to implement the same functionality as the cumulative algorithm provided by the example.

9. Analyze the implementation logic of *NSPolicySelect::MajorFilter_*.

10. Analyze the implementation logic of *IsArrayEmpty*.

11. Try to construct a template policy object, that is, a policy object with a template as its value. Try to introduce macros to simplify the definition of the corresponding policy object.
12. The heterogeneous dictionaries developed in this chapter contain the method *Get*, which is used to obtain different types of data objects based on key values. But, for now, the method *Get* copies the object in the dictionary and then returns the copied results when returning an object. For some data structures, the expenses of replication are relatively high. We can consider using move semantics to reduce the additional costs of replication. Based on the existing code, introduce a new function *Get* for *VarTypeDict::Values*, which is called when the object of *VarTypeDict::Values* itself is a rvalue. When the new function *Get* is called, the underlying data object will be returned by movement.
13. Try to write two metafunctions, *AddItem* and *DelItem*, which add or remove elements for heterogeneous dictionaries at compile time. For example, in the following code snippet:

```
using MyDict = VarTypeDict<struct A, struct B>;
using DictWithMoreItems = AddItem<MyDict, struct C>;
using DictWithLessItems = DelItem<MyDict, A>;
```

The types of *DictWithMoreItems* are *VarTypeDict<A, B, C>*, and the type of *DictWithWithLessItems* is *VarTypeDict<B>*.

Note that *AddItem* and *DelItem* should be able to handle boundary situations. For example, calling *AddItem<MyDict, A>* or *DelItem<MyDict, C>* will incur errors: the former adds a duplicate key and the latter removes a key that does not exist.

# THE DEEP LEARNING FRAMEWORK

# Chapter 3

# A Brief Introduction to Deep Learning

Deep learning is a branch of artificial intelligence, which has been widely used in many fields such as speech, image, and natural language processing. This book is not intended to discuss deep learning in depth—it focuses more on implementing such a framework using metapro-gramming than the mathematical principles of deep learning algorithms. Nevertheless, a preliminary understanding of the background of deep learning is a prerequisite for the follow-up discussion.

This chapter provides an overview of deep learning and the framework to be implemented, giving the reader a holistic understanding of the framework to be implemented.

## 3.1 Introduction to Deep Learning

Readers of the computer industry must have heard of deep learning more than once, and more or less know its breakthrough achievements in fields such as image processing and speech recognition. For example, AlphaGo, a deep learning-based chess(go) program developed by DeepMind for Google, shocked the world by beating top human chess players Lee Sedol and Ke Jie. However, the application of deep learning did not stop there. In fact, deep learning (or a more basic concept: machine learning) has permeated every aspect of our lives.

For example, when we drive or walk in a public area of a busy city, images captured by high-definition cameras deployed in the corner of the city are transferred to the relevant systems for automatic number-plate recognition, facial recognition, collision detection, etc. to ensure public safety throughout the city; when we pay by credit card at a convenience store, banks' data centers employ this technology to automatically determine whether it is an identity theft; when we use search engines, search algorithms running on server clusters adopt deep learning to match users' input with massive amounts of data and return results to satisfy users; when we use social or newsletter software, algorithms supported by deep learning are deployed on servers to more or less analyze users' interaction with software, providing a relatively personalized service to users.

Although the media often use philosophical metaphors such as "simulating the human brain" to introduce deep learning techniques to the public, thereby making the public more or less aware that it is a powerful and mysterious technology. However, it often misleads the public to some extent. This book avoids using such biological metaphors and introduces the basics of the technology from programmers' perspective instead.

Readers may often see deep learning and machine learning mentioned together, but in fact deep learning is an important subdomain of machine learning.

## 3.1.1 From Machine Learning to Deep Learning

As programmers, you no doubt understand how to write computer programs to solve practical problems. When we need to implement a program, which waits for users' input and then displays different contents based on their input, we will naturally tear down the entire functionality into the form that the sequences, loops, and branches can express. When the problem is a little more complicated, such as sorting elements in an array based on certain information, it's natural to come up with using some sorting algorithms. Further, when designing large-scale projects, we will refer to classic design patterns to ensure reuse and flexibility among modules.

However, consider the following question: we need to implement a program that determines whether a cat or a person is drawn in a picture based on the picture entered by users. Programmers who don't know anything about machine learning may be not aware of what to do next after making the program read the pixel value of a picture into an array. Some programmers might try to write the program like this: if the pixel value of some area is within a certain range, then the system decides that a cat is depicted on it. Such a procedure, in today's view, is undoubtedly ridiculous—if measured by accuracy, then this program may only be a little more accurate than randomly guessing a category of it. Even if it is a same cat, the pixel value on different pictures will vary according to their camera angle and shooting time.

If we make this problem a little easier, assuming a magical machine that can tell us how many feet the creature in the picture has after a picture is entered, then we can use the information to determine. If the machine returns that the creature in the picture has 4 feet, then we consider it as a cat; if there are two feet, then there is a person.

We can't guarantee that this judgment is 100% accurate. For example, because of the limitation of the camera angle, the cat's feet might be obstructed. Then according to the previous judgment, the cat in the picture may be regarded as a person. In another case, an old man in the picture is holding a cane and our program misjudges it as the third foot—then our program will not be able to deal with such situations.

In addition, assuming that the magical machine can tell us more information, such as whether the creature has a beard on its face, the density of its body hair, and so on. Again, the information can be error-prone, but even so, when combined with more information, our program can still have a much more accurate prediction about whether the creature in the picture is a person or cat than a random guess.

If our goal is to construct such a program, then there are two problems to solve. Firstly, assuming that the magical machine already exists, how to maximize the information it provides to improve the accuracy of the classification? Secondly, how to construct the "magical machine" mentioned earlier, to provide us with such information?

The first question is relatively intuitive. For example, we can consider constructing a model whose input is information such as the number of feet, whether there is a beard on the face, how many hairs there are on the body, and so on. Then we can convert each message into a numerical representation, give them certain weights, and then combine these values with the weights, thus multiplying the values corresponding to each input by their weights and summing them. If the result is greater than a certain value, it is considered a human; otherwise it is considered a cat. How can we determine the weight for each message? We can choose the weights from the best results through continuous experiments. But a better way is to find a large number of pictures containing cats or people, and let the system automatically derive these weights.

As discussed, it is a typical problem of machine learning. If the problem can't be solved by explicit programming, we can use machine learning algorithms to generalize specific models from training data. In order to learn from training data, we need to construct a model, and design a training algorithm, which describes how to use the information provided by the training data and how the specific parameters contained in the model can be adjusted. Then we need to extract information from the training data (such as how many legs the creature in the picture has, whether it has a beard, etc.)—such information is called features in machine learning. The training dataset contains a large number of samples, each of which may contain the output we want in addition to features. Through these samples and specific training algorithms, we can adjust the parameters contained in the model and finally obtain the trained model—this is the training process of a model. On the other hand, using a trained model and entering new features, we can use the parameters in the model to obtain corresponding prediction results—it is the prediction process of a model.

Of course, that's not the whole story of machine learning and we're just briefly introducing a branch of machine learning here—supervised learning. Machine learning also includes many other branches, such as unsupervised learning, reinforcement learning, and so on. But learning from data and learning with features is the common concept of machine learning.

So, what does it have to do with deep learning? In fact, it involves the second question described earlier—how to construct that magical machine, that is, how to extract features from the original input information?

Before the advent of deep learning, the problem relied heavily on experts and algorithms in specific fields. For example, we may need some specialized algorithms in the image field in order to extract how many legs the creatures in the image have. With strong limitations, these algorithms that extract features effectively in the field of image processing may be difficult to apply to the field of speech. In fact, such feature extraction has been so difficult that it has developed a specialized field: feature engineering.

Feature engineering is laborious, and the effect of artificial feature extraction is often not ideal. So, can we make the computer extract features itself? Based on this idea, people have carried out long-term researches. In the 1990s, Mr. Yann LeCun and other scholars proposed LeNet, employing a multilayer artificial neural network to automatically learn features from the original input pixels and using extracted features to predict which number from 0 to 9 is in the image, which has achieved quite good results. However, LeNet is much more complex than traditional artificial neural networks and the corresponding training is tougher, and there was no great progress after LeNet's release. Until 2006, a famous scholar Geoffrey Hinton published a related paper, which has solved the problem of training complex networks to some extent, thus creating a new climax in the study of multilayer neural networks. Multilayer neural network can effectively extract features from raw data through its own learning, which advantage the traditional machine learning does not have. Accordingly, the method of stacking complex neural networks together to form a very "deep" structure, automatically extracting features, and completing model learning is called deep learning.

### *3.1.2 A Wide Variety of Artificial Neural Networks*

#### *3.1.2.1 Artificial Neural Networks and Matrix Operations*

Deep learning system is born out of artificial neural network. Figure 3.1 shows a simple artificial neural network.

In Figure 3.1, the input is $p_1, p_2, \ldots, p_R$ and the output is $a_1, a_2, \ldots, a_S$. For any $a_i$, there's $a_i = f\left(\sum_{j=1}^{R} p_j w_{i,j} + b_i\right)$, where $f$ is a nonlinear transformation. Typical nonlinear transformations include $\tanh(x) = \dfrac{e^x - e^{-x}}{e^x + e^{-x}}$, $sigmoid(x) = \dfrac{1}{1 + e^{-x}}$, and so on. We can write the calculation formula for $a_i$ as the following form of vector:

$$\vec{a} = F\left(W\vec{p} + \vec{b}\right)$$

Arrows are added on the top of $a, b, p$ to indicate that they are vectors. $W$ is a matrix and $F$ indicates nonlinear transformations of each element in the vector.

Using matrix operations to represent artificial neural networks not only simplifies the representation of networks, but also allows us to expand them more flexibly. For example, if the nonlinear transformation $F$ is treated as an operation of a vector rather than that of each element in a vector, we can construct a more complex nonlinear transformation, such as a nonlinear operation

$$Softmax(a_1, \ldots, a_n) = \left(\frac{e^{a_1}}{\sum_i e^{a_i}}, \ldots, \frac{e^{a_n}}{\sum_i e^{a_i}}\right)$$

is a relatively complex vector transformation that maps each element in a vector to a value between (0,1) and makes those values amount to 1. We can use this transformation to simulate a probability distribution. The researchers also invented dropout, maxout, layer-normalization, and other complex transformations, which can be considered as special forms of matrix operations.

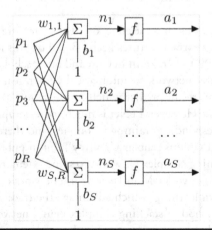

**Figure 3.1　A simple artificial neural network, originally selected from *Neural Network Design*.**

### 3.1.2.2 Deep Neural Network

Simply stacking artificial neural networks create a Deep Neural Network (DNN):

$$\vec{a_1} = F\left(W_0 \vec{a_0} + \vec{b_0}\right)$$

$$\vec{a_2} = F\left(W_1 \vec{a_1} + \vec{b_1}\right)$$

......

$$\vec{a_n} = F\left(W_{n-1} \vec{a_{n-1}} + \vec{b_{n-1}}\right)$$

The input of the network is $\vec{a_0}$ with the output as $\vec{a_n}$. $\vec{a_n}$ is the result of several layers of nonlinear transformations from $\vec{a_0}$. Assuming that we want to recognize the decimal values contained in an image, $\vec{a_0}$ can be pixels in the image and $\vec{a_n}$ can be a vector with ten elements, representing the probability of the number (0 to 9) corresponding to the image respectively.

### 3.1.2.3 Recurrent Neural Networks

The size of input vector in a DNN is fixed, while a Recurrent Neural Network (RNN) is good at handling sequences of variable lengths. A typical RNN is as follows:

$$\vec{h_n} = F(\vec{h_{n-1}}, \vec{x_n})$$

If the input sequence is $\vec{x_1}, \ldots, \vec{x_n}$ and $\vec{h_0}$ is a preset parameter, then $\vec{h_n}$ will contain all the information of $\vec{x_1}, \ldots, \vec{x_n}$. Because RNN can naturally handle the case of input as a sequence, it is widely used in natural language processing, speech recognition, and other fields.

### 3.1.2.4 Convolutional Neural Networks

Another common neural network is Convolutional Neural Network (CNN), which is aimed at splitting the data to be processed into small pieces, each acting with a convolution matrix to extract features. Figure 3.2 shows a typical convolution in image processing:

### 3.1.2.5 Components of Neural Networks

The above is just a quite simple introduction to DNN, RNN, and CNN. These network structures can also be mutant and combined to meet specific demands. The internal network structure of a practical deep learning system can be quite complicated to perform challenging tasks like machine translation and autonomous driving.

To make deep learning systems easier to maintain, we tend to divide a complex system into smaller components and adopt these components to construct the entire system like building blocks. For example, for basic DNNs, we can maintain components for matrix multipliers, for vector additions and for nonlinear transformations, which can be used to construct a fully connected network structure that represents $\vec{a} = F\left(W\vec{p} + \vec{b}\right)$, and then further treat this structure as a component, thus stacking it to form a DNN.

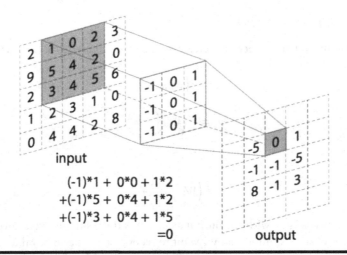

**Figure 3.2    Convolution calculation. (Source: http://vis.pku.edu.cn.)**

The introduction of components is a typical idea of divide and conquer. Maintaining smaller components is relatively cheaper than directly maintaining complex deep learning systems and a common component can be reused in the deep learning framework (of course, different objects instantiated from same component may contain different parameters, but their computational logic is same.) Neural networks also have another good feature—it can mathematically decompose the parameter optimization of the entire network into the process of parameter optimization for each component. It is for this reason that we can construct a complex deep learning system to ensure the correctness of the system training process.

### 3.1.3 Organization and Training of Deep Learning Systems

Neural network structures in deep learning systems can be quite complex and contain a large number of parameters. The so-called training of a deep learning system is to adjust the parameters contained in the network to make them meet demands of related tasks. For example, if we want to use CNNs for image recognition, we need to adjust the parameters of the convolution matrix in the network to improve the system's recognition accuracy.

#### 3.1.3.1 Network Structure and Loss Function

Before solving practical problems through deep learning systems, we should first choose the neural network structure and optimization objectives contained in the deep learning system. As mentioned earlier, different network structures are also applicable in different areas. If dealing with sequence-related issues, we can consider introducing structures such as RNN; CNN may be a good choice for image processing; for more complex problems, it requires a specialized structure or a complex network constructed by combining multiple structures.

Another practical problem is how to describe optimization objectives of the network quantificationally. In general, we need to convert optimization objectives of the network into mathematical representations and use some optimization algorithms to adjust the network parameters in the deep learning system in the subsequent training process, so that the behavior of the network will be more and more inclined to our optimization objective. Typically, the optimization objective is expressed as a loss function and the learning process of the system is the process of constantly adjusting network parameters so that the value of the loss function decreases gradually on the training set. Take the task of judging whether there is a cat or a person in a picture described earlier as an example. Assuming that we construct a deep learning system with input as pixels in the picture and output as two probability values $p_c$, $p_p$ representing the probability of a cat and a person, respectively. Given $N$ samples and the real category of sample $i$ as $y_i$, then we can define the following loss function:

$$loss = \frac{-1}{N} \sum_{i=1}^{N} \left\{ \delta_{y_i=y_c} \log p_c^i + \delta_{y_i=y_p} \log p_p^i \right\}$$

$p_c^i$ and $p_p^i$ represent the probability that the output of the current system is a cat or a person respectively for sample $i$. When $y_i$ is a cat, the value of $\delta_{y_i=y_c}$ is 1, otherwise it is 0. Similarly, when $y_i$ is a person, the value of $\delta_{y_i=y_p}$ is 1, otherwise it is 0. It is not difficult to realize that the value of the formula will gradually decrease with the classification accuracy of the system increasing. The training process of the network is indeed the process of gradually reducing the loss function by adjusting the network parameters.

As the developers of deep learning frameworks, we do not need to pay too much attention to how to choose the structure of the network and loss function but we should provide a series of modules to make it convenient to build the corresponding network structure after determining the network structure and loss function.

## 3.1.3.2 Model Training

After defining the network structure and loss function, we can adopt them to build a neural network model. The model usually contains a large number of parameters. The training process of the model is the process of adjusting the model parameters according to training samples, in order to make the loss function as small as possible. The training processes for different network structures and loss functions are different, but in general, the training of a whole model includes following steps:

- **Parameter initialization**: at the beginning of model training, we need to initialize the parameters contained therein. In general, these parameters can be assigned initial values with random initialization. But in order to ensure that the model eventually works well, we should limit the distribution of initialization parameters—such as initializing them according to a certain distribution or ensuring that the initialized parameters have certain properties. The deep learning framework needs to provide a variety of initialization methods for users to choose from.
- **Forward propagation and backward propagation**: after assigning parameters in the model with initial values, the parameters need to be adjusted according to training samples. The process of adjustment is mainly composed of forward and backward propagation. In forward propagation, the input of each sample is passed in turn; the system calculates the output of the system under the current parameters of the model, and the corresponding loss function value of the output. In backward propagation, the value of the loss function is used to calculate the gradient and feed it back to each component of the neural network along a path opposite to the forward propagation, in which the components calculate the gradient of

the parameters contained. The components that the data experience in forward propagation are exactly the same as the components in backward propagation but the orders are exactly the opposite. The deep learning framework needs to maintain the processes of forward and backward propagation, ensuring that the right results are obtained at each step with enough efficiency of computations.

■ **Parameter update**: after forward and backward propagation of one or more samples, the system accumulates parameters' gradients, which can be used to update the parameter values later. The most basic way to update is to multiply a gradient value with a factor and add the result to the original parameter. Of course, there are other ways to update parameters, each of which has its pros and cons, and the deep learning framework needs to provide a variety of update methods for users to choose from.

It is not difficult to be aware that the deep learning framework plays an important role in every step of model training. A mature deep learning framework may also contain several extended features. For example, deep learning frameworks may be required to support multi-machine concurrent training to speed up training because the calculation speed of forward and backward propagation is relatively slow. What's more, a good deep learning framework should be able to output some intermediate results for debugging.

### 3.1.3.3 Predictions with Models

After a model is trained, it can be used for prediction. The so-called prediction refers to the process of entering samples into the model, executing forward propagation and calculating the output results. From the perspective of neural networks, the prediction process of the model only involves forward propagation, without backward propagation or parameter update, so it is simpler than model training. Meanwhile, since the model prediction only involves forward propagation, so it doesn't need to record some intermediate variables probably required for backward propagation, which spares room for optimization.

An excellent deep learning framework should not only support the training of models, but also further optimize the prediction using models in order to improve the speed of prediction and reduce the use of resources.

## 3.2 The Framework Achieved in This Book—MetaNN

### 3.2.1 From Computing Tools of Matrices to Deep Learning Frameworks

The basis of deep learning is artificial neural networks and the core of artificial neural networks is matrix operations. Therefore, the core of a deep learning framework is matrix operations.

There are many common tools that provide matrix computation, such as Matlab, Octave, and so on. So is it feasible to use these software directly for deep learning? In theory, it is possible because the computational logic provided by these software can already meet demands of deep learning. However, the particularity of deep learning system itself leads to the result that these software can construct deep learning systems, but the effect is often not good enough.

Firstly, a deep learning system is a compute-intensive system, in which there are a large number of highly complex calculations of matrices and smooth running of the system needs high speed of processing. In fact, for such kind of systems, CPU cannot even meet requirements of matrix computation and it may require other computing devices (such as GPUs, FPGAs, etc.) to achieve fast matrix computation. Software such as Matlab and Octave are required to solve general-purpose tasks and computing speed (especially the speed of matrix operations) is not one of the most important goals of concern. As a result, systems constructed with general software like these are often unacceptably slow when training a medium- to high-scale deep learning model.

Secondly, deep learning systems are often complex and have unique architectures. In model training, for example, the training process consists of forward and backward propagation. The former produces the corresponding output based on the sample input, while the latter calculates the gradient of network parameters based on the loss function. Forward and backward propagation both contain the corresponding methods of calculation—some methods are more complex, and the common software for matrix computation often do not organize these algorithms well to help users easily use them to complete the task of deep learning. If users want to adopt common software for matrix computation for deep learning, they may need to introduce a secondary development on the basis of these software, resulting in high expenses of development and maintenance.

Deep learning is a quite fast-growing field. It is no exaggeration to say that there are papers proposing new technologies or improving existing algorithms almost every month. By introducing a dedicated deep learning framework, the development of the framework can be separated from the use of it—the developer of the framework is responsible for implementing and maintaining the existing algorithms, introducing new algorithms to ensure the efficiency and scalability of the algorithms, while users of the framework focus on using the existing framework to apply deep learning to the real world, so as to solve practical problems or to conduct a theoretical study of deep learning. With the emergence of this division of labor, deep learning researchers are becoming more and more dependent on frameworks. Today, we can say that the quality of a deep learning framework even determines the success or failure of its deep learning tasks to a certain extent.

It is in such background that many deep learning frameworks emerge. Nowadays, many open-source deep learning frameworks can be found on the Internet. Research institutions and users of deep learning are even spending time and money developing their own deep learning frameworks—the goal is to make the framework more responsive to their demands. There are some famous frameworks, including TensorFlow, Theano, PaddlePaddle, Caffe, and so on, which all have their own strengths and can be applied to different deep learning systems. In this field, different factions and styles of science have been developing simultaneously.

### 3.2.2 Introduction to MetaNN

This book will implement a deep learning framework, MetaNN. "Meta" represents the use of metaprogramming and "NN" is an acronym for Neural Network. A natural question is: why do we want to achieve a new framework, given that there are so many deep learning frameworks?

We want to use this framework as a carrier to discuss the technique of C++ metaprogramming. There are many books on C++ but not many books on C++ metaprogramming. Even when there is a discussion of metaprogramming, the focus of the discussion is often laid on techniques involved in metaprogramming—relatively small points of knowledge, independent, and lacking in consistency. The discussion of using metaprogramming to develop large-scale frameworks is even more rare. Thus, many readers regard metaprogramming as flashy "tricks" after reading some books about it. Because we don't understand how to link these technologies together to form a complete system that can develop large programs.

The deep learning framework is complex enough that, in fact, there are a large number of research results produced in the field of deep learning. If these findings are to be incorporated into a framework, the framework itself is complex enough and can't be achieved relying on some so-called "small tricks." We want to prove that metaprogramming is perfectly capable of constructing such a system. There are rules for the process of constructing it, whose essence is the programming technique of "sequence, branches, and loops" discussed in Chapter 1. As long as we are proficient in these technologies, it is entirely possible to construct such a complex set of systems. The process of reading this book is just the process of being skilled in these programming techniques.

Deep learning systems are complex and a good deep learning framework must be able to cover up the complexity to some extent, providing users with interfaces easy to configure and use. On the other hand, a key point of deep learning systems is to provide efficient computing power to meet actual requirements of usage. It is difficult to reconcile the two to some extent and each framework needs to maintain a balance between the two. For this point, different frameworks adopt different strategies. For example, the Theano framework uses Python as the user interface. Python is easy to use but slow to execute. In order to speed up the system, Theano converts Python source code internally and calls the C++ compiler to compile the converted code, using the compiled results for actual model training. Although this approach solves the problem of ease of use and high performance to some extent, it is not conducive to debugging and in-depth analysis—the framework is not actually running the code written by users but the product processed by the C++ compiler. So, it may be burdensome for average users to understand what happened in the process of conversion. When encountering a complex problem, it is difficult for them to go deep into the bottom of the system and really analyze the problem.

TensorFlow and Caffe use C++ as the low-level programming language for implementation, which takes advantage of the high-performance features of C++, while providing interfaces at the upper level using more user-friendly languages such as Python for user calls. Although this approach does not involve secondary compilation, they are traditionally object-oriented programming in C++—so the performance will be sacrificed to some extent to ensure ease of use. These frameworks are simple to use and well suited for academic researches. But when providing direct external services with it as the low-level implementation (such as providing online high-throughput prediction services), it may be constrained by the characteristics of the framework itself and not be able to achieve the full performance of the underlying hardware system. For example, Caffe organizes the components of deep learning in "layers," each of which maintains its own calculations. It causes that calculations that could have been merged or optimized in some cases can be only called one by one because of the existence of layers, which adversely affects performance. In this case, in order to provide high-volume network services, we may need to develop a dedicated on-line system for prediction, rewrite the entire predictive logic, introduce a lot of optimization, or use specialized hardware (such as Google's TPU) to further improve the performance of the system.

This trade-off is not only reflected in the sacrifice of performance for ease of use, but also in the sacrifice of ease of use for performance and effect. For example, the *SoftmaxLoss* layer was introduced in Caffe, which is mathematically equivalent to a two-layer structure (such as *Softmax+Log*). Caffe contains the *Softmax* layer and the *Log* layer. One of the main reasons for the introduction of additional *SoftmaxLoss* layer is to reduce instability of the system due to rounding errors in calculations, in addition to merging layers to speed up operations. In order to improve the stability of the system, when using Caffe, if we want to perform Log calculations immediately after *Softmax*, we need to use the *SoftmaxLoss* layer instead of explicitly constructing the two-layer structure of *Softmax+Log*. There are similar limitations in other deep learning frameworks—typical examples of sacrificing ease of use for performance.

Similar to frameworks such as TensorFlow and Caffe, MetaNN is also a deep learning framework built on C++, which also provides abstract interfaces at the upper level to cover up the complex logic within the system—thereby improving ease of use. However, because MetaNN internally contains a large number of metaprogramming techniques, additional optimization can be introduced to the calculation processes of models with metafunctions and compile-time calculations. It gives the system a natural advantage in terms of speed while maintaining ease of use—which is difficult to obtain through traditional methods of object-oriented programming. Meanwhile, MetaNN does not have to introduce constructs such as *SoftmaxLoss*[1] to improve performance.

But the use of metaprogramming technology also has its drawbacks—the strong reliance on metaprogramming technology makes it difficult for MetaNN to provide an interface like Python in the mainstream deep learning framework. In fact, it is not completely unable to provide a Python interface for users who are not familiar with C++. But if such an interface is provided, we will need to encapsulate the results of C++ metaprogramming, which will affect the logic of optimization for the program to some extent, resulting in losing the advantages of metaprogramming. Therefore, MetaNN will not provide a Python interface to the outside.

### 3.2.3 *What We Will Discuss*

Deep learning is a fast-growing and widely-used field. Accordingly, a complete deep learning framework contains a lot of contents. A typical deep learning framework should be able to handle high-dimensional matrices (primarily for image, video, etc.), execute concurrent training (to cope with excessive training data), and use different processors (such as CPU/GPU) for model training and prediction (to accommodate different scenarios).

If these issues are discussed one by one, it will undoubtedly greatly increase the thickness of this book. In addition, this book takes the deep learning framework as the carrier for discussion the core technique of template metaprogramming. From this perspective, there is no need for an in-depth discussion of every aspect probably covered in a deep learning framework. The deep learning framework is complex and we'll limit it to the core parts. Although only the most central elements of this framework are included in subsequent discussions, MetaNN is scalable enough to include the functionality that should be in the deep learning framework. Therefore, if readers are not satisfied after reading the contents of this book, it is entirely possible to use the techniques learned in this book to further develop and enrich the framework, so that it can meet demands of specific tasks.

The core components of the entire framework can be divided into four levels from bottom to up: data, operations, layers, and evaluations. On the basis of these concepts, networks can be built for training and prediction. The follow-up discussion of this book will also focus on these concepts.

### 3.2.3.1 *Data Representation*

The kernel of the entire framework is data. Typically, data is represented as matrices, but the specific form of the data varies for different tasks.

For example, for tasks in natural language processing, the basic unit to be processed is the word. If a word is expressed in a vector, the data dealt with in the framework is usually one-dimensional vectors. Concatenating words together can form sentences, and accordingly, arranging the vectors

---

[1] As we will see in Chapter 8 of this book, MetaNN does not need to introduce layers like *SoftmaxLoss*. The system will judge the connection of the layers at compile time and if it finds that there is a *Log* layer immediately following the *Softmax* layer, the corresponding optimization will be automatically introduced to increase the calculation speed while maintaining the stability of calculations.

that represent words can form a two-dimensional matrix. For systems that process a sentence at a time (such as a translation system), the basic unit to be processed is a two-dimensional matrix. If we want to further increase the throughput of our system and support multiple sentences for simultaneous processing, the data to be processed is a three-dimensional tensor. In cases where each input element can be represented as a one-dimensional vector, it is common to process data up to the level of three-dimensional tensors.

But for image processing, the framework may be required to support data of higher dimensions—a black-and-white image can be represented as a two-dimensional matrix, while for color images, each pixel usually contains three components (red, green, and blue). Therefore, the system that processes color images needs to use a three-dimensional tensor to represent an image. If we want to increase system throughput and process multiple images at once, we need to use a four-dimensional tensor to represent the image group. Therefore, the system that processes images is required to introduce tensors of higher dimensions to represent the data.

In this book, we discuss data up to three-dimensional tensors—they meet requirements of most tasks in natural language processing, which is not enough for some image-processing tasks. But if needed, we can also extend MetaNN to introduce new underlying data types to support four-dimensional data to meet demands of such tasks.

### 3.2.3.2 Matrix Operations

The deep learning framework should support a variety of methods in matrix operations, such as the dot product of two matrix or calculating tanh values for elements in the matrix. The development of deep learning is changing rapidly and many new operations are being invented constantly. Accordingly, the deep learning framework should also be able to support computational expansion and can easily introduce new operations.

MetaNN divides matrix calculation into two steps: construction of computation expressions and evaluation of computation expressions. The former is to construct an expression template that represents the result of an operation while the latter is to execute an actual calculation of the expression template to obtain the result. For example, an operation adding two matrices produces an expression template that represents the result of an operation. This expression template can be evaluated later to obtain the result matrix, but we cannot obtain the values of the elements in the result matrix through the expression template until the evaluation finished.

The reason for this design is that, on the one hand, the construction of an expression template representing the results of the operation is quite fast compared to the evaluation; on the other hand, separating the construction of expressions from the evaluation makes it possible to optimize specifically for evaluation and improve system performances. We'll use a specific chapter to discuss matrix operations and construction of expression templates.

Because operations are divided into two steps and the evaluation will be discussed separately, we mainly focus on the process of constructing operation expressions when discussing the "operations" in MetaNN. The "operation" we discuss in Chapter 5 also mainly refers to the construction of operation expressions while the evaluation will be discussed in Chapter 8.

### 3.2.3.3 Layers and Automatic Derivation

In MetaNN, there is an abstract concept above matrix operations: layers. Some deep learning frameworks combine the concept of operation with that of layers. But distinguishing between the two concepts can make better abstractions, thereby improving their ease of use.

Layers are based on matrix operations and provide a higher level of abstraction. As mentioned earlier, model training in deep learning systems involves both forward and backward propagation. Both processes require the introduction of matrix operations. One of the main tasks for layers is to associate the matrix operations used by forward propagation and backward propagation while encapsulating details so that users do not have to pay attention to specific implementations.

The gradients need to be calculated during the training of the deep learning model, while the calculation of gradients involves (partial) derivation and the backward propagation of the calculation results. Derivatives involved in the deep learning framework can be divided into two categories, which correspond to the two types of layers in MetaNN.

1. **Basic layers**: these layers encapsulate code of forward propagation and corresponding backward propagation code required for derivation calculation—the code is not complex and can be easily written and written right.
2. **Composite layers**: layers made up of basic layers. Composite layers can also be further composited, that is, larger composite layers consisting of small composite layers and basic layers.

Theoretically, a composite layer can call its sublayers to achieve forward propagation and backward propagation of data. However, in backward propagation of data, the chain rule is needed for derivation. The concept of the chain rule is not complex in itself, but if a composite layer involves too many sublayers, it can be cumbersome to write accordingly and prone to errors. In fact, it is entirely possible to encapsulate the corresponding logic according to the basic principles of the chain rule and use it to execute automatic derivation in the composite layer. In this way, as long as it is ensured that the encapsulation of the chain rule is correct, we can ensure that the derivation of the composite layer is correct, too.

This book will focus on the implementation of automatic derivation for composite layers in a specific chapter.

## 3.2.3.4 Evaluation and Performance Optimization

Matrix operations are the core of the deep learning framework. Although we can construct expression templates quickly, it is ultimately up to evaluate the expression templates to get the final results. It can be said that improving the evaluation or the actual speed of matrix computation is critical to improving the overall performance of a system. In general, deep learning frameworks increase the speed of matrix computation in both hardware and software.

On the hardware side, a deep learning framework supports computing devices in addition to CPU (such as GPUs, FPGAs, and so on), taking advantage of the unique performance benefits of these cells to speed up. On the software side, a deep learning framework can consider calling specialized matrix libraries and optimizing performance by combining computations.

In this book, we only discuss using CPU for calculation without introducing other matrix computation libraries. Because "using a dedicated computing device" and "using a matrix library" for matrix operations is beyond the topics discussed in this book. MetaNN reserves extended interfaces to support computing devices in addition to CPU. Meanwhile, we will discuss the way to optimize program performance by combining computations—with these basic concepts, it is not complicated to introduce a matrix library on this basis.

### 3.2.4 Topics Not Covered in This Book

In addition to the topics discussed, there are some other topics that deep learning frameworks are required to include, which this book will not cover. The main reason is that they have little to do with template metaprogramming, or the metaprogramming knowledge involved has been discussed in this book. These topics include:

- **Concurrent training**: that is, how to increase the speed of training by concurrent methods in case of massive data. On the basis of realizing the core logic of MetaNN, multi-machine concurrent training can be achieved by extending the framework. The key point of multi-machine concurrent training lies in data transmission, and network communication, which involves less metaprogramming. The topic of this book is to discuss metaprogramming techniques, so we won't discuss concurrent training.
- **Update of model parameters**: some algorithm is required to update the parameters the model contains during model training. This book won't discuss this section because the metaprogramming techniques used in the processes are already embodied in other central parts of the framework.

## 3.3 Summary

This chapter provided an overview of backgrounds about deep learning and a brief overview of the Deep Learning Framework (MetaNN) to be discussed later. Deep learning is a very fast-growing field with many achievements. This book will not discuss all of them but describe only some of the core issues of the framework design. Nevertheless, MetaNN reserves enough extension interfaces for easy expansion of functionality.

Next, we'll walk through the design details of MetaNN.

# Chapter 4

# Type System and
# Basic Data Types

Data is the cornerstone of the entire framework. This chapter discusses the type system and basic data types used in MetaNN.

As a deep learning framework, MetaNN involves a large number of matrix operations, and correspondingly, the data types involved in MetaNN are matrix-based. We can use arrays to store elements in a matrix and, on this basis, construct the data type that represents the matrix, but this is only one kind of representation of matrices. The characteristics of matrices involved in different application scenarios are also different. For the specific characteristics of a matrix, choosing the right representation can reduce the space and time complexity required for data-related operations, and provide more space for the overall optimization of the subsequent framework while simplifying programs.

In addition to matrices, MetaNN also works with other data types. Typically, the dot product of two vectors (which can be viewed as matrices of single row or column) is a scalar and the related operations of scalars are incorporated into the type system of the entire framework. In addition to matrices and scalars, MetaNN can also deal with lists of matrices or scalars, supporting more complex calculations.

To provide greater flexibility for data representation, many deep learning frameworks introduce the concept of tensor, which can represent a collection of data in any dimension. Individual numbers (scalars) can be represented by zero-dimensional tensors; one-dimensional tensors for vectors or arrays; two-dimensional tensors for matrices; and so on. MetaNN does not introduce tensors to represent all possible data types; on the contrary, it is aimed at more obvious distinctions among purposes of data by introducing different data types. For example, a one-dimensional array can represent a list of scalars or a vector. The two concepts will be confusing if we use tensors as a uniform representation, not conducive to the development of large-scale programs. Conversely, if these two forms are assigned with different types (class templates), we can explicitly distinguish between their purposes according to the names of types. *Introducing unique data types for different purposes of data is one of the characteristics of MetaNN.*

In fact, we deliberately design MetaNN a type-rich system. For every mathematical concept (such as a matrix), there may be multiple representations (expressed as distinct classes or class templates) in MetaNN—each with its own unique role. Meanwhile, MetaNN is scalable—a new representation (i.e., new types) of a same mathematical concept can be added to MetaNN. These types can seamlessly dock with existing algorithms as long as they meet some basic requirements. In order to be possible to manage these types while facilitating extension, MetaNN introduces a dedicated system of types to classify them. As we move forward, we'll see relatively complex data types in the latter sections of this chapter. Even quite complex types can be incorporated to the entire type system, of which the design principle permeates the entire construction of MetaNN. Thus, understanding the type system is the foundations of understanding the entire framework.

In fact, the type system and its typical implementations can be seen as a paradigm that can apply not only to the MetaNN framework itself, but also to other generic systems. The first half of this chapter will discuss the type system used in MetaNN from this perspective so as to bring readers a higher level of awareness of it. On this basis, the second half of this chapter describes the specific data types used in MetaNN. These data types will serve as the bottom of the framework, providing rudimentary capabilities of data storage and access.

## 4.1 The Type System

### 4.1.1 Introduction to the Type System

In any system, if we want it to support different data types and easily introduce new data types for extensions, then a mechanism is required to manage the data types therein. This book refers to this mechanism of managing data types as the type system. One of the most important tasks for the type system is to group diverse data types: each group is called a category, representing a unique concept and several specific implementations for it.

Each programming approach can introduce its own management system for data types. For instance, in an object-oriented system, the typical way is to classify by derivation—types in each category are derived directly or indirectly from a base class, which represents the concept described by the corresponding category. A base class defines the interfaces corresponding to the concept in the form of virtual functions. Derived classes can choose to inherit or rewrite virtual functions in the base class, providing a situation-appropriate implementation that complies with the requirements of the concept.

C++ supports object-oriented programming, so the type system can be defined in the above way. Nonetheless, this book is about metaprogramming. Within the framework of generic metaprogramming, there are other ways to handle data, such as through tags.

Tags are nothing new. In fact, the C++ Standard Library we use every day contains tags: it uses a tagging system to manage iterators and classify them into categories. Each iterator category requires specific interfaces and behaviors. The requirements for interfaces are not explicitly introduced through base classes and virtual functions but are given in documents. There is no common base class among diverse data types belonging to the same category. As a result, the organizational relationship is relatively loose among iterators of a same category in a tag-based type system compared to a derivation-based type system.

Compared with derivation-based type systems, tag-based type systems have their inherent performance advantages. In a derivation-based type system, base classes and derived classes are linked through virtual functions and derived classes need to inherit or modify the virtual functions defined in base classes to implement their specific logic. Users, on the other hand, need to call virtual functions to access interfaces. Access to virtual functions involves pointers dereference, which introduce performance losses themselves. Getting rid of limitations of virtual functions can improve the performance of systems to some extent. In addition, because there is no limitation of virtual functions, there will be more freedom for different types when implementing interfaces.[1]

Of course, compared with derivation-based type systems, there are also inconveniences of tag-based type systems. The main usage limit is still related to compile-time computing. In a derivation-based type system, we can declare a function that receives references or pointers of base classes and passes the object of the derived class into it, which is a typical implementation of polymorphism and processed at runtime, therefore also known as dynamic polymorphism. However, we will lose this polymorphic nature of runtime when using a tag-based type system. All types are specified at the compile time and cannot be flexibly adjusted at runtime. Because of this, whether a tag-based type system should be used is also up to the circumstances. Furthermore, we can combine tag-based type systems with derivation-based type systems to take advantage of both.

In MetaNN, we will primarily use the tag-based type system, supplemented by the derivation-based type system. The derivation-based type system is mainly used at runtime of the program. When discuss the concept of layers in Chapter 6, we introduce a derived dynamic type system *DynamicData* to save the intermediate results of calculations in the deep learning framework. Meanwhile, Chapter 6 will discuss ways to combine the two types of systems.

In addition to the special cases covered in Chapter 6, MetaNN will primarily use the tag-based type system to maintain the collection of data it uses. We need a system to represent the various data types used by the framework, each of which has a specific purpose. If the network constructed by the deep learning framework can be clarified at compile time,[2] correspondingly the data types used in this network can be clarified at compile time. The advantages of fastness and scalability in tag-based type systems will be manifest.

Tag-based generic type systems are not original in MetaNN—the C++ Standard Template Library (STL) uses a tagging system to manage the type of iterator. MetaNN, on the other hand, draws on and extends this technique to manage the data used with a similar tagging system. Before understanding the data tagging system in MetaNN, we need to first look at the tagging system used to manage iterators in C++.

## 4.1.2 Classification Systems of Iterators

Readers who have used the C++ STL must be no stranger to iterators. STL classifies iterators into several categories and specifies the interfaces that each iterator category needs to implement. For example:

- Input iterators support increment operations and can dereference to get corresponding values. An input iterator can be compared with another input iterator to determine whether they are equal.
- Random-access iterators support more operations than input iterators. For example, we can add or subtract an integer to move the position where the iterator points; it supports relational operators to be compared with one another; two random-access iterators can subtract one another to calculate the distance between them.

---

[1] For example, when a derived class implements a virtual function for a base class in C++, it can modify the signature of the function, such as modifying the return type of the function. But there are quite a lot of limitations for modifications. There are far fewer corresponding restrictions in a tag-based type system.

[2] This is also a prerequisite for this book.

The types of iterators vary widely, but after they are classified into several categories, the algorithm can be designed or optimized for a specific iterator category. For example, some algorithms only support random-access iterators, and with an input iterator as the argument, the algorithm will not work. As another example, some algorithms can choose to optimize in an appropriate way when passing in a random-access iterator as the argument to speed up itself.

Iterator tags are introduced to represent the categories of iterators in C++. For example, *input_iterator_tag* is used to represent an input iterator, while *random_access_iterator_tag* represents a random-access iterator. Meanwhile, C++ requires the introduction of a special structure, *iterator_traits* for each iterator, which correlates the iterator's tag (category) with the specific iterator type. For example:

```
1   template<typename T>
2   struct iterator_traits<const T*>
3   {
4       typedef random_access_iterator   iterator_category;
5       // ...
6   };
```

This indicates that any pointer type can be regarded as a random-access iterator.

Conventional C++ development involves more operations of an iterator's own and not directly the iterator's category tags. But in fact, it is precisely because of the existence of iterator tags that there is the possibility of optimization for algorithms. Take the *std::distance* algorithm as an example[3]:

```
1   template<typename _InputIterator>
2   inline auto __distance(_InputIterator b, _InputIterator e,
3                           input_iterator_tag)
4   {
5       typename iterator_traits<_InputIterator>::difference_type n = 0;
6
7       while (b != e) {
8           ++b; ++n;
9       }
10
11      return n;
12  }
13
14  template<typename _RandomAccessIterator>
15  inline auto __distance(_RandomAccessIterator b,
```

---

[3] Note that the C++ standard only regulates the behaviors an algorithm should have and does not indicate the implementation details of an algorithm. What is given here is only a possible implementation, which is simplified without details not pertinent to the discussion.

```
16                          _RandomAccessIterator e,
17                          random_access_iterator_tag)
18
19  {
20      return e - b;
21  }
22
23  template<typename _Iterator>
24  inline auto distance(_Iterator b, _Iterator e)
25  {
26      return __distance(b, e, __iterator_category(b));
27  }
```

*distance* is used to calculate the distance between two iterators and its implementation is a typical compile-time branch structure. The function *distance* calls *__iterator_category(b)* to construct the variable that represents the category of the iterator *b*, and then the compiler uses this variable to select one of the two *__distance* to execute: for input iterators, the distance between the two can only be calculated in a gradual increment, with a time complexity of *O(n)*; for random-access iterators, one iterator can be subtracted from the other directly to calculate the distance between the two, with a time complexity of *O(1)*.

From the described code snippet, we can realize the differences between a type and a category. Iterators may be of a variety of types but each type belongs to a specific category, such as the integer pointer is a type of iterators and the category to which the iterator belongs is the random-access iterator. The relationship between the two is built by *iterator_traits*.

### 4.1.3  Use Tags as Template Parameters

Consider the described code snippet again: The implementation of *__distance* contains three function parameters, the third of which represents the category of the iterator and is used to select functions by the compiler. But in the internal logic of *__distance*, the object corresponding to this parameter is not used. Therefore, there is no need to assign the appropriate parameter name to it.

In fact, in addition to introducing tags as function parameters, we can introduce them as template parameters. The following code snippet is a rewrite of *distance*, using template parameters to deliver the information about tags:

```
1  template<typename TIterTag, typename _InputIterator,
2          enable_if_t <is_same<TIterTag,
3                              input_iterator_tag>::value>* = nullptr>
4  inline auto __distance(_InputIterator b, _InputIterator e)
5  {
6      typename iterator_traits<_InputIterator>::difference_type n = 0;
7
8      while (b != e) {
```

```
 9              ++b; ++n;
10      }
11
12      return n;
13  }
14
15  template <typename TIterTag, typename _RandomAccessIterator,
16              enable_if_t <is_same<TIterTag,
17                                  random_access_iterator_tag>::value>*
18                          = nullptr>
19  inline auto __distance(_RandomAccessIterator b,
20                          _RandomAccessIterator e)
21
22  {
23      return e - b;
24  }
25
26  template<typename _Iterator>
27  inline auto distance(_Iterator b, _Iterator e)
28  {
29      using TagType
30          = typename iterator_traits<_Iterator>::iterator_category;
31      return __distance<TagType>(b, e);
32  }
```

Using function parameters to deliver information of tags like STL means that we need to specify an additional parameter for the function that will not be used directly, which affects the understanding of the function to some extent. Meanwhile, it may mean that we should construct and deliver an additional tag object not used at all. While many compilers can optimize away the construction and delivery of this tag object, the compiler can also choose not to optimize. If so, it means that we need to pay the corresponding costs of runtime. In turn, delivering information about tags with template parameters will not result in any additional runtime costs. MetaNN assigns the appropriate category tags to the data types it uses and delivers information about tags with template parameters in operations in a similar way to the described code snippet.

After a brief understanding of how tags for iterator categories work, we'll dive into the type system and specific category tags that MetaNN uses.

## 4.1.4 The Type System of MetaNN

As a deep learning framework, the basic data type processed in MetaNN is matrices. In addition, MetaNN should be able to process other types of data to meet demands of different deep learning tasks.

The simplest data type is a scalar. One of the principal tasks of the deep learning framework is encapsulating matrix operations. Matrix operations also involve scalars. For example, the addition of a matrix and a scalar is a typical operation involving both matrices and scalars. Correspondingly, the deep learning framework has to deal with scalars.

In addition to scalars and matrices, deep learning frameworks may also involve batch processing. A large number of experiments manifest that the batch processing of calculations of the same kind is often more efficient than executing each calculation in turn. You have no doubt heard the word *SIMD*, which means "Single Instruction, Multiple Data" and is one of the main methods of computing optimization in CPU. We can use such instructions to add and multiply multiple sets of floating point numbers at once. Similarly, executing multiple matrix calculations of the same type together can also improve execution efficiency. MetaNN introduces specialized data categories to represent the input and output of batch processing.

Currently, MetaNN introduces a total of four data tags, which are placed in the structure for unified management:

```
1  struct CategoryTags
2  {
3      struct Scalar;              // Scalar
4      struct Matrix;              // Matrix
5      struct BatchScalar;         // List of scalars
6      struct BatchMatrix;         // List of matrices
7  };
```

The tagging system of MetaNN supports extensions and new tag categories can be added to it if needed.

There are two points to highlight about this tagging system.

Firstly, MetaNN does not distinguish between vectors and matrices. A vector can be thought of as a matrix with a single row (or column) and the operations it involves can also be expressed as matrix operations. Therefore, MetaNN does not specifically distinguish between vectors and matrices, which are represented by the tag *Matrix* uniformly.

Secondly, there is no hierarchical relationship among the tags of MetaNN—unlike the tagging system of iterators. The tagging system of the STL iterators presents a hierarchy: for example, a random-access iterator is also an input iterator, which is explicitly described by introducing derivation between the tag classes of iterators. However, in the type system introduced by MetaNN, the conceptual affiliations between tags are not obvious and we deal with each type of tags separately. It means that when a data operation function is called, it should be ensured that the category of the incoming argument exactly matches the category required by the function, otherwise an error will occur.[4]

---

[4] In contrast, in the tagging system of the STL iterators, if the function specifies input iterators as arguments, then the object of a random-access iterator can also be arguments.

## 4.1.5 Metafunctions Related to the Type System

After defining the tags that represent the categories, the next step is to associate them with specific data types—only by this way can category tags play their practical roles. MetaNN introduces two sets of metafunctions to associate tags with specific data types.

### 4.1.5.1 Metafunction IsXXX

Given any data type, the metafunction *IsXXX* is used to determine whether the type belongs to a certain tag. For each tag, there is a corresponding metafunction *IsXXX*. For example, for tags of type *BatchMatrix*, the corresponding metafunction is defined as follows:

```
1    template <typename T>
2    constexpr bool IsBatchMatrix = false;
3
4    template <typename T>
5    constexpr bool IsBatchMatrix<const T> = IsBatchMatrix<T>;
6
7    template <typename T>
8    constexpr bool IsBatchMatrix<T&> = IsBatchMatrix<T>;
9
10   template <typename T>
11   constexpr bool IsBatchMatrix<const T&> = IsBatchMatrix<T>;
12
13   template <typename T>
14   constexpr bool IsBatchMatrix<T&&> = IsBatchMatrix<T>;
15
16   template <typename T>
17   constexpr bool IsBatchMatrix<const T&&> = IsBatchMatrix<T>;
```

Five specializations (4–17 lines) are defined here to remove constants and reference symbols from the types—making metafunctions more common. For example, after the introduction of these specializations, *IsBatchMatrix<const int>* and *IsBatchMatrix<int>* will produce the same result: this is what we usually want to see.

In the basic definition of *IsBatchMatrix*, it returns *false* directly, indicating that the tag for a specific data type is not *BatchMatrix* by default. Assuming that as the program develops; we need to introduce a new type *A*, which is a list of matrices. Then we can describe it with the following specialization in the program:

```
1    template <>
2    constexpr bool IsBatchMatrix<A> = true;
```

In this way, the metafunction *IsBatchMatrix<A &>*, *IsBatchMatrix<const A>*, etc. will return *true* in subsequent code.

The definitions of *IsScalar*, *IsMatrix*, and *IsBatchScalar* are basically the same as *IsBatchMatrix*, which will not be further elaborated here.

## 4.1.5.2 Metafunction DataCategory

The metafunction *DataCategory* is also used to associate a specific type with its tag. But, unlike *IsXXX*, it receives a specific type and returns the category tag for that type.

```
1   template <typename T>
2   struct DataCategory_
3   {
4   private:
5       template <bool isScalar, bool isMatrix, bool isBatchScalar,
6                   bool isBatchMatrix, typename TDummy = void>
7       struct helper;
8
9       template <typename TDummy>
10      struct helper<true, false, false, false, TDummy> {
11          using type = CategoryTags::Scalar;
12      };
13
14      template <typename TDummy>
15      struct helper<false, true, false, false, TDummy> {
16          using type = CategoryTags::Matrix;
17      };
18
19      template <typename TDummy>
20      struct helper<false, false, true, false, TDummy> {
21          using type = CategoryTags::BatchScalar;
22      };
23
24      template <typename TDummy>
25      struct helper<false, false, false, true, TDummy> {
26          using type = CategoryTags::BatchMatrix;
27      };
28
29  public:
30      using type = typename helper<IsScalar<T>, IsMatrix<T>,
31                                    IsBatchScalar<T>,
32                                    IsBatchMatrix<T>>::type;
33  };
34
35  template <typename T>
36  using DataCategory = typename DataCategory_<T>::type;
```

*DataCategory* calls *DataCategory_* to implement its principal logic. A simple branch is used in *DataCategory_*to implement the mapping between the type and the tag.

The metafunction *DataCategory* is implemented by calling the metafunction *IsXXX*, so if we modify the behavior of the metafunction *IsXXX*, the behavior of the corresponding metafunction *DataCategory* will change. For example, if there is no corresponding category tag associated with a data type, calling the metafunction *DataCategory* will incur a compilation error—meaning that the data type cannot be used in the framework of MetaNN. But if you introduce the following specialization as discussed:

```
1   template <>
2   constexpr bool IsBatchMatrix<A> = true;
```

Then *DataCategory<A>* will return *CategoryTags::BatchMatrix*.

The described process completes the construction of the tagging system for categories in MetaNN. In the second half of this chapter, we'll discuss the basic data types introduced by MetaNN in turn. MetaNN is type-rich and supports type extensions. The types it uses can vary, but there is a certain rule to follow in the design of each type. These rules form the design concepts of the data types in MetaNN together. Before diving into specific data types, we need to discuss some of the design concepts in MetaNN, which will help understand each specific data type. Meanwhile, understanding these design concepts is critical to understanding the whole framework of the system.

## 4.2 Design Concepts

### 4.2.1 Support for Different Computing Devices and Computing Units

Various data types contained in MetaNN involve operations related to storage space. So, they also have some commonalities.

The entire framework wants to support different computing devices—although the book focuses on CPU-based computational logic, the entire framework should be easier to be extended to support other computing devices such as GPU or FPGA. The characteristics of different devices are also distinct: for example, GPU memory is allocated differently from CPU memory. Frameworks should be able to cover differences like this between these devices to some extent and provide relatively consistent interfaces for users to call.

In addition, the units of data involved in the calculations may differ for a same computing device. For instance, when using CPU for calculations, we can choose *float* or *double* as the type for data storage units—the former takes up less space and the latter is more accurate. When using FPGA for calculations, we may also consider using floating points or fixed-point numbers as units to introduce a trade-off between accuracy and speed. Therefore, in addition to computing devices, data types should be able to support diverse units of computations and provide relatively uniform interfaces and behaviors.

Based on the discussed considerations, our data types need to be capable of encapsulating different computing devices and units and provide interfaces to expose the appropriate information.

To support different computing devices and facilitate expansion, MetaNN introduced the structure *DeviceTags* to describe computing devices:

```
1   struct DeviceTags
2   {
3       struct CPU;
4   };
```

It contains declarations for different devices internally. Currently, CPU is the only supported device, but we can add device names such as GPU and FPGA to it, if needed.

Data structures that support different computing devices cannot be mixed up with each other. In order to clearly describe computing devices and units, most data types in MetaNN are designed as class templates that receive two parameters, which represent the computing unit and the computing device respectively.

In the case of a matrix, the template is declared as:

```
1   template<typename TElem, typename TDevice>
2   class Matrix;
```

The first template parameter is the computing unit, and the second template parameter represents the computing device.

## 4.2.2 Allocation and Maintenance of Storage Space

Some data types in the MetaNN framework involve the maintenance of storage space. Typically, a matrix with $N$ rows and $M$ columns needs to allocate and maintain an array of size $N{\times}M$ to store the data it contains. Further, there are differences in how storage space is allocated, released, and used by different devices. We want to encapsulate the differentiation to provide a relatively uniform interface, which in turn eliminates requirements for the upper layer to pay attention to the details of storage operations.

MetaNN maintains storage space through two class templates, *Allocator* and *ContinuousMemory*. *Allocator* contains the logic of allocation and release for storage space, while *ContinuousMemory* maintains the allocated storage space.

### 4.2.2.1 Class Template Allocator

The declaration of the class template *Allocator* is as follows:

```
1   template <typename TDevice>
2   struct Allocator;
```

It receives a parameter assigned with a device type defined in *DeviceTags*. Diverse instances of *Allocator* can be introduced through specializations and execute allocation and release of storage space using device-related logic.

Here is a specialization of the template *Allocator* for allocating CPU memory:

```
1   template <>
2   struct Allocator<DeviceTags::CPU>
3   {
4       template <typename TElem>
5       static std::shared_ptr<TElem> Allocate(size_t p_elemSize) {
6         return std::shared_ptr<TElem>
7             (new TElem[p_elemSize], [](TElem* ptr) { delete[] ptr; });
8       }
9   };
```

Each version of *Allocator* specialization contains the function template *Allocate*, which receives the data type to be allocated as the template parameter and the number of elements to be allocated as the function parameter, allocates the storage space internally and returns the results of allocation in the smart pointer of type *std::shared_ptr*. This is achieved in the described version of specialization.

From its name, *Allocate* implements the allocation of storage space. But in practice, it also contains the logic of releasing storage space, which is given in the constructor *std::shared_ptr*. Take the discussed implementation as an example: *std::shared_ptr* uses *delete* to free up memory by default, which is appropriate for allocating a single element. But what we're allocating here is an array of elements, so we need to use the version receiving two parameters when constructing *std::shared_ptr*. The second parameter specifies how memory is freed up by a lambda expression: call *delete[]* to release the memory of the array.

The reason why the class template *Allocator* is introduced instead of calling *new* directly for memory allocation is that in addition to encapsulating different allocation methods,[5] we can also introduce more complex logic to implement more efficient memory usage. For instance, we can build a memory pool in the *Allocator* to save memory no longer in use, and the next time *Allocator* is called, the memory can be obtained directly from the memory pool for reuse if possible. It reduces the expenses of memory allocation and release. We need to modify the logic of the second argument of the constructor *std::shared_ptr* to achieve this goal.

Memory pools and associated techniques are beyond the scope of this book. So here's just one of the simplest implementations. Interested readers can refer to the inner implementation of MetaNN to learn how to utilize memory pools to replace the operation *delete[]* here.

### 4.2.2.2 Class Template ContinuousMemory

The class template *ContinuousMemory* maintains the memory allocated by *Allocator*. It is defined as follows:

```
1   template <typename TElem, typename TDevice>
2   class ContinuousMemory {
3       static_assert(std::is_same<RemConstRef<TElem>, TElem>::value);
```

---

[5] For example, we can't use *new* to allocate the memory used by GPU.

```
4          using ElementType = TElem;
5    public:
6          explicit ContinuousMemory(size_t p_size)
7        : m_mem(Allocator<TDevice>::template Allocate<ElementType>(p_size))
8              , m_memStart(m_mem.get())
9          {}
10
11         ContinuousMemory(std::shared_ptr<ElementType> p_mem,
12             ElementType* p_memStart)
13             : m_mem(std::move(p_mem))
14             , m_memStart(p_memStart)
15         {}
16
17         auto RawMemory() const { return m_memStart; }
18
19         const std::shared_ptr<ElementType> SharedPtr() const {
20             return m_mem;
21         }
22
23         bool operator== (const ContinuousMemory& val) const {
24           return (m_mem == val.m_mem) && (m_memStart == val.m_memStart);
25         }
26
27         bool operator!= (const ContinuousMemory& val) const {
28             return !(operator==(val));
29         }
30
31         size_t UseCount() const {
32             return m_mem.use_count();
33         }
34
35    private:
36         std::shared_ptr<ElementType> m_mem;
37         ElementType* m_memStart;
38    };
```

It receives two template parameters: *TElem* represents the type of the computing unit and *TDevice* represents the device type limited to the declaration in *DeviceTags*.

*ContinuousMemory* first ensures that the type of the computing unit does not contain references and const qualifiers—for deep learning frameworks, it is usually meaningless if an element in a matrix used for calculation is a reference or of type const. *ContinuousMemory* uses the metafunction *RemConstRef* to remove information of references or const that may occur in *TElem* and compare the output type of the metafunction with *TElem*. If the two are the same ones, then

*TElem* does not contain information of references or const. Otherwise, static assertions will be triggered with reporting errors.

*ContinuousMemory* then constructs two data members using the type information about the computing unit: *m_mem* maintains the smart pointer assigned by *Allocator* and *m_memStart* records the starting position of the data. Typically, *m_memStart* points to the beginning of *m_mem*, but in the case involving a submatrix (which is discussed later in this chapter), *m_memStart* may point to the middle of *m_mem*. *m_mem* is only used to save the allocation results of *Allocator*, ensuring that the reference counting of the corresponding smart pointer is correct. Reading data is always executed through *m_memStart*.

*ContinuousMemory* provides two constructors. The first form receives the number of elements as an argument delivered to *Allocator* to allocate memory. The other constructor is used to construct a submatrix (we'll mention the corresponding logic of construction when discussing submatrices). Meanwhile, the class provides the appropriate interface to return internally stored data (lines 17–21).

*ContinuousMemory* also contains two interfaces to determine whether two instances of *ContinuousMemory* are equal. If two instances point to the same memory region, they are equal. The evaluation operation provides the corresponding support for the optimization of evaluation, and Chapter 8 of this book discusses the evaluation, where we will re-examine the purpose of the evaluation operation.

In addition to the discussed interface, *ContinuousMemory* also provides an interface, *UseCount*, which serves to return the reference count of the underlying smart pointer. It doesn't seem necessary because the reference count is used only in general to facilitate the underlying logic to determine if memory recycling can be executed. Why is it exposed to the upper level? To account for this, it involves another design concept for MetaNN: shallow copy and detection of write operations. Similar to memory maintenance, this design concept runs through the various data types of MetaNN.

## 4.2.3 Shallow Copy and Detection of Write Operations

Shallow copy and detection of write operations are also two design principles of data types for MetaNN. These two principles are closely related to the concept of "element-level reading and writing." This section begins with a discussion of element-level reading and writing, which leads to the specific meaning of shallow copy and detection of write operations.

In addition to scalars, the data types operated in the deep learning framework—whether it's matrices, data for batch processing, or other data types, they are basically a set of data. A common operation for data sets is to access elements on the side of CPU for reading and writing. This operation is called element-level reading and writing.

### 4.2.3.1 Data Types without Requirements of Support for Element-level Reading and Writing

No matter whether it's a matrix or a list of matrices, their core function is to store data sets needed for computing. It seems that interfaces should be provided to access each of these elements. But a closer analysis shows that element-level reading and writing is unnecessary in many cases.

This is, above all, a cost issue. In general, reading and writing of data involves interaction with the CPU memory—we can read data from memory or write data back into memory. If the storage space to be read from and written into is not CPU-controlled memory—such as a matrix for GPU operations, whose data is stored in the GPU memory. In order to achieve element-level reading and writing, a copy between the GPU memory and the CPU memory is required. For example, when data is read from the GPU, data from the GPU memory is first copied to the CPU before it can be read by users. The cost of copying storage space is often quite high compared to reading and writing data itself, so supporting this form of reading and write leads to an additional burden on the system. In general, when it comes to interactions between different types of computing devices, what we need is not to read and write an element, but to read and write to the entire set of data—such as copying a matrix in the CPU into the GPU as a whole, or vice versa. As a result, the framework can achieve the required functionality by simply providing replication of data at the level of abstract data types (such as the level of matrices) between the CPU and a particular device. The replication handles multiple data items at once, so as to take full advantage of the bandwidth provided by the computing device and improve replication efficiency.

Secondly, some special types of data structures are not necessary to support element-level reading and writing. Typical data structures include a distinctive matrix of all 0s or 1s, which has a special purpose in the system. It makes no sense to execute write operations with it—because all elements have the same value.

## 4.2.3.2 Element-level Writing and Shallow Copy

Even if a data type does need to support operations of element-level reading and writing on the side of CPU, the statuses of reading and writing are distinct. In general, operations of reading can be performed at any time but whether write operations are supported depending on the timing of operations. We will take matrices as an example to discuss the causes of this phenomenon.

Numerous operations of deep learning frameworks involve the replication of data—for example, copying the output of one network as the input to another. Typically, a data type uses an array inside it to store its element values. The replication of arrays is relatively time-consuming. If each time of replication involves the replication of each element in the data, the speed of the entire framework will be significantly affected. To solve this problem, MetaNN uses shallow copy for data replication—for a matrix in the general sense: the data type contains objects of type *ContinuousMemory* internally and the core logic of replication is done by copying the objects. *ContinuousMemory* uses the default method of replication, which is essentially replication of the smart pointer *std::shared_ptr* contained inside the *ContinuousMemory*. The target object involved in replication will point to the same memory as the original object—which can greatly improve the performance of the system.

However, this design has a side effect: writing on an object will affect other objects that point to the same memory region. In general, this is not the way we want. A typical scenario is that we save the intermediate results of forward propagation in the network to ensure that backward propagation is performed correctly. However, intermediate results may share memory with the input matrix. If we modify the contents of the input matrix (i.e., operations of writing) after forward propagation, the intermediate results saved in the corresponding network will also be modified, then subsequent calculations will go wrong. For complex networks, it is likely that the behavior of the system will be abnormal due to incorrect write operations without precautionary measures. More unfortunately, such anomalies are often difficult to trace. In order to prevent this from happening, it is necessary to take special care of write operations—if the object currently performing element-level writing does not share memory with other objects, then the operation can be done; conversely, if the object shares memory with other objects, the write operation should be prohibited.

The smart pointer *std::shared_ptr* uses reference count internally to implement the maintenance of resources. Its reference count can be obtained by its member function *use_count*: it indicates that there is no other *std::shared_ptr* pointing to the same memory when the count is 1, and the write operation is safe and does not affect other objects. That's why we introduce the function *UseCount* in *ContinuousMemory*—before writing, we can call the function first to obtain the corresponding reference count and guarantee the security of write operations.

## 4.2.4 Expansion of Underlying Interfaces

The constraint of write operations reflects the consideration of system security in MetaNN. For the same purpose, MetaNN also introduces more restrictions on the underlying data. For example, it does not allow users to directly access the saved data through the head pointer of the array. Users should only have limited access to data through the external interfaces provided by MetaNN.

On the other hand, the limited interfaces also limit system optimization. Take matrix computations as an example: MetaNN provides the *Matrix* template[6] to describe matrices and functions to support matrix operations. *Matrix* classe provide interfaces for element-level reading and writing but they can only access one element at a time. Actual matrix computations often require access to all elements of matrices (i.e., matrix-level reading and writing) and it is not friendly to use an element-level access interface.

Firstly, a function calls itself produces costs. Although the compiler can choose to inline element-level reading and writing functions, it is hard to guarantee that the compiler will definitely do so. If the compiler does not turn inline the corresponding functions, the speed will be significantly affected when we try to call such an interface to get data for the entire matrix.

Secondly, *Matrix* adds an assertion to the interface function of element-level reading and writing to determine the legitimacy of the incoming parameters of rows and columns: each time the interface is called, the corresponding assertion statement is triggered. Relatively speaking, when accessing the entire matrix, we only need to ensure the range of incoming rows and columns to be legitimate without having to confirm each element accordingly.

More importantly, in order to expedite the system, we often need to ask for third-party libraries for specialized matrix calculations. For instance, we can use MKL libraries for acceleration in a CPU environment and use libraries like Cuda to implement matrix multiplication and other operations in a GPU environment. The external interfaces provided by these third-party libraries often require pointers to the array of elements corresponding to the incoming matrix, as well as other auxiliary parameters, enabling access to the entire matrix. Matrix templates do not have relevant interfaces exposing such information.

Various data structures in MetaNN are faced with similar problems. Of course, we can introduce more interfaces with more openness to these data structures, enabling them to work more efficiently with other libraries. But that's not what we want: if such interfaces are provided, in addition to third-party libraries, users of the framework can use these interfaces too. But in fact, we don't want users of the framework to use them. The central purpose of introducing a

---

[6] We'll discuss the specific implementation of the *Matrix* template later in this chapter.

more open interface is to increase computing speed. Nevertheless, these interfaces lose security we want to ensure to some extent in the meantime. It is not required for users of the MetaNN framework to be concerned with details of the calculation. Although they also read and write specific data structures, the frequency of reading and writing data is relatively low compared to computing processes of the entire network. Using more secure interfaces has an impact on the speed of operations, but what is affected is a small part of processes in the entire system. In turn, for framework users, we are more concerned with helping them use safely and reducing the risks that may occur during usage. Therefore, we want to hide these more efficient yet risky interfaces from end users.

MetaNN is a generic framework, and all the code is contained in the header file. In theory, users of the framework can see all details of its implementation. In such an environment, it is hard to hide such efficient but more risky interfaces from users. Nonetheless, at least we can implement hiding to some extent—that is, to achieve matrix-level access in a special way. MetaNN employs a middle tier to achieve a certain degree of user blocking:

```
1   template<typename TData>
2   struct LowerAccessImpl;
3
4   template <typename TData>
5   auto LowerAccess(TData&& p)
6   {
7       using RawType = RemConstRef<TData>;
8       return LowerAccessImpl<RawType>(std::forward<TData>(p));
9   }
```

*LowerAccess* is the underlying interface to access, which should only be invoked by the frame MetaNN itself.

*LowerAccessImpl* is a template for exposing information that is not intended to be exposed to frame users but intended to be exposed to other components of MetaNN. In theory, *LowerAccessImpl* can be utilized to expose the underlying information of any class: to simply specify each data type that we want to provide additional access support for. *LowerAccess*, on the other hand, is a function that assigns a given data to get the appropriate class supporting underlying access.

We'll take a look at the application of *LowerAccess* as we discuss concrete data structures later in this chapter.

### 4.2.5 Type Conversion and Evaluation

We have discussed the tagging system in the previous section. The tagging system is used to classify the data involved in MetaNN. Each tag represents a category that may correspond to one or more specific data types. Given the computing unit and the computing device, there is one most generic type of all types for a tag, which is referred to as the principal type in MetaNN. It can be said that any other type of the same tag is a special case of the principal type. For example, *Matrix<float, DeviceTags::CPU>* is the principal type of matrices, which uses an array to represent the values of elements in the matrix. We can construct a certain data type to represent a zero matrix, but obviously a zero matrix can also be represented by *Matrix<float, DeviceTags::CPU>*.

Given the tag of the category, the computing unit and the computing device, the corresponding principal type is determined: the metafunction *PrincipalDataType* is used to get the principal type in MetaNN:

```
1   template <typename TCategory, typename TElem, typename TDevice>
2   struct PrincipalDataType_;
3
4   template <typename TElem, typename TDevice>
5   struct PrincipalDataType_<CategoryTags::Matrix, TElem, TDevice>
6   {
7       using type = Matrix<TElem, TDevice>;
8   };
9
10  // Other specializations of PrincipalDataType_
11  // ...
12
13  template <typename TCategory, typename TElem, typename TDevice>
14  using PrincipalDataType
15      = typename PrincipalDataType_<TCategory, TElem, TDevice>::type;
```

For example, *PrincipalDataType<CategoryTags::Matrix, float, DeviceTags::CPU>* will return *Matrix<float, DeviceTags::CPU>*, which is the principal type of matrices with *float* as the computing unit and *DeviceTags::CPU* as the computing device.

The principal type is typically used to interact with the user. For example, users can define the input matrix using the principal type and send the input matrix to the deep learning system for calculation. In order to read the values of each element in the result matrix, users also need to convert the calculation result to the principal type. The process of converting a specific data type to the corresponding principal type is called evaluation.

The process of evaluation itself can be quite complicated and involve most computational operations in a deep learning framework, which are often time-consuming. Increasing the speed of evaluation is key to increasing the speed of a deep learning system. For faster evaluation of the system, we need to introduce a set of mechanisms. It is precisely because of the significance and complexity of evaluation that a separate chapter is required to discuss it. This book will discuss evaluation in Chapter 8.

### 4.2.6 *Data Interface Specifications*

MetaNN uses category tags to classify the type system. There is a loose organizational structure between different types that belong to the same category. The interfaces that each type needs to provide are given in the form of a document description. Based on the discussion, this section provides an overview of the interfaces to be supported by existing categories of MetaNN.

- Each data type requires two type definitions, *ElementType* and *DeviceType*, which represent the computing unit and the computing device associated with it. For example, for a data type *A*, *A::DeviceType* represents the computing device it corresponds to.

■ Each data type requires the introduction of a specification of the metafunction in the form of *IsXXX* to indicate the category it falls within. For instance, for a data type *A*, it is necessary to introduce the specification of Is*Matrix<A>=true* to it if it is a matrix.

■ Each data type requires the provision of the appropriate evaluation logic to be converted to the corresponding principal type. The evaluation logic actually corresponds to a series of interfaces, including *EvalRegister* for registration of evaluation and several interfaces to determine whether objects are equal. We'll discuss the usage of these interfaces in Chapter 8.

■ If a type belongs to the category of matrices, it needs to provide interfaces *RowNum* and *ColNum* to return the number of rows and columns of the matrix.

■ If a type is a list, it needs to provide the interface *BatchNum* to return the number of "elements" it contains. Typically, a list of matrices would require *BatchNum* to return the number of matrices in it, while a list of scalars would require *BatchNum* to return the number of scalars in it.

■ Other interfaces for data types are not mandatory, especially that they are not required to provide interfaces for element-level reading and writing. However, *LowerAccessImpl* should be provided for specific data types to access their underlying data, if necessary.

We have discussed the design concepts and interface specifications for data types in MetaNN, which will run through the framework. Next, we'll talk about basic data types contained in MetaNN, starting with the scalars.

## 4.3 Scalars

The status of scalars in the deep learning framework is quite special. In general, a deep learning framework should provide specialized abstract data types to represent data structures such as matrices. But for scalars, it is not necessary to introduce specialized data types. For example, a deep learning framework based on C++ can choose to use built-in data types (such as *float/double*) to represent scalars.

MetaNN choose to encapsulate scalar as classes, that is, introducing specific abstract data type is introduced for scalars. There are two reasons for this design: to ensure a degree of consistency in the underlying data structure and to make the use of scalars more flexible.

The first thing is consistency. As we have seen in section 4.1, there are corresponding requirements for each category of data in MetaNN, including providing several member functions, type definitions, and so on. Such information is aimed at maintaining the entire framework system in MetaNN. If we use the built-in data type of C++ to represent scalars, the built-in data type of C++ does not meet the corresponding requirements for the data type of MetaNN. So we have to introduce specialized logic of processing for scalars. Furthermore, as discussed in Chapter 3, the concept of operations is introduced in MetaNN and the core of operations is to build an expression template. Imagine that the result of a certain operation is a scalar and the corresponding expression template that represents the scalar provides several member functions and type definitions, which is essentially different from the scalars basically constructed using the built-in data type of C++. The inconsistency also increases the complexity of the framework maintenance. Conversely, encapsulating scalars into specialized data types can largely ensure that they behave in a similar way to other data structures (such as matrices), thus simplifying the maintenance of the entire system.

Secondly, encapsulating scalars can also make them more flexible to use. MetaNN supports multiple levels of expansions, one of which is to support different computing devices. Currently, MetaNN only supports CPU. But we can extend it to support GPU, FPGA, and more. Different devices may use different storage regions, such as the CPU uses the CPU memory, while the GPU reads from and writes into the GPU memory. Typically, scalars are stored in the CPU memory, but it does not preclude situations where space needs to be allocated for scalars to be saved in other storage regions. MetaNN encapsulates scalars and can handle scalars in different storage regions in a relatively uniform way.

## 4.3.1 Declaration of Class Templates

MetaNN introduces a special class template for scalars, which is declared as follows:

```
1   template <typename TElem, typename TDevice = DeviceTags::CPU>
2   struct Scalar;
3
4   template <typename TElem, typename TDevice>
5   constexpr bool IsScalar<Scalar<TElem, TDevice>> = true;
```

It receives two parameters, representing the computing unit and the type of the computing device. The type of the computing device has the default value as *DeviceTags::CPU*, indicating that a scalar is stored in the CPU memory by default.

Here is also a declaration of a specialization, setting *IsScalar<Scalar<...>>* as *true*. In this way we associate the category tag *CategoryTags::Scalar* with the class template *Scalar*. According to the previous discussion, the system also returns the *Scalar* tag when *DataCategory* is called.

## 4.3.2 A Specialized Version Based on CPU

Scalars can be specialized for different devices. In this book, we'll limit the scope of the discussion to the CPU. So here's just a specialized version for CPU of scalars. The interfaces and data members included are as follows:

```
1    template <typename TElem, typename TDevice = DeviceTags::CPU>
2    class Scalar
3    {
4    public:
5        using ElementType = TElem;
6        using DeviceType = TDevice;
7
8    public:
9        Scalar(ElementType elem = ElementType())
10            : m_elem(elem) {}
11
12        auto& Value() { return m_elem; }
13
```

```
14          auto Value() const { return m_elem; }
15
16          // Interfaces related to evaluation
17          bool operator== (const Scalar& val) const;
18
19          template <typename TOtherType>
20          bool operator== (const TOtherType&) const;
21
22          template <typename TData>
23          bool operator!= (const TData& val) const;
24
25          auto EvalRegister() const;
26
27  private:
28          ElementType m_elem;
29  };
```

### 4.3.2.1 Type Definitions and Data Members

As mentioned earlier, each data type in MetaNN should contain two declarations: *ElementType* and *DeviceType*, which represent the computing unit and the computing device type respectively. They can be considered as interfaces. In general, for a data type *X* used in MetaNN, information about the appropriate device and computing unit can be obtained through *X::DeviceType* and *X::ElementType*. Meanwhile, *Scalar* uses the type of the computing unit to declare its unique data member, *m_elem*.

In addition to type definitions and declarations of data members, the template *Scalar* contains several interfaces that describe operations supported for scalars. These operations can be divided into the following categories.

### 4.3.2.2 Construction, Assignment, and Movement

*Scalar* explicitly declares a constructor that receives a data member of type *ElementType* as an argument, using the data member to initialize the value of scalars. If no arguments are passed in to *Scalar* in the process of constructing it, the default value constructed by *ElementType()* will be saved in it.

Apart from this constructor, the class template *Scalar* does not declare any other constructor, assignment function, and movement function. The compiler automatically synthesizes the corresponding copy of constructor, assignment function, and movement function for it according to the C++ standard.

### 4.3.2.3 Reading and Writing Elements

The template *Scalar* provides the interface *Value* to obtain the value of the element, which has two overloaded versions. The non-const version can be used to modify the value of the element.

### 4.3.2.4 Evaluating Related Interfaces

In addition to constructors and *Value*, the other interfaces provided by the template *Scalar* are used for evaluation. Evaluation is a relatively complex process. In order to support evaluation, we need to provide two types of interfaces.

1. Determine whether data items are "equal"—lines 17–23 of the described code snippet define several functions for given two data members used in MetaNN to determine whether they are "equal." Note that "equal" is quoted here, where the equality judgment here is different to the general mathematical judgment of equality for performance issue.
2. Registration of evaluation—each data type used in MetaNN requires the interface *EvalRegister* to be registered for evaluation.

As for details of evaluation, we will leave it to Chapter 8 for discussion. The analysis of these two types of interfaces will also be left to Chapter 8, which will not be elaborated here.

### 4.3.3 The Principal Type of Scalars

Scalars are relatively simple data structures without many variations. So far, only one template implementation has been introduced for scalars in the underlying data types of MetaNN, that is, the *Scalar* discussed earlier.[7]

"Scalar" is also a tag in MetaNN. As we have discussed earlier—a corresponding principal type should be introduced for each tag. Although the category of scalars currently contains only one class template, it is also necessary to introduce a principal type for it:

```
1   template <typename TElem, typename TDevice>
2   struct PrincipalDataType_<CategoryTags::Scalar, TElem, TDevice>
3   {
4       using type = Scalar<TElem, TDevice>;
5   };
```

The principal type of scalars is the type instantiated from the class template *Scalar* based on the computing unit and the computing device.

Having finished the discussion of scalars, we'll look at the implementation of the category of matrices in MetaNN. Matrices bear many similarities to scalars but there are several data types in matrices. The next section discusses the purpose of these data types and their connections.

## 4.4 Matrix

In the existing MetaNN system, the largest distinction between scalars and matrices is that there are several data types in the category of matrices. As mentioned earlier, one of these types will be a "principal type" and each specific data type provides a corresponding method of evaluation to

---

[7] Note that this chapter only discusses the basic data types of MetaNN. Chapter 5 discusses operations, which construct expression templates. An expression template can be considered a composite data type and it can be a scalar.

be converted to the principal type. The principal type of matrices is represented by the template *Matrix*. Let's first look at the definition of this class template.

## 4.4.1 Class Template **Matrix**

### 4.4.1.1 Declarations and Interfaces

The class template Matrix is declared as follows:

```
1  template<typename TElem, typename TDevice>
2  class Matrix;
3
4  template <typename TElem, typename TDevice>
5  constexpr bool IsMatrix<Matrix<TElem, TDevice>> = true;
```

Similar to the template *Scalar*, this template also receives two parameters: *TEelem* represents the type of computing unit, and *TDevice* represents the computing device associated with the matrix. On this basis, we introduced the specialization of *IsMatrix* to tag types like *Matrix<TElem, TDevice>* with the category of matrices.

Similar to *Scalar*, this book will only discuss the template's specialization for the CPU:

```
1   template <typename TElem>
2   class Matrix<TElem, DeviceTags::CPU>
3   {
4   public:
5       using ElementType = TElem;
6       using DeviceType = DeviceTags::CPU;
7
8   public:
9       Matrix(size_t p_rowNum = 0, size_t p_colNum = 0);
10
11      // Interfaces related to dimensions
12      size_t RowNum() const { return m_rowNum; }
13      size_t ColNum() const { return m_colNum; }
14
15      // Interfaces for read/write access
16      void SetValue(size_t p_rowId, size_t p_colId, ElementType val);
17      const auto operator () (size_t p_rowId, size_t p_colId) const;
18      bool AvailableForWrite() const;
19
20      // Interface for a submatrix
21      Matrix SubMatrix(size_t p_rowB, size_t p_rowE,
22              size_t p_colB, size_t p_colE) const;
23
```

```
24        // Interfaces related to evaluation
25        // ...
26
27  private:
28    Matrix(std::shared_ptr<ElementType> p_mem, ElementType* p_memStart,
29        size_t p_rowNum, size_t p_colNum, size_t p_rowLen);
30
31  private:
32    ContinuousMemory<ElementType, DeviceType> m_mem;
33    size_t m_rowNum;
34    size_t m_colNum;
35    size_t m_rowLen;
36  };
```

A matrix is a two-dimensional structure, so two arguments need to be passed in to represent the number of rows and columns of the matrix when constructing the object *Matrix*. Two objects, *m_rowNum* and *m_colNum*, are also required inside the class to hold both values. *m_mem* points to the beginning of the array that holds the matrix elements. The elements in the matrix are stored in row-major order, that is, the first row of the elements in the matrix is saved in the front of the array, followed by the second row, and so on.

This specialized version has a lot in common with *Scalar*: for example, they both use the default semantics for copying and moving and both provide interfaces related to evaluation. These are discussed previously and will not be repeated. Here's a look at the unique features of *Matrix* compared to *Scalar*.

## 4.4.1.2 Dimensional Information and Element-level Reading and Writing

Matrices are two-dimensional and the class template *Matrix* provides *RowNum* and *ColNum* to return the number of rows and columns of a matrix.

Lines 16 and 17 of the code snippet provide two functions for element-level reading and writing. As mentioned earlier, the status of read operations is different from that of write operations, so read and write operations cannot be provided simultaneously through the following interfaces:

```
1  TElem& operator () (size_t p_rowId, size_t p_colId);
```

It is because if we use such an interface, the matrix object itself will not be able to distinguish whether the call is for a write or read operation.

Read operations are secure and we use *operator()* as its interface, which returns a copy of elements inside a matrix rather than references or pointers, which ensures that subsequent operations do not change the internal state of the matrix object. A specialized function *SetValue* is introduced for write operations. The function determines the value of the reference count internally. Write operations can only be executed if the current storage space is exclusive:

```
1  const auto operator () (size_t p_rowId, size_t p_colId) const
2  {
3        assert((p_rowId < m_rowNum) && (p_colId < m_colNum));
```

```
4            return (m_mem.RawMemory())[p_rowId * m_rowLen + p_colId];
5        }
6
7        bool AvailableForWrite() const
8        {
9            return m_mem.UseCount() == 1;
10       }
11
12       void SetValue(size_t p_rowId, size_t p_colId, ElementType val)
13       {
14           assert(AvailableForWrite());
15           assert((p_rowId < m_rowNum) && (p_colId < m_colNum));
16           (m_mem.RawMemory())[p_rowId * m_rowLen + p_colId] = val;
17       }
```

When *m_mem.UseCount() == 1* is *true*, it indicates that the current object does not share memory with other objects. *SetValue* will only proceed with subsequent actions under this premise, that is, when *AvailableForWrite()* returns *true*, or otherwise the assertion will fail.

## 4.4.1.3 Submatrix

The class template *Matrix* uses a continuous array internally to represent elements in a matrix. The elements in a matrix are arranged in row-major order. Meanwhile:

- The first element of the storage space represents the first element of the matrix;
- The last element of each row in the matrix is adjacent to the first element of the next row.

In some cases, we may be required to access the submatrix of a matrix. For example, for a 100×100 matrix, we want to get the elements in 20–30 rows and 15–55 columns and use them as a submatrix.

Similar to the case of matrix replication, we also don't wish to involve a large number of memory copies when constructing submatrices. We hope to share storage space with the submatrix with its parent matrix in an approach similar to "shallow copy." Now let's consider what treatments should be introduced to achieve this.

Obviously, if a submatrix is required to share storage space with the parent matrix, the two properties mentioned earlier can no longer be maintained in the submatrix. Because the first element of the submatrix may not be the first element of the parent matrix, and if the number of columns of the submatrix is fewer than the number of columns of the parent matrix, there will be a "gap" between the last element of each row and the first element of the next row in the submatrix.

Because of the absence of these two properties, we need additional information to identify the correct location of elements of the matrix: we introduced *m_memStart* to represent the position of the first element of the matrix in the *ContinuousMemory* class, and *m_rowLen* to represent the original length of a row in the *Matrix* template. If one matrix is not a submatrix of another matrix, then *m_memStart* will point to the starting position of the allocated memory (i.e., the position that the member variable *ContinuousMemory::m_mem* points to), while its *m_rowLen* and *m_colNum* are of the same value (i.e., the length of each row in the matrix is the number of columns in the

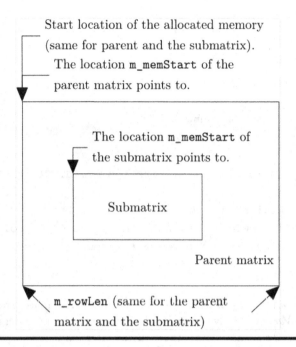

Start location of the allocated memory (same for parent and the submatrix). The location **m_memStart** of the parent matrix points to.

The location **m_memStart** of the submatrix points to.

Submatrix

Parent matrix

**m_rowLen** (same for the parent matrix and the submatrix)

**Figure 4.1   Data members' relationships in the parent matrix and the submatrix.**

matrix). For the submatrix, however, *m_memStart* may no longer point to the starting position of the allocated memory, while the value of *m_rowLen* is consistent with the value of *m_rowLen* of its parent matrix: the distance between the start of two adjacent rows in the parent matrix is the same as that of the submatrix, which is preserved in *m_rowLen*. Figure 4.1 shows the relationship between data members in the parent matrix and the submatrix.

*SubMatrix* implements the logic of constructing a submatrix based on the previous ideas, which receives four parameters, representing the first and last rows, the first and last columns of the submatrix. A new instance of *Matrix* is constructed based on these four parameters and returns:

```
1   Matrix SubMatrix(size_t p_rowB, size_t p_rowE,
2                     size_t p_colB, size_t p_colE) const
3   {
4       assert((p_rowB < m_rowNum) && (p_colB < m_colNum));
5       assert((p_rowE <= m_rowNum) && (p_colE <= m_colNum));
6
7       TElem* pos = m_mem.RawMemory() + p_rowB * m_rowLen + p_colB;
8       return Matrix(m_mem.SharedPtr(),
9                     pos,
10                    p_rowE - p_rowB,
11                    p_colE - p_colB,
12                    m_rowLen);
13  }
```

Line 7 calculates the new starting location and lines 8–12 call a private constructor of *Matrix* to implement the construction of the submatrix. This private constructor calls the second constructor (which received pointers) of *ContinuousMemory* internally to implement the pointer's replication.

SubMatrix follows the STL style of front-closed and back-open intervals when determining intervals for parameters: the submatrix contains rows $[p\_rowB, p\_rowE)$ and the columns $[p\_colB, p\_colE)$. The instance returned by the function shares memory with the original matrix, but the $(i, j)$ element of the new instance is actually the $(i + p\_rowB, j + p\_colB)$ element of the original instance.

### 4.4.1.4 Underlying Access Interfaces of Matrix

Previously, we mentioned a specialized mechanism in the framework for accessing underlying data. The template *Matrix* adopts this mechanism to provide a relatively convenient but less secure interface for other components in MetaNN.

To implement this interface, we first declare the friend type in the template *Matrix*:

```
1   template <typename TElem>
2   class Matrix<TElem, DeviceTags::CPU>
3   {
4       // ...
5       friend struct LowerAccessImpl<Matrix<TElem, DeviceTags::CPU>>;
6       // ...
7   };
```

After that, the following class template specialization is introduced:

```
1   template<typename TElem>
2   struct LowerAccessImpl<Matrix<TElem, DeviceTags::CPU>>
3   {
4       LowerAccessImpl(Matrix<TElem, DeviceTags::CPU> p)
5           : m_matrix(p) {}
6
7       auto MutableRawMemory() {
8           return m_matrix.m_mem.RawMemory();
9       }
10
11      const auto RawMemory() const {
12          return m_matrix.m_mem.RawMemory();
13      }
14
15      size_t RowLen() const {
16          return m_matrix.m_rowLen;
```

```
17          }
18
19   private:
20          Matrix<TElem, DeviceTags::CPU> m_matrix;
21   };
```

It exposes the data storage region inside the template *Matrix* with the form of a pointer.

Based on this construct, we can declare an object as follows and access the head pointer of the array corresponding to the matrix:

```
1   Matrix<XXX, DeviceTags::CPU> X;
2   auto lower_X = LowerAccess(X);
3   auto ptr = lower_X.RawMemory();
```

*ptr* points to the underlying storage space of the matrix allocated by MetaNN. Other components of MetaNN can use this memory pointer for fast data access without calling the (relatively time-consuming) interface for element-level reading and writing each time the data is accessed.

Meanwhile, objects of type *LowerAccessImpl<Matrix<...>>* also provide the function *RowLen*, which exposes the row length of *Matrix*. For element-level operations, this piece of information does not have to be exposed. Nonetheless, when we manipulate an array of elements stored inside the matrix, it is necessary to determine the boundaries of the data with the information.

Calling interfaces related to *LowerAccessImpl<Matrix<...>>* can impose some impact on the security of the system compared to calling the inherent interfaces in *Matrix*. For example, we can call *MutableRawMemory* to obtain an array pointer and use it to write. This interface does not determine if there is a problem of memory sharing and the abuse of it may lead to the side effects introduced by write operations as described earlier. Again, we don't want users of the framework to gain access to the underlying array pointers for unsafe operations. *LowerAccessImp* and its related components are introduced only for the internal implementation of the framework. This intention is also manifested when the additional *LowerAccessImp* is used instead of providing access to pointers in the methods of Matrix.

MetaNN uses the template *Matrix* to represent a matrix in the general sense. *Matrix* maintains an array internally where each array element corresponds to only one matrix element, and vice versa. In theory, we can employ this template to represent any matrix. However, the actual task may involve special matrices, which have their own characteristics and will be both memory-wasting and not conducive to computing optimization if represented as *Matrix*. Conversely, the effect may be better if it is represented in a different form. Currently, MetaNN contains three special matrices: the trivial matrix, the zero matrix, and the one-hot vector.

## 4.4.2 Special Matrices: Trivial Matrix, Zero Matrix, and One-hot Vector

### 4.4.2.1 Trivial Matrix

If each element in a matrix is of the same value, then we call the matrix "trivial." Trivial matrices are typically used as input to certain networks in deep learning frameworks and do not involve element modifications.

The template *TrivalMatrix* is adopted to represent trivial matrices in MetaNN and the definition of this class template is as follows:

```
1   template<typename TElem, typename TDevice, typename TScalar>
2   class TrivalMatrix
3   {
4   public:
5        using ElementType = TElem;
6        using DeviceType = TDevice;
7
8   public:
9        TrivalMatrix(size_t p_rowNum, size_t p_colNum, TScalar p_val);
10
11       // Interfaces related to dimensions
12       size_t RowNum() const;
13       size_t ColNum() const;
14
15       // Interfaces for read/write access
16       auto ElementValue() const;
17
18       // Interfaces related to evaluation
19       // ...
20
21   private:
22       TScalar m_val;
23       size_t m_rowNum;
24       size_t m_colNum;
25
26       // Caching the results of evaluation
27       EvalBuffer<Matrix<ElementType, DeviceType>> m_evalBuf;
28   };
```

After discussing the class templates *Scalar* and *Matrix*, the author assumes that readers have learned some of the general design principles in MetaNN. So in the following discussion, we'll skip these similar concepts and focus on sections specific to each class.

Compared to *Matrix*, *TrivalMatrix* contains an additional template parameter that represents the type of scalars it stores. According to the previous discussion, a scalar contains other information in addition to its value, such as the device where the scalar value itself is located, which determines the behavior details of *TrivalMatrix*.

The class *TrivalMatrix* also provides *ElementType* and *DeviceType*, which can be understood as the computing unit and the computing device corresponding to the results of evaluation after it is evaluated. For example, assuming that MetaNN supports GPU as a computing device, then *TrivalMatrix<float, GPU, ...>* means that we will allocate some space in the GPU memory to store the results of evaluation after it is evaluated.

The third template parameter of *TrivalMatrix* (scalar) also contains information about the computing unit and the computing device, which can be different from the first two template parameters of *TrivalMatrix*. For example, *TrivalMatrix<float, GPU, Scalar<int, CPU>>* can be declared—it means that although a *float* matrix stored in the GPU memory will be constructed after the evaluation of *TrivalMatrix*, each value in this matrix is a copy of an *int* value stored in the CPU.

We allow *TrivalMatrix* and the scalar it contains to differ in computing units and computing devices to some extent, provided that the following conditions are met:

■ The computing unit of the scalar can be implicitly converted into the computing unit of *TrivalMatrix*.
■ The computing device type of the scalar is the CPU or the same as that of *TrivalMatrix*. It indicates that we can set the element values in a trivial matrix on the side of CPU or can construct a matrix in the same device with scalars stored in a certain device. However, it is not currently supported to obtain scalar values from a particular device (such as the GPU memory) and construct a corresponding trivial matrix in another device (such as FPGA), which is not common.

The constructor of *TrivalMatrix* receives three parameters: the number of rows and columns in the matrix and the corresponding scalar object. The scalar object is saved in the *m_val*: only this scalar value needs to be recorded inside the matrix object and there is no need to specifically allocate an array to represent each element in the matrix—in this sense, the space complexity of *TrivalMatrix* is much less than Matrix. In addition, *TrivalMatrix* provides a specialized function, *ElementValue* to access the scalar objects in it. This is also different from *Matrix*.

Another difference between *TrivalMatrix* and *Matrix* is that it has an additional data member, *m_evalBuf*, which is used to save the results of evaluation. We'll discuss it in the Chapter 8.

After implementing a trivial matrix, we need to specialize *IsMatrix* to associate it with the matrix tag in MetaNN:

```
1   template <typename TElem, typename TDevice>
2   constexpr bool IsMatrix<TrivalMatrix<TElem, TDevice>> = true;
```

This step is quite important and equivalent to tagging *TrivalMatrix* accordingly. Only by introducing this specialization can *TrivalMatrix* be associated with the entire type system of MetaNN.

There's one more point about *TrivalMatrix*. Constructing objects of *TrivalMatrix* directly is complex—we should provide the computing unit, the computing device and the type of the scalar. A function is provided to simplify the construction of *TrivalMatrix* in MetaNN:

```
1   template<typename TElem, typename TDevice, typename TVal>
2   auto MakeTrivalMatrix(size_t rowNum, size_t colNum, TVal&& m_val)
3   {
4       using RawVal = RemConstRef<TVal>;
5
6       if constexpr (IsScalar<RawVal>)
7       {
```

```
 8          // Checking if RawVal::DeviceType == TDevice or CPU
 9          // ...
10          return TrivalMatrix<TElem, TDevice, RawVal>(rowNum, colNum,
11                                                      m_val);
12      }
13   else
14   {
15          TElem tmpElem = static_cast<TElem>(m_val);
16          Scalar<TElem, DeviceTags::CPU> scalar(std::move(tmpElem));
17          return TrivalMatrix<TElem, TDevice,
18                         Scalar<TElem, DeviceTags::CPU>>
19                              (rowNum, colNum, std::move(scalar));
20      }
   }
```

It receives two forms of input: if the third parameter of the input is a scalar, it is asserted that the scalar has the same device type as the trivial matrix to be constructed, or the device type of the scalar is CPU. Then the corresponding trivial matrix is constructed using the type of the scalar (*RawVal*). If the third parameter entered is a numeric value, it is used to construct a scalar with the CPU as the device type and then the trivial matrix is further constructed with the constructed scalar.

### 4.4.2.2 Zero Matrix

A zero matrix can be considered as a special "trivial matrix": all the element values in the matrix are 0. If the system can understand that a trivial matrix used in a deep learning framework is essentially a zero matrix, more optimization can be introduced based on the information. For example, the sum of two matrices, $A+B$, is to be calculated. If $B$ is a trivial matrix, the calculation can be simplified to adding each element of $A$ to the element values stored in $B$ (*B.ElementValue()*). If we can further determine that $B$ is a zero matrix, the result of the calculation is the same as that of $A$. The class template *ZeroMatrix* is introduced to represent a zero matrix in MetaNN, which contains only two data fields: the number of rows and the number of columns. Its implementation is basically similar to a trivial matrix, which will not be repeated here.

### 4.4.2.3 One-hot Vector

Vectors can be regarded as matrices with one row or one column and has the same calculation logic as matrices. Therefore, data structures are not specifically introduced to represent vectors in MetaNN. But the one-hot vector is an exception.

Various applications of deep learning require a vector representation associated with the basic unit of each processing. For example, in tasks related to natural language processing, the system may associate a vector representation for each word and the sequence of words entered is converted to a corresponding vector sequence to participate in the operations. These vector representations are called *embedding*.

A deep learning system may put all the *embedding* vectors together to form an *embedding* matrix. Subsequent calculations are performed with selecting several rows or columns of the matrix based on the input information. The process of selection can be considered as the process of multiplying the matrix by the vector. Take the row vector as an example: suppose the size of the *embedding* matrix is $N \times M$—it contains $N$ row vectors and the length of each vector is $M$. If it is multiplied with $(0, ..., 0, 1, 0, ..., 0)$, a row vector with a length of $N$ (i.e., a vector with only the k'th element as 1 and the rest of the elements as 0) on its left side, then multiplication is equivalent to taking out the k'th row of the embedding matrix.

As a mechanism of input selection, the one-hot vector has special purposes in deep learning frameworks. The vectors involved in MetaNN are primarily row vectors.[8] Accordingly, the one-hot vectors implemented in MetaNN are also row vectors. The implementation is quite similar to that of a trivial matrix and it records only the information that must be saved. The code is not included in this book and readers can refer to the source code of MetaNN to understand how to implement a one-hot vector.

### 4.4.3 Introducing a New Matrix Class

After the preceding discussion, the author believes that readers will be able to grasp the differences between categories and types, at least to some extent. In MetaNN, a matrix is a category that can correspond to many different types, including a matrix in the general sense, a trivial matrix, a zero matrix, and so on. Each type has its own application scenarios and we can optimize data structures of matrices for a specific application scenario. The connections among different matrix classes are loose. Although they are utilized to represent matrices, they are not derived from a certain base class. MetaNN describes the relationship between matrix types and matrix categories through specializations of the template *IsMatrix*.

One of scalabilities of MetaNN is the ability to introduce new data types. For example, if we need to introduce a data structure to represent the unit matrix,[9] we should:

1. Define a new class or class template to store the number of rows or columns of the unit matrix;
2. Introduce corresponding interfaces in the class (class template), including the interfaces related to evaluation, the interface representing the computing unit and the computing device and the interface that returns the number of rows and columns;
3. Specialize *IsMatrix* to indicate that a matrix is introduced.

Above, we discuss basic matrix types in MetaNN. Scalars and matrices are basic data types that deep learning frameworks typically should support. On this basis, more complex data structures can be introduced. For example, we can arrange multiple scalars or matrices into a group to form the structure of a list. Next, we'll discuss the list structure in MetaNN.

---

[8] This is because if we take a column vector in a matrix, the adjacent elements in the column vector do not have adjacent storage space—which complicates optimization. Therefore, the vectors supported by MetaNN are primarily row vectors.

[9] That is, a matrix with diagonal elements as 1 and the other elements as 0.

## 4.5 List

Lists are introduced to facilitate batch computing and thus improve system performance. In batch computing, each operand involved in computing can be regarded as a data series that contains a set of (ordered) raw data, usually with the same dimension and type. For instance, if we want to execute matrix multiplication, the dimensions of matrices involve in multiplication are $M \times N$ and $N \times K$ respectively, and the result is an $M \times K$ matrix. Now, we wish to speed up by batch computing: each $B$ matrices is grouped together and the calculation is executed all at one. For each multiplication, the multipliers will actually be two matrix sequences, each containing $B$ matrices with dimensions as $M \times N$ and $N \times K$. The result is a matrix sequence, containing $B$ matrices with dimensions as $M \times K$.

If we hope to support batch computing, the framework must provide data structures to represent the sequences in which batch computing is performed. The simplest way to represent data in batch computing is to ascend the dimension. For example, if the original data involved in computing is a one-dimensional vector, then we can use a two-dimensional matrix to represent the list of vectors; if the original data involved in computing is a two-dimensional matrix, then we can use a three-dimensional tensor to represent the list of matrices. But the author argues that this approach is too simplistic and rough, which can lead to conceptual confusions—a same matrix can be used in the pattern of batch computing to represent the list of vectors and a separate matrix in the other patterns, which can introduce procedural confusions. To avoid the confusions, two categories of lists are introduced to specifically represent the operands required for batch computing in MetaNN.

Lists in MetaNN actually correspond to two categories: *BatchScalar* for lists of scalars and BatchMatrix for lists of matrices. In this section, we'll take the list of matrices as an example. The list of scalars is similar to the list of matrices, so its specific implementation will be left for readers to analyze.

This section begins with basic list types and two special list types will be discussed: *Array* and *Duplicate*.

### 4.5.1 *Template* Batch

The template *Batch* is used to represent the basic list type and declared as follows:

```
1   template <typename TElement, typename TDevice, typename TCategory>
2   class Batch;
```

It receives three template parameters that represent the computing unit, the computing device, and the categories of each element in the list. Further, we can use the following specializations to represent a list of scalars and a list of matrices respectively:

```
1   //A list of scalars
2   template <typename TElement, typename TDevice>
3   class Batch <TElement, TDevice, CategoryTags::Scalar>;
4
5   //A list of matrices
6   template <typename TElement, typename TDevice>
7   class Batch <TElement, TDevice, CategoryTags::Matrix>;
```

After introducing declarations of types, we can associate the class template *Batch* with the tagging system in MetaNN by introducing specializations of metafunctions:

```
1   template <typename TElement, typename TDevice>
2   constexpr bool IsBatchMatrix<Batch<TElement, TDevice,
3                                       CategoryTags::Matrix>> = true;
4
5   template <typename TElement, typename TDevice>
6   constexpr bool IsBatchScalar<Batch<TElement, TDevice,
7                                       CategoryTags::Scalar>> = true;
```

It suggests that the specific tag of the class template *Batch* may be the list of matrices or scalars and its value depends on the category given by its third template parameter.

Next, let's take the list of matrices as an example to discuss the implementation details of the class template *Batch*. The main definitions of the list of matrices class are as follows (for brevity, we overlook interfaces related to evaluation):

```
1   template <typename TElement, typename TDevice>
2   class Batch<TElement, TDevice, CategoryTags::Matrix>
3   {
4   public:
5       using ElementType = TElement;
6       using DeviceType = TDevice;
7
8       friend struct LowerAccessImpl<Batch<TElement, TDevice,
9                                     CategoryTags::Matrix>>;
10
11  public:
12      Batch(size_t p_batchNum = 0, size_t p_rowNum = 0,
13            size_t p_colNum = 0);
14
15      // Interfaces related to dimensions
16      size_t RowNum() const { return m_rowNum; }
17      size_t ColNum() const { return m_colNum; }
18      size_t BatchNum() const { return m_batchNum; }
19
20      // Interfaces related to evaluation...
21
22      // Interfaces for read/write access
23      bool AvailableForWrite() const;
24      void SetValue(size_t p_batchId, size_t p_rowId,
25            size_t p_colId, ElementType val);
26      const auto operator [] (size_t p_batchId) const;
```

```
27
28          // Interface for a submatrix
29          auto SubBatchMatrix(size_t p_rowB, size_t p_rowE,
30                              size_t p_colB, size_t p_colE) const;
31
32  private:
33          ContinuousMemory<ElementType, DeviceType> m_mem;
34          size_t m_rowNum;
35          size_t m_colNum;
36          size_t m_batchNum;
37          size_t m_rowLen;
38          size_t m_rawMatrixSize;
39  };
```

*Batch* stores data internally in a one-dimensional array and uses *ContinuousMemory* to maintain elements in the array. In the array, matrices in the list are positioned one by one, that is, the array contains all the elements of the No. 0 matrix first, then the No. 1 matrix, and so on. Elements in the matrix are organized in a row-first manner.

When constructing a *BatchMatrix* object, we should provide the number of matrices contained (i.e., the parameter *p_batchNum* in the constructor) in addition to the number of rows and columns in each matrix in order to construct a list of matrices. Correspondingly, the list of matrices also provides an additional function *BatchNum* to return the number of matrices contained in the list.

Similar to *Matrix*, the class template *Batch* also should distinguish between read and write operations, so it provides an interface *AvailableForWrite* to check whether it is safe to write; the interface *SetValue* to write data; the interface *operator []* to read data.

Here we need to explain the interface *operator []* that reads data. *Matrix* provides *operator ()* to access data elements, which receives two parameters. Here *operator []* is employed in *Batch*, which receives only one parameter—the index of matrices, to obtain a temporary object of type *Matrix* returned by the system. In this way, we can access elements of a matrix in the list as follows (e.g., the element in the third row and fifth column of the second matrix):

```
1  Batch<int, DeviceTags::CPU, CategoryTags::Matrix> bm...;
2  auto x = bm[2](3, 5);
```

Overloading different operands is intentional: the behaviors of a list is more similar to an array. Arrays are generally indexed with square brackets in C++, so *operator []* is overloaded here to obtain elements in the list. The matrix itself requires two indexes to access the data in it, so it is necessary to overload *operator ()*. By overloading different operators, the hierarchy of data in the list of matrices can be manifested more clearly: the list of matrices contains matrices and the matrices contain data elements.

Finally, the list of matrices also provides an interface to get a list of submatrices, its behavior is to obtain the corresponding submatrices for each matrix contained therein, and forms a new list of matrices. In retrospect, we introduce an intermediate variable *m_rowLen* to ensure that the parent matrix and the submatrix share storage space in the definition of *Matrix*. Similarly, to ensure that the parent matrix and the submatrix share storage space, we also need to introduce a variable *m_rawMatrixSize* to represent the size of each matrix (i.e., the result of the number of rows multiplied with the number of columns) in the original list of matrices. Readers can analyze how to locate elements in the submatrix based on this field.

*Batch* is the most basic class template of lists, which uses arrays to store data and requires that the matrices (or scalars) in the list are continuous—it may improve computing performance in some cases,[10] but it also leads to the loss of some flexibility. Next, we'll discuss a special list *Array*, which focuses more on flexibility and is a beneficial supplement to *Batch*.

## 4.5.2 *Template* Array

The relationship between *Batch* and *Array* is much like that between the built-in array in C++ and linear containers in the STL. For the former, the space allocated is kept unchanged and data items are stored continuously, which provides better performance for accessing storage space. For the latter, the size can change dynamically and the system does not guarantee that data items must be continuously stored, with slightly worse performance for accessing storage space.

### 4.5.2.1 *Introduction of the Template* Array

The declaration of the Array template is as follows:

```
1   template <typename TData>
2   class Array;
```

Unlike *Batch*, *Array* receives only one template parameter, which is the type of elements it contains (such as matrix or scalar). *Array* can derive information such as the corresponding computing unit, computing device, and so on based on the interface provided by the type.

Next, in order to incorporate *Array* into the entire type system, we need to introduce the corresponding specializations of *IsXXX*:

```
1   template <typename TData>
2   constexpr bool IsBatchMatrix<Array<TData>> = IsMatrix<TData>;
3
4   template <typename TData>
5   constexpr bool IsBatchScalar<Array<TData>> = IsScalar<TData>;
```

The described code snippet is not hard to understand: if the elements stored in *Array* are matrices, then *Array* is obviously a list of matrices; if the elements stored in *Array* are scalars, then Array is the list of scalars.

After the declaration of *Array*, let's turn to its implementation. Here's a problem: a list of matrices and a list of scalars require different interfaces. For example, a list of matrices should provide

---

[10] For example, if we want to multiply multiple vectors by a matrix, we can arrange multiple vectors into a list and then call the matrix multiply interface, passing the first pointer to the vector list and the first pointer of the matrix list into this method. The result of multiplying each vector against the matrix can be calculated with a single call.

an interface to return the number of rows and columns of the matrix and a list of scalars does not need to provide such an interface—although they belong to the same class template, the interfaces are different. So, their implementations are obviously distinct. We should provide different implementations for different categories. To achieve this, we introduce an auxiliary class, *ArrayImp*:

```
1   template <typename TData, typename TDataCate>
2   class ArrayImp;
3
4   template <typename TData>
5   class ArrayImp<TData, CategoryTags::Matrix> {
6       // ...
7   };
8
9   template <typename TData>
10  class ArrayImp<TData, CategoryTags::Scalar> {
11      // ...
12  };
13
14  template <typename TData>
15  class Array : public ArrayImp<TData, DataCategory<TData>>
16  {
17  public:
18      using ElementType = typename TData::ElementType;
19      using DeviceType = typename TData::DeviceType;
20      using ArrayImp<TData, DataCategory<TData>>::ArrayImp;
21  };
```

The most important part of the preceding code snippet is line 15—*Array* inherits from *ArrayImp*. *Array* delegates its logic to *ArrayImp*. Compared to *Array*, *ArrayImp* contains an additional template parameter that represents the category of its data elements (also specified in the derivation in line 15). *ArrayImp* can employ the information to introduce specializations to provide interfaces that the category should support.

### 4.5.2.2 *Class Template* ArrayImp

Next, let's look at one implementation of *ArrayImp*, which is specialized with *CategoryTags::Matrix* and implements lists of matrices. The implementation of lists of scalars is similar and will not be elaborated here.

*ArrayImp* specialized with *CategoryTags::Matrix* is mainly defined as follows:

```
1   template <typename TData>
2   class ArrayImp<TData, CategoryTags::Matrix>
3   {
4   public:
```

```
 5          using ElementType = typename TData::ElementType;
 6          using DeviceType = typename TData::DeviceType;
 7
 8          ArrayImp(size_t rowNum = 0, size_t colNum = 0);
 9
10          template <typename TIterator,
11                  std::enable_if_t<IsIterator<TIterator>>* = nullptr>
12          ArrayImp(TIterator b, TIterator e);
13
14   public:
15          size_t RowNum() const { return m_rowNum; }
16          size_t ColNum() const { return m_colNum; }
17          size_t BatchNum() const { return m_buffer->size(); }
18
19          // Interface compatible with the STL
20          // push_back, size...
21
22          // Interfaces related to evaluation
23          // ...
24
25          bool AvailableForWrite() const {
26                  return (!m_evalBuf.IsEvaluated()) &&
27                      (m_buffer.use_count() == 1);
28          }
29
30   protected:
31          size_t m_rowNum;
32          size_t m_colNum;
33          std::shared_ptr<std::vector<TData>> m_buffer;
34          EvalBuffer<Batch<ElementType, DeviceType,
35                              CategoryTags::Matrix>> m_evalBuf;
36   };
```

It contains two constructors, the first of which receives two parameters: the number of rows and columns. They will be recorded in *m_rowNum* and *m_colNum*. When we add a matrix to it later, it is required that the number of rows and columns for each newly added matrix should be equal to *m_rowNum* and *m_colNum* respectively. The second constructor receives a set of iterators (*std::enable_if_t<IsIterator<TIterator>>* = nullptr* limits *TIterator* to be of type iterator and the specific implementation of *IsIterator* will be discussed later). This constructor assumes that each element in the iterator is of type *TData* and initializes the list object *Array* with the interval corresponding to the iterator arguments. It is assumed in the process of construction that each matrix in the interval has the same number of rows and columns, which the number of rows and columns in the list of matrices will be set as.

Similar to the class template *Batch*, *ArrayImp* also provides *RowNum*, *ColNum*, and *BatchNum* to return the number of rows and columns and the number of matrices in the list respectively. Unlike *Batch*, however, *ArrayImp* provides several STL-compatible interfaces to add matrices (such as *push_back*) to it for dynamic growth of the list.

It's necessary to talk about write operations in *ArrayImp*. We want to achieve that multiple instances of *ArrayImp* can share storage space, as in *Matrix*. Therefore, *m_buffer* is set here as a shared pointer to ensure that the replication of *ArrayImp* does not involve much replication of data items. But again, data sharing requires the protection of write operations: *ArrayImp* contains write operations and calling *push_back* to add a matrix to it is a typical one. We don't want to allow writing when there are multiple copies of the same *ArrayImp*, which can incur unpredictable side effects. To solve this problem, we also introduce the function *AvailableForWrite*, in which *m_buffer.use_ count()==1* is judged.

But the function *ArrayImp::AvailableForWrite* also contains another judgment: *!m_evalBuf. IsEvaluated()*, which involves a part of evaluation logic. We'll discuss the process of evaluation in details in the Chapter 8, but here's a brief mention of the functionality of this function. As mentioned earlier, evaluations can be considered as processes of converting a particular data type to the principal type of the category to which it belongs. The principal types of the list of matrices are *Batch<TElem, TDevice, CategoryTags::Matrix>*, so a corresponding *EvalBuffer* (lines 34 and 35) is included in the class template *ArrayImp* to store the results of evaluation.

*EvalBuffer* contains an internal state that indicates whether the evaluation has been completed before. For a general data object, if it has been evaluated before, it will return the results of evaluation stored in *EvalBuffer* directly the next time it is evaluated, thus avoiding repeated evaluations of the same data and thereby improving the system performance.

Here's the problem that *ArrayImp* itself contains functions for write operations, such as *push_back*, which can alter the data inside it. If we complete an evaluation of *ArrayImp* and then call *push_back* to change its internal data, the system will return the evaluation result stored in *EvalBuffer* when it is evaluated again. The result no longer matches the current state of *ArrayImp*, resulting in an evaluation error.

The primary cause of the error is a conflict between the evaluation operation and the write operation. MetaNN solves this problem by forbidding write operations later if the evaluation operation is executed. This is also the reason for another judgment in *AvailableForWrite*: if the evaluation operation has been executed, then *m_evalBuf.IsEvaluated()* will be *true* and AvailableForWrite will return *false*, correspondingly.

### 4.5.2.3 *Metafunction* IsIterator

So far, we've basically completed the discussion of the *ArrayImp* object. But there is one detail omitted here: the implementation of the metafunction *IsIterator*. This metafunction determines whether the input is an iterator in C++ STL. In fact, such a metafunction is not available in the C++ STL, and therefore we need to implement it by ourselves. The logic of implementation is quite skillful, so it's specially discussed here.

The metafunction is defined as follows:

```
1   template <typename T>
2   struct IsIterator_
3   {
4       template <typename R>
```

```
5        static std::true_type Test(typename std::iterator_traits<R>
6                                               ::iterator_category*);
7
8        template <typename R>
9        static std::false_type Test(...);
10
11       static constexpr bool value = decltype(Test<T>(nullptr))::value;
12  };
13
14  template <typename T>
15  constexpr bool IsIterator = IsIterator_<T>::value;
```

The core of this code snippet is the declaration of the two functions *Test* (lines 4–9), which is equivalent to overloading the *Test* function. According to the matching principle for overloaded functions in C++, the function with parameters in the form of "…" will be matched the least. That is to say, for a function call, if there is another overloaded version that matches the function call, the compiler will not select the function with parameters in the form of "…". The compiler will select the function with parameters in the form of "…" only if all other overloaded versions cannot match the call statement.

Now consider the evaluation process for *IsIterator_<T>::value*. In order to evaluate, the compiler needs to choose between two overloaded *Test* functions. If *T* is an iterator, then there is *std::iterator_traits<R>::iterator_category* with the category of iterators as its "value." In this case, the compiler can select the declaration of the first *Test*, that is, the function declaration with type *std::true_type* as the return type.

Conversely, if *T* is not an iterator, the first *Test* will not match the call of *Test<T>(nullptr)*. Based on the SFINAE principle, the compiler will not immediately report an error but try to match other function declarations. Here the compiler can only select to match the declaration of the second *Test*, that is, the version with type *std::false_type* as the return type.

*decltype(Test<T>(nullptr))* will return the result type of the expression *Test<T>(nullptr)*. That is, *std::true_type* or *std::true_type*. *std::true_type* and *std::true_type* both contain the data member *value* which can be accessed at compile time—the values are *true* and *false* respectively. Line 11 of the code snippet converts the question of whether *T* is an iterator type to the value of *decltype(Test <T>(nullptr))::value*, which will be used as the output of the metafunction *IsIterator_<T>*.

Here's another point to note: *Test* only requires declaring other than defining. In fact, the compile-time behavior here only involves the selection of overloaded functions and the process of selection only involves function declarations, so it is unnecessary to introduce the definition for *Test*.

### 4.5.2.4 Construction of Array Objects

The class *ArrayImp* is not used directly by users. What users construct is the class *Array* with the element type as its template argument, for example:

```
1  Array<Matrix<int, DeviceTags::CPU>> check(10, 20);
```

It creates a list of matrices *check*, where each element is a matrix of type *Matrix<int, DeciveTags::CPU>*, each with 10 rows and 20 columns. *Array* automatically inherits the interfaces provided in *ArrayImp*, which users can use to add matrices to the list. The category tag *Array<Matrix<int, DeciveTags::CPU>>* will be deduced to be *CategoryTags::BatchMatrix* automatically.

In addition, if users want to construct a list of matrices based on an array of matrices or a vector, it is feasible to choose the following method:

```
1  vector<Matrix<int, DeviceTags::CPU>> vec;
2  vec.push_back(...)
3
4  Array<Matrix<int, DeviceTags::CPU>> check(vec.begin(), vec.end());
```

When constructing a list, the system detects to ensure that the number of rows and columns for each matrix is the same. So the number of rows and columns for each matrix in *vec* must be the same.

The described code snippet should specify the specific type of matrices when constructing *check*. MetaNN provides the function *MakeArray* to simplify the way to call, and thus freeing users from explicitly providing type declarations:

```
1  template <typename TIterator>
2  auto MakeArray(TIterator beg, TIterator end)
3  {
4      using TData = typename std::iterator_traits<TIterator>:
        :value_type;
5      using RawData = RemConstRef<TData>;
6
7      return Array<RawData>(beg, end);
8  }
```

Based on this function, users can construct the list of matrices as follows:

```
1  vector<Matrix<int, DeviceTags::CPU>> vec;
2  vec.push_back(...)
3
4  auto check = MakeArray(vec.begin(), vec.end());
```

*Array* is a special list that provides the ability to dynamically add elements for a list. But it's not the only special list, and we can also introduce other special lists in MetaNN to meet different requirements. For now, MetaNN introduces another special list, *Duplicate*. Let's look at the functionality and implementation of this list.

### 4.5.3 *Duplication and Template* Duplicate

#### 4.5.3.1 *Introduction of the Template* Duplicate

Consider a multiplication network: the network contains a matrix $A$ and it outputs $AX$ given any input matrix $X$. Now we want to achieve batch computing: given multiple matrices $X_1, X_2, ..., X_n$ as input, the network should output $AX_1, AX_2, ..., AX_n$.

In the implementation, we can put $X_1, X_2, ..., X_n$ in a *Batch* object. How to deal with $A$? Or in other words, how can we represent the behavior of multiple matrices multiplied by a matrix?

The problem can be resolved at the level of matrix computations. It is provided that the *Batch* list of matrices can be multiplied by a matrix object, in which each element in the *Batch* list is multiplied by the matrix object and the results are collected to form a new *Batch* object. Under this provision, we can introduce concrete implementation logic for a matrix multiplying a matrix, a matrix multiplying a list of matrices, a list of matrices multiplying a matrix, and a list of matrices multiplying a list of matrices.

Nevertheless, this approach turns clearly not perfect: on the one hand, the number of functions we want to implement may increase exponentially as the categories increase—which is not conducive to writing or maintenance of the code; on the other hand, much logic of these functions is the same and the entire process of implementation is time-consuming and tedious. To solve this problem, we can divide the calculation process into two steps: the first step is to determine whether it is a matrix multiplying the list of matrices, and if so, convert the matrix to the list of matrices; in the second step, we only need to implement two versions—matrix multiplication and a list of matrices multiplying a list of matrices. For each type of multiplication, we need to implement the type conversion, whose costs are not high. The main logic of computations is in the second step, but the second step involves only two implementations. So, the whole process is much easier to implement than to implement each multiplication alone.

Now let's focus on the first step, that is, how to convert a matrix into a list of matrices. We notice that in this case, each matrix in the list is the same. Of course, we can use the class template *Batch* to construct this list of matrices, but it will deprive us of the information that "every matrix in the list is the same." To preserve the information for evaluation optimization, we introduce the template *Duplicate* to implement a replicable list like this:

```
1   template <typename TData, typename TDataCate>
2   class DuplicateImp;
3
4   template <typename TData>
5   class Duplicate : public DuplicateImp<TData, DataCategory<TData>>
6   {
7   public:
8       using ElementType = typename TData::ElementType;
9       using DeviceType = typename TData::DeviceType;
10      using DuplicateImp<TData, DataCategory<TData>>::DuplicateImp;
11  };
12
13  template <typename TData>
14  constexpr bool IsBatchMatrix<Duplicate<TData>> = IsMatrix<TData>;
15
16  template <typename TData>
17  constexpr bool IsBatchScalar<Duplicate<TData>> = IsScalar<TData>;
```

Similar to the template *Array*, the template *Duplicate* is derived from a base class: *DuplicateImp*, which is responsible for determining whether a scalar or a matrix is replicated. If *TData* is a matrix (scalar), Duplicate<TData> is a list of matrices (scalars).

### 4.5.3.2 *Class Template* DuplicateImp

The definition of the template *DuplicateImp* for matrices is as follows (the part for lists of scalars is also omitted here):

```
1   template <typename TData, typename TDataCate>
2   class DuplicateImp;
3
4   template <typename TData>
5   class DuplicateImp <TData, CategoryTags::Scalar> {
6        // ...
7   };
8
9   template <typename TData>
10  class DuplicateImp<TData, CategoryTags::Matrix>
11  {
12  public:
13       using ElementType = typename TData::ElementType;
14       using DeviceType = typename TData::DeviceType;
15
16       DuplicateImp(TData data, size_t batch_num)
17               : m_data(std::move(data))
18               , m_batchNum(batch_num)
19       {
20               assert(m_batchNum != 0);
21       }
22
23  public:
24       size_t RowNum() const { return m_data.RowNum(); }
25       size_t ColNum() const { return m_data.ColNum(); }
26       size_t BatchNum() const { return m_batchNum; }
27
28       const TData& Element() const { return m_data; }
29
30       // Interfaces related to evaluation
31       // ...
32  protected:
33       TData m_data;
34       size_t m_batchNum;
35       EvalBuffer<Batch<ElementType, DeviceType,
36                   CategoryTags::Matrix>> m_evalBuf;
37  };
```

The constructor of this class receives two parameters: the elements stored in the list and the number of elements, which are stored in *m_data* and *m_batchNum* respectively. In addition to interfaces related to evaluation, this class provides an interface *Element* to return the duplicated element in the list.

Compared with *ArrayImp*, the logic of *DuplicateImp* is simpler—it doesn't support write operations.[11] Therefore, there is no need to provide a function such as *AvailableForWrite* for judgment of write operations.

### 4.5.3.3 Construction of the Duplicate Object

We can construct a *Duplicate* object as follows:

```
1   ZeroMatrix<int, DeviceTags::CPU> mat(100, 200);
2
3   Duplicate<ZeroMatrix<int, DeviceTags::CPU>> batch_matrix(mat, 10);
```

Line 3 constructs a list of 10 matrices, each with the same content as *mat*.

When constructing a list of matrices in this way, we need to specify the type of *batch_matrix*. The main part of the declaration for this type is to give the type of template parameters in *Duplicate*, that is, the type of *mat* in the previous example. In some cases, it may be hard to explicitly specify the type of the matrix *mat* but we still want to construct a list of matrices based on it. To achieve this, MetaNN offers two *MakeDuplicate* functions:

```
1   template<typename TData>
2   auto MakeDuplicate(size_t batchNum, TData&& data)
3   {
4     using RawDataType = RemConstRef<TData>;
5     return Duplicate<RawDataType>(std::forward<TData>(data), batchNum);
6   }
7
8   template<typename TData, typename...TParams>
9   auto MakeDuplicate(size_t batchNum, TParams&&... data)
10  {
11    using RawDataType = RemConstRef<TData>;
12    RawDataType tmp(std::forward<TParams>(data)...);
13    return Duplicate<RawDataType>(std::move(tmp), batchNum);
14  }
```

Based on the function *MakeDuplicate*, the list of matrices can be constructed as follows:

```
1   ZeroMatrix<int, DeviceTags::CPU> mat(100, 200);
2   auto batch_matrix = MakeDuplicate(10, mat);
3
```

---

[11] Because the purpose of *Duplicate* is to replicate an existing matrix or scalar and all the information it needs is provided at the time of construction, it does not need to change over the lifetime of the object.

```
4   // or
5   auto batch_matrix
6       = MakeDuplicate<ZeroMatrix<int, DeviceTags::CPU>>(10, 100, 200);
```

## 4.6 Summary

This chapter discussed the basic data types introduced by MetaNN.

A flexible deep learning framework can involve multiple data types. These data types can be classified into different categories. Object-oriented programming handles this scenario by declaring base classes to represent categories and then deriving types from the base classes. But, as a metaprogramming framework, MetaNN adopts a typical generic programming idea: there are no derivation relationships among different types belonging to the same category—the organization is loose and designed to be more flexible.

On the other hand, we should conceptually classify the types in MetaNN: a category tag is introduced for each type through the tagging system and the sets of interfaces that are required for types belonging to the same category are specified. It is implemented through virtual functions in object-oriented programming, while generic programming does not use virtual functions so as to be looser and more efficient—at least in the process of calling these functions, we do not have to bear the additional expenses of calling introduced by virtual functions.

Generic programming and object-oriented programming are not incompatible. In the implementation of *Array* and *Duplicate*, we combine generic programming with object-oriented techniques of inheritance to provide an implementation scheme for the introduction of different interfaces for different categories. Learning generic programming does not mean abandoning the typical concepts in object-oriented programming. Conversely, using the appropriate concepts at the appropriate scenario enables us to develop more elegant and robust programs.

In this section, we are aware that the interfaces provided by classes are not limited to functions and declarations such as *DeviceType* and *ElementType* can also be considered interfaces to provide information (such as computing devices) for subsequent extensions.

## 4.7 Exercises

1. This chapter discusses the usage of tags. There is also the concept of tags in the Standard Template Library (STL) that we often use. STL classifies iterators and assigns different iterators with different tags (such as bidirectional iterators, random-access iterators, and so on). Search the Internet for relevant concepts, learn and understand the usage of tags in STL, and compare them with the usage of tags in this chapter.

2. In this chapter, we discussed using function parameters or template parameters to deliver category tags. Tags are delivered as function parameters in the STL, one of whose advantages is that they can automatically process the inheritances of tags. There is a derivation hierarchy among iterator tags in the STL. For example, the forward iterator is a special input iterator, that is, the tag of forward iterators, *forward_iterator_tag*, is derived from the tag *input_iterator_tag* in the tagging system. For the implementation of *__distance* discussed in this chapter, if the third argument is a forward iterator, the compiler automatically selects

the version of the input iterator for calculation. If, as discussed in this chapter, using template parameters to deliver iterator tags, we cannot simply achieve similar results by comparing *std::is_same*. Try to introduce a new metafunction to implement similar tag matching in the algorithm that uses template parameters to deliver iterator categories. More specifically, the implemented metafunction should be able to be called as follows:

```
template<typename TIterTag, typename _InputIterator,
        enable_if_t <FUN<TIterTag,
                         input_iterator_tag,
                         forward_iterator_tag,
                         bidirectional_iterator_tag>>*= nullptr>
inline auto __distance(_InputIterator b, _InputIterator e);
```

*FUN* is a metafunction to be implemented. The described call indicates that if *TIterTag* is *input_iterator_tag* (for input iterators), forward_iterator_tag (for forward iterators) or bidirectional_iterator_tag (for bidirectional iterators), the compiler will select the current version of *__distance*.

3. There is another benefit for delivering tag information using template parameters instead of function parameters—there is no longer need to provide definitions for tag types. In order to deliver tag information based on function parameters, the STL has to introduce a type definition like this:

```
struct output_iterator_tag {};
```

However, if the tag is delivered using template parameters, the corresponding definition of the type can be omitted:

```
struct output_iterator_tag;
```

Analyze the reason why this happens.

4. The STL provides a metafunction, *is_base_of*, to determine whether a class is the base class of another. Use this metafunction to modify the declaration of *__distance* in the section 4.1.2 to make it more concise. Consider question 3 again that is based on the modified declaration of the metafunction: do we need a type definition for the iterator tag here? Why?

5. When discussing the implementation of *DataCategory_*, we introduced an auxiliary metafunction called *helper* declared inside *DataCategory_*. Try to extract it to the outside of *DataCategory_*. Consider whether this modification will reduce the number of instances constructed at compile time as discussed in Chapter 1. Try to verify your idea.

6. This chapter describes the matrix class *Matrix* used in MetaNN, considering the following declaration:

```
vector<Matrix<int, DeviceTags::CPU>> a(3, { 2, 5 });
```

Our intention is to declare a vector consisting of three matrices. After that, we want to assign values to each of the three matrices in the vector. Think about whether this works. If not, what's the problem (hint: the replication of matrices in MetaNN is shallow copy)?

7. In the discussion of submatrices, we determine the distance between two rows by introducing *m_rowLen*. In addition to this approach, we can also mark the number of elements between the end of the previous row and the beginning of the next row in two consecutive lines. Compare the pros and cons of this approach and the way this book uses.

8. Read and analyze the implementation code for scalars in *Batch*, *Array*, and *Duplicate*.

9. Read and analyze the implementation code for *OneHotVector* and *ZeroMatrix*.

10. One of *ArrayImp*'s constructors introduces the metafunction *IsIterator* to ensure that the input parameters are iterators. Can we remove this metafunction and declare it with the following function?

```
template <typename TIterator>
ArrayImp(TIterator b, TIterator e)
```

Why?

11. When discussing *ArrayImp*, we mentioned that it cannot be modified after evaluation. So is there the same problem with class templates *Matrix* or *Batch*? In fact, these two templates are somewhat special. Even if they are evaluated and then modified, their semantics are correct. Consider the reason.

12. Some data structures discussed in this chapter include data members such as *EvalBuffer* to store results after evaluation. But class templates like *Matrix* do not contain similar data members. Consider the reason.

# Chapter 5

# Operations and Expression Templates

Chapter 4 discusses the basic data types introduced in MetaNN. On this basis, this chapter discusses how MetaNN uses these data types to implement computational logic.

In MetaNN, operations are offered in the form of functions, which can receive one or more parameters, perform specific calculations, and return the corresponding results. Undoubtedly, readers of this book are no strangers to the implementation of functions. Theoretically, according to the principles or formulas of an algorithm, it is not a tough task to implement the corresponding functions. So why do we utilize a specific chapter to discuss function implementations?

In fact, it is pertinent to the design principles of MetaNN: we hope MetaNN to be scalable; meanwhile, the framework should offer enough space for optimization. For data, the tag system is introduced to support scalability. For sufficient space for optimization, various data types are introduced. The design of operations in MetaNN also embodies these two principles—in order to supply a better and more convenient approach to extend, we extract similar logic from different operations to form a hierarchy on the implementation of the operation logic; for the sake of sufficient optimization space, we introduce expression templates as a bridge between operations and results. These contents will be dived into in this chapter.

Although our discussion is based on "operations," readers will find that much of this chapter revolves around "data types." Data types are the core of operations and what this chapter talks about is no longer basic data types, but a specialized structure that is made up of basic data types—expression templates. Let's start from this point and begin the design of computing modules.

## 5.1 Introduction to Expression Templates

Expression templates are bridges connecting operations with data. On the one hand, they encapsulate operations; on the other hand, they provide interfaces to represent the results of operations. Let's introduce the concept of expression templates with a simple example.

Given two matrices $A$ and $B$. In order to calculate "$A+B$," we can save it in an expression template that represents the result of the calculation:

```
1   template <typename T1, typename T2>
2   class Add
3   {
4   public:
5       Add(T1 A, T2 B)
6           : m_a(std::move(A))
7           , m_b(std::move(B)) {}
8
9       size_t RowNum() const
10      {
11          assert(m_a.RowNum() == m_b.RowNum());
12          return m_a.RowNum();
13      }
14
15      // ...
16
17  private:
18      T1 m_a;
19      T2 m_b;
20  };
```

*Add* is a class template that receives two template parameters, *T1* and *T2*. The constructor of this class requires the data object corresponding to the template parameters (i.e., the input parameters of the operation) to be passed in. By setting the type of input parameters to be a template, there is no need to limit the specific data type of operands: as long as operands provides specific interfaces or conforms to specific concepts, the appropriate template instances can be constructed accordingly.

Assuming that *T1* and *T2* are matrices, and accordingly, *Add* is an expression template that encapsulates operations of matrix addition. Even though it is a simple example of the class, we can still grasp some features of expression templates from it.

◼ Expression templates encapsulate operations and can represent the results of operations as an abstract data type. For instance, the result of adding two matrices is still a matrix. So *Add* should satisfy the requirements for the matrix in the framework. Typically, it requires an interface *RowNum* to return the number of rows of the matrix as well as other interfaces the matrix type must support. Meanwhile, objects of type *Add* represent matrices conceptually, so it should also be classified into the matrix category, tagged with *CategoryTags::Matrix*.

◼ Although expression templates are equivalent to results of operations conceptually, there are many distinctions between them and results of operations. For example, expression templates do not support write operations. If we adopt Matrix<float, DeviceTags::CPU> to preserve the addition results of matrices, then we can then modify the values of specific elements in the resulting object. Nonetheless, expression templates are more about "expression" than "preservation." For expression templates, it is quite tough to define the behavior of their write operations. Not only element-level write operations, but also matrix-level write operations are not supported. In extreme cases, we can influence the results by modifying operands saved in the expression template object (*m_a* or *m_b*). But the effect is indirect and not as intuitive as directly modifying the calculation results.

In Chapter 4, we mentioned that a matrix can be unable to support write operations and *Add* is such a matrix type, which is a composite data type composed of basic data types of matrices.

Expression templates are just encapsulations of data operations and there seem not much they can handle. So why do we introduce expression templates? In fact, expression templates provide a prerequisite for subsequent optimization of the system.

A common method of system optimization is called Lazy Evaluation. The idea is to postpone the actual process of calculation and execute computations only when fully necessary. In some cases, it will reduce the amount of computations for the entire system. Expression templates embody the idea of Lazy Evaluation.

In the case of matrix addition, if the program ends up requiring just the values of some elements instead of the entire result matrix, the expression template can be required to offer an interface to get the corresponding elements and only the matrix elements at particular locations need to be evaluated[1]:

```
1  class Add
2  {
3  public:
4      float operator() (size_t r, size_t c) const
5      {
6          return m_a(r, c) + m_b(r, c);
7      }
8      // ...
9  };
```

If all that is ultimately needed are the values of some elements in the result matrix, we will save most expenses associated with calculating the entire matrix.

But in fact, for a deep learning framework, what we require most often is exactly all the elements of the result. For example, the system needs to obtain the values of each element in the result matrix for matrix addition. Even so, the idea of Lazy Evaluation is instrumental: because if the timing of evaluation is postponed, we may accumulate multiple calculations together when the final calculation is executed. Also take the example of matrix addition: assuming that there are multiple operations of matrix addition in the network, it is possible to accumulate these operations together and complete the calculations at once. In Chapter 4, we mentioned that executing calculations of the same type together has the potential to improve the overall performance of the system. Lazy Evaluation here takes advantage of this feature, sparing the system more space for optimization. It is on the basis of the described considerations that all operations in MetaNN are essentially constructing instances of expression templates and using them to put off the actual process of calculation.

There is another benefit of expression templates that an object of them can be treated as composite data. Accordingly, an expression template object can also be utilized as an argument for

---

[1] The following code snippet assumes that both *m_a* and *m_b* supply interfaces to access its internal elements.

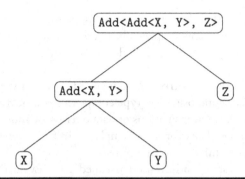

**Figure 5.1    The tree structure of *Add<Add<X, Y>, Z>*.**

another expression template. For example, we can construct an expression template object such as *Add<Add<X, Y>, Z>*, which receives data objects of type *Add<X, Y>* and adds them to data objects of type *Z* to represent the result of addition.

An expression template can be represented in a tree structure: in addition to leaf nodes in the tree, each subnode corresponds to an operation. Leaf nodes represent the input of operations, and the root of the tree is the output of the entire operation. In the case of *Add<Add<X, Y>, Z>*, it can be represented in a tree structure as shown in Figure 5.1.

## 5.2  The Design Principles of Operation Templates in MetaNN

### 5.2.1  *Problems of the Operation Template* Add

Previously, we used the template *Add* to demonstrate the basic idea of expression templates. As an example of code, the template *Add* is sufficient to illustrate the core concept. But, if applied directly to the MetaNN framework as a component, the template *Add* is not up to the task.

Firstly, the template *Add* lacks a mechanism to represent the category tags of operands and the results. In the previous section, we assume that the input parameters and output of *Add* are both matrices, which is not strictly limited in the code and might lead to the misuse of the template. In the meantime, the corresponding expression template will not be able to be the input to other operations due to the missing information of categories corresponding to the expression template's evaluation result.

Secondly, the template *Add* is not scalable enough, which is a major problem. After implementing matrix addition, we may also consider implementing matrix subtraction, which can be introduced by another template, *Sub*. Many functions of *Sub* are fully consistent with the implementation of *Add* (such as the interface *RowNum*). For every expression template to implement an operation, we hope not to rewrite all the logic associated with that template.

To solve these two problems, we should systematically design expression templates for the representation of operations in MetaNN. We refer to the expression templates specifically adopted to represent operations as operation templates in MetaNN. This section discusses the design of operation templates. First, let's take a closer look at how an operation template should behave.

### 5.2.2  *Behavior Analysis of Operation Templates*

An operation template is the bridge between its operation and data. On the one hand, it preserves the input of the operation inside its object, which is essentially an abstraction of the operation behavior; on the other hand, the computing template object itself provides an interface to represent the result of the operation, which is the abstraction of the data. This section analyzes the tasks an operation template needs to accomplish and the reuse of logic that may occur during its life cycle by dividing in detail the construction and use of operation templates in MetaNN.

In MetaNN, the construction and use of operation templates involve the following aspects.

### 5.2.2.1 Validation and Derivation of Types

In the previous chapter, we established the data type system in MetaNN, which is also used in computational operations. Operations require the system to determine the validity of its input parameters and to determine the category to which the corresponding output belongs.

- **To verify the category of input operands for the expression to ensure the validity of the input.** An operation is not valid for all types of data. For example, the matrix multiplication needs to receive two matrices as operands. If the arguments are two scalars, the operation is invalid. The system should be capable of detecting this error and prompt the corresponding information. In general, this part of logic is unlikely to be reused because each operation checks the validity of its parameters in diverse ways.

- **To determine the category of the operation output.** The output category of the operation is closely pertinent to the category of its input parameters. For example, in the addition operation, the result should be a matrix when two matrices add together and the result of adding two lists of matrices should be a list of matrices. An operation template, as a composite data type, may serve as an input to other operation templates. So it should derive the category tag for results of operations. The category tag is also relevant to the operation, but the output category of an operation is likely to be consistent with the input category in general. For instance, if the category of the input parameter of an operation is a matrix, it is more likely that the output category will be a matrix. We can use this feature to construct the most basic inference system of output types. First, it determines whether the input parameters of an operation belong to the same category. If so, the category of input parameters in the operation can be returned to represent the category of the output. The logic is valid for most operations. For special operations not in line with the logic, specializations are required to derive the actual output categories.

### 5.2.2.2 Division of Object Interfaces

After determining the category of the composite data type that an operation represents, most interfaces that the corresponding operational object needs to provide are determined. For example, if the result of an operation is a matrix, it needs to provide the number of rows and columns of the result matrix, as well as the corresponding interface of evaluation to construct a matrix of type *Matrix*. These interfaces can be classified into the following categories:

- **Interfaces to represent the computing unit and the computing device.** As we mentioned in Chapter 4, MetaNN can be extended to support different computing units and computing devices. To achieve this, we introduce declarations of both *ElementType* and *DeviceType* into the data structure contained in MetaNN, which will act as an interface about the computing unit and the computing device. As an intermediate result, the operation template also ought to provide both interfaces. In general, the inputs of an operation have the same computing unites and computing devices, which we can utilize to set the corresponding information of the operation results. However, in some special cases, the inputs of operations may have different computing units and computing devices. In this case, we need a metafunction to derive the computing unit and computing device based on the information of the input parameters.

■ **Interfaces related to dimensions**. Interfaces related to dimensions offer the dimensions of operation results. Also take addition as an example. If two matrices are added, the number of rows and columns of the result should be consistent with the number of rows and columns of the input matrices. If two lists of matrices are added, the number of matrices contained in the output and the number of rows and columns of each matrix should be in accordance with the input parameters. Similar to determining the output category of an operation, we can also introduce a default implementation for interfaces related to dimensions. We determine whether all input parameters are of the same dimensions. If true, the dimensions of the input parameters are returned directly. The logic can be adopted to handle most operations. If we encounter a situation that does not conform to the logic, then specializations for the corresponding operation to implement the unique logic of dimensions can be introduced.

■ **Interfaces related to evaluating**. An operation template is a template expression that represents an intermediate state of an operation. The expression template delays the calculation, but ultimately, we need to convert this intermediate state into the result of the operation. The operation templates in MetaNN provide interfaces related to evaluation. These interface functions require calling specific evaluation logic internally to accomplish the calculation. The calculation method will vary depending on the specific operation logic. It is daunting to reuse this part of the logic between different operations.

### 5.2.2.3 Auxiliary Class Templates

According to the previous analysis, it is natural to be aware that distinct parts involved in operations can be reused logically to different degrees. Depending on the degree of reuse, MetaNN introduces several auxiliary class templates for each operation template to determine the validity of the input parameters, derive the category tag for the output, and supply interfaces related to dimensions and evaluation.

Note that these auxiliary class templates are conceptually orthogonal. If we combine a few auxiliary class templates, it can impose an impact on the reuse of code. For instance, if we combine auxiliary templates related to dimensions and evaluation into one, we should write the same calculation logic of dimensions repeatedly when introducing diverse computational logic for diverse operations.

After the introduction of these auxiliary class templates, operations in MetaNN are no longer isolated expression templates but they form a subsystem. Next, we'll first discuss the framework of this subsystem and then take specific computational logic as examples to discuss the implementation based on the subsystem.

## 5.3 Classification of Operations

MetaNN is scalable, which is reflected in the design of the computational logic: the current MetaNN already contains some operations and it is convenient to add new operations to it. Computing subsystems are provided to maintain scalability of computing in MetaNN. Similar to the basic data system discussed in Chapter 4, MetaNN also classifies the operations it contains in order to better support extensions. Currently, they are classified according to the number of operands required for operations:

```
1   struct UnaryOpTags {
2         struct Sigmoid;
3         struct Tanh;
4         struct Transpose;
5         // ...
6   };
7
8   struct BinaryOpTags {
9         struct Add;
10        struct Substract;
11        struct ElementMul;
12        // ...
13  };
14
15  struct TernaryOpTags {
16        struct Interpolate;
17        // ...
18  };
```

Here are three structures defined to represent unary, binary, and ternary operations. Each structure contains numerous declarations of types, each of which corresponds to an operation. For example, *Sigmoid* is a unary operation that allows the *Sigmoid* function to transform each element in a matrix or list of matrices. It receives a matrix or list of matrices and returns data of the same category as the input. The values of each element in the result come from the transformation of values of each element in the input parameter.

MetaNN supports two kinds of extensions by introducing the previous structure: we can add new unary, binary, and ternary operations, or new types of operations. For example, if an operation requires four parameters, we can introduce a new structure to include the newly introduced quaternary operator.

It should be noted that the current method of classification may not be the only feasible one and operations can be classified in other ways. As more and more operations are introduced into the framework, we may need to adjust the grouping of operations. For example, it is entirely possible to sort the operations commonly used in CNN into a group. Meanwhile, it is entirely practicable to sort subgroups in large groups:

```
1   struct MajorOperGroup {
2         struct MinorOperGroup
3         {
4               struct Oper1;
5               // ...
```

```
6          };
7          // ...
8      };
```

The organization of computing is quite flexible.

## 5.4  Auxiliary Templates

In the previous section, we mentioned that operations require support for several secondary templates, which are briefly described in this section.

### 5.4.1  The Auxiliary Class Template OperElementType_/OperDeviceType_

The definitions of *OperElementType_* and *OperDeviceType_* are as follows:

```
1   template <typename TOpTag, typename TOp1, typename...TOperands>
2   struct OperElementType_ {
3       using type = typename TOp1::ElementType;
4   };
5
6   template <typename TOpTag, typename TOp1, typename...TOperands>
7   struct OperDeviceType_ {
8       using type = typename TOp1::DeviceType;
9   };
```

They are utilized to specify types of the computing unit and computing device for a given operation template. As mentioned earlier, the operands of an operation template have the same computing unit and computing device typically. We can get the appropriate information from the first operands of the operation—which is also the default implementation of *OperElementType_* and *OperDeviceType_*.

Assuming a particular operation, *MyOper*, which contains two operands, the computing unit and computing device of its result are determined according to the second operand. Then we can introduce the following specialization:

```
1   template <typename TOp1, typename TOp2>
2   struct OperElementType_<MyOper, TOp1, TOp2> {
3       using type = typename TOp2::ElementType;
4   };
5
6   template <typename TOp1, typename TOp2>
7   struct OperDeviceType_<MyOper, TOp1, TOp2> {
8       using type = typename TOp2::DeviceType;
9   };
```

## 5.4.2 *The Auxiliary Class Template* OperXXX_

For each specific operation *XXX*, we introduce a class template, *OperXXX_*, to determine the validity of input parameters and construct a template expression that represents the operation when the input parameters are valid. This template is not introduced through specialization. We'll see an example of the template as we discuss specific operations later.

## 5.4.3 *The Auxiliary Class Template* OperCateCal

*OperaCal* is a metafunction that infers the category of results of an operation based on the operation tags and category of input parameters. It is defined as follows[2]:

```
1  template <typename TOpTag, typename THead,
2              typename...TRemain>
3  using OperCateCal
4      = typename CateInduce_<TOpTag,
5                        Data2Cate<THead, TRemain...>>::type;
```

Its input is the tag of the operation and the type of each parameter, and the output is the category tag of the result of the operation. As follows:

```
1  OperCateCal<BinaryOpTags::Add,
2          Matrix<float, DeviceTags::CPU>,
3          TrivalMatrix<float, DeviceTags::CPU>>
```

It will return *CategoryTags::Matrix*, which means that two matrices (a matrix in the general sense and a trivial matrix) are added and the result is a matrix. As we can see from this example, *OperCateCal* is concerned with the category the operands fall within rather than the specific type of operands, which is quite reasonable. For addition, as long as the two matrices are involved, the operation is valid and the result must be a matrix no matter what the specific types of the two matrices are.

In addition, the input template parameters of *OperCateCal* are specific data types instead of categories for ease of use. In order to extract the information of categories from types, we ought to use the metafunction *DataCategory* introduced in Chapter 4. In the meantime, *OperCateCal* should convert each type of input parameters required for the operation in this way. So we introduce an additional metafunction, *Data2Cate*, to convert each type of input parameters in turn, which is essentially a loop:

```
1  template <typename TCateCont, typename...TData>
2  struct Data2Cate_
3  {
4      using type = TCateCont;
5  };
6
```

---

[2] In order to keep typography concise, the definition here omits information relevant to namespace, of which the full definition can be found in the source code.

```
7    template <typename...TProcessed, typename TCur, typename...TRemain>
8    struct Data2Cate_<std::tuple<TProcessed...>, TCur, TRemain...>
9    {
10       using tmp1 = DataCategory<TCur>;
11       using tmp2 = std::tuple<TProcessed..., tmp1>;
12       using type = typename Data2Cate_<tmp2, TRemain...>::type;
13   };
14
15   template <typename THead, typename...TRemain>
16   using Data2Cate = typename Data2Cate_<std::tuple<>,
17                                        THead, TRemain...>::type;
```

The core of the loop is lines 7–13. In this partial specialization, *std::tuple<TProcessed...>* indicates the sequence in which type-to-category conversion has been completed. *TCur* is the type currently to be processed. *TRemain...* is the remaining types to deal with. Lines 10–12 are a typical sequence logic at compile time. Firstly, *DataCategory* is called to obtain the category of the current type, which is preserved in *tmp1*. Then *tmp1* is "attached" to the category array. Finally, *Data2Cate* is recursively called to process subsequent types.

When each type of input parameters is converted to the appropriate category, the compiler selects the primary template for *Data2Cate*, which returns the result of conversions directly: *std::tuple<...>* and each element in *tuple* is a category tag.

After obtaining category tags for the input types, *OperCateCal* calls *CateInduce_* to infer the category of the output. The implementation of *CateInduce_* is as follows:

```
1    template <typename TOpTag, typename TCateContainer>
2    struct CateInduce_;
3
4    template <typename TOpTag, typename...TCates>
5    struct CateInduce_<TOpTag, std::tuple<TCates...>>
6    {
7        using type = typename OperCategory_<TOpTag, TCates...>::type;
8    };
```

The introduction of specialization here indicates that its second template parameter must be in the form of *std::tuple*. On this basis, *CateInduce_* extracts the contents of *tuple* and calls *OperCategory_*.

The default version of *OperCategory_* derives the category of results of operations based on the following code snippet:

```
1    template <typename TOpTag, typename THeadCate, typename...TRemainCate>
2    struct OperCategory_
3    {
4        static_assert(SameCate_<THeadCate, TRemainCate...>::value,
5                      "Data category mismatch.");
```

```
6      using type = THeadCate;
7    };
```

Here *SameCate_* is an auxiliary metafunction utilized to assert the consistency of elements in the information of categories, *THeadCate* and *TRemainCate*.... On this basis, *THeadCate* is returned, which is the category of operands.

This design makes sense for most operations. Considering the situation of matrix addition, the template *OperCategory_* will be instantiated as follows.

```
1    struct OperCategory_<BinaryOpTags::Add,
2                         CategoryTags::Matrix, CategoryTags::Matrix>
3    {
4        static_assert(SameCate_<CategoryTags::Matrix,
5                                CategoryTags::Matrix>::value,
6                                "Data category mismatch.");
7        using type = CategoryTags::Matrix;
8    };
```

This metafunction returns *CategoryTags::Matrix* as the output type of the operation.

Of course, there are also special operations that may cause the default version of *OperCategory_* to be invalid. In these cases, we should specialize the metafunction to offer the corrected behavior—we'll see an example like this later.

### 5.4.4 *The Auxiliary Class Template* OperOrganizer

The class template *OperOrganizer* is adopted to supply interfaces relevant to dimensions. It is declared as follows:

```
1    template <typename TOpTag, typename TCate>
2    class OperOrganizer;
```

It receives two parameters: *TOpTag* for the operation tag and *TCate* represents the category tag for the operation result. For instance, the corresponding instance of *OperOrganizer* is *OperOrganizer* *<BinaryOpTags::Add, CategoryTags::Matrix>* for matrix addition.

Distinct data categories require different interfaces for dimensions. For example, a matrix should provide *RowNum* and *ColNum* to represent the number of rows and columns; a list of matrices should provide an additional interface *BatchNum* to represent the number of matrices in it. As a result, *OperOrganizer* needs to specialize various data categories and introduce the appropriate implementation of interfaces in each version of specializations.

#### 5.4.4.1 *Specialization for Scalars*

The specialized version of *OperOrganizer* for scalars is as follows:

```
1    template <typename TOpTag>
2    class OperOrganizer<TOpTag, CategoryTags::Scalar>
```

```
3  {
4  public:
5      template <typename THead, typename...TRemain>
6      OperOrganizer(const THead&, const TRemain&...) {}
7  };
```

It's actually a trivial implementation. MetaNN does not impose any requirements on scalar's interface of dimensions. Accordingly, the specialized version for scalars does not require the introduction of any interfaces pertinent to dimensions. Nonetheless, we introduce the specialization of the template *OperOrganizer* for scalars: *OperOrganizer* will be employed as the base class of operation templates and the introduction of this specialization ensures that all operation templates can be derived from the corresponding base class *OperOrganizer* without having to pay attention to whether the result of operations is a scalar or not.

It should be noted that all specialized versions of *OperOrganizer* contain a template constructor, which receives input parameters of operations and calculates dimensions of results lines 5 and 6). Although scalars do not contain any dimension interfaces, we introduce this constructor which simplifies the call of *OperOrganizer*. As we'll see later, the constructor of the base class *OperOrganizer* can be called in a uniform way in operation templates due to uniform forms of constructors.

## 5.4.4.2 Specialization for Lists of Scalars

Compared to the version of scalars, the version of OperOrganizer for lists of scalars offers the logic of dimensions that ought to be supported by lists of scalars:

```
1  template <typename TOpTag>
2  class OperOrganizer<TOpTag, CategoryTags::BatchScalar>
3  {
4  private:
5      template <typename THead, typename...TRemain>
6      bool SameDim(const THead&, const TRemain&...)
7      {
8          return true;
9      }
10
11     template <typename THead, typename TCur, typename...TRemain>
12     bool SameDim(const THead& head, const TCur& cur,
13                  const TRemain&...rem)
14     {
15         const bool tmp = (head.BatchNum() == cur.BatchNum());
16         return tmp && SameDim(cur, rem...);
17     }
18
19 public:
```

```
20          template <typename THead, typename...TRemain>
21          OperOrganizer(const THead& head, const TRemain&... rem)
22              : m_batchNum(head.BatchNum())
23          {
24              assert(SameDim(head, rem...));
25          }
26
27          size_t BatchNum() const { return m_batchNum; }
28
29  private:
30          size_t m_batchNum;
31  };
```

A list of scalars should provide the interface *BatchNum()* to return the number of elements in the list. Based on the design principles of operation templates in MetaNN, we here supply a default implementation of dimension interfaces, which assumes that all input parameters received by operations are lists of scalars and that *BatchNum()* of each list should have the same value (i.e., the same dimensions). On the basis, the value of *BatchNum()* for the first argument is utilized as the number of elements in the result of operations.

To achieve this default implementation, this specialization of *OperOrganizer* introduces the function *SameDim* internally to determine whether dimensions of input parameters conform to the requirements. In its constructor, *OperOrganizer* calls this function to assert and preserves the number of elements in the first parameter (*head*) and returned when the interface *BatchNum()* is called by the upper layer (line 27).

### 5.4.4.3 Other Specialized Versions

Similar specializations for *CategoryTags::Matrix* and *CategoryTags::BatchMatrix* are introduced in *OperOrganizer*. The logic of these specializations is similar to the specialization for *CategoryTags::Batch Scalar* and will not be elaborated here. Only the following two points should be noted:

1. *OperOrganizer<TOpTag, CategoryTags::Matrix>* provides the interfaces *RowNum()* and *ColNum()* for returning the number of rows and columns of the result matrix.
2. *OperOrganizer<TOpTag, CategoryTags::BatchMatrix>* further provides the interface *BatchNum()* for returning the number of matrices contained in the result matrix list.

### 5.4.5 The Auxiliary Class Template OperSeq

*OperSeq* is the last auxiliary template to encapsulate the logic associated with evaluation. This metafunction calls a series of auxiliary (meta)functions to implement the evaluation of an operation template together.

In Chapter 4, we mention that data types should provide evaluation interfaces to be converted to the appropriate principal data types. As a composite type, operation templates are no exception. The evaluation logic of operation templates invokes the corresponding logic of computation in *OperSeq* to complete the conversion to principal data types.

Each operation requires the introduction of the corresponding *OperSeq* specialization, and an *OperSeq*-specialized version may encapsulate several evaluation methods. Each evaluation method corresponds to a specific computational scenario in which the program selects the appropriate method for evaluating according to the actual context at compile time and run time—all to ensure the efficiency and stability of the evaluation. We will discuss the logic of this section in detail in Chapter 8.

## 5.5 Framework for Operation Templates

With the support of auxiliary templates discussed earlier, we can construct the framework for operation templates. MetaNN introduces three class templates:

```
1   template <typename TOpTag,
2             typename TData>
3   class UnaryOp;
4
5   template <typename TOpTag,
6             typename TData1, typename TData2>
7   class BinaryOp;
8
9   template <typename TOpTag,
10            typename TData1, typename TData2, typename TData3>
11  class TernaryOp;
```

They receive the operation tag and the corresponding type of operands as template arguments, which are used to represent unary, binary, and ternary operations.

Next, we'll explain their implementation with the example of the unary operation template, *UnaryOp*. The remaining two templates are simply receiving different numbers of input parameters, which are not fundamentally different from *UnaryOp* and will not be elaborated here. With auxiliary templates introduced previously, the implementation logic of operation templates will be much simplified. We'll first introduce category tags for operation templates and then look back at the definitions of operation templates.

### 5.5.1 Category Tags for Operation Templates

The operation template can be considered a composite data type. All data types in MetaNN are associated with the appropriate category tags, and the operation template is no exception. For *UnaryOp*, we specify its tags as follows:

```
1   template <typename TOpTag, typename TData>
2   constexpr bool IsScalar<UnaryOp<TOpTag, TData>>
3       = std::is_same<OperCateCal<TOpTag, TData>,
4                      CategoryTags::Scalar>::value;
5
```

```
6    template <typename TOpTag, typename TData>
7    constexpr bool IsMatrix<UnaryOp<TOpTag, TData>>
8         = std::is_same<OperCateCal<TOpTag, TData>,
9                        CategoryTags::Matrix>::value;
10
11   template <typename TOpTag, typename TData>
12   constexpr bool IsBatchScalar<UnaryOp<TOpTag, TData>>
13        = std::is_same<OperCateCal<TOpTag, TData>,
14                       CategoryTags::BatchScalar>::value;
15
16   template <typename TOpTag, typename TData>
17   constexpr bool IsBatchMatrix<UnaryOp<TOpTag, TData>>
18        = std::is_same<OperCateCal<TOpTag, TData>,
19                       CategoryTags::BatchMatrix>::value;
```

An operation template is the abstraction of operation results, and the category tag of an operation template is the category tag of the operation results. The described code categorizes operation templates with category tags for the operation results.

These metafunctions call *OperCateCal<TOpTag, TData>* to obtain the categories of operation results and compare them with tags such as *CategoryTags::BatchScalar* to calculate the operation result types. *OperCateCal* receives the type of input parameters and returns the category tag of the output. On this basis, we use *std::is_same* to judge returned tags and set specializations of the metafunction *IsXXX* based on the result. In this way, we give the category tag for the current operation.

### 5.5.2 Definition of UnaryOp

*UnaryOp* is defined as follows[3]:

```
1    template <typename TOpTag, typename TData>
2    class UnaryOp
3        : public OperOrganizer<TOpTag, OperCateCal<TOpTag, TData>>
4    {
5        static_assert(std::is_same<RemConstRef<TData>, TData>::value,
6                      "TData is not an available type");
7    public:
8       using ElementType = typename OperElementType_<TOpTag, TData>::type;
9       using DeviceType = typename OperDeviceType_<TOpTag, TData>::type;
10
11   public:
12       UnaryOp(TData data)
```

---

[3] Similar to the discussion in Chapter 4, we omit the interfaces pertinent to evaluation here, which will be discussed in Chapter 8 unifiedly.

```
13                : OperOrganizer<TOpTag, Cate>(data)
14                , m_data(std::move(data)) {}
15
16        // Interfaces related to evaluation
17        // ...
18
19        const TData& Operand() const
20        {
21                return m_data;
22        }
23
24  private:
25        TData m_data;
26
27        // Data members related to evaluation
28        // ...
29  };
```

This class receives two template parameters: *TOpTag* represents the operation tag and *TData* represents the type of operand. Because a unary operator contains only one parameter, *UnaryOp* only needs one template parameter to represent the operand in addition to *TOpTag*.

After determining the operation tag and the type of operands, we can implement the class template *UnaryOp*, which is derived from *OperOrganizer<TOpTag, OperCateCal<TOpTag, TData>>*—the class offers the interface of dimensions that *UnaryOp* ought to provide. *UnaryOp* utilizes *OperElementType_* and *OperDeviceType_* internally to obtain the corresponding computing units and computing devices. In interfaces relevant to evaluation, *UnaryOp* calls *OperSeq* to implement actual operations.

In addition to the described interfaces, *UnaryOp* also should preserve the corresponding input parameters internally in order to be capable of accomplishing the evaluation later. *UnaryOp* declares *m_data* to hold the operands. Specific objects of operands are passed in with the constructor. *UnaryOp* does not provide methods to alter operands, that is, there are no interfaces for writing—as discussed earlier, providing write operations in an expression template does not make much sense. However, *UnaryOp* supplies the read interface *Operand* for returning input parameters. During the process of evaluation, we can adopt this interface to obtain the information inside expression templates for evaluation optimization.

## 5.6 Examples of Operation Implementations

### 5.6.1 Sigmoid *Operation*

Here we take the operation *Sigmoid* as the first example to discuss the implementation of specific operations. The logic of this operation is quite simple and does not involve adjustments to the default logic of *OperOrganizer* and *OperCategory_*, which offer the default behavior that already conforms to the requirements of *Sigmoid*.

*Sigmoid* is an operation in neural networks that maps a real number into an interval of (0,1), of which the formula is:

$$S(x) = \frac{1}{1 + e^{-x}}$$

When $x$ tends to be positive or negative infinity, the value of this function tends to 1 or 0. The function is usually used in neural networks as layers of nonlinear transformation.

The main processing unit of a neural network is a matrix. Accordingly, we ought to implement the operation *Sigmoid* that receives a matrix as arguments and calculates the *sigmoid* value for each element in the matrix. In addition, we hope this operation to support lists of matrices so as to support processing multiple matrices at the same time. Therefore, the operation *Sigmoid* should be valid for both matrices and lists of matrices.

### 5.6.1.1 Function Interface

The function interface for the operation *Sigmoid* is defined as follows:

```
1    template <typename TP,
2            std::enable_if_t<OperSigmoid_<TP>::valid>* = nullptr>
3    auto Sigmoid(TP&& p_m)
4    {
5            return OperSigmoid_<TP>::Eval(std::forward<TP>(p_m));
6    }
```

It is a function template that receives objects of type *TP* and returns the object of the operation template corresponding to *Sigmoid*. Let's take a closer look at this code snippet and see what it implements.

Firstly, as a function template, *Sigmoid* contains two template parameters. But its second template parameter is actually a metafunction *enable_if_t*. Please recall the knowledge about this metafunction as we discussed in Chapter 1, it is not hard to be aware that this parameter actually constitutes the logic of selection. The code corresponding to it will only compile when *OperSigmoid_<TP>::valid* is *true*, or otherwise the SFINAE mechanism will be triggered and it will be rejected by the compiler.

In other words, *OperSigmoid_<TP>::valid* is essentially a selector to ensure the validity of the input parameters. If *TP* is a valid type of parameters, the metafunction will return *true*, triggering compilation; otherwise the metafunction will return *false* with the compilation rejected. It is because this is the only version of the function *Sigmoid*. If the compiler refuses to associate a *Sigmoid* call to the function, a compilation error will occur, prompting users that the function *Sigmoid* is misused.

We'll analyze the implementation of *OperSigmoid_<TP>::valid* in the next section. Before that, let's finish the discussion about function *Sigmoid*. Line 3 of the function gives its signature. Please notice that the return type of the function is set here as *auto*, which is a feature in C++ 14, indicating that its actual return type is determined by the return statement in the function body.

The function body of this function contains only one statement (line 5), which calls the function *OperSigmoid_<TP>::Eval* and forwards the input parameters to it via *std::forward*. The function *Sigmoid* returns the result of *OperSigmoid_<TP>::Eval* and the return type of the function *Sigmoid* corresponds to that of *OperSigmoid_<TP>::Eval*, accordingly.

From the analysis of the discussed code snippet, it is natural to realize that the core logic of the entire code snippet is encapsulated in the template *OperSigmoid_*. As discussed at the beginning of this chapter, *OperSigmoid_* is an auxiliary template for operation templates. In this case, the role of *OperSigmoid_* is to determine the validity of the *Sigmoid* parameters and construct the object of *UnaryOp* corresponding to the *Sigmoid* operation.

### 5.6.1.2 Template OperSigmoid_

The template *OperSigmoid_* is defined as follows:

```
1   template <typename TP>
2   struct OperSigmoid_
3   {
4   private:
5       using rawM = RemConstRef<TP>;
6
7   public:
8       static constexpr bool valid = IsMatrix<rawM> ||
9                                     IsBatchMatrix<rawM>;
10
11  public:
12      static auto Eval(TP&& p_m)
13      {
14          using ResType = UnaryOp<UnaryOpTags::Sigmoid, rawM>;
15          return ResType(std::forward<TP>(p_m));
16      }
17  };
```

The template receives the template parameter *TP*, which represents the type of input parameters. Internally, it first utilizes *RemConstRef* to remove information of constants and references (if any) in the type and preserves the type without such information in *rawM*.

Lines 8 and 9 define the constant *valid*. The function *Sigmoid* only supports matrices or lists of matrices, so we detect the category tag of the input parameter here with *IsMatrix* and *IsBatchMatrix* and preserve the results in *valid*. The compile-time constant will be adopted in the interface of the function *Sigmoid* as input to *std::enable_if_t*.

*OperSigmoid_::Eval* receives the input parameter *p_m*, infers inside it the type of operation templates *UnaryOp<UnaryOpTags::Sigmoid, rawM>* that should be returned, and then utilizes *p_m* as the parameter to construct the *UnaryOp* object and return it.

### 5.6.1.3 User Calls

So far, we've done half the work of the operation *Sigmoid*,[4] which constructs the *UnaryOp* object and returns it to users. Based on the logic, users can use the operation *Sigmoid* with the following code snippet:

---

[4] The other half is to construct the logic related to evaluation, which is left to Chapter 8 for discussion.

```
1   Matrix<...> mat;
2   Batch<Matrix<...>> bmat;
3
4   // Add data to matrices & lists of matrices ...
5
6   auto s1 = Sigmoid(mat);
7   auto s2 = Sigmoid(bmat);
8   auto s3 = Sigmoid(1.0);     // Error
```

The function *Sigmoid* is called in lines 6 and 7 for matrices and lists of matrices respectively, forming the object of the operation template. Here are two points to explain. Firstly, a matrix or a list of matrices can be used as an argument for the function *Sigmoid*. The system automatically constructs the corresponding operating object according to the category tag of the operand. Conversely, the call in line 8 incurs a compilation error because the function *Sigmoid* we defined does not support the type *double*.

Secondly, the types of operation objects constructed with a matrix or a list of matrices are distinct. But users of the framework don't need to be concerned with specific data types. The feature *auto* in C++ 11 is employed here to declare the types of *s1* and *s2* and the specific types of *s1* and *s2* will be deduced by the compiler.

So far, we've seen the details of the logic in the interfaces of *Sigmoid* during the construction of operation templates. The template *Sigmoid* is a relatively simple implementation of operations but some of its design principles are also utilized in more complex logic of operations.

## 5.6.2 *Operation* Add

The operation *Add* is more complicated than *Sigmoid* since it is a binary operator that processes three types of parameters, including scalars, matrices, and lists of matrices.

Currently, MetaNN does not support operations of scalar addition which usually we don't need. Because operations like the addition of two floating-point scalars can be done directly through the built-in operations provided in C++. Nonetheless, we ought to support many kinds of additions beyond that, such as the following ones.

- **A scalar is added to a matrix**: the operation is to add the scalar to each element of the matrix.
- **A scalar is added to a list of matrices**: the operation is to add the scalar to each element of the list of matrices.
- **A matrix is added to a matrix**: the operation is to add the corresponding elements of the matrices.
- **A matrix is added to a list of matrices**: the operation is to add each element in the list of matrices to another operand (matrix).
- **Lists of matrices are added**: the two lists of matrices should contain the same number of matrices. On this basis, the corresponding matrices in the two lists are added.

Considering that the commutative property is applied in addition, we ought to deal with more combinations of input parameters.

### 5.6.2.1 Function Interface

Although there are many types of additions to support, we would not like to provide a complete set of implementation logic for each addition. In contrast, we want to maximize the reuse of code. In MetaNN, there is only one interface that represents the addition of operands[5]:

```
1   template <typename TP1, typename TP2,
2           std::enable_if_t<OperAdd_<TP1, TP2>::valid>* = nullptr>
3   auto operator+ (TP1&& p_m1, TP2&& p_m2)
4   {
5       using Cate1 = DataCategory<TP1>;
6       using Cate2 = DataCategory<TP2>;
7       return OperAdd_<TP1, TP2>:: template Eval<Cate1, Cate2>
8               (std::forward<TP1>(p_m1), std::forward<TP2>(p_m2));
9   }
```

Firstly, as a function template, *operator+* introduces three template parameters: the first two template parameters represent the type of operands and the last template parameter is used to introduce restrictions—ensuring that the compilation of this template will be triggered only when *OperAdd_<TP1, TP2>::valid* is *true*.

Two types, *Cate1* and *Cate2*, are calculated from the operands type, representing the category tags of the two input parameters. On this basis, this function calls the function template *OperAdd_::Eval* constructs the template expression corresponding to addition and returns it.

Notice that it is distinct from *Sigmoid* here: *OperSigmoid_::Eval* is not a function template because it does not require different implementations to be introduced depending on the category of input parameters. But for *Add*, it supports diverse additions through an interface, which is essentially logic of branches. We implement the branch at compile time by introducing template parameters for *OperAdd_::Eval*.

*OperAdd_<TP1,TP2>::Eval* receives the category tags corresponding to *TP1* and *TP2* as template parameters. In order to clarify it in C++ that it is a function template and let the compiler interprets the angle brackets behind *Eval* as the beginning of a template parameter rather than a less-than sign, we should give the keyword *template* explicitly before *Eval*, which is also specified in the C++ standard.

The logic for the rest of this function is similar to the function *Sigmoid*, except that *Sigmoid* is a unitary operator and addition is a binary operator, which involves delivery of more parameters.

Next, let's take a look at the implementation of *OperAdd_* and see how it handles different types of additions.

### 5.6.2.2 The Implementation Framework of OperAdd_

The implementation framework of *OperAdd_* is shown as follows[6]:

---

[5] Of course, as a function template, this interface may be instantiated by the compiler in multiple versions.

[6] For the sake of typography, two auxiliary metafunctions are introduced here: *Imp* is used to call *std::is_same* to determine whether the two types are the same, and *CT* is a shorthand for *CategoryTags*. These two lines do not exist in the source code.

```
1    template <typename TP1, typename TP2>
2    struct OperAdd_
3    {
4        // valid check
5    private:
6        using rawM1 = RemConstRef<TP1>;
7        using rawM2 = RemConstRef<TP2>;
8
9    public:
10       static constexpr bool valid
11           = (IsMatrix<rawM1> && IsMatrix<rawM2>) ||
12             (IsMatrix<rawM1> && IsScalar<rawM2>) ||
13             (IsScalar<rawM1> && IsMatrix<rawM2>) ||
14             (IsBatchMatrix<rawM1> && IsMatrix<rawM2>) ||
15             (IsBatchMatrix<rawM1> && IsBatchMatrix<rawM2>);
16
17       template <typename X1, typename X2>
18       constexpr static bool Imp = std::is_same<X1, X2>::value;
19
20       using CT = CategoryTags;
21
22       template <typename T1, typename T2,
23                 std::enable_if_t<Imp<T1, T2>>* = nullptr>
24       static auto Eval(TP1&& p_m1, TP2&& p_m2);
25
26       template <typename T1, typename T2,
27                 std::enable_if_t<Imp<CT::BatchMatrix, T1>>* = nullptr,
28                 std::enable_if_t<Imp<CT::Matrix, T2>>* = nullptr>
29       static auto Eval(TP1&& p_m1, TP2&& p_m2)
30
31       // Other Eval functions...
32   };
```

Here, we have only implemented part of combinations for addition described previously. Even so, *OperAdd_* is much more complicated than *OperSigmoid_*—the main reason is that it supports diverse categories of parameters.

Firstly, *OperAdd_* enumerates the types of combinations for addition it supports and assigns them with the member *valid*. For instance, it supports matrix addition (defined in line 11) and addition of matrices and scalars (defined in lines 12 and 13).

After that, *OperAdd_* introduce the appropriate function templates *Eval* for each possible addition operation. Note that here the first two template parameters in the template *Eval* are the category tags for operands, and not the types of operands. The template *Eval* utilizes the information to construct the corresponding branch, ensuring that the compiler can select the correct version of *Eval*.

### 5.6.2.3 The Implementation of OperAdd_::Eval

*OperAdd_::Eval* introduces a corresponding implementation for each addition scenario. This section will select only a few of them for discussion. On this basis, readers can refer to the source code and understand the rest of the implementation logic.

If the two parameters involved in addition belong to the same category (e.g., both parameters in addition are both matrices and lists of matrices), then the implementation of *OperAdd_::Eval* is trivial:

```
1   template <typename T1, typename T2,
2              std::enable_if_t<Imp<T1, T2>>* = nullptr>
3   static auto Eval(TP1&& p_m1, TP2&& p_m2)
4   {
5       static_assert(std::is_same<typename rawM1::DeviceType,
6                       typename rawM2::DeviceType>::value,
7           "Matrices with different device types cannot add directly");
8       static_assert(std::is_same<typename rawM1::ElementType,
9                       typename rawM2::ElementType>::value,
10          "Matrices with different element types cannot add directly");
11
12      using ResType = BinaryOp<BinaryOpTags::Add, rawM1, rawM2>;
13      return ResType(std::forward<TP1>(p_m1),
        std::forward<TP2>(p_m2));
14  }
```

It first determines whether the device types and the element types of the two operands are same (lines 5–10). If not, they cannot be added. On this basis, the corresponding *BinaryOp* object is constructed and returned (lines 12 and 13).

The addition of a matrix and a scalar is more complicated: we cannot pass in a matrix and a scalar directly into the equation when constructing *BinaryOp*, or otherwise it will result in different tags for the input parameters of operations. According to the previous discussion, the default method for operation templates to determine the category tag for results of operations is to first ensure that the category tag for operands is consistent and return the category tag for the first operand on that basis. If the category tags for inputs of an operation are distinct, then we will be unable to take advantage of this default method and have to introduce the corresponding specialization for special treatment.

MetaNN cleverly avoids this problem using the trivial matrix as discussed in Chapter 4:

```
1   template<typename T1, typename T2,
2              std::enable_if_t<Imp<CT::Scalar, T1>::value>* = nullptr,
3              std::enable_if_t<Imp<CT::Matrix, T2>::value>* = nullptr>
4   static auto Eval(TP1&& p_m1, TP2&& p_m2)
5   {
6       using ElementType = typename rawM2::ElementType;
```

```
7          using DeviceType = typename rawM2::DeviceType;
8          auto tmpMatrix
9              = MakeTrivalMatrix<ElementType, DeviceType>(p_m2.RowNum(),
10                                                         p_m2.ColNum(),
11                                                         p_m1);
12
13         using ResType = BinaryOp<BinaryOpTags::Add,
14                                  RemConstRef<decltype(tmpMatrix)>,
15                                  rawM2>;
16         return ResType(std::move(tmpMatrix), std::forward<TP2>(p_m2));
17     }
```

For the situation that the first operand is a scalar and the second operand is a matrix, we can construct a trivial matrix corresponding to the first operand (lines 6–11) according to the information of the second operand. Then the trivial matrix is utilized as the operand in addition.

The commutative property is applied in addition, so with addition of a matrix and a scalar, it is easy to implement addition of a scalar and a matrix:

```
1   template <typename T1, typename T2,
2             std::enable_if_t<Imp<CT::Matrix, T1>>* = nullptr,
3             std::enable_if_t<Imp<CT::Scalar, T2>>* = nullptr>
4   static auto Eval(TP1&& p_m1, TP2&& p_m2)
5   {
6       return OperAdd_<TP2, TP1>::
7           template Eval<T2, T1>(std::forward<TP2>(p_m2),
8               std::forward<TP1>(p_m1));
9   }
```

Other editions of *OperAdd_::Eval* are implemented with a similar mechanism. For instance, when implementing addition of a matrix and a list of matrices, it converts a matrix into a list of matrices of type *Duplicate* and then constructs a template for lists of matrices to add. The relevant code is left to readers for self-analysis.

Addition has a common feature with *Sigmoid*: they do not modify the default behavior of *OperOrganizer* and *OperCategory_*. Most operations in MetaNN have this characteristic. However, there are also special operations that require modifications to the default behavior of both class templates. The operation transpose is a typical example.

### 5.6.3 Operation Transpose

Transpose is a unary operation of matrices that receives a matrix $x$ of $N \times M$ and returns a matrix $y$ of $M \times N$, which satisfies $x(i, j) = y(j,i)$. MetaNN extends it to support lists of matrices: the operation is to transpose each matrix in the list, combine the results into a new list of matrices, and return it.

Compared to *Add*, *Sigmoid*, etc., the most significant difference of transpose is to modify the default behavior of *OperOrganizer*: the numbers of rows and columns of its input and output matrices are no longer the same. We need to introduce a specialization of *OperOrganizer* to describe the variation:

```
1   template <>
2   class OperOrganizer<UnaryOpTags::Transpose, CategoryTags::Matrix>
3   {
4   public:
5       template <typename TData>
6       OperOrganizer(const TData& data)
7           : m_rowNum(data.ColNum())
8           , m_colNum(data.RowNum())
9       { }
10
11      size_t RowNum() const { return m_rowNum; }
12      size_t ColNum() const { return m_colNum; }
13
14  private:
15      size_t m_rowNum;
16      size_t m_colNum;
17  };
18
19  template <>
20  class OperOrganizer<UnaryOpTags::Transpose, CategoryTags::BatchMatrix>
21      : public OperOrganizer<UnaryOpTags::Transpose, CategoryTags::Matrix>
22  {
23      using BaseType = OperOrganizer<UnaryOpTags::Transpose,
24                                     CategoryTags::Matrix>;
25  public:
26      template <typename TData>
27      OperOrganizer(const TData& data)
28          : BaseType(data)
29          , m_batchNum(data.BatchNum())
30      { }
31
32      size_t BatchNum() const { return m_batchNum; }
33
34  private:
35      size_t m_batchNum;
36  };
```

*OperOrganizer* receives two template parameters: the operating tag and the category of operation result. For transpose operations, the tag is *UnaryOpTags::Transpose*. Transpose operations ought to support both matrices and lists of matrices, so we should introduce corresponding specializations for each of the two operand types.

For the specialization of matrices, when we construct an *OperOrganizer* object, the number of columns and rows of the operand can be assigned to the number of rows and columns of the *OperOrganizer* object respectively, so as to represent the change in the dimensions of the matrix caused by transpose operation (lines 7 and 8). The specialized version of lists of matrices is derived from the specialized version of matrices, which utilize the specialized version of matrices to record the number of rows and columns and only maintaining the number of matrices in the derived class. Although in MetaNN, we do not regard lists of matrices as a special kind of matrix, both matrices and lists of matrices provide interfaces for the number of rows and columns, so the derivation can simplify the code writing to some extent.

In addition to the discussed differences, the other part of transpose is quite similar to *Sigmoid*.

Transpose modifies the default logic of *OperOrganizer* to change the dimensions of the operation result. In addition, we can modify *OperCategory_* to support operations with different categories of input and output.

### 5.6.4 *Operation* Collapse

The operation *collapse* is a typical operation with distinct categories of input and output. Its input is a list of matrices, which adds the matrices in the list and generates the resulting matrix to output. It does not conform to the default behavior of *OperCategory_*—the category tag for input and output is consistent. When implementing this operation, we ought to specialize *OperCategory_*.

```
1    template <>
2    struct OperCategory_<UnaryOpTags::Collapse,
3                         CategoryTags::BatchMatrix>
4    {
5        using type = CategoryTags::Matrix;
6    };
```

In addition to the described specialization, the logic of the other parts in the operation *collapse* is similar to other operations, which will not be elaborated here.

## 5.7 The List of Operations Supported by MetaNN

So far, we have completed the targeted discussion of design methods for operations in MetaNN. In the course of the discussion, we do not list the full details of operations in MetaNN but focus on the design principles in the form of examples. Currently, there are not quite a lot of operations introduced in MetaNN and we can introduce more and more abundant operations for MetaNN in the way discussed in this chapter. This section briefly lists the operations that MetaNN currently supports.

For convenience of illustration, the input parameters are represented by markers like $x$ or $x_1$, $x_2$, $x_3$ and $y$ is used for the output. For a matrix $x$, the element in the $i$-th row and $j$-th

**Table 5.1   Unary Operations Currently Supported by MetaNN**

| Operation Names | Categories of Input | Categories of Output | Implementation Logic |
|---|---|---|---|
| Abs | Matrix | Matrix | $y(i, j) = \lvert x(i, j) \rvert$ |
| | List of matrices | List of matrices | $y^k(i, j) = \lvert x^k(i, j) \rvert$ |
| Sign | Matrix | Matrix | $y(i, j) = sign(x(i, j))$ |
| | List of matrices | List of matrices | $y^k(i, j) = sign(x^k(i, j))$ |
| Collapse | List of matrices | Matrix | $y(i, j) = \sum_k x^k(i, j)$ |
| Sigmoid | Matrix | Matrix | $y(i, j) = 1 / (1 + e^{-x(i,j)})$ |
| | List of matrices | List of matrices | $y^k(i, j) = 1 / (1 + e^{-x^k(i,j)})$ |
| Tanh | Matrix | Matrix | $y(i, j) = \tanh(x(i, j))$ |
| | List of matrices | List of matrices | $y^k(i, j) = \tanh(x^k(i, j))$ |
| VecSoftmax | Matrix | Matrix | $y(0, i) = e^{x(0,i)} / \sum_j e^{x(0,j)}$ |
| | List of matrices | List of matrices | $y^k(0, i) = e^{x^k(0,i)} / \sum_j e^{x^k(0,j)}$ |

column is represented as $x(i, j)$. For a list of matrices $x$, the element in the $i$-th row and $j$-th column of the $k$-th matrix is represented as $x^k(i, j)$. For a list of scalars $x$, $x^i$ represents the $i$-th element.

## 5.7.1  Unary Operations

Table 5.1 lists the unary operations currently supported by MetaNN. The names of operations in the first column of the table correspond to names of functions required to call the operation. For example, if we want to calculate *Sigmoid* for matrix $x$, we can call *Sigmoid*($x$) to do so.

*VecSoftmax* serves to normalize the input matrix. In the current version, *VecSoftmax* requires that the input matrix should contain only one line—that is, actually a row vector. If we use a list of matrices as the input to *VecSoftmax*, each matrix in the list is required to be a row vector. Of course, we can break this limit by extension: for instance, allowing the input matrix to contain multiple rows can help *VecSoftmax* to normalize it by rows.

## 5.7.2  Binary Operations

Table 5.2 lists the binary operations that MetaNN currently supports.

**Table 5.2  Binary Operations Currently Supported by MetaNN**

| Operation Names | Categories of Input | | Categories of Output | Implementation Logic |
|---|---|---|---|---|
| | $x_1$ | $x_2$ | | |
| +−*/ | Matrix | Matrix | Matrix | $y(i,j) = x_1(i,j)°x_2(i,j)$ |
| | Matrix | Scalar | Matrix | $y(i,j) = x_1(i,j)°x_2$ |
| | Scalar | Matrix | Matrix | $y(i,j) = x_1°x_2(i,j)$ |
| | List of matrices | List of matrices | List of matrices | $y^k(i,j) = x_1^k(i,j)°x_2^k(i,j)$ |
| | Matrix | List of matrices | List of matrices | $y^k(i,j) = x_1(i,j)°x_2^k(i,j)$ |
| | List of matrices | Matrix | List of matrices | $y^k(i,j) = x_1^k(i,j)°x_2(i,j)$ |
| | Scalar | List of matrices | List of matrices | $y^k(i,j) = x_1°x_2^k(i,j)$ |
| | List of matrices | Scalar | List of matrices | $y^k(i,j) = x_1^k(i,j)°x_2$ |
| Dot | Matrix | Matrix | Matrix | $y(i,j) = \sum_k x_1(i,k)x_2(k,j)$ |
| | List of matrices | Matrix | List of matrices | $y^k(i,j) = \sum_m x_1^k(i,m)x_2(m,j)$ |
| | Matrix | List of matrices | List of matrices | $y^k(i,j) = \sum_m x_1(i,m)x_2^k(m,j)$ |
| | List of matrices | List of matrices | List of matrices | $y^k(i,j) = \sum_m x_1^k(i,m)x_2^k(m,j)$ |
| NegativeLog Likelihood | Matrix | Matrix | Scalar | $y = -\sum_{i,j} x_1(i,j)\log(x_2(i,j))$ |
| | List of matrices | List of matrices | List of scalars | $y^k = -\sum_{i,j} x_1^k(i,j)\log(x_2^k(i,j))$ |
| VecSoftmax Derivative | Matrix | Matrix | Matrix | $y = Dot(x_1, D(x_2))$ |
| | List of matrices | List of matrices | List of matrices | $y^k = Dot(x_1^k, D(x_2^k))$ |
| Sigmoid Derivative | Matrix | Matrix | Matrix | $y(i,j) = x_1(i,j)x_2(i,j)(1 - x_2(i,j))$ |
| | List of matrices | List of matrices | List of matrices | $y^k(i,j) = x_1^k(i,j)x_2^k(i,j)(1 - x_2^k(i,j))$ |
| Tanh Derivative | Matrix | Matrix | Matrix | $y(i,j) = x_1(i,j)(1 - x_2(i,j)^2)$ |
| | List of matrices | List of matrices | List of matrices | $y^k(i,j) = x_1^k(i,j)(1 - x_2^k(i,j)^2)$ |

There are more kinds and more complex calculations in binary operations than unary operations. Here is a simple explanation of the entries in Table 5.2.

Firstly, addition, subtraction, multiplication, and division can be executed between matrices, between a matrix and a scalar, and so on. For two matrices $A$ and $B$, we can realize the four operations of the corresponding elements in the matrix in the form of $A+B$, $A*B$, and so on—the actual operation is represented by ° in Table 5.2.

In addition to multiplying the corresponding elements, the matrix also needs to support dot product, which adopts the function *Dot* as an interface. *Dot (A, B)* returns the operation template, representing the dot product of $A$ and $B$. *Dot* can also be executed between a matrix and a list of matrices or between lists of matrices, which is to calculate dot product of the corresponding matrices in the list.

*VecSoftmaxDerivative* corresponds to the differentiation of *VecSoftmax*. The input is the gradient $(x_1)$ transmitted from the upper layer and the result of the previous *Softmax* operation $(x_2)$. $x_2$ will be first transformed within the operation, constructing a *Jacobian* matrix:

$$D(x_2)_{i,j} = \begin{cases} -x_2(0,i)x_2(0,j), \ i \neq j \\ x_2(0,i)(1-x_2(0,i)), \ i = j \end{cases}$$

The dot product of $x_1$ and $D(x_2)$ will be returned.

*SigmoidDerivative* and *TanhDerivative* correspond to the differentiation of *Sigmoid* and *Tanh* respectively. Take the former as an example, because for *Sigmoid*, there is:

$$S(x) = \frac{1}{1+e^{-x}}$$

So,

$$S'(x) = \frac{e^{-x}}{(1+e^{-x})^2} = S(x)(1-S(x))$$

When the input of the operation is $x$, $S(x)(1-S(x))$ is the value of $S'(x)$. This value will be multiplied by the input gradient and continues to propagate as the output gradient. Therefore, this operation receives two parameters: the input gradient $x_1$ and the result of *Sigmoid* $x_2$. On this basis, the new gradient value is the output.

### 5.7.3 Ternary Operations

MetaNN currently supports two ternary operations: *NegativeLogLikelihoodDerivative* and *Interpolate*.

*NegativeLogLikelihoodDerivative* corresponds to the derivative of *NegativeLogLikelihood*. It receives three input parameters, the input gradient $(x_1)$ transmitted from the upper layer, the tag information $(x_2)$, and the prediction result of the neural network $(x_3)$. Among them:

■ If the calculation result of the tag and the neural network are matrices, the corresponding output is a scalar, which are calculated as follows:

$$y(i,j) = -x_1 x_2(i,j) \,/\, x_3(i,j)$$

■ If the calculation result of the tag and the neural network are lists of matrices, the corresponding output is a list of scalars, which are calculated as follows:

$$y^k(i,j) = -x_1^k x_2^k(i,j) \,/\, x_3^k(i,j)$$

The function *Interpolate* receives three parameters: $x_1$ and $x_2$ are two matrices or lists of matrices, and $x_3$ is a matrix or list of matrices of interpolation factors. For versions with matrices as input:

$$y(i,j) = x_1(i,j)x_3(i,j) + x_2(i,j)(1 - x_3(i,j))$$

For versions with lists of matrices as input:

$$y^k(i,j) = x_1^k(i,j)x_3^k(i,j) + x_2^k(i,j)(1 - x_3^k(i,j))$$

That's all the operations MetaNN can currently implement. Deep learning is a quite fast-growing field and new approaches are emerging constantly. At present, the purpose of MetaNN is not to introduce a large number of operations, but to discuss the writing of operations in this framework by introducing a number of typical operations. MetaNN itself is scalable and we can introduce more operations to it in the way discussed in this chapter.

# 5.8 The Trade-off and Limitations of Operations

## 5.8.1 The Trade-off of Operations

Usually, the main problem involved in introducing operations is not the writing of code, but the trade-off between "using an existing combination of operations" and "introducing new functions for operations"—more of a design issue. Various operations can be combined with other operations. A typical example: for elements in a matrix, addition and multiplication can be combined to form subtraction:

$$A - B = A + (-1) \times B$$

So, is it necessary to introduce subtraction? Essentially, an expression template itself can be considered a tree structure. If we choose to use a combination of existing operations to form new operations, it will deepen the entire expression tree—for example, with the introduction of subtraction operations, we only need one root node to represent the result of the operation and two leaf nodes represent operands in order to construct a tree structure that represents subtraction. However, if we combine addition with multiplication to "simulate" subtraction, then the constructed subtraction tree needs five nodes to indicate—three nodes are needed to represent the input and output of the multiplication, and the other two nodes represent the other operand and the final operation result respectively. Increased depth of the tree increases the difficulty of subsequent optimization.

On the other hand, we can't introduce new operational expressions for every possible combination of operations, which will greatly raise the number of operational expressions and are detrimental to system maintenance. A better trade-off is to introduce specialized functions to represent operations that may be used frequently in the deep framework. If an operation is not used so frequently, it can be combined with multiple suboperations.

### 5.8.2 Limitations of Operations

An operation is a construct based on data and forms new data by combining and transforming the original data. It is often employed in deep learning frameworks, but it is also a relatively underlying construct with some limitations in usage.

Firstly, it can be tough for users who don't know much about deep learning systems to determine when and what operations to use. The author does not mention too much computational deduction in the discussion of this chapter, most of which states conclusions directly, for instance, how to calculate the derivative corresponding to *Softmax*, etc. It is because these mathematical deductions are beyond the scope of this book. But on the other hand, readers unfamiliar with these mathematical principles may raise some questions about which operation to choose to represent the derivative calculation for another operation when reading this section. In fact, if an operation is offered directly to end users, they may have the same questions. This is not what we want.

Secondly, there is a risk that operations could be misused. For example, for *SigmoidDerivative*, it requires the output of *Sigmoid* as its input. In other words, assuming that the input of *Sigmoid* input is $x$ and the output is $y$, then we have to use $y$ as the input of *SigmoidDerivative* to obtain its derivative of $x$. Nonetheless, it is not embodied in the declaration and definition of the function *SigmoidDerivative*. A typical misuse is to take the input of *Sigmoid* as input to *SigmoidDerivative*— if $x$ is used as input to *SigmoidDerivative*, then the result will be wrong.

The limitation forces us to introduce more advanced constructs that provide interfaces, which are convenient and not error-prone. We'll discuss the concept of "layers" in the next chapter, which, as the upper-level component of operations, will better combine and encapsulate operations.

## 5.9 Summary

This chapter discussed the design and implementation of operations in MetaNN.

MetaNN adopts template expressions to represent operations. A template expression is a bridge between operations and data that encapsulates operations and supplies the interfaces that data needs to support. Through template expressions, we postpone the evaluation process of operations to provide more space for optimization.

As a deep learning framework, MetaNN ought to support various operations and offer enough convenient interfaces for extension. To achieve this, we introduced several auxiliary class templates, which encapsulate different parts involved in operations. We can introduce various operations by specializing these auxiliary class templates.

This chapter presented specific examples of several operations' implementations and listed the operations that MetaNN currently supports, which can be helpful references for implementations of operations.

Template expressions that represent operations encapsulate a lot of implementation details, simplifying their interfaces as much as possible. But even so, interfaces provided by operations are not friendly enough and have some limitations—too many operations can make it hard for users to choose and they may be misused. To solve this problem, the concept of "layers" will be introduced in the next chapter, further encapsulating them and providing better interfaces.

## 5.10 Exercises

1. In this chapter, we introduce the metafunction *OperCategory_*:

   ```
   template <typename TOpTag, typename THeadCate,
             typename...TRemainCate>
   using OperCategory_ = ...
   ```

   If we change the declaration of this metafunction to the following form:

   ```
   template <typename TOpTag, typename TCates...>
   using OperCategory_ = ...
   ```

   What is the difference between the behaviors of the former version and the modified metafunction? Please analyze which one is better.
2. *OperCateCal* calls the metafunction *CateInduce_*, unpacks the input array *tuple*, extracts the elements therein and calls *OperCategory_*. Can we make *OperCateCal* call *OperCategory_* directly? What are the pros and cons of this design?
3. Read and analyze the implementation code for *BinaryOp* and *TernaryOp*.
4. Read and analyze the operations currently supported in MetaNN to understand how concrete operations are associated with the operation framework through auxiliary functions.
5. Not all operations need to introduce the corresponding operations of differentiation. For instance, the basic arithmetic operations of matrices and the operation of dot product do not introduce the corresponding operations of differentiation in MetaNN. Analyze the reasons for this design (readers can analyze it with the discussion of layers in the next chapter).
6. Implement the operation *ReLU*. *ReLU* is a unary operator that can receive a matrix or a list of matrices and calculate $y = \max(0,x)$ for each data element $x$ in the matrix or list of matrices. Please write programs to verify the correctness of the implementation.
7. Implement the operation *ReLUDerivative*, corresponding to the differentiation of *ReLU*. Before implementing it, please consider how many parameters it should have. Write programs to verify the correctness of the implementation.

# Chapter 6

# Basic Layers

Chapter 5 discusses the operations in MetaNN, which are represented as template expressions and postpone the entire process of calculation, providing a prerequisite for the overall optimization of the system. But the end of Chapter 5 also mentions that operations are not user-friendly interfaces. Therefore, we should encapsulate on the basis of operations with the introduction of the concept, "layer." We'll discuss the implementation of layers in MetaNN in two chapters: present chapter discusses the basic layers in MetaNN and Chapter 7 discusses the composite and recurrent layers in MetaNN.

Layers encapsulate operations to provide user-friendly interfaces. Users can organize the deep learning network through "layers" in MetaNN to train and predict models. It can be stated that "layer" is a concept quite attached to end-users. Deep learning is a fast-growing field with emerging new technologies. In order to support more technologies, on the one hand, we should simplify the introduction of new layers to the entire framework; on the other hand, existing layers ought to be flexible enough to support different formulations and adjust details of their behaviors. These are all what MetaNN needs to consider when designing the concept of layers. It is precisely because of the flexibility that we need to discuss the details of implementation through two chapters.

Present chapter discusses the basic layers, whose main function is to encapsulate operations and form the most basic logic of execution. The composite layers discussed in Chapter 7 are combinations of the basic layers, which are a typical composite pattern. The composite layers and the basic layers share some design concepts, so understanding the design principle of basic layers is also a prerequisite for understanding composite layers.

Similar to previous chapters, before actual development, it's significant to analyze what features the concept of "layers" should contain and how to introduce them—these contents constitute the design principles of layers. Let's begin with this and dive into the discussion of layers.

## 6.1 Design Principles of Layers

### 6.1.1 Introduction to Layers

From users' point of view, layers are the basic units that make up a deep learning network. A deep learning network usually requires two types of operations: training and prediction. Layers also should offer appropriate support for both.

163

Deep neural networks contain a large number of parameters, which are generally stored in the form of matrices in the layers that constitute deep neural networks. Model training refers to the process of optimizing parameter matrices in networks by training data. A typical form of training is supervised training: given a training dataset $(x_1, y_1), (x_2, y_2) \ldots (x_n, y_n)$, each $(x_i, y_i)$ is a sample, $x_i$ is the information of input of the sample and $y_i$ is the labeling corresponding to the sample. The purpose of training models is to adjust parameter matrices so that when the input of a model is $x_i$, its output is as close as possible to $y_i$. A typical training method for deep neural networks is to input $x_i$ to the network, calculate the output value of the network in the case of the current parameter matrices, compare the value with the label $y_i$, obtain the difference between the two,[1] and then adjust the parameters in the network according to the difference.

Model training can be divided into two steps: calculating prediction results of the network based on the input and adjusting the parameter matrices according to the performance of the network. Network predictions are in reverse order to gradient calculations. We assume that a feed-forward network contains two layers, $A$ and $B$. During the prediction, the input is first fed into $A$, the output of $A$ is passed to $B$, and the output of $B$ is the output of the entire network. Then, during the calculation of the gradient, the gradient representing the difference is passed to $B$ first, the result is then passed to $A$ after being processed by $B$, and $A$ will use the input gradient $B$ passes to it to calculate the gradient corresponding to its internal parameter matrix.

We use **forward propagation** to describe the process of prediction in the network and **backward propagation** to describe the process of gradient calculation of network parameters. For any layer, the information of input received in forward propagation is called the **input feature** (or **input** for short) and the information of output is called the **output feature** (or **output** for short); the information of input received in backward propagation is called the **input gradient** and the information of output is called the **output gradient**. If the layer needs to update the parameter matrix it contains, then it should calculate the parameter gradient with the input gradient, which will serve to update the parameter matrix after backward propagation.

Corresponding to the prediction process of the described example, $A$ receives the input and generates output, the output of $A$ is equally the input of $B$ and the output of $B$ is the output of the whole network. In backward propagation, $B$ receives its input gradient, calculates the gradient corresponding to its internal parameter matrix and output gradient. The output gradient of $B$ is delivered to $A$ as the input gradient of $A$, and $A$ uses that gradient to calculate the internal parameter gradient and output gradient. The output gradient is further transmitted outward.

When the entire backward propagation is completed, we get the parameter gradients for each matrix to be updated, which can be subsequently employed to update the network parameters.

To support the training process, a layer needs to provide two interfaces for forward and backward propagation. For tasks of pure prediction, there is no need for backward propagation. As a deep learning framework that supports training and prediction, it needs to provide interfaces for both forward and backward propagation. MetaNN introduces *FeedForward* and *FeedBackward* in each layer as abstract interfaces for forward and backward propagation. Arguably, they are the most critical interfaces in each layer of MetaNN.

It should be noted that not all layers contain parameter matrices within them. In fact, most of the basic layers we will see later don't contain parameter matrices—they just serve to transform the input. However, these layers also require backward propagation functions to produce the input gradients required by other layers in the network.

---

[1] The difference is usually expressed by the loss function, which receives the true label and the prediction results of the network and returns a value to measure the prediction.

Support for forward and backward propagation is of great significance, but far from all the features supplied by layers. In fact, layers in MetaNN have worked on many implementation details in order to satisfy both flexibility and efficiency. Next, let's take the life cycle of layer objects as a clue to comprehend the design details of layers in MetaNN.

## 6.1.2 Construction of Layer Objects

In general, we all hope layers to be more versatile—especially basic layers as the basis for forming composite layers. The generality is often embodied when we want a layer to have some basic behavior and it can be fine-tuned with parameters. For instance, for a layer with a parameter matrix during training, it would normally calculate the parameter gradient in backward propagation for subsequent adjustments. Nevertheless, in some special cases, we want the parameter matrix contained in the layer to remain unchanged but parameter matrices contained in other layers in the network are adjusted. At this point, the layer does not need to calculate the parameter gradient. Similarly, we may also adjust the behavior details of a layer in other ways. We wish the layer to support versatility to some extent—to supply interfaces that allow users to decide on the details of behaviors, which can be determined at the beginning of the construction of layer objects and will remain unchanged in the use of layers. Therefore, a layer should provide interfaces to receive the parameters that control its behavior when constructed.

If implementing based on object-oriented programming, we can adopt classes to represent various layers and introduce parameters into constructors of classes to control the subsequent behavior of objects. Nonetheless, MetaNN is a framework for generic programming. In addition to introducing parameters into constructors, we can also set a layer as a class template to specify behavior details by introducing template parameters for it. It is an inherent advantage of templates: for instance, *stack* defined in the STL is a template, which can be implemented with *vector, deque,* or other linear structures at the low level. We can set the details of its underlying data structure by specifying the template parameters of *stack*. Similarly, we can specify the details of its behavior by introducing template parameters into layers in MetaNN.

There is one benefit of specifying behavior details using template parameters: constructors can only be called at runtime and template parameters are processed at compile time. Specifying parameters at compile time allows us to introduce better optimization using some characteristics of compile time, which is not available for runtime parameters. Also consider the example of *stack*. If its underlying data structure is specified through stack's constructor in the STL, its implementation will be a lot more complex. Nevertheless, it is using template parameters that *stack* can optimize data structures at compile time to enhance its performance. For layers in MetaNN, we deliver a few parameters in the constructor, using template parameters to specify most of its behaviors.

### 6.1.2.1 Information Delivered through Constructors

In MetaNN, if necessary, we specify the name of a layer in the form of a string in the constructor, as well as information such as the dimensions of the input parameters and the output. A deep learning network may contain several layers, each of which may contain corresponding parameter matrices. In order to make a distinction between different parameter matrices in the layers, we ought to assign each matrix a name. MetaNN will name a layer that contains parameter matrices, and the layer uses its name as a prefix to nominate the parameter matrices it contains. For example, if a layer named "MyLayer" contains two parameter matrices, the layer can name the parameter matrices it contains as "MyLayer-1" and "MyLayer-2."

If a layer contains parameter matrices, we need to specify the appropriate name for it as one of the layer's constructor arguments. On the other hand, if the layer does not contain parameter matrices, it does not need to introduce a corresponding name. It is tantamount to assigning names to each matrix in the entire neural network in this way. If we can ensure that the name in the constructor passed to each layer is unique to the entire network, then we can also guarantee that the parameter matrix contained in the layer is not shared with other layers. If we hope various layers to share a same set of parameter matrices, we only need to assign a same name to those layers.

The name of the matrix is of type string, more user-friendly to the framework than other forms of naming. As we discussed earlier, it is daunting to use data of type string as template parameters, so the information is delivered through constructors. Another message to be passed through constructors is the dimensions of input parameters and output results of layers (such as the number of rows and columns of the output matrix). Layers ought to specify the information when constructing parameter matrices contained inside it. Typically, the layer used to calculate the dot product of the input vector and a matrix requires these two messages to infer the number of rows and columns of the parameter matrix it maintains.

The information of dimensions can theoretically be placed in template parameters, but MetaNN chooses to deliver them in constructors because passing as template arguments cannot provide great help with optimization of performance introduced at compile time. If passed as a template argument, it will boost the burden on the compiler with few benefits. So, MetaNN delivers the information in constructors.

### 6.1.2.2 Information Specified through Template Parameters

Most messages required for construction of layers are passed in as template arguments. These messages are diverse, and different layers require distinct information. For instance, for a layer that contains a parameter matrix, it should know whether to calculate the corresponding parameter gradient during training; for a layer without parameter matrices, this message is redundant. Some parameters only make sense for a particular layer, while others may be meaningful for most layers.

Parameters of layers vary widely, which is distinct from the data and operations discussed previously. Although data and operations are implemented as templates in MetaNN, the number of parameters and the meaning of each parameter in these templates are basically constant (e.g., there are usually two parameters in class templates that represent basic data types, indicating the type of computing unit and device, respectively). For layers, it is totally different in this aspect. To deal with the disparity effectively, we should utilize the Policy template implemented in Chapter 2. Hopefully, you still remember the details of this module. If not, refer back to this part.

Specifically, a layer is implemented as a class template, declared as follows:

```
1   template <typename T>
2   class XXXLayer;
```

*T* is a container *PolicyContainer* that contains the template parameters required for the layer.

### 6.1.3 Initialization and Loading of Parameter Matrices

To construct layer objects, we should specify the appropriate template parameters for a layer and deliver the appropriate values in constructors. If the layer contains a parameter matrix, the next step after constructing the layer object is assigning a value to the parameter matrix contained therein. The data sources of assignments can be roughly divided into two types: if the layer has not been involved in training before, then we need to initialize the parameter matrix through an initializer so that the parameter matrix is assigned with a specific value (such as 0) or distribution (e.g., normal distribution); or we can adopt an existing matrix to assign the parameter matrix—for example, obtain the results of model training previously from files and load them into the current parameter matrix.

In order to initialize and load parameters: on the one hand, MetaNN introduce the function template *Init* in layers as an interface for initialization and model loading[2]; on the other hand, MetaNN introduces a network-level initialization module to initialize all the layers contained in the entire network. We'll discuss both in more detail later in this chapter.

### 6.1.4 Forward Propagation

Each layer ought to provide a function template *FeedForward* as an interface to be called during forward propagation. The interface should receive information of input passed to it by its predecessor layer in the network, calculate the result and return it to be utilized by its successor layer in the network.

Here's a problem: each layer varies in the number and meaning of the inputs and outputs. For example, the number of input parameters corresponding to the layers that represents addition of matrices or transpose of a matrix is not the same; if a layer indicates subtraction of matrices, the statuses of the subtrahend and minuend are also distinct—when passed to the layer as arguments, they are non-interchangeable.

One straightforward way to specify the meaning of each parameter is to introduce multiple parameters for *FeedForward*. For example, it is written as follows:

```
1   template <typename TMinuend, typename TSubtrahend>
2   auto FeedForward(TMinuend&& minuend, TSubtrahend&& subtrahend);
```

Through the names of arguments, we can distinguish between the meanings of the two parameters (subtrahend and minuend). This approach is intuitive, but may lead to a number of problems. First of all, we still can't prevent the function from being misused—for example, for two matrices *A* and *B*, we want to subtract *B* from *A*. However, if users accidentally write the two in wrong positions when calling the function:

```
1   FeedForward(B, A);
```

The system will continue to work but the results will be wrong, which will not directly lead to compilation errors and run failures, therefore difficult for error debugging.

Another major problem is the fact that it leads to a difference among the interfaces *FeedForward* defined by distinct layers: the number of parameters it receives varies accordingly with different functions of the layers. If we're dealing with a single layer, it's not a big deal. But if we want to introduce a unified set of logic to handle the combinations of layers,[3] the disparity among the forms of the interface *FeedForward* in each layer will intensify the complexity of programming.

---

[2] Not all layers require this interface. If a layer does not contain a parameter matrix, it does not need to provide it.

[3] Composite layers are discussed in Chapter 7.

We want to unify this interface in different layers to facilitate subsequent calls and management. So, how can we resolve the problem?

One way is to utilize the list structure as a container for input and output of a function: to distinguish among parameters by artificially defining the meaning of each element in the list. For example, for a layer that represents matrix subtraction, we can require that the input of the layer should be a vector list, which can contain only two elements, the first as the subtrahend and the second as the minuend. The output of the layer is also a list that contains an element to represent the result of the subtraction of the two matrices.[4]

Nonetheless, there are two problems with this approach. Firstly, it does not fundamentally reduce the likelihood of misuse. It is because we need to artificially specify the meaning of each element in the list, which is not displayed in the program code and there may still be misuse and also more difficult to debug. In addition, the class of lists typically requires each element to be of the same type, but one of MetaNN's main design principles is to introduce rich types to improve system performance. Typically, two input items to an addition layer may come from the basic class template *Matrix* and the operation template formed by an operation—where the types of parameters passed in to the layer are distinct. Of course, we can evaluate the input data, convert it to the same type constrainedly, and then call *FeedForward*. However, it is not consistent with our design principle: our goal is to postpone the evaluation process, thus providing the possibility of optimization. The benefits of introducing rich types, operation templates, and other mechanisms will be ruined if we evaluate simply to match interfaces of layers.

How to resolve this problem? Some readers may have found the answer, which is to use the **heterogeneous dictionary** we discussed in Chapter 2. First of all, the module is essentially a dictionary and each entry in the dictionary is a key-value pair—the types of values in different entries can be distinct. We can utilize it to solve the problem of type differentiation; secondly, we should explicitly give the key names for the module to read and write, which will reduce the possibility of parameter misuse.[5] Heterogeneous dictionaries are containers that hold heterogeneous data structures. In the process of forward and backward propagation, the received input and the resulting output are stored in the corresponding container. The input and output containers of the same layer may be different (e.g., for a layer that represents the addition of two matrices, two parameters are required in the input container and only one result is required in the output container). However, for each layer, the input container of it in backward propagation must be the same as the output container in forward propagation; the output container in backward propagation must be the same as the input container in forward propagation. Therefore, a layer ought to correlate two containers: one to store the forward input and backward output, and one to store the forward output and backward input. We refer the former to the **input container** and the latter to the **output container**.

One more thing to note about *FeedForward*: it's a function template rather than a trivial function, so it's designed to receive input of different types and produce output of different types. Consider a layer that calculates *Sigmoid*, which calculates the *Sigmoid* result of the input and returns it. Depending on the type of input, it constructs the corresponding calculation template as the returning result. Thus, although layers are introduced in MetaNN, they do not generate too many side effects on computational performance during forward

---

[4] In fact, this is the way used in many deep learning frameworks, such as the famous deep learning framework *Caffe*.

[5] In fact, the two modules discussed in Chapter 2 are used here in layers. If readers are not familiar with this part, the author recommends reading the relevant content again.

propagation—we are still constructing operation templates, the entire computing process can be deferred to the end, and we can take advantage of the benefits of Lazy Evaluation to improve system performance.

If *FeedForward* is set as a function, or if we require that its return result must be some type, then we will lose that advantage to some extent. Typically, we may need to return the results after evaluating the results in the layer, thus losing the meaning of introducing rich types and computational templates.

## 6.1.5 Preservation of Intermediate Results

In the case of the operation *Sigmoid*, which is encapsulated in the layer *SigmoidLayer* and is provided to the outside. If we want to support backward propagation, we need a place to hold the intermediate result that *SigmoidLayer* produces when calling *FeedForward*—the result can be utilized to calculate the output gradient in backward propagation. We can select two places to preserve these intermediate results: to place intermediate results with input and output, or to preserve intermediate results in the layer. MetaNN selects the second approach because we think the layer represents a collection of operations related to the layer itself, which can be better associated with these intermediate results. Conversely, if intermediate results are delivered together with input and output, the correspondence between the data and the intermediate results will be lost (i.e., how the intermediate result is obtained with the data).

In MetaNN, however, there is a problem with preserving intermediate results: *FeedForward* is a function template and the type of the intermediate result it produces during calculation depends on the type of argument entered. If we introduce a data field into the layer to hold intermediate results, what is the type of the data field?

A simple resolution is to set the type of the intermediate result as the principal type.[6] The intermediate results are then converted to the principal type and saved during forward propagation. But this conversion is essentially an evaluation, which leads to a forward movement of the evaluation process and is not what we would like to happen.

To solve this problem, we introduced a type "*DynamicData*," which encapsulates intermediate result types, thus masking differences among specific types. Constructing dynamic types does not involve actual matrix computations and the expense of construction is relatively low. Dynamic types also provide an interface for evaluation, which essentially forwards the input to the type it encapsulates for calculation.

The introduction of dynamic types makes it possible to preserve intermediate results, but the introduction of this construct comes at an additional cost: in order to unify types, it is equivalent to discarding some information—which complicates subsequent optimization processes for evaluation.

With regard to intermediate results, it is also significant to point out that the field used by the layer to save intermediate results is not simply *DynamicData*, but a stack of *DynamicData*. Because a certain layer object may be used multiple times in forward propagation.[7] The corresponding intermediate results ought to be recorded for each usage. In backward propagation, the intermediate results of the last calculation will be used first, which is typical logic of "Last In, First Out" and most reasonable to be expressed in a stack.

---

[6] Principal types are discussed in Chapter 4.

[7] We'll see this case in Chapter 7 when discussing recurrent layers.

## 6.1.6 Backward Propagation

In backward propagation, the layer's interface *FeedBackward* is called. Similar to forward propagation, the interface is also a template. The intermediate results produced in forward propagation will be utilized in the calculation of backward propagation.

There are two points to note about backward propagation. Firstly, each layer should provide interfaces for backward propagation. However, not all backward propagation interfaces will be called. If a layer is only used for prediction instead of training, then backward propagation is not requisite and we ought to optimize for that.

Secondly, it is also significant that in some cases, even if the layer's interface for backward propagation is called, it can choose not to calculate the output gradient. With regard to this point, it is worth focusing on its analysis: in deep neural networks, each layer involves forward propagation to produce results and output outwards, but backward propagation does not necessarily require calculating the output gradient. Backward propagation generates an output gradient because the gradient will be delivered to other layers and adopted by these layers to calculate the parameter gradient. If we do not have to update the parameter matrix for some layers in the network, then the layer does not need to receive output gradients from other layers. It results in some layers that do not require substantial calculations in backward propagation (because they are not required to offer the information of gradients for other layers), thus reducing the amount of computations.

To achieve optimization at this level, we introduce a parameter *IsFeedbackOut* for each layer, to indicate whether the output gradient needs calculation for backward propagation. If its value is *false*, we will omit the calculation of the output gradient in backward propagation of the layer.

In general, *IsFeedbackOut* does not require manual settings of users because its value is pertinent to whether other layers require parameter updates. We'll see that the information can be automatically deduced by methods of metaprogramming when discussing composite layers in the next chapter.

If a layer's *IsFeedbackOut* is set to be *false*, then we can acquire an additional benefit: in many cases, we no longer need to introduce *DynamicData* into the layer to support calculations of backward propagation. In this way, the logic of forward propagation will be simplified and we will obtain more space to optimize system performance.

## 6.1.7 Update of Parameter Matrices

In the process of backward propagation, if the parameter matrix contained in the layer needs to be updated, then the layer will save the corresponding parameter gradient, which will be unified after backward propagation to update the corresponding parameters.

Note that the backward propagation of gradients and the update of parameters are two processes. When *FeedBackward* is called, it can only record the parameter gradient and cannot update the parameter with the gradient at the same time. Firstly, when the parameter matrix is shared by multiple layers in the network, if a certain layer updates the parameter matrix when it calls *FeedBackward*, it may affect the gradient calculation of another layer. Secondly, some update algorithms will adjust the parameter gradient generated in backward propagation and the adjustment may be built on all the parameter gradients obtained, which requires us to update the parameters uniformly after the backward propagation of the entire network is completed.

The last benefit of updating parameter uniformly is also about the computation speed. Essentially, the parameter gradients we preserve are also objects of type *DynamicData*. We only need to evaluate objects of this type uniformly before updating the parameter gradient—which facilitates the consolidation of calculations and boosts efficiency.

MetaNN introduces *GradCollect* to collect parameter gradients and each layer containing the parameter matrix should provide this interface. We'll see the specific form of the interface later.

### 6.1.8 Acquisition of Parameter Matrices

If a layer contains a parameter matrix, it should be preserved for prediction after the completion of training. MetaNN requires each layer with a parameter matrix to provide an interface *SaveWeights* to obtain the parameters of the matrix. Of course, if the layer does not contain a parameter matrix, it is unnecessary to provide this interface.

### 6.1.9 Neutral Detection of Layers

Layer objects may need to save intermediate results in forward propagation for calculations of backward propagation. From the perspective of intermediate results, forward and backward propagation just constitute the "producer-consumer" relationship. During a round of training, the intermediate results produced in forward propagation should be completely consumed in backward propagation. We call the layer "without any intermediate results stored" a "neutral layer." The layer should be neutral at initial state; after each call of forward and backward propagation and obtaining the corresponding parameter gradient, the layer should return to the neutral state.

If a layer in MetaNN needs to preserve intermediate information, it will provide an interface *NeutralInvariant* to assert that the layer is neutral. Typically, this function can be called after a round of training. If the layer is not neutral, the function prompts an exception indicating that there is an error in some parts of the system.

Like most interfaces, not all layers provide the interface *NeutralInvariant*. If a layer does not need to save variables in the intermediate state, it is needless to provide this function.

So far, we have learned the basic design principles of layers. From the above analysis, it is natural to realize that a layer is not only the package of operations but has numerous features also. It is these features that make its introduction will not impact on the performance of the system too much, but help the system to be more user-friendly. In the second half of this chapter, we'll dive into the implementation details of layers to illustrate how to embody these principles in the specific code.

Nonetheless, before discussing the specific implementation of layers, we should implement some auxiliary logic: for example, initialization modules for the entire network, dynamic type *DynamicData*, and so on. Meanwhile, we ought to introduce a series of template parameters for layers to control their behaviors. These contents will be discussed in the next section.

## 6.2 Auxiliary Logic for Layers

### 6.2.1 Initializing the Module

As mentioned earlier, in order to achieve initialization, we introduce the interface *Init* for the layers that contain parameter matrices. But simply introduction of this interface is not enough. A practical deep learning model may contain layers that together form a network. The layers in the network interact with each other, which can lead to the complexity of the actual initialization and parameter loading process. The following cases are typical ones.

- We may hope to introduce distinct initialization methods for different parameter matrices, such as normal distribution initialization for parameters contained in some layers and zero initialization for parameters contained in others.
- For some applications (such as transfer learning), some layers of the network may have been trained before and previously trained matrices need loading, while others have not previously participated in training and need to be initialized.
- MetaNN provides string names for each layer that contains parameters. Layers with the same name share a parameter matrix, which indicates that updating a parameter matrix for a certain layer will affect layers with the same name. Initialization and parameter loading must guarantee that these layers share a set of parameter matrices.
- In many cases, we may construct multiple instances of networks in a single process, and whether the parameter matrix is shared among these network instances depends on the actual situation. For instance, if the construction of multiple network instances is for parallel training, they typically cannot share parameters to prevent an update of one network from affecting other networks.[8] In another case, however, assuming that we construct multiple networks for parallel prediction, the parameter matrices in the corresponding networks will not be updated, so multiple networks can usually share a set of parameter matrices, which saves storage space. The initialization logic should support users to select whether to share parameters among networks.

From the discussed analysis, it is effortless to be aware that there are interactions among layers—the same for networks. So, initialization and model loading cannot be solved simply by introducing the function *Init* inside the layer. We should bring in a network-level module to maintain the logic of initialization. This section will discuss how this module is implemented in MetaNN.

### 6.2.1.1 Using the Initialization Module

Before constructing the module of initialization, we should consider how to define the module's interface to support the scenarios mentioned earlier. Here is how to use the initialization module in MetaNN:

```
1    auto initializer
2        = MakeInitializer<float,
3                    PInitializerIs<struct Gauss1>,
4                    PWeightInitializerIs<struct Gauss2>>()
5          .SetFiller<Gauss1>(GaussianFiller{ 0, 1.5 })
6          .SetFiller<Gauss2>(GaussianFiller{ 0, 3.3 });
7    Matrix<float, CPU> mat;
8    initializer.SetMatrix("name1", mat);
9    map<string, Matrix<float, DeviceTags::CPU>> loader;
10   layer.Init(initializer, loader);
```

---

[8] Assuming that we construct multiple threads in the process, each thread contains a network and networks sharing a parameter matrix. If thread *A* is in the process of updating the network parameters and thread *B* is in forward and backward propagation, then the result of *B* is obviously wrong.

Lines 1–8 of the code snippet construct an instance of the initialization module; line 9 constructs a container that holds intermediate results to support parameter sharing; line 10 passes both of them to the layer for initialization.

One of the main functions of the initialization module is to specify the initializer. The initializer represents a specific approach of initialization. For instance, *GaussianFiller{0, 1.5}* is an initializer that represents the initialization using a normal distribution with a mean of 0 and a standard deviation of 1.5. Each initializer corresponds to an initialization tag (such as *Gauss1* in the previous code) and the initialization module associates the initializer with a specific layer by the initializing tag.

In the example of the previous code snippet, we specify a generic initializer tag as *Gauss1*. For the weight matrix, the initializer corresponding to the tag *Gauss2* serves to initialize it. After that, lines 5 and 6 of the code snippet give the initializers for *Gauss1* and *Gauss2* via *SetFiller*.

In addition to configuring initializers, *initializer* can also deploy parameter matrices such as the parameter matrix *name1* in line 9 of the code snippet.

*layer.Init* needs to be implemented in the following way[9]:

- It examines if the second argument contains the parameter matrix that requires loading. If so, it obtains the matrix directly—indicating that it will share the parameter matrix with some other layer.
- Otherwise, it examines if the initialization module contains the parameter matrix that requires loading. If so, it obtains the corresponding parameter matrix from the initialization module. The loaded matrix is preserved in the second argument in the meantime—indicating that the current parameters are explicitly loaded and their parameters can be shared by other matrices with the same name.
- Otherwise, an initializer (such as *Gauss1* in this example) is selected based on the property of the current layer to initialize—corresponding to an explicit initialization process.

The kernel of the difference between the first two initialization methods is that if the parameter matrix is obtained from *loader*, the obtained parameter matrix must be shared with the other layers; if the parameter matrix is obtained from the initialization module, the obtained parameter matrix must be independent and not shared with other layers.

Based on such structure, let's consider how to support the several scenarios of initialization mentioned earlier.

- In order to support the initialization of distinct parameter matrices in various ways, the initialization module can introduce multiple instances of initializers to be selected by the specific layers for the appropriate instances.
- The initialization module can output the parameter matrix at the same time when the initializer is configured, so as to support the occurrence of both initialization and parameter loading.
- Because of the introduction of *loader*, the successor layers that load the parameters can share the parameter matrix with the predecessor layers that previously load the parameters in the network.

---

[9] We'll give the implementation code later when discussing the specific layers.

■ If we want to share parameters among networks, we can continue to initialize the other networks using *initializer* and *loader* after calling *Init* on one network. The next initialized networks can obtain the parameters in *loader* directly to share the parameters.

■ If we do not want to share parameters among networks, we can empty *loader* and then initialize the other networks after calling *Init* on one network.

After designing the interface for the initialization module, let's look at how to implement the initialization module.

## 6.2.1.2 MakeInitializer

*MakeInitializer* is the entry point for the entire initialization module. It's obvious from the previous usage that it actually utilizes two techniques provided in Chapter 2—adopting policy templates to tag initializers and using heterogeneous dictionaries to configure initializers for tags. For instance, the following code:

```
1   MakeInitializer<float,
2                   PInitializerIs<struct Gauss1>>()
3     .SetFiller<Gauss1>(GaussianFiller{ 0, 1.5 });
```

Line 2 sets policy, while line 3 essentially calls a heterogeneous dictionary to set up the initializer.
MetaNN introduces three policy object templates for the initialization module:

```
1   struct InitPolicy {
2       using MajorClass = InitPolicy;
3
4       struct OverallTypeCate;
5       struct WeightTypeCate;
6       struct BiasTypeCate;
7
8       using Overall = void;
9       using Weight = void;
10      using Bias = void;
11
12      // ...
13  };
14
15  TypePolicyTemplate(PInitializerIs, InitPolicy, Overall);
16  TypePolicyTemplate(PWeightInitializerIs, InitPolicy, Weight);
17  TypePolicyTemplate(PBiasInitializerIs, InitPolicy, Bias);
```

*Overall*, *Weight*, and *Bias* represent the tags of the default initializer, the weight initializer, and the bias initializer,[10] respectively. The default values of the three policies are void, representing an invalid initializer tag. We can set a valid tag by introducing a policy object.

---

[10] The weight and bias initializers are used for the initialization of parameters in the *WeightLayer* and *BiasLayer* and the implementation of these two layers is shown later.

*PInitializerIs* serves to set the default initializer; *PWeightInitializerIs* and *PbiasInitializerIs* are employed to configure the weight and bias initializers, respectively. For initialization, the weight layer searches for tags set by *PWeightInitializerIs*—if void, it obtains the tags set by *PInitializerIs*. The bias initializer is similar.

Based on the introduction of the above policy object template, *MakeInitializer* is implemented as follows:

```
1   template <typename TElem, typename...TPolicies>
2   auto MakeInitializer()
3   {
4       using npType = FillerTags2NamedParams<TPolicies...>;
5       using FilDictType = RemConstRef<decltype(npType::Create())>;
6       return ParamInitializer<TElem,
7                               PolicyContainer<TPolicies...>,
8                               FilDictType>
9                                   (npType::Create());
10  }
```

It calls *FillerTags2NamedParams* to obtain the tag name of the incoming policy object and execute dereplication,[11] and use the dereplicated tag to construct objects of type *VarTypeDict* (i.e., objects of a heterogeneous dictionary). The object of type *ParamInitializer* is then constructed.

### 6.2.1.3 Class Template ParamInitializer

The class template *ParamInitializer* contains the main logic of the initialization module. Its main definitions are as follows:

```
1   template <typename TElem, typename TPolicyCont, typename TFillers>
2   class ParamInitializer
3   {
4   public:
5       using PolicyCont = TPolicyCont;
6
7       ParamInitializer(TFillers&& filler)
8           : m_filler(std::move(filler)) {}
9
10      // Configuration and acquisition interfaces of the initializer
11      template <typename TTag, typename TVal>
12      auto SetFiller(TVal&& val) && ;
13
14      template <typename TTag>
```

---

[11] The logic of the metafunction *FillerTags2NamedParams* is left to readers to analyze.

```
15        auto& GetFiller();
16
17        // Configuration and acquisition interfaces of the parameter matrix
18        template <typename TElem2, typename TDevice2>
19        void SetMatrix(const std::string& name,
20                       const Matrix<TElem2, TDevice2>& param);
21
22        template <typename TElem2, typename TDevice2>
23        void GetMatrix(const std::string& name,
24                       Matrix<TElem2, TDevice2>& res) const;
25
26        bool IsMatrixExist(const std::string& name) const;
27
28    private:
29        TFillers m_filler;
30        std::map<std::string, Matrix<TElem, DeviceTags::CPU>> m_params;
31    };
```

It contains two data members, *m_filler* and *m_params*. *m_filler* is actually an instance of a heterogeneous dictionary that holds the object of the initializer. *ParamInitializer* provides two interfaces *SetFiller* and *GetFiller* to configure and acquire the initializer in it.

*m_params* contains the matrix parameters preserved in the initializer. *ParamInitializer* provides *SetMatrix* and *GetMatrix* to configure and acquire the appropriate parameter matrix. The function *MatrixExist* is offered meanwhile, which is given the name of the argument matrix to determine its existence.

Note that when using *SetMatrix* and *GetMatrix* to configure and acquire matrix parameters, the computing unit and the computing device of the matrix can be different from those in *m_params*. *ParamInitializer* calls a function *DataCopy* inside its member functions to convert among different matrix types. In addition to supporting type conversion of different computing units and devices, the function *DataCopy* itself has the semantics of deep replication: in MetaNN, if the operations of copy and assignment of the matrix are executed directly, the new matrix is constructed to share storage space with the source matrix. On the contrary, if the function *DataCopy* is used, the new matrix constructed corresponds to a different storage space from the source matrix. It is because of the introduction of this function that there will be no data sharing among the parameters obtained from *ParamInitializer* (this is a feature we hope *ParamInitializer* to support).

### 6.2.1.4 *Class Template* Initializer

*Initializers* are represented as class templates in MetaNN. Currently, MetaNN implements the class templates for the following initializers:

■ *ConstantFiller* initializes the contents of the matrix to a constant;
■ *GaussianFiller* uses normal distribution to initialize matrix parameters;

- *UniformFiller* uses uniform distribution to initialize matrix parameters;
- *VarScaleFiller* implements *variance_scaling_filler* in Tensorflow and thus constructs *XavierFiller* and *MSRAFiller*.

The specific implementation of initializers is not the focus of this chapter's discussion. Due to the limited space available, they will not be elaborated here. The code is left to interested readers to refer to.

## 6.2.2 *Class Template* DynamicData

The class template *DynamicData* is a encapsulation of data that masks most information contained in a specific data type and exposes only the most basic properties of that data type, including the computing unit, supported devices, and category tags. It is declared as follows:

```
1  template <typename TElem, typename TDevice, typename TDataCate>
2  class DynamicData;
```

It is a pointer-like construct, which is implemented internally using the smart pointer *shared_ptr* of C++. The goal of this section is to implement *DynamicData*. Next, let's look at how MetaNN is building the class template *DynamicData* by hiding specific data types step by step.

### 6.2.2.1 *Base Class Template* DynamicCategory

The more intuitive way to mask specific data types is to introduce an inheritance hierarchy: if we can introduce a base class and derive based on it, then we can use the pointers of the base class to access the methods of derived classes. In the discussion of the previous chapters, we can realize that the data structures involved in MetaNN are not derived from a certain base class, which is designed to reduce unnecessary restrictions. Nonetheless, it does not hinder us from introducing a base class to construct derived structures when necessary.

The base class we're introducing is still essentially a class template: *DynamicCategory*, declared as follows:

```
1  template <typename TElem, typename TDevice, typename TDataCate>
2  class DynamicCategory;
```

The declaration is quite similar to *DynamicData* and also includes the computing units, supported devices, and category tags as template parameters. Distinct data categories support various sets of operational interfaces, so we should specialize according to different category tags:

```
1  template <typename TElem, typename TDevice>
2  class DynamicCategory<TElem, TDevice, CategoryTags::Matrix>
3  {
4  public:
5      using ElementType = TElem;
6      using DeviceType = TDevice;
```

```
7       using EvalType = PrincipalDataType<CategoryTags::Matrix,
8                                          ElementType,
9                                          DeviceType>;
10
11  public:
12      template <typename TBase>
13      DynamicCategory(const TBase& base)
14          : m_rowNum(base.RowNum())
15          , m_colNum(base.ColNum()) {}
16
17      virtual ~DynamicCategory() = default;
18
19      size_t RowNum() const { return m_rowNum; }
20      size_t ColNum() const { return m_colNum; }
21
22      // Interfaces related to evaluation
23      // ...
24
25  private:
26      size_t m_rowNum;
27      size_t m_colNum;
28  };
29
30  template <typename TElem, typename TDevice>
31  class DynamicCategory<TElem, TDevice, CategoryTags::BatchMatrix>
32  {
33      ...
34  };
```

Currently, *DynamicCategory* introduces specialization only for matrices and lists of matrices, but it doesn't obstruct us from introducing the corresponding specialization for scalars and lists of scalars—*DynamicCategory* supports extensions. If needed, we can introduce corresponding specializations for other category tags in the type system. Here we only list the definition specific for the specialization of *CategoryTags::Matrix*. Let's check what's in it.

Functions such as *RowNum* and *ColNum* are introduced in the specialization of matrices, as well as the interfaces related to evaluation—they are all functions the matrix category should support. However, the interfaces related to evaluation are declared as virtual functions and the standard approach of object-oriented design is applied here: virtual functions are introduced as the interfaces in the base class to supply the implementation of the function in the derived class.

Meanwhile, the class *DynamicCategory* declares its destructor as a virtual function because we will utilize references or pointers from this base class to access objects of the derived class at a later stage. At this point, we should declare the destructor of the base class as a virtual function to guarantee the correctness of the logic for destructors.

## 6.2.2.2 *Derived Class Template* DynamicWrapper

With the base class, the next step is to construct the derived class. The data classes and operation templates in MetaNN do not have a common base class. In order to associate them with the
base class, we ought to introduce an additional class template as an intermediate layer, which is
*DynamicWrapper*.

   *DynamicWrapper* is defined as follows:

```
1   template <typename TBaseData>
2   class DynamicWrapper
3       : public DynamicCategory<typename TBaseData::ElementType,
4                                typename TBaseData::DeviceType,
5                                DataCategory<TBaseData>>
6   {
7       using TBase = DynamicCategory<typename TBaseData::ElementType,
8                                    typename TBaseData::DeviceType,
9                                    DataCategory<TBaseData>>;
10
11  public:
12      DynamicWrapper(TBaseData data)
13          : TBase(data)
14          , m_baseData(std::move(data)) {}
15
16      // ...
17  private:
18      TBaseData m_baseData;
19  };
```

It receives specific data types or types of operation templates as template arguments. Based
on the information, it can derive the computing units, computing devices, and category tags
supported by the type and select the appropriate base class *DynamicCategory* for derivation
(lines 3–5).

   *DynamicWrapper* must be constructed with objects of type *TBaseData*—that is, objects of
the data type specified by its template parameters. *DynamicWrapper* itself completes the process of "encapsulating" the object, which is to convert it into a dynamic data type. Meanwhile,
*DynamicWrapper* includes a data member *m_baseData* to preserve the incoming object instances
so as to support subsequent evaluations.

   *DynamicCategory* already provides interfaces pertinent to category tags (for instance,
matrix classes offer functions such as *RowNum*), so *DynamicWrapper* no longer needs to
implement these interfaces—it only ought to implement evaluation-related interfaces. We'll
discuss evaluation in Chapter 8 and the implementations of relevant interfaces will be elaborated there.

   After implementing this class template, we can access objects of type *DynamicWrapper*
with a pointer of type *DynamicCategory*—that's the purpose of object-oriented programming.

The primary usage of data is to serve as operands to operations. However, it is not a friendly method to operate directly with the pointer of the base class because operations in MetaNN do not receive pointers as arguments. For instance, we can't add the data of type *shared_ptr<DynamicCategory>* to the *Matrix* objects. In the meantime, we are reluctant to adjust the operations that have been implemented and introduce new interfaces receiving pointers as operands due to the introduction of pointers. We should bring in another layer of encapsulation to mask this inconsistency of operation parameters that result from pointers. The layer of encapsulation is *DynamicData*.

## 6.2.2.3 *Encapsulating Behaviors of Pointers with* DynamicData

Similar to *DynamicCategory*, *DynamicData* specializes different data categories accordingly. Here's its specialization for matrices:

```
1   template <typename TElem, typename TDevice>
2   class DynamicData<TElem, TDevice, CategoryTags::Matrix>
3   {
4       using BaseData = DynamicCategory<TElem, TDevice,
5                                        CategoryTags::Matrix>;
6   public:
7       using ElementType = TElem;
8       using DeviceType = TDevice;
9
10      DynamicData() = default;
11
12      template <typename TOriData>
13      DynamicData(std::shared_ptr<DynamicWrapper<TOriData>> data)
14      {
15          m_baseData = std::move(data);
16      }
17
18      size_t RowNum() const { return m_baseData->RowNum(); }
19      size_t ColNum() const { return m_baseData->ColNum(); }
20
21      // Interfaces related to evaluation
22      // ...
23  private:
24      std::shared_ptr<BaseData> m_baseData;
25  };
```

The implementation of this class is intuitive: it provides all the interfaces that the matrix category should provide and keeps the pointer object *std::shared_ptr<BaseData>* internally at the same time. The operations related to obtaining the number of rows and columns of the matrix and evaluation are forwarded to the object.

## 6.2.2.4 Category Tags

*DynamicData* is also a form of data in MetaNN, so we should introduce the appropriate category tag for it. For example:

```
1  template <typename TElem, typename TDevice>
2  constexpr bool IsMatrix<DynamicData<TElem, TDevice,
3                                  CategoryTags::Matrix>> = true;
```

They are trivial and we can determine the category of *DynamicData* based on the third template parameter.

## 6.2.2.5 Auxiliary Functions and Auxiliary Meta Functions

In addition to the basic constructs discussed earlier, MetaNN also introduces some external functions and metafunctions to assist in the construction of dynamic type objects.

    *DynamicData* is a data structure with relatively special status—serves to encapsulate diverse data types. So, here we introduce an additional tag for it to detect whether a data type is an instance of the class template *DynamicData*:

```
1   template <typename TData>
2   constexpr bool IsDynamic = false;
3
4   template <typename E, typename D, typename C>
5   constexpr bool IsDynamic<DynamicData<E, D, C>> = true;
6
7   template <typename E, typename D, typename C>
8   constexpr bool IsDynamic<DynamicData<E, D, C>&> = true;
9
10  template <typename E, typename D, typename C>
11  constexpr bool IsDynamic<DynamicData<E, D, C>&&> = true;
12
13  template <typename E, typename D, typename C>
14  constexpr bool IsDynamic<const DynamicData<E, D, C>&> = true;
15
16  template <typename E, typename D, typename C>
17  constexpr bool IsDynamic<const DynamicData<E, D, C>&&> = true;
```

On this basis, MetaNN supplies the function *MakeDynamic* to easily convert a data type to the corresponding dynamic type:

```
1   template <typename TData>
2   auto MakeDynamic(TData&& data)
3   {
```

```
4         if constexpr (IsDynamic<TData>)
5         {
6             return std::forward<TData>(data);
7         }
8         else
9         {
10            using rawData = RemConstRef<TData>;
11            using TDeriveData = DynamicWrapper<rawData>;
12            auto baseData = std::make_shared<TDeriveData>
13                            (std::forward<TData>(data));
14            return DynamicData<typename rawData::ElementType,
15                        typename rawData::DeviceType,
16                        DataCategory<rawData>>(std::move(baseData));
17        }
18    }
```

If the type of the input parameter is already an instance of *DynamicData*, *MakeDynamic* returns the input object itself, or otherwise it will derive and return the corresponding *DynamicData* type based on its computing unit, supported devices, and category tag.

### 6.2.2.6 DynamicData *and Dynamic Type System*

When discussing type systems in Chapter 4, we mentioned that the main type system employed in MetaNN is a type system based on category tags—a static type system that can be used for compile-time computing. *DynamicData* dealt with in this section can be regarded as reorganizing the types in the tagging system through inheritance in object-oriented programming, thus constructing a dynamic type system.

The type system based on *DynamicData* is dynamic because *DynamicData* itself masks most information about a specific data type—we cannot execute operations based on the hidden information at compile time. These hidden pieces of information, or the specific behaviors of the type encapsulated by *DynamicData*, are embodied dynamically when called at runtime.

A dynamic type system and a static type system have their pros and cons, respectively. A dynamic type system can mask the differences of specific types and represent various specific data types through an abstract data type, thus simplifying the writing of code; a static type system does not hide specific type information, so that optimization can be executed at compile time according to the information. When writing code, we ought to select the appropriate type system in order to take full advantage of both.

A dynamic type system and a static type system can also be converted to each other. In this section, *DynamicData* to encapsulate specific data types is introduced, which is essentially the process of transforming a static type system into a dynamic type system. We then bring in the corresponding category tags for *DynamicData*, which is essentially the process of incorporating the abstract data types of dynamic type systems into static type systems. The two types of systems work together and can produce more subtle changes to cope with complex scenarios.

### 6.2.3 *Common Policy Objects for Layers*

As mentioned earlier, MetaNN uses policy objects to control specific behaviors of layers. Some policy objects that control behaviors are unique to a particular layer and some are used by many layers. This section discusses the main template parameters introduced by MetaNN, which are typically adopted by numerous layers. The method of parameter definitions discussed in this section is rooted in policy templates discussed in Chapter 2.

#### 6.2.3.1 *Parameters Relevant to Update and Backward Propagation*

Parameters associated with update and backward propagation are defined in the structure *FeedbackPolicy*:

```
1   struct FeedbackPolicy
2   {
3       using MajorClass = FeedbackPolicy;
4
5       struct IsUpdateValueCate;
6       struct IsFeedbackOutputValueCate;
7
8       static constexpr bool IsUpdate = false;
9       static constexpr bool IsFeedbackOutput = false;
10  };
11  ValuePolicyObj(PUpdate, FeedbackPolicy, IsUpdate, true);
12  ValuePolicyObj(PNoUpdate, FeedbackPolicy, IsUpdate, false);
13  ValuePolicyObj(PFeedbackOutput, FeedbackPolicy,
14                 IsFeedbackOutput, true);
15  ValuePolicyObj(PFeedbackNoOutput, FeedbackPolicy,
16                 IsFeedbackOutput, false);
```

It contains two policies: *IsUpdate* indicates whether to update the parameters of a layer and *IsFeedbackOutput* represents whether the layer is required to calculate the output gradient. Definitions such as *PUpdate* denote specific policy objects.

It should be noted that, although *IsFeedbackOutput* here is introduced to configure whether the layer ought to produce an output gradient, the information usually does not need setting explicitly According to the previous discussing, it is pertinent to the value of *IsUpdate* in its predecessor layer. We'll discuss in the next chapter how to infer and modify the parameter *FeedbackIsOutput* of the current layer with the information from the predecessor layer.

#### 6.2.3.2 *Parameters Relevant to Input*

The input-related parameters received by layers are defined in *InputPolicy*:

```
1   struct InputPolicy
2   {
3       using MajorClass = InputPolicy;
```

```
4
5        struct BatchModeValueCate;
6        static constexpr bool BatchMode = false;
7   };
8   ValuePolicyObj(PBatchMode, InputPolicy, BatchMode, true);
9   ValuePolicyObj(PNoBatchMode, InputPolicy, BatchMode, false);
```

*BatchMode* indicates whether the layer receives input in the form of a list. MetaNN's layers support batch computing with input in the form of lists.

### 6.2.3.3 Parameters Relevant to Operations

A layer is an encapsulation of operations and the parameters associated with operations are located in *OperandPolicy*:

```
1   struct OperandPolicy
2   {
3       using MajorClass = OperandPolicy;
4
5       struct DeviceTypeCate : public MetaNN::DeviceTags {};
6       using Device = DeviceTypeCate::CPU;
7
8       struct ElementTypeCate;
9       using Element = float;
10  };
11  TypePolicyObj(PCPUDevice, OperandPolicy, Device, CPU);
12  TypePolicyTemplate(PElementTypeIs, OperandPolicy, Element);
```

Currently, MetaNN only supports CPU as the computing device and the discussion in this book is restricted to floating point numbers of type *float* as the computing unit. So, the definition of *OperandPolicy* is trivial. However, we can easily extend it to support other types of computing units (such as *double*) or other computing devices (such as GPU).

## 6.2.4 Metafunction InjectPolicy

According to the discussion in Chapter 2, in order to use policy templates, we should place policy objects into *PolicyContainer* and use the metafunction *PolicySelect* to acquire a specific value of policy. For the sake of employing the above mechanism in a layer, we require the layer to have the following form of declaration:

```
1   template <typename TPolicyContainer>
2   class XXLayer;
```

*TPolicyContainers* is a type in the form such as *PolicyContainer<X1,X2...>*. Based on this convention, we can pass in template arguments for the layer in the following way:

```
1   using SpecLayer = XXLayer<PolicyContainer<PUpdate, ...>>;
```

To simplify the writing of code, MetaNN introduce the metafunction *InjectPolicy*:

```
1   template<template <typename TPolicyCont> class T, typename...TPolicies>
2   using InjectPolicy = T<PolicyContainer<TPolicies...>>;
```

In this way, we can simplify the declaration of *XXLayer* with the following statement:

```
1   using SpecLayer = InjectPolicy<XXLayer, PUpdate, ...>;
```

## 6.2.5 Universal I/O Structure

Layers will utilize heterogeneous dictionaries discussed in Chapter 2 as an input/output container for forward and backward propagation. In order to use a heterogeneous dictionary, we should also bring in some definitions to represent the specific container and the names of elements. Various layers have similar I/O structures and we extract the I/O structures that we might use frequently to form some common structure definitions:

```
1   struct LayerIO : public NamedParams<LayerIO> {};
2
3   struct CostLayerIn : public NamedParams<CostLayerIn,
4                                   struct CostLayerLabel> {};
```

Many layers are single-input or single-output. For such layers, *LayerIO* can be used as its input or output container. The container contains only one element and *LayerIO* will also serve as the index for that element.

Note that the definition in line 1 contains two *LayerIO*s, the first of which is the container name and the second is the index keyword. They have distinct meanings and purposes but can be represented by the same name.

The last layer of the training network often serves to calculate the value of the loss function, which usually adopts the output of its predecessor layer and the labeled data tagged as input to determine the similarity between the two. Therefore, a generic I/O structure *CostLayerIn* is defined here as an input container for the loss function layer, which contains two elements, *CostLayerIn* for the output of the predecessor layer and *CostLayerLabel* for label information.

## 6.2.6 Universal Operation Functions

As mentioned earlier, all layers should provide interfaces *FeedForward* and *FeedBackward* for forward and backward propagation. But not all layers need to support functions such as parameter loading—only layers that contain parameter matrices need to provide such interfaces. The design avoids introducing various unnecessary interface functions into the layer but might contributes to the complexity of usage for users—they may call the interface *Init* to a layer that does not support parameter initialization, resulting in a compilation error.

To solve this problem, MetaNN introduces a series of common operation functions:

```
1    // Parameter initialization and loading
2    template <typename TLayer, typename TInitializer, typename TBuffer,
3             typename TInitPolicies = typename TInitializer::PolicyCont>
4    void LayerInit(TLayer& layer, TInitializer& initializer,
5                   TBuffer& loadBuffer, std::ostream* log = nullptr);
6
7    // Collecting parameter gradients
8    template <typename TLayer, typename TGradCollector>
9    void LayerGradCollect(TLayer& layer, TGradCollector& gc);
10
11   // Preserving the parameter matrix
12   template <typename TLayer, typename TSave>
13   void LayerSaveWeights(const TLayer& layer, TSave& saver);
14
15   // Neutral detection
16   template <typename TLayer>
17   void LayerNeutralInvariant(TLayer& layer);
18
19   // Forward propagation
20   template <typename TLayer, typename TIn>
21   auto LayerFeedForward(TLayer& layer, TIn&& p_in);
22
23   // Backward propagation
24   template <typename TLayer, typename TGrad>
25   auto LayerFeedBackward(TLayer& layer, TGrad&& p_grad);
```

The first parameters for these functions are layer objects for users to call the specific interfaces of the layer. For instance, assuming that *A* is a layer object, *LayerInit (A, …)* can serve to invoke the initialization operation.

Forward and backward propagation should be supported by each layer, so *LayerFeedForward* and *LayerFeedBackward* will call the corresponding functions of the layer object directly to implement. Nonetheless, other interfaces don't need to be supported by each layer. If the input layer object does not support an operation, calling the corresponding universal interface will not produce any side effect.

Let's take *LayerNeutralInvariant* as an example to consider how common interfaces are implemented:

```
1    template <typename L>
2    std::true_type NeutralInvariantTest(decltype(&L::NeutralInvariant));
3
4    template <typename L>
5    std::false_type NeutralInvariantTest(...);
```

```
6
7   template <typename TLayer>
8   void LayerNeutralInvariant(TLayer& layer)
9   {
10    if constexpr (decltype(NeutralInvariantTest<TLayer>(nullptr))::value)
11      layer.NeutralInvariant();
12  }
```

Chapter 4 discusses the implementation of the metafunction *IsIterator*. A similar implementation is adopted here: *NeutralInvariantTest* has two overloaded versions, one of which receives *decltype (&L::NeutralInvariant)* as an argument and returns *std::true_type*. If the layer's implementation of its class template contains the member function *NeutralInvariant*, the compiler will match this version; otherwise the compile will match the version with ... as the argument and infer its return value type as *std:false_type*.

The call of *decltype...* in *LayerNeutralInvariant* triggers the compiler to select one of the two overloaded versions and obtains the constant *value* in the return type. The evaluation result in *if constexpr* is *true* only when the first overloaded version is matched, which causes the system to execute *layer. NeutralInvariant()*, or otherwise *LayerNeutralInvariant* will do nothing and return directly.

Until now, we have discussed most auxiliary logic required to construct layers. There is also some auxiliary logic closely relevant to the implementation of layers. We'll explain it later when we discuss specific implementations of layers.

## 6.3 Specific Implementations of Layers

This section will clarify how to construct a class template that represents a base layer according to the auxiliary logic mentioned previously. The way layers utilize the logic varies depending on their characteristics. We'll start with a relatively simple layer.

### 6.3.1 AddLayer

*AddLayer* is a relatively simple layer implemented by MetaNN that receives two matrices of two matrix lists, which add them and return the result of addition.

*AddLayer* is a two-input and one-output layer, so we should first define its input container and utilize *LayerIO* as its output container directly:

```
1   using AddLayerInput = VarTypeDict<struct AddLayerIn1,
2                                     struct AddLayerIn2>;
```

On this basis, *AddLayer*'s class template is defined as follows:

```
1   template <typename TPolicies>
2   class AddLayer
3   {
4       static_assert(IsPolicyContainer<TPolicies>,
```

```
5                          "TPolicies is not a policy container.");
6         using CurLayerPolicy = PlainPolicy<TPolicies>;
7
8    public:
9         static constexpr bool IsFeedbackOutput
10            = PolicySelect<FeedbackPolicy,
11                           CurLayerPolicy>::IsFeedbackOutput;
12        static constexpr bool IsUpdate = false;
13        using InputType = AddLayerInput;
14        using OutputType = LayerIO;
15
16   public:
17        template <typename TIn>
18        auto FeedForward(const TIn& p_in)
19        {
20            const auto& val1 = p_in.template Get<AddLayerIn1>();
21            const auto& val2 = p_in.template Get<AddLayerIn2>();
22
23            using rawType1 = std::decay_t<decltype(val1)>;
24            using rawType2 = std::decay_t<decltype(val2)>;
25
26            static_assert(!std::is_same<rawType1, NullParameter>::value,
27                          "parameter1 is invalid");
28            static_assert(!std::is_same<rawType2, NullParameter>::value,
29                          "parameter2 is invalid");
30
31            return OutputType::Create()
32                .template Set<LayerIO>(val1 + val2);
33        }
34
35        template <typename TGrad>
36        auto FeedBackward(TGrad&& p_grad)
37        {
38            if constexpr (IsFeedbackOutput)
39            {
40                auto res = p_grad.template Get<LayerIO>();
41                return AddLayerInput::Create()
42                    .template Set<AddLayerIn1>(res)
43                    .template Set<AddLayerIn2>(res);
44            }
45            else
46            {
```

```
47              return AddLayerInput::Create();
48          }
49      }
50  };
```

It receives *TPolicies* as its template parameters and requires *TPolicies* to be *PolicyContainer*[12] internally (lines 4 and 5). On this basis, it filters the parameters using *PlainPolicy* and acquires the list of trivial parameters according to the current layer *CurLayerPolicy*.

We haven't discussed *PlainPolicy* before, which is a metafunction and introduced mainly pertinent to composite layers. We'll cover this metafunction in Chapter 7. For now, readers only need to understand that *PlainPolicy*'s output is also a *PolicyContainer* and that its input and output are almost identical for the base layer.

Once we've got *CurLayerPolicy*, we can get some policy information from it next. For instance, the value of *IsFeedbackOutput* is obtained in lines 9–11, indicating whether the layer needs to output a gradient. *AddLayer* only needs this piece of information—it doesn't contain a parameter matrix internally. So, the value *IsUpdate* is introduced here and set as *false*, denoting that there is no requirement of parameter updates for the layer.

It's significant to note that although *AddLayer* need no updates, we still require it to offer the value of *IsUpdate*. In fact, this value, along with *IsFeedbackOutput*, is the information that each layer should provide. In Chapter 7, we ought to adjust the value *IsFeedbackOutput* of the layer. In order to adjust it, we have to know the values *IsUpdate* and *IsFeedbackOutput* in other layers of the network.

In addition to these two points, a layer should also provide *InputType* and *OutputType* as the type of input and output containers, which will be also adopted in composite layers. From the above definitions, it is effortless to realize that *AddLayer*'s input container is *AddLayerInput* and the output container is *LayerIO*.

*AddLayer::FeedForward* serves for forward propagation and its implementation logic is quite simple—obtaining two input parameters based on the key, determining that the input parameters are not empty (lines 23–29), then adding the two input parameters and preserving the result in the output container to return.

*AddLayer::FeedBackward* receives input gradients and calculates the output gradient corresponding to *AddLayerIn1* and *AddLayerIn2*. The function uses *constexpr if* internally to implement the corresponding logic, which is designed to introduce different logic based on the value of *IsFeedbackOutput*. If *IsFeedbackOutput* is *true*, then the output gradient needs calculating and the first branch will be compiled. For *AddLayer*, it means that the input gradient is copied to *AddLayerIn1* and *AddLayerIn2*, respectively. In turn, if *IsFeedbackOutput* is *false*, it denotes there is no need to calculate the output gradient and we simply construct an empty container of type *AddLayerInput* and return it.

The previously discussed is the main implementation code for *AddLayer*, which does not maintain a parameter matrix internally and does not need to maintain intermediate information to assist in its backward propagation. Therefore, there is no need to introduce interfaces such as *Init* for it. From this point of view, it is a relatively simple layer.

---

[12] Here the metafunction *IsPolicyContainer* is adopted to determine, of which the definition is in Chapter 2.

## 6.3.2 ElementMulLayer

*ElementMulLayer* receives two matrices (or lists of matrices) to multiply the corresponding elements therein, generate a new matrix (or list of matrices) and output.

*ElementMulLayer* is quite similar to *AddLayer*, except that the former is element multiplication and the latter is element addition. Because *ElementMulLayer* is to multiply elements, the input of forward propagation is required when the output gradient is calculated. Specifically, if the input parameters of forward propagation are $A$ and $B$ respectively, the input gradient of backward propagation is $G$, then the output gradient corresponding to the first parameter is $G°B$ and the output gradient corresponding to the second parameter is $G°A$ (° means that the corresponding multiplications of elements). From this analysis, it is natural to be aware that we should record the input information during forward propagation to calculate gradient for backward propagation.

### 6.3.2.1 Recording Intermediate Results

In order to calculate the output gradient, we need to preserve the input of forward propagation as an intermediate result in the layer. Nonetheless, note that the intermediate information is only stored meaningfully when the output gradient needs to be calculated. The main implementation of *ElementMulLayer* is as follows (some similar logic discussed in *AddLayer* is omitted here):

```
1    using ElementMulLayerInput =
2    VarTypeDict<struct ElementMulLayerIn1,
3              struct ElementMulLayerIn2>;
4
5    template <typename TPolicies>
6    class ElementMulLayer
7    {
8        using CurLayerPolicy = PlainPolicy<TPolicies>;
9    public:
10       static constexpr bool IsFeedbackOutput = ...
11       static constexpr bool IsUpdate = false;
12       using InputType = ElementMulLayerInput;
13       using OutputType = LayerIO;
14
15   public:
16       template <typename TIn>
17       auto FeedForward(const TIn& p_in);
18
19       template <typename TGrad>
20       auto FeedBackward(const TGrad& p_grad);
21
22       void NeutralInvariant();
23
24   private:
```

```
25        using BatchMode
26            = PolicySelect<InputPolicy, CurLayerPolicy>::BatchMode;
27
28        using ElemType
29            = typename PolicySelect<OperandPolicy,
30                                    CurLayerPolicy>::Element;
31
32        using DeviceType
33            = typename PolicySelect<OperandPolicy,
34                                    CurLayerPolicy>::Device;
35
36        using DataType
37            = LayerInternalBuf<IsFeedbackOutput,
38                               BatchMode, ElemType, DeviceType,
39                               CategoryTags::Matrix,
40                               CategoryTags::BatchMatrix>;
41        DataType m_data1;
42        DataType m_data2;
43  };
```

Similar to *AddLayer*, we first define the container *ElementMulLayerInput*, which acts as an input container for *ElementMulLayer*.

Inside *ElementMulLayer*, we acquire *ElementType*, *DeviceType*, and *BatchMode*, representing the compute units, device units, and whether the arguments are matrices or lists of matrices, respectively. Using the information, we call *LayerInternalBuf* to construct the type *DataType* for storing intermediate results:

If we don't need to output gradient information (i.e., *IsFeedbackOutput* is *false*), then *LayerInternalBuf* will return the type *NullParameter*—it just acts as a placeholder and doesn't actually participate in the calculation.

Conversely, if we need to output the gradient, *LayerInternalBuf* will construct a data type *std:: stack<DynamicData<...>>*. Whether matrices or lists of matrices are saved in *std::stack* is determined by the value of *BatchMode*.

*ElementMulLayer* adopts *DataType* to declare two variables: *m_data1* and *m_data2*, which will serve to store intermediate results.

### 6.3.2.2 Forward and Backward Propagation

After the introduction of the above data members, the next step is to employ them in forward and backward propagation. Let's first consider the implementation of forward propagation:

```
1   template <typename TIn>
2   auto FeedForward(const TIn& p_in)
3   {
4       const auto& val1 = p_in.template Get<ElementMulLayerIn1>();
```

```
5          const auto& val2 = p_in.template Get<ElementMulLayerIn2>();
6
7          // ... Omitting some input checks
8
9          if constexpr (IsFeedbackOutput)
10         {
11             m_data1.push(MakeDynamic(val1));
12             m_data2.push(MakeDynamic(val2));
13         }
14         return LayerIO::Create().template Set<LayerIO>(val1 * val2);
15  }
```

Similar to *AddLayer*, the two input parameters in the container are obtained first. The input parameters are then saved in *m_data1* and *m_data2* if the gradient ought to be output in backward propagation. Eventually, *FeedForward* constructs a container of type *LayerIO* and preserves the result of multiplication of the two input parameters in that container to return.

The implementation of backward propagation is not laborious:

```
1   template <typename TGrad>
2   auto FeedBackward(const TGrad& p_grad)
3   {
4       if constexpr (IsFeedbackOutput)
5       {
6           if ((m_data1.empty()) || (m_data2.empty()))
7           {
8               throw std::runtime_error("...");
9           }
10
11          auto top1 = m_data1.top();
12          auto top2 = m_data2.top();
13          m_data1.pop();
14          m_data2.pop();
15
16          auto grad_eval = p_grad.template Get<LayerIO>();
17
18          return ElementMulLayerInput::Create()
19              .template Set<ElementMulLayerIn1>(grad_eval * top2)
20              .template Set<ElementMulLayerIn2>(grad_eval * top1);
21      }
22      else
23      {
24          return ElementMulLayerInput::Create();
25      }
26  }
```

If the gradient is not required transferring outwards, it is sufficient to return the empty container of *ElementMulLayerInput* directly, or otherwise it calculates the output gradient using the intermediate result previously saved and places it in the container *ElementMulLayerInput*.

### 6.3.2.3 Neutral Detection

Since variables are introduced to record intermediate results, we should bring the logic of neutral detection into implementations of layers, which guarantees that layers are still neutral after a round of training—it ensures correctness of the training process to some extent:

```
1   void NeutralInvariant()
2   {
3       if constexpr(IsFeedbackOutput)
4       {
5           if ((!m_data1.empty()) || (!m_data2.empty()))
6           {
7               throw std::runtime_error("NeutralInvariant Fail!");
8           }
9       }
10  }
```

If *m_data1* and *m_data2* in the layer still contain elements when *NeutralInvariant* is called, the system will prompt an exception to indicate the failure of neutral detection.

That's the kernel logic of *ElementMulLayer*. As we can see, in order to support output gradients in backward propagation, we ought to introduce additional data fields in layers to record intermediate results. In fact, in addition to supporting the calculation of output gradients, there is another purpose for recording intermediate results—to calculate parameter gradients. Neither of the two layers mentioned earlier does contain a parameter matrix, so there is no issue of parameter updates. Next, we'll seek how the layers that contain parameter matrices calculate the parameter gradients through intermediate variables.

## 6.3.3 BiasLayer

*BiasLayer* and *AddLayer* have similar functions, which both implement addition of matrices or lists of matrices. Unlike *AddLayer*, however, *BiasLayer* maintains a matrix parameter internally. The layer receives only one matrix in forward propagation, add the received matrix to its internally maintained matrix and outputs the result.

### 6.3.3.1 Basic Framework

The basic framework for the class template *BiasLayer* is as follows:

```
1   template <typename TPolicies>
2   class BiasLayer
3   {
```

```
4          using CurLayerPolicy = PlainPolicy<TPolicies>;
5      public:
6          static constexpr bool IsFeedbackOutput = ...
7          static constexpr bool IsUpdate
8              = PolicySelect<FeedbackPolicy, CurLayerPolicy>::IsUpdate;
9          using InputType = LayerIO;
10         using OutputType = LayerIO;
11
12     private:
13         using ElementType = ...
14         using DeviceType = ...
15
16     public:
17         BiasLayer(std::string p_name, size_t p_vecLen);
18         BiasLayer(std::string p_name, size_t p_rowNum, size_t p_colNum);
19
20     public:
21         template <typename TInitializer, typename TBuffer,
22         typename TInitPolicies = typename TInitializer::PolicyCont>
23         void Init(TInitializer& initializer, TBuffer& loadBuffer,
24                   std::ostream* log = nullptr);
25
26         template <typename TSave>
27         void SaveWeights(TSave& saver);
28
29         template <typename TIn>
30         auto FeedForward(const TIn& p_in);
31
32         template <typename TGrad>
33         auto FeedBackward(const TGrad& p_grad);
34
35         template <typename TGradCollector>
36         void GradCollect(TGradCollector& col);
37
38         void NeutralInvariant() const;
39
40     private:
41         const std::string m_name;
42         size_t m_rowNum;
43         size_t m_colNum;
44
45         Matrix<ElementType, DeviceType> m_bias;
```

```
46
47        using DataType
48            = LayerInternalBuf<IsUpdate,
49                               BatchMode, ElemType, DeviceType,
50                               CategoryTags::Matrix,
51                               CategoryTags::BatchMatrix>;
52
53        DataType m_grad;
54    };
```

The parameter matrix that *BiasLayer* maintains internally is considered as part of parameters in the entire network. Therefore, the layer should supply features such as model loading, storage, and update. *BiasLayer* includes *Init*, *SaveWeights*, and other interfaces to provide operations relevant to parameters.

In addition to these interfaces, *BiasLayer* utilizes template parameters to infer the value of *IsUpdate* (lines 7 and 8), which is different from the two layers discussed earlier. Since it contains a parameter matrix, it needs the information to determine whether to update the parameters it maintains.

*BiasLayer* offers two constructors and the first arguments they receive are of type string, representing the name of the parameter matrix inside. In addition to the name of parameter matrices, *BiasLayer* also ought to receive dimensional information to spare space for parameter matrices.

*BiasLayer* can receive two forms of dimensional information (corresponding to two constructors). If only one value is entered, *BiasLayer* will construct a (row) vector; if two values are entered, *BiasLayer* will then construct a parameter matrix according to them. The constructed vector or matrix is preserved in the data field *m_bias*.

Similar to *ElementMulLayer*, *BiasLayer* employs *LayerInternalBuf* to determine the data type of intermediate variables. But unlike *ElementMulLayer*, *BiasLayer* uses *IsUpdate* instead of *IsFeedbackOutput* as the first argument for this metafunction. It is because we need to save the intermediate results only if parameters are required to be updated.

## 6.3.3.2 *Initialization and Loading of Parameters*

*BiasLayer* implements the initialization and loading of its internal parameter matrix through *Init*:

```
1    template <typename TInitializer, typename TBuffer,
2             typename TInitPolicies = typename TInitializer::PolicyCont>
3    void Init(TInitializer& initializer, TBuffer& loadBuffer,
4             std::ostream* log = nullptr)
5    {
6        if (auto cit = loadBuffer.find(m_name); cit != loadBuffer.end())
7        {
```

```
8          const Matrix<ElementType, DeviceType>& m = cit->second;
9          if ((m.RowNum() != m_rowNum) || (m.ColNum() != m_colNum))
10         {
11             throw std::runtime_error("...");
12         }
13         m_bias = m;
14         ... // Output log information
15         return;
16     }
17     else if (initializer.IsMatrixExist(m_name))
18     {
19       m_bias = Matrix<ElementType, DeviceType>(m_rowNum, m_colNum);
20       initializer.GetMatrix(m_name, m_bias);
21       loadBuffer[m_name] = m_bias;
22       ... // Output log information
23       return;
24     }
25     else
26     {
27       m_bias = Matrix<ElementType, DeviceType>(m_rowNum, m_colNum);
28       using CurInitializer
29           = PickInitializer<TInitPolicies, InitPolicy::BiasTypeCate>;
30       if constexpr (!std::is_same<CurInitializer, void>::value)
31       {
32           size_t fan_io = m_rowNum * m_colNum;
33           auto& cur_init
34               = initializer.template GetFiller<CurInitializer>();
35           cur_init.Fill(m_bias, fan_io, fan_io);
36           loadBuffer[m_name] = m_bias;
37           ... // Output log information
38       }
39       else
40       {
41           throw std::runtime_error("...");
42       }
43     }
44 }
```

Because initialization and loading are handled at the same time, the declaration of the interface *Init* is relatively complicated. It receives the following parameters:

- *TInitializer& initializer*: An instance of the initialization module.
- *TBuffer& loadBuffer*: To store the matrices initialized by other layers.

■ *std::ostream\* log*: A pointer to the output stream. If not empty, it will be used to output log information to indicate the source of the initialized data.
■ *TInitPolicies*: The Policy to decide which initializer in the initialization module to use for initialization. The parameter supports the initialization of composite layers. We'll discuss the purpose of this parameter in Chapter 7 with regard to composite layers.

The function tries to initialize/load the arguments internally by the following three ways in turn:

1. If there is a matrix in *loadBuffer* with the same name as the matrix to be initialized, then the matrix with the same name in *loadBuffer* will be copied to *m_bias* (lines 6–16), which allows the current layer to share matrix parameters with other layers in the network.
2. Otherwise, if initializer has a matrix that corresponds to the name of the current layer, the value of the matrix is loaded into *m_bias* (lines 17–24).
3. Otherwise, an initializer is selected to initialize (lines 26–43).

The logic of the first two parts is more intuitive and here we focus on the logic of the third part.

When selecting the initializer for initialization, the system first calls *PickInitializer* to obtain the tag for the initializer. The second parameter of this metafunction is *InitPolicy::BiasTypeCate*, which indicates that the initializer to be acquired serves to initialize the matrix associated with the bias layer. *PickInitializer* will first try to use *InitPolicy::BiasTypeCate* to acquire the initialization tag internally. If the tag has not been set (i.e., acquiring the type *void*), then it will attempt to use *InitPolicy::OverallTypeCate* to obtain the common initialization tag—that is, obtain the default initializer.

Once the corresponding initializer tag is obtained, if the tag is a valid initializer tag (i.e., not *void*), the system will call *GetFiller* to get the corresponding initializer based on this tag and call *Fill* to initialize the parameter matrix with the acquired initializer. The function *Fill* receives the parameter matrix to be initialized, as well as the number of input and output of the matrix elements as arguments.[13] The number of *BiasLayer*'s input elements is the same as the number of its output elements, which is equal to the number of elements in the parameter matrix. Therefore, *m_rowNum\*m_colNum* is passed directly to the function here.

If the tag for the initializer is invalid (i.e., *void*), the system will prompt an exception indicating that it cannot be initialized.

### 6.3.3.3 Obtaining Parameters

*BiasLayer* offers the interface *SaveWeights* for callers to obtain the parameter matrix stored in it:

```
template <typename TSave>
void SaveWeights(TSave& saver) const
{
    auto cit = saver.find(m_name);
    if ((cit != saver.end()) && (cit->second != m_bias))
    {
```

[13] Some initialization algorithms require these two values as parameters.

```
7           throw std::runtime_error(...);
8       }
9       saver[m_name] = m_bias;
10  }
```

It receives a *saver* as an argument and *saver* is also a dictionary that preserves the correspondence between names and matrices. It first searches the dictionary for a matrix with the same name. If there is, it may be due to multiple layers sharing common matrix parameters, or otherwise there is an error in the network. We use *cit->second!=m_bias* to determine whether the two matrices point to different memory, and if it returns *true*, the system will prompt the corresponding information of exception.

## 6.3.3.4 Forward and Backward Propagation

*BiasLayer*'s code for forward propagation is quite simple:

```
1   template <typename TIn>
2   auto FeedForward(const TIn& p_in)
3   {
4       const auto& val = p_in.template Get<LayerIO>();
5       return LayerIO::Create().template Set<LayerIO>(val + m_bias);
6   }
```

It acquires the parameter with the key as *LayerIO* directly from the input container, adds it to the *m_bias*, and writes the result to the output container to return.

For backward propagation, the appropriate logic should be introduced to record the gradient required to update parameters:

```
1   template <typename TGrad>
2   auto FeedBackward(const TGrad& p_grad)
3   {
4       if constexpr (IsUpdate)
5       {
6           const auto& tmp = p_grad.template Get<LayerIO>();
7           assert((tmp.RowNum() == m_bias.RowNum()) &&
8                   (tmp.ColNum() == m_bias.ColNum()));
9
10          m_grad.push(MakeDynamic(tmp));
11      }
12      if constexpr (IsFeedbackOutput)
13          return p_grad;
14      else
15          return LayerIO::Create();
16  }
```

If *IsUpdate* of the current class is *true*, the function will preserve the information of *p_grad* in the stack of *m_grad*.

If *IsFeedbackOutput* is *true*, then *BiasLayer* should construct the information for the output gradient. *BiasLayer*'s output gradient is the same as the input gradient, so it is sufficient to return the input parameters of *FeedBackward* directly. If *IsFeedbackOutput* is *false*, then it constructs an empty *LayerIO* container to return.

### 6.3.3.5 Collecting Parameter Gradients

*BiasLayer* maintains a parameter matrix internally, so it is necessary to provide interfaces to collect parameter gradients for subsequent parameter updates after the completion of backward propagation. *BiasLayer* supplies *GradCollect* to collect parameter gradients:

```
1   template <typename TGradCollector>
2   void GradCollect(TGradCollector& col)
3   {
4       if constexpr (IsUpdate)
5       {
6           MatrixGradCollect(m_bias, m_grad, col);
7       }
8   }
```

*GradCollect* receives parameters of type *TGradCollector*, which requires an interface *Collect* to collect parameter gradients. *GradCollect* determines whether the current layer involves parameter updates internally. If so, *MatrixGradCollect* is called to collect the corresponding gradients:

```
1   template <typename TWeight, typename TGrad, typename TGradCollector>
2   void MatrixGradCollect(const TWeight& weight,
3                          TGrad& grad,
4                          TGradCollector& col)
5   {
6       while (!grad.empty())
7       {
8           auto g = grad.top();
9           grad.pop();
10          col.Collect(weight, g);
11      }
12  }
```

### 6.3.3.6 Neutral Detection

Intermediate variables are introduced in *BiasLayer*, so interfaces for neutral detection are also required:

```
1    void NeutralInvariant() const {
2        if constexpr(IsUpdate)
3        {
4            if (!m_grad.empty())
5            {
6                throw std::runtime_error("NeutralInvariant Fail!");
7            }
8        }
9    }
```

The implementation of this interface is basically the same as the function with the same name in *ElementMulLayer*. The main difference is that neutral detection will be performed here only if *IsUpdate* is *true*.

## 6.4 Basic Layers achieved in MetaNN

From these examples, we have seen the design principles and construction techniques of basic layers in MetaNN. In theory, we can construct a variety of layers in the previously described ways. MetaNN adopts these techniques to achieve several basic layers. This chapter does not analyze their implementations one by one but only outlines their interfaces and functionality in this section—the specific code is left for readers to refer to.

### *AbsLayer*

- **Functional overview:** it receives a matrix or list of matrices and evaluates the absolute value of each element to return.
- **Input/output container:** *LayerIO*.

### *AddLayer*

- **Functional overview:** it receives two matrices or lists of matrices and returns the result of their addition.
- **Input container:** *AddLayerInput*.
- **Output container:** *LayerIO*.

### *BiasLayer*

- **Functional overview:** it receives a matrix or a vector, calculates the addition of the input and the matrix or vector in the layer, and returns the result. The layer contains a parameter matrix internally, which is initialized using the initializer specified by *InitPolicy::BiasTypeCate*, if needed.
- **Input/output container:** *LayerIO*.

## ElementMulLayer

- **Functional overview:** it receives two matrices or lists of matrices, returning the result of their multiplication.
- **Enter container:** *ElementMulLaterInput.*
- **Output container:** *LayerIO.*

## InterpolateLayer

- **Functional overview:** it receives three matrices or lists of matrices and executes the operation *Interpolate* on them.
- **Enter container:** *InterpolateLayerInput.*
- **Output container:** *LayerIO.*

## SigmoidLayer

- **Functional overview:** it receives a matrix or list of matrices and executes the operation *Sigmoid* on it.
- **Input/Output Container:** *LayerIO.*

## SoftmaxLayer

- **Feature overview:** it receives a matrix or list of matrices and execute the operation *VecSoftmax* on it.
- **Input/output container:** *LayerIO.*

## TanhLayer

- **Functional Overview:** it receives a matrix or list of matrices and executes the operation *Tanh* on it.
- **Input/output container:** *LayerIO.*

## WeightLayer

- **Functional overview:** it receives a matrix or a list of matrices, calculates the dot product of the input and the matrix inside the layer and output the result. The layer contains a parameter matrix internally, which is initialized using the initializer specified by *InitPolicy::WeightTypeCate*, if needed.
- **Input/output container:** *LayerIO.*

## NegativeLogLikelihoodLayer

- **Function overview:** it receives the label and the output of the predecessor layer and calculates the Negative Log Likelihood as a loss function.
- **Enter container:** *CostLayerIn.*
- **Output container:** *LayerIO.*

## 6.5 Summary

This chapter discussed the basic layers in MetaNN.

On the one hand, a layer is first and foremost the encapsulation of operations, which associates the operations required for forward and backward propagation and puts them in a class template; on the other hand, a layer is not restricted to the encapsulation of operations, which can modify their behavior through the policy object, thus supplying a more flexible way to use the operations.

The flexibility comes at a price. As we can see in this chapter, in order to support different behaviors flexibly and efficiently, we ought to introduce a large number of compile-time branching operations (e.g., the introduction of diverse branches based on whether to update the parameter matrix). In general, such branches are introduced within functions: distinct behaviors can be selected depending on compile-time parameters. In this case, the corresponding code can be well organized using *constexpr if* in C++ 17 without the need for relatively complex branch implementations such as template specializations.

In order to allow layers to support gradient calculations, we introduce the dynamic data type *DyanmicData*, which wraps a layer beyond a specific data type, masking variations among different data types. The introduction of the type enables us to save intermediate results of forward and backward propagation in layers, thus offering a prerequisite for subsequent updates of parameter gradients. However, this approach has an adverse effect on subsequent optimization of code: in essence, the introduction of *DyanmicData* is the process of removing information from specific data types. Only by removing these specific data types can we preserve them in the data field of the layer without distinctions. Nonetheless, the information of these specific data types is quite helpful for the optimization of the evaluation process and we can "recover" some of the lost information in some ways. But it is almost impossible to retrieve all the lost information—the loss of some information will make us lose some of the possibility of evaluation optimization.

Despite potential problems, layers in general can be a good data structure, which is user-friendly and easy to utilize. Although this chapter is based on quite basic layers to discuss development techniques, the same techniques can also be adopted to implement more complex layers.

Yes, in theory, we can use the techniques discussed in this chapter to develop complicated layers. But in practice, it is usually not a good idea. As the complexity of layers grows, the difficulty of writing and the likelihood of errors will be intensified, too. As we'll see in the next chapter, by introducing specialized components, we can easily combine basic layers to construct complex layers with the reduction of difficulty in writing and possibility of errors.

## 6.6 Exercises

1. *BiasLayer::Init* has the following logic:

```
if constexpr (!std::is_same<CurInitializer, void>::value)
    // ...
else
    throw std::runtime_error("...");
```

The *throw* statement in the case is used to handle cases where the initialization tag is invalid. Discarding exceptions usually happens at runtime. If we modify it to the behavior of compile time, for example, in the following way:

```
if constexpr (!std::is_same<CurInitializer, void>::value)
    // ...
else
    static_assert(DependencyFalse<CurInitializer>);
```

Is it okay? Think about it and rewrite the code to verify your ideas.

2. Due to limited space, this chapter discusses only the concepts and design principles of the layers and does not analyze the relevant code in the MetaNN line by line. Please read the code relevant to basic layers in MetaNN, especially *WeightLayer*'s code, to make sure you understand its implementation in details.

3. Based on the operations *ReLU* and *ReLUDerivative* implemented in Chapter 5, write a *ReLU* layer.

4. Currently, the *Get* method used in layers' *FeedForward* and *FeedBackward* is to return the elements to be acquired by copying—it is unnecessary in some cases. In the exercises in Chapter 2, we implement a method of obtaining elements through movement. On this basis, please optimize functions like *FeedForward* and *FeedBackward* in layers to decrease the times of copying elements. (Tip: variables are all *lvalues*, so we can't obtain parameters directly from the input of functions with the semantics of movement, but need to forward them with *std::forward*)

# Chapter 7

# Composite and Recurrent Layers

Chapter 6 discusses the writing of basic layers and defines the set of interfaces that the layers should implement in MetaNN. In theory, we can use the approaches discussed in the previous chapter to implement all the layer structures in deep learning networks. However, in practice, if the logic of layers is relatively complicated, it is tough and error-prone to construct directly using the methods mentioned in the previous chapter.

A complex layer usually contains several operations that may affect each other in a certain form. In this case, writing the correct code of forward propagation can be challenging while it is more intricate for backward propagation. We consider deep learning systems to be complex, which is in large part because it is relatively strenuous to write the correct code of forward and backward propagation with the increasing complexity of the network. Furthermore, when the system becomes complex, it can be quite challenging to find errors by debugging if there are errors in the logic of layers.

There is another aspect to be considered in developing complex layers: we need to adjust the behaviors of layers in the form of policy objects. As layers become more complicated, there will be more adjustments. It is feasible to introduce relatively simple branching logic with the approach of policy combined with branches mentioned in the previous chapter, while dealing with complex behavior adjustments makes it difficult to maintain the code—all of which should be addressed.

In response to these problems, MetaNN introduces the concept of composite layers. A composite layer is a combination of basic layers—a typical composite pattern. The basic layers in a composite layer constitute a structure of a directed acyclic graph. The composite layer automatically derives how to perform forward and backward propagation based on its internal diagram structure. The most prominent benefit of composite layers is that we can simplify the writing and maintenance of code by splitting the original complex computational logic into a sequence of relatively simple computational logic. On the one hand, a composite layer is a combination of basic layers. In order to ensure the logical correctness of a composite layer, we should guarantee that the logic of each basic layer contained therein is correct. Obviously, it is much easier to ensure the latter compared to the former. On the other hand, to ensure that a composite layer works correctly, we should also assure that the logic of forward and backward propagation, etc. derived within the composite layer is correct. It can be relatively challenging but this part of logic is fairly reusable. As long as we spend a certain amount of time in this part of correct logic, then it can be reused within all the instances in composite layers.

A composite layer is a combination of basic layers. To construct a complex deep learning network, most deep learning frameworks provide a way to integrate relatively basic components. One of the most noteworthy differences between the composite layers in MetaNN and other deep learning frameworks is that many operations (for instance, the logic of deriving forward and backward propagation based on graph structures) are completed at compile time. It is consistent with the overall design of MetaNN. We hope to make the most of metaprogramming and compile-time computing to simplify the logic at runtime so as to provide possibilities for system optimization.

This chapter focuses on the construction of composite layers. Similar to other components in MetaNN, we first ought to design the interfaces for composite layers and clarify how to use the components for users. Based on the interfaces that have been designed, we will discuss specific implementations that include two parts: the inheritance of policy and constructing the kernel logic of composite layers.

Based on the discussion of the core logic of composite layers, we will construct recurrent layers. Recurrent layers constitute the Recurrent Neural Network[1] essentially. We'll discuss how to construct a recurrent layer based on a classic component of the Recurrent Neural Network: *GatedUnitedUnit* (GRU). The implementation of GRU can also be regarded as a typical application of composite layers.

# 7.1 Interfaces and Design Principles of Composite Layers

## 7.1.1 Basic Structure

Composite layers can be considered a typical pattern of combination and its external interfaces should conform to the basic requirements of MetaNN for "layers." For a layer, the two primary operations are forward and backward propagation. A composite layer also needs to offer both interfaces.

A composite layer is a combination of basic layers, yet it does not necessarily contain only basic layers but can include other composite layers, which can compose a more complex structure. For the convenience of subsequent discussions, we refer to layers contained in a composite layer as its "sublayer." A sublayer can be either a basic layer or another composite layer. Chapter 6 mentioned the concepts of input and output containers for forward and backward propagation introduced by MetaNN. Forward propagation receives the input container object, returning the output container object. Backward propagation receives the output container object, returning the input container object. The interfaces for forward and backward propagation in composite layers also ought to configure the corresponding input and output containers, which should be capable of being connected to the sublayers contained in composite layers. After a sublayer receives the parameters delivered to the composite layer, it will calculate and output the result. The resulting output may be connected to other sublayers or act as the overall output of the composite layer.

Figure 7.1 shows the internal structure of a composite layer from the perspective of forward propagation.

---

[1] Readers can refer to the relevant content in Chapter 3 for a brief description of the Recurrent Neural Network.

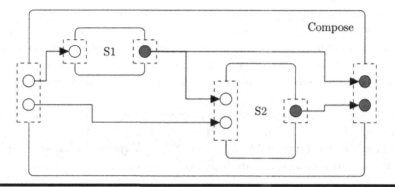

**Figure 7.1    The internal structure of a typical composite layer**

In this diagram, each layer with a frame is represented with solid lines, the input and output containers for the layer with frames with dotted lines; hollow dots for the elements in the input container and solid dots for the elements in the output container.

The structure of a composite layer displayed in this diagram is not complicated but it is sufficient for our discussion. The composite layer *Compose* contains two sublayers, *S1* and *S2*. One of *Compose*'s input elements is delivered to the input container of *S1*. The output of *S1* along with another input element from *Compose* serves as the input for *S2*. The output of *S2* will act as one of the output elements of *Compose*. Another output of *Compose* comes from the output of *S1*.

## 7.1.2 Syntax for Structural Description

As Figure 7.1 shows, in addition to defining input and output containers, we should also provide four types of information in order to describe a composite layer.

- Defining which sublayers are included in the composite layer.
- Defining that the input of certain sublayers comes from the input of the composite layer.
- Defining that the output of certain sublayers constitutes the output of the composite layer.
- Defining that the output of certain sublayers constitutes the input of some other sublayers.

MetaNN introduces four class templates as the carriers of these four types of information.

1. *SubLayer<LayerTag, LayerType>* defines sublayers. This class template describes the tag (*LayerTag*) and the type (*LayerType*) of the sublayer. The tag represents the "name" of the sublayer, while the type specifies the function of it. *AddLayer*, for example, is a sublayer type that means that the layer is used to add two matrices or lists of matrices. There may be multiple sublayers of the same type in a composite layer, but each sublayer has a unique name, which will serve to refer to the corresponding layer object.
2. *InConnect<InName, InLayertag, InLayerName>* is utilized to associate an element in the input container of the composite layer with an element in the input container of its sublayer. *InName* represents an element in the input container of the composite layer while *InLayerName* corresponds to an element in the input container of its sublayer.
3. *OutConnect<OutLayerTag, OutLayerName, OutName>* serves to associate an element in the output container of the composite layer with an element in the output container of its

sublayer. *OutName* represents an element in the output container of the composite layer while *OutLayerName* corresponds to an element in the output container of its sublayer.

4. *InternalConnect<OutLayerTag, OutName, InLayerTag, InName>* is employed to "connect" two sublayers in the composite layer, indicating an element in the output container of a certain sublayer will serve as an input element in the input container of another sublayer.

For example, in Figure 7.1, it is assumed that the input container of the composite layer contains two elements *Input1* and *Input2* and the output container contains two elements *Output1* and *Output2*. Meanwhile, the types of *S1* and *S2* are *SigmoidLayer* and *AddLayer* respectively. The composite layer can then be described in the following way:

```
1   using ComposeIn = VartypeDict<struct Input1, struct Input2>;
2   using ComposeOutput = VarTypeDict<struct Output1, struct Output2>;
3
4   SubLayer<S1, SigmoidLayer>
5   SubLayer<S2, AddLayer>
6   InConnect<Input1, S1, LayerIO>
7   InConnect<Input2, S2, AddLayerIn2>
8   InternalConnect<S1, LayerIO, S2, AddLayerIn1>
9   OutConnect<S1, LayerIO, Output1>
10  OutConnect<S2, LayerIO, Output2>
```

*ComposeIn* and *ComposeOut* represent the input and output containers of the composite layer respectively. On this basis, lines 4 and 5 define two sublayers; lines 6 and 7 declare how the input elements of the composite layer are connected to the sublayer; line 8 indicates that the output of *S1* is connected to *AddLayerIn1* of *S2*[2]; the last two lines (9 and 10) show that the output of *S1* and *S2* will act as the output of the composite layer itself.

The internal structure of a composite layer contains most information needed to construct it. On this basis, we can further adjust the behavior details of a composite layer. In MetaNN, the designation of layer behaviors is mainly implemented by policy and a composite layer is no exception. However, unlike basic layers, there are relationships of including and being included in a composite layer and the corresponding designation of behaviors becomes more complicate. Next, let's turn to how to easily specify the behavior details of a composite layer by extending the original mechanism of policy templates.

### 7.1.3 The Inheritance Relationship of Policies

Basic layers can compose composite layers; composite layers and basic layers can be further combined to form more complex structures. As the structure of layers becomes more intricate, there will be more and more aspects of their behaviors that can be adjusted. For basic layers, we can specify the details of their behaviors by introducing the appropriate policy object. For composite layers, it is challenging to specify behavior details in turn for each sublayer it contains—a composite layer that may contain hundreds of foundation layers directly or indirectly, in which specifying behavior details for each basic layer would be boring and error-prone.

---

[2] Note that *S1* is *SigmoidLayer*, which contains only one element indicated with *LayerIO* in the input/output container. The details can be found in Chapter 6.

The introduction of policies to adjust the behaviors of layers often lie in two situations. Firstly, each layer in MetaNN has its default behavior—corresponding to the default value of policies. In general, if we want to alter a certain behavioral detail, it is usually the corresponding details of all the sublayers in the composite layer that should be adjusted. By default, for example, each layer in the network receives input in a non-batch way (*BatchMode* is *false*). We might wish all the sublayers in a certain composite layer to handle the input in a *Batch* way—that is, to alter *BatchMode* to be *true*.

Another scenario is that most sublayers in a composite layer serve to satisfy the requirements but the policy corresponding to only a few sublayers is required adjusting. For instance, we hope most sublayers to update parameters during the training phase and some layers not to update parameters contained therein. In fact, when configuring the policy for the composite layer, we can solve most problems by dealing with both of the discussed situations.

There are relationships of including and being included between a composite layer and its sublayers. Based on such structures, a natural solution to the policy adjustment is that we can specify a policy for the composite layer, which will be applied to all the sublayers it contains. In addition, sublayers can specify their own behaviors. The policy specified by sublayers can override the policy specified by the composite layer. Assuming that there are two policy objects *P1* and *P2*, we hope most sublayers in the composite layer to possess the behavior specified by *P1* and a sublayer *SubX* to possess the behavior specified by *P2*. Then the policy of the composite layer can be declared as follows:

```
1   PolicyContainer<P1, SubPolicyContainer<SubX, P2>>
```

*SubPolicyContainer* is a container in MetaNN that assigns the sublayers the appropriate policy object. When using the discussed code to define template parameters for the composite layer, the sublayers except *SubX* will correspond to *PolicyContainer<P1>* while *SubX* corresponds to *PolicyContainer<P1,P2>* or *PolicyContainer<P2>*, which depends on whether *P1* and *P2* conflict (i.e., whether their major and minor categories are the same). If *P1* does not conflict with *P2*, then *SubX* corresponds to *PolicyContainer<P1,P2>*, which can be considered as *SubX* "inheriting" the corresponding behavior from its parent container; otherwise if *P1* and *P2* conflict, then *SubX* corresponds to *PolicyContainer<P2>*, indicating that the behavior specified for *SubX* overrides the behavior specified by the policy of the composite layer.

We call this extension of policy the inheritance of policy. The inheritance of policy can be further promoted. For instance, *SubX* also contains a sublayer *SubY*, and can be written as follows:

```
1   PolicyContainer<P1,
2               SubPolicyContainer<SubX, P2,
3                       SubPolicyContainer<SubY, P3>>>
```

Such a structure specifies the policy for each sublayer in the composite layer with a relatively simple syntax. We'll consider later in this chapter how to implement the inheritance of policy.

## 7.1.4 Correction of Policies

The correction logic of policy is also involved in the composite layer. Chapter 6 introduced the policy *IsFeedbackOutput*, which indicates whether a layer needs to calculate the output gradient. In general, the information should be derived from the relationships between layers. Specifically in composite layers, this involves the problem of policy correction.

A deep learning framework will eventually construct a network of several layers. From the perspective of forward propagation, some layers are used first, while others continue to process with the results of their predecessors. If a layer *A* directly or indirectly uses the results of a layer *B* as input, then we refer to *B* as the predecessor layer and *A* as the successor layer. In backward propagation, the interfaces for backward propagation of the successor layer are called first, and then the predecessor layer. It raises a problem that if the predecessor layer needs to update parameters, then the information used to calculate the gradient should be provided by its successor layer. In other words: if *B* needs to update its parameters, then *A* must calculate the output gradient.

Assume that *A* and *B* are in a composite layer and that *A*'s policy does not explicitly declare that the output gradient is calculated. Then the composite layer ought to correct the policy of *A* according to the relationship between *A* and *B*, so that *A* calculates the output gradient and delivers it *B*.

## 7.1.5 Constructors of Composite Layers

The basic structures of composite layers and policies are specified at compile time. But there is some information to specify at runtime when constructing instances of a composite layer. For example, we need to call the constructors of each sublayer to pass in the information required for construction (such as the names of layers, the dimensions of the arguments it contains, and so on). To do this, we should also discuss specialized constructors of each composite layer.

Next, we'll take a concrete example to denote how a composite layer is constructed and display how to write constructors of composite layers.

## 7.1.6 An Example of Complete Construction of a Composite Layer

Consider the following example: the basic layers *WeightLayer* and *BiasLayer* were introduced in Chapter 6 and now we wish to construct a composite layer *LinearLayer* based on the two layers. The input of the composite layer will first pass through *WeightLayer* and then through *BiasLayer*. In order to construct this composite layer, we should first define its internal structure:

```
1   struct WeightSublayer;
2   struct BiasSublayer;
3
4   using Topology
5       = ComposeTopology<SubLayer<WeightSublayer, WeightLayer>,
6                         SubLayer<BiasSublayer, BiasLayer>,
7                         InConnect<LayerIO, WeightSublayer, LayerIO>,
8                         InternalConnect<WeightSublayer, LayerIO,
9                         BiasSublayer, LayerIO>,
10                        OutConnect<BiasSublayer, LayerIO, LayerIO>>;
11
12  template <typename TPolicies>
13  using Base = ComposeKernel<LayerIO, LayerIO, TPolicies, Topology>;
```

*ComposeTopology* integrates most structural information required for the composite layer within it, which is also the focus of this chapter. On this basis, we use *ComposeKernel* to introduce a class template and we can modify the behavior details of the composite layer by passing in a policy for the template (we'll also discuss the implementation details of *ComposeKernel* in this chapter).

One point to note is that the sequence of all statements in *ComposeTopology* can be adjusted at will. In other words, if it is written as follows:

```
1   using Topology
2       = ComposeTopology<InConnect<LayerIO, WeightSublayer, LayerIO>,
3                         SubLayer<WeightSublayer, WeightLayer>,
4                         OutConnect<BiasSublayer, LayerIO, LayerIO>,
5                         SubLayer<BiasSublayer, BiasLayer>,
6                         InternalConnect<WeightSublayer, LayerIO,
7                         BiasSublayer, LayerIO>>;
```

The behavior of the program will remain unchanged.

With these two steps in, as mentioned earlier, we also ought to introduce a reasonable constructor for the composite layer to pass in the parameter required for the construction of the runtime object. To achieve this, we need to introduce the inheritance:

```
1   template <typename TPolicies>
2   class LinearLayer : public Base<TPolicies>
3   {
4       using TBase = Base<TPolicies>;
5
6   public:
7       LinearLayer(const std::string& p_name,
8           size_t p_inputLen, size_t p_outputLen)
9           : TBase(TBase::CreateSubLayers()
10                  .template Set<WeightSublayer>(p_name + "-weight",
11                                      p_inputLen, p_outputLen)
12                  .template Set<BiasSublayer>(p_name + "-bias",
13                                      p_outputLen))
14      { }
15  };
```

*CreateSubLayers* is also an auxiliary function supplied by *ComposeKernel*, which can serve to specify the appropriate parameters for each sublayer. For instance, if the arguments delivered into *LinearLayer* are "root," 10 and 3, then the composite layer will construct two sublayers inside it, named "*root-weight*" and "*root-bias*." The former uses dot product to change the dimensions of the input vector from 10 to 3, while the latter is added to another vector with the length of 3 and returns the result.

That's all the work to construct a composite layer—we don't have to explicitly introduce forward and backward propagation, parameter initialization, and so on. These operations are fully implemented by *ComposeTopology* and *ComposeKernel* internally. The focus of this chapter is how to implement these two modules. But before that, let's start by discussing the implementation of policy inheritance and correction—*CompuseKernel* invokes the interfaces for policy inheritance and correction to derive the policy of the sublayer.

## 7.2 Implementation of Policy Inheritance and Correction

### 7.2.1 Implementation of Policy Inheritance

#### 7.2.1.1 The Container SubPolicyContainer and the Functions Related

In order to achieve policy inheritance described earlier, we should first introduce containers that can store the policy of a sublayer:

```
1   template <typename TLayerName, typename...TPolicies>
2   struct SubPolicyContainer;
3
4   template <typename T>
5   constexpr bool IsSubPolicyContainer = false;
6
7   template <typename TLayer, typename...T>
8   constexpr bool
9   IsSubPolicyContainer<SubPolicyContainer<TLayer, T...>> = true;
```

There is nothing special in the declaration of *SubPolicyContainer*. Its template parameters include two parts: *TLayerName* represents the name tag of the layer and *TPolicies...* corresponds to the policy to be set for the layer.

We also introduce a metafunction *IsSubPolicyContainer* to determine whether the input type is an instance of *SubPolicyContainer*, which simplifies the writing of code of policy-related logic later.

With the introduction of the preceding structures, we specify that *PolicyContainer* may contain general policy objects or subcontainers of *SubPolicyContainer*.

#### 7.2.1.2 The Implementation of PlainPolicy

The introduction of *SubPolicyContainer* is tantamount to broaden the range *PolicyContainer* can include, which is beneficial for composite layers as well as for policy inheritance. But the new *PolicyContainer* will not be available directly for *PolicySelect*. To solve this problem, we introduce the metafunction *PlainPolicy* to remove all sublayer-related policies in *PolicyContainer*. It basic behavior is to traverse all the elements in *PolicyContainer*—if it is a policy object, it will remain or otherwise be discarded. For example, for the following policy containers:

```
1   using Ori = PolicyContainer<P1,
2                               SubPolicyContainer<...>,
3                               P2,
4                               SubPolicyContainer<...>>;
```

After *PlainPolicy<Ori>* is called, *PolicyContainer<P1, P2>* will be constructed.

In Chapter 6, for a basic layer, *PlainPolicy* will be called before the policy is obtained:

```
1   template <typename TPolicies>
2   class AddLayer
3   {
4       static_assert(IsPolicyContainer<TPolicies>,
5                     "TPolicies is not a policy container.");
6       using CurLayerPolicy = PlainPolicy<TPolicies>;
7       ...
8   };
```

It is used to filter out unnecessary information of sublayer settings and prevent it from affecting subsequent calls of *PolicySelect*.

*PlainPolicy*'s implementation is essentially a loop judgment. The author believes readers can read such code easily so far. Therefore, the relevant code is left to readers to analyze.

### 7.2.1.3 The Metafunction SubPolicyPicker

*SubPolicyPicker* is defined as follows:

```
1   template <typename TPolicyContainer, typename TLayerName>
2   using SubPolicyPicker
3       = typename SubPolicyPicker_<TPolicyContainer, TLayerName>::type;
```

It receives two template parameters, representing the composite layer's policy container and the tag of the sublayer to be obtained. A policy container for the sublayer is constructed based on them. For instance, we suppose that the contents of the policy container in the composite layer are as follows:

```
1   using PC =
2       PolicyContainer<P1,
3               SubPolicyContainer<SubX, P2,
4                       SubPolicyContainer<SubY,
                                P3>>>;
```

Then calling *SubPolicyPicker<PC,SubX>* will construct the following container[3]:

```
1   PolicyContainer<P2,
2           SubPolicyContainer<SubY, P3>,
3           P1>
```

The above policy container includes all the policies that we want to assign to *SubX*.

---

[3] It is assumed that there is no conflict between *P1* and *P2*.

Here are a few points to note:

■ Based on the discussion in Chapter 2, it is natural to find that the position of the policy object in the policy container does not impact on its behavior. Here we put *P1* in the back end of the entire policy container for code simplification.

■ *SubPolicyPicker* can only parse one tier at a time. For the discussed example, if we want to acquire the policy of *SubY*, we must call *SubPolicyPicker* twice:

```
1   using T1 = SubPolicyPicker<PC, SubX>;
2   using T2 = SubPolicyPicker<T1, SubY>; //Obtaining the
    policy of SubY
```

■ The previous example manifests that there is no conflict between *P1* and *P2*. If there is conflict between the two, the generated policy container should be *PolicyContainer<P2, SubPolicy Container<SubY,P3>>*.

■ A composite layer may contain multiple sublayers, some of which do not configure a separate policy. For instance, we assume that *SubZ* is included in the composite layer in addition to *SubX* and *SubY*. Then *SubPolicyPicker<PC, SubZ>* will return *PolicyContainer <P1>* to indicate that the layer's policy is consistent with the composite layer.

After carefully analyzing the discussed examples and instructions, it is not tough to propose a basic solution of *SubPolicyPicker*'s implementation: to traverse all the *SubPolicyContainer*s and determine if one of them corresponds to the sublayers to be extracted. If there is no *SubPolicyContainer* corresponds to it, then the policy set by the composite layer will be returned; if there is a corresponding *SubPolicyContainer* and its first template parameter has the same name as the layer to be extracted, then we should construct a corresponding policy container based on it to return. When constructing a new container, we need to consider the policy object in the original container to determine whether it conflicts with the object in the current container. If they do not conflict, we add it to the new container.

*SubPolicyPicker_* realizes the implementation logic called by *SubPolicyPicker*. In order to simplify the code, there are several adjustments to the discussed logic in *SubPolicyPicker_*, as follows:

```
1   template <typename TPolicyContainer, typename TLayerName>
2   struct SubPolicyPicker_
3   {
4       using tmp1 = typename SPP_<TPolicyContainer, TLayerName>::type;
5       using tmp2 = PlainPolicy<TPolicyContainer>;
6       using type = PolicyDerive<tmp1, tmp2>;
7   };
```

*tmp1* looks for the result of *SubPolicyContainer*. If there is no explicit designation of policy for the sublayer to be processed in the policy container of the composite layer, then *SPP_* will return *PolicyContainer<>*, which is an empty container. Otherwise, the *PolicyContainer* it returns contains the policy object contained in *SubPolicyContainer*.

*tmp2* calls *PlainPolicy* to acquire the policy object in the policy container of the composite layer. On this basis, *type* calls *PolicyDerive* to add the contents of *tmp2* to *tmp1*—note that only non-conflicting policy objects will be added.

It should be pointed out that *SPP_* will only search for the first *SubPolicyContainer* which conform to the requirements in the policy container. Take the following policy container for example:

```
1   using Ori = PolicyContainer<P1,
2                       SubPolicyContainer<Sub, ...>,
3                       SubPolicyContainer<Sub, ...>>;
```

When *SubPolicyPicker<Ori, Sub>* is called, the contents of the second *SubPolicyContainer* will be omitted. Readers can modify the logic here to enable them to access all the policies in *SubPolicyContainer* that satisfy the requirements.

### 7.2.2 Implementation of Policy Correction

MetaNN introduces the metafunction *ChangePolicy* to modify objects in the policy container. *ChangePolicy* is not restricted to modifying the output gradient policy mentioned earlier, but is designed to be more versatile:

```
1   template <typename TNewPolicy, typename TOriContainer>
2   using ChangePolicy
3       = typename ChangePolicy_<TNewPolicy, TOriContainer>::type;
```

It receives two template parameters: the first is a policy object that we hope to introduce after modification and the second is the original policy container. It traverses each element in the policy container, removes the policy object that conflicts with the object we want to introduce, and adds the policy object that we want to introduce to the tail of the newly constructed container. Due to limited space, the specific implementation code of this metafunction is not listed here. Interested readers can refer to it from the source code.

On the basis of realizing the inheritance and correction of policy, we can adopt them to realize the kernel logic of the composite layer, which we'll discuss later. As mentioned earlier, the kernel logic of the composite layer is encapsulated in two templates, *ComposeTopology* and *ComposeKernel*. *ComposeTopology* analyzes the "syntax for structural description" discussed earlier and sort the sublayers in the composite layer based on the relationship among the layers. The sorting results will guide forward and backward propagation. According to the results, *ComposeKernel* implements the interfaces that layers should offer, including forward and backward propagation, parameter initialization and loading, etc. We'll start with the implementations pertinent to *ComposeTopology* and we'll discuss the implementation of *ComposeKernel* on that basis.

## 7.3 The Implementation of *ComposeTopology*

### 7.3.1 Features

*ComposeTopology* is a class template primarily used to analyze the "syntax for structural description" introduced previously and thus find out the sequence of calls for sublayers. On this basis, the class also provides a metafunction for passing in a policy container to instantiate the sublayers contained in a composite layer.

*ComposeTopology's* input is a syntax for structural description, which consists of four clauses that describe the sublayers contained in a composite layer, the input/output connections among the sublayers and the input/output connections between sublayers and the composite layer. MetaNN assumes that the complex connections described are essentially a directed acyclic graph in which the nodes represent the sublayers and the arcs among nodes depict the directions of the data in the sublayers during forward propagation. The sublayers inside the composite layer constitute a graph structure. When the forward and backward propagation of data is executed actually, the data will flow through each layer in a certain order, which cannot be confused or otherwise there will be logical errors.

In Figure 7.1, for example, the composite layer contains two sublayers, *S1* and *S2*. During forward propagation, the data delivered into the composite layer can only pass through *S1* first and then through *S2*. If this order is reversed, since the input of *S2* depends on the output of *S1*, so the interfaces for forward propagation in *S2* are called when *S1* has not produced the correct output. Therefore, correct results are naturally not available. It is similar in backward propagation where the gradient information entered into the composite layer must pass through *S2* first and then through *S1*. Deriving the sequence of propagation is the basis for ensuring that the composite layer behaves correctly, which is also the most significant task for *ComposeTopology*.

How can we transform the structure of the diagram into such a sequence? If familiar with data structures and algorithms, readers may have put forward a solution: topological sorting. In fact, it is a classic problem of topological sorting. The source of *ComposeTopology's* name is that it essentially implements topological sorting of sublayers within the composite layer.

The topological sorting given by *ComposeTopology* embodies the order of layers in which data should pass through in turn during forward propagation. Accordingly, in backward propagation, we can achieve automatic calculation of gradients by going through the layers in completely reverse order of forward propagation. Of course, there are still many implementation details for forward and backward propagation. These details will be discussed later in this chapter.

**Unlike the general implementation of topological sorting, *ComposeTopology's* topological sorting is executed at compile time and fully utilizes metaprogramming techniques to implement the entire algorithm.** The implementation of *ComposeTopology* is a comprehensive application of metaprogramming techniques. It can be said that readers can be relatively proficient in using the various basic methods of metaprogramming if fully understanding the implementation code of topological sorting. Next, let's review the topology sorting algorithm and then dive into the implementation details of *ComposeTopology*.

### 7.3.2 Introduction to the Topological Sorting Algorithm

The input for topological sorting is a directed acyclic graph and the output is a sequence which contains all the nodes in the directed acyclic graph. If there is an edge pointing from node *A* to node *B* in the original graph, *A* must be in front of *B* in the output sequence. For the same input, there may be more than one sequence conforming to the discussed requirements, but we only need to select one of the many available sequences in general. Meanwhile, please note that this algorithm is only valid for a directed acyclic graph—the directed graph denotes the sequence of the nodes; the graph must be acyclic, or otherwise it is unable to construct a sequence that satisfies the discussed requirements.

The idea of the algorithm is not complicated. First, we construct an empty queue *L* to hold the output. Next, the input graph is processed: since there is a directed acyclic graph, we can certainly find one or more nodes without input arcs. We place these nodes in $L$ (entering the queue) and then remove them with their output arcs from the original graph, which is equivalent to constructing a subgraph based on the original graph. The discussed operations are repeated on the subgraph and more nodes can be transferred into $L$ while the original graph is narrowed down. Until the graph contains no nodes, $L$ is then output as the result we want.

If the input graph is cyclic, then in the execution of the algorithm, it will occur that we can no longer add any nodes to $L$ when $L$ still does not contain all the nodes in the input graph. At this point, the algorithm ought to prompt an error.

Next, we'll implement the algorithm at compile time.

### 7.3.3 Main Steps Included in ComposeTopology

*ComposeTopology* implements topological sorting internally. In order to achieve the algorithm, it first analyzes the "syntax for structural description" of the input and "constructs" a directed acyclic graph conceptually. In the meantime, *ComposeTopology* generates some intermediate results that can be used by *ComposeKernel* subsequently.

The process of *ComposeTopology* can be roughly divided into the following steps:

1. The clauses about the four kinds of information in the "syntax for structural description" are classified and placed in the corresponding containers, thus facilitating the subsequent processing.
2. Based on the results of the previous step, it checks the validity of the constructed graph. For invalid cases, an assertion is given and it prompts a compilation error.
3. The operation of topological sorting is performed when ensuring input to be valid.
4. Based on the results of topological sorting, the metafunction *Instances* is provided to instantiate each sublayer on the basis of a given policy.

Let's consider each step one by one.

### 7.3.4 Clauses for Structural Description and Their Classification

We introduce the "syntax for structural description" as described earlier, which depicts the internal structure of a composite layer. The syntax contains four kinds of clauses and each clause is actually a class template. We can also regard them as four metafunctions that allow users to obtain the information contained in it through specific interfaces. Let's first look at the definitions of these four metafunctions:

■ The template *SubLayer<TLayerTag,TLayer>* receives two template parameters, representing the name (*TLayerTag*) and the type (*TLayer*) of the sublayer. It contains two declarations inside to obtain information of *TLayerTag* and *TLayer*:

```
1   template <typename TLayerTag, template<typename> class TLayer>
2   struct SubLayer {
3       using Tag = TLayerTag;
4       template <typename T> using Layer = TLayer<T>;
5   };
```

Note *TLayer* and *SubLayer::Layer* are class templates. It is because there is no need to specify policy information when users enter this clause. For example, in *SubLayer<S1, SigmoidLayer>*, *TLayer* corresponds to *SigmoidLayer <typename TPolicyCont>*. The class template *SigmoidLayer* can be truly instantiated into a type only if specific policy containers are subsequently entered as template parameters for the class template *SigmoidLayer*.

■ *InConnect<TInName, TInLayerTag, TInLayerName>* receives three template parameters that denote how the composite layer is connected to the input containers of its sublayers. The layers in MetaNN adopt the "heterogeneous dictionary" discussed in Chapter 2 as input and output containers. This module can contain data of different types, each with a key name for indexing. *TInName* and *TInLayerName* in *InConnect* represent the names of the keys in the input container of the composite layer and the sublayer respectively. *TInLayerTag* indicates the name of the sublayer. *InConnect* also supplies several interfaces internally to access the information it contains:

```
1   template <typename TInName,
2             typename TInLayerTag, typename TInLayerName>
3   struct InConnect {
4       using InName = TInName;
5       using InLayerTag = TInLayerTag;
6       using InLayerName = TInLayerName;
7   };
```

■ *OutConnect<TOutLayerTag, TOutLayerName, TOutName>* represents how the composite layer is connected to the output container of the sublayer and its definition is similar to the definition of *InConnect*, except that *TOutLayerName* and *TOutName* correspond to the key names in the output containers of the sublayers and composite layer respectively.

```
1   template <typename TOutLayerTag, typename TOutLayerName,
2             typename TOutName>
3   struct OutConnect {
4       using OutLayerTag = TOutLayerTag;
5       using OutLayerName = TOutLayerName;
6       using OutName = TOutName;
7   };
```

■ *InternalConnect<TOutLayerTag, TOutName, TInLayerTag, TInName>* describes the connections among sublayers inside the composite layer. During forward propagation, the contents corresponding to the key *TOutName* in the output container of the sublayer *TOutLayerTag* are delivered to the elements corresponding to the key *TInName* in the input container of the layer *TInLayerTag*.

```
1   template <typename TOutLayerTag, typename TOutName,
2             typename TInLayerTag, typename TInName>
```

```
3    struct InternalConnect {
4        using OutTag = TOutLayerTag;
5        using OutName = TOutName;
6        using InTag = TInLayerTag;
7        using InName = TInName;
8    };
```

When describing the structure of a composite layer, the discussed clauses may be compounded together. To facilitate subsequent operations, *ComposeTopology* should first classify them into different categories.

*ComposeTopology* first introduces four containers for storing the four clauses divided:

```
1    template <typename...T> struct SubLayerContainer;
2    template <typename...T> struct InterConnectContainer;
3    template <typename...T> struct InConnectContainer;
4    template <typename...T> struct OutConnectContainer;
```

On this basis, MetaNN brings in the metafunction *SeparateParameters_* to complete the classification of clauses:

```
1    template <typename...TParameters>
2    struct SeparateParameters_
3    {
4        // Auxiliary logic
5
6        using SubLayerRes = ...       // The array of SubLayerContainer
7        using InterConnectRes = ...   // The array of InterConnectContainer
8        using InConnectRes = ...      // The array of InConnectContainer
9        using OutConnectRes = ...     // The array of OutConnectContainer
10   };
```

The metafunction *SeparateParameters_* is essentially recurrent processing of the input parameters (structural descriptions contain several clauses), which then places the results of the disposition into members such as *SubLayerRes*. *ComposeTopology* calls the metafunction *SeparateParameters_* to obtain the corresponding results:

```
1    template <typename...TParameters>
2    struct ComposeTopology
3    {
4        using SubLayers
5            = typename SeparateParameters_<TParameters...>::SubLayerRes;
6        using InterConnects = ...
```

```
7        using InputConnects = ...
8        using OutputConnects = ...
9
10       // ...
11    };
```

## 7.3.5  Examination of Structural Validity

After classifying the clauses of structural descriptions, the next step is to examine the validity. Even though, clauses of structural description construct a directed acyclic graph in essence and the directionality of arcs in the graph is guaranteed by the semantics of clauses of structural descriptions. The topological algorithm itself can examine whether there are cycles in the graph. In addition to these two aspects, specifically to the application of composite layers, there are numerous items to check. Currently, MetaNN has introduced a total of eight examinations, which are outlined as follows. Readers can consider whether there is anything else that should be detected.

- A composite layer should contain one or more sublayers, that is, *ComposeTopology::SubLayers* cannot be empty.
- Each sublayer in the same composite layer should have distinct names. Note that different sublayers can be of the same type (e.g., all of type *AddLayer*) but their names (i.e., the first parameter for *SubLayer*) cannot be the same. It is because names will serve to describe the connections among sublayers. If there are different sublayers with a same name, the connections among layers cannot be accurately described.
- In an *InternalConnect* description, the input layer and the output layer cannot be the same one, or otherwise a cycle will be formed in the directed graph. It is the simplest case of detecting the existence of cycles—that is, whether a single sublayer forms a cycle inside itself. For the input of users, there may be multiple sublayers forming a cycle, which can be detected by the topology sorting algorithm.
- The data source for the input container must be unique. For instance, there can't be multiple *InConnect* statements with exactly the same *InLayerTag* and *InLayerName*. If this happens, it means that there are multiple sources of data for particular elements in a certain input container during forward propagation. Then the system will be unable to select which source as the actual input for the layer *InLayerTag*.[4]
- The names of the layers in *InternalConnect*, *InConnect,* and *OutConnect* clauses must appear in the *SubLayer* clauses. Otherwise, the name of the layer cannot be associated with the type of the layer.
- Similar to the previous one, the name of the layer introduced with the *SubLayer* clauses must also appear in *InternalConnect*, *InConnect*, and *OutConnect*, or otherwise the layer would not be involved in forward and backward propagation, which is essentially a "zombie layer."

---

[4] Note that the output is not subject to the restriction, that is, the output container of the layer can deliver a result to multiple locations, which makes sense. For example, the sublayer *S1* in Figure 7.1 delivers the output to the input of *S2* and the output of the composite layer respectively.

- The output of *InternalConnect* serves as either the input to a sublayer or the output of a composite layer, or otherwise it cannot be processed during backward propagation.
- Similar to the previous one, the output of layers that appears in *InConnect* is connected to either *InternalConnect* or *OutConnect*.

MetaNN adopts metafunctions in the previous examinations. For instance, MetaNN introduced *SublayerCheck* for the second one:

```
1    template <typename TCheckTag, typename...TArray>
2    struct TagExistInLayerComps
3    {
4        // Omitting internal logic
5    };
6
7    template <typename TSublayerCont> struct SublayerCheck;
8
9    template <typename...TSublayers>
10   struct SublayerCheck<SubLayerContainer<TSublayers...>>
11   {
12       template <typename...T>
13       struct CheckUniqueLayerTag
14       {
15           static constexpr bool value = true;
16       };
17
18       template <typename TSubLayer, typename...T>
19       struct CheckUniqueLayerTag<TSubLayer, T...>
20       {
21           using CurTag = typename TSubLayer::Tag;
22
23           static constexpr bool tmp
24               = !(TagExistInLayerComps<CurTag, T...>::value);
25           static constexpr bool value
26               = AndValue<tmp, CheckUniqueLayerTag<T...>>;
27       };
28
29       constexpr static bool IsUnique
30           = CheckUniqueLayerTag<TSublayers...>::value;
31   };
```

*SublayerCheck* receives an instance of the container *SublayerContainer* and constructs a nested loop inside it. The outer loop *SublayerCheck::CheckUniqueLayerTag* traverses each element in the container, obtains the name tags, and calls the inner loop *TagExistInLayerComps* to compare the tag with the element behind in the container. If there appears to be elements with a same name, then *IsUnique* is set as *false*, or otherwise *true*.

Inside *ComposeTopology*, the following assertion is introduced based on *SublayerCheck*:

```
1   static_assert(SublayerCheck<SubLayers>::IsUnique,
2               "Two or more sublayers have same tag.");
```

Due to limited space, the examinations will not be elaborated here. Readers can refer to and analyze the relevant code.

## 7.3.6 *Implementation of Topological Sorting*

MetaNN introduces the metafunction *TopologicalOrdering_* to encapsulate the kernel logic of topological sorting. The main code of this metafunction is implemented as follows:

```
1   template <typename TSubLayerArray, typename TInterArray>
2   struct TopologicalOrdering_;
3
4   template <typename...TSubLayerElems, typename...TInterElems>
5   struct TopologicalOrdering_<SubLayerContainer<TSubLayerElems...>,
6                               InterConnectContainer<TInterElems...>>
7   {
8       // ...
9       using SublayerPreRes =
10          SublayerPreprocess_<SubLayerContainer<>,
11                              SubLayerContainer<>,
12                              TSubLayerElems...>;
13
14      using OrderedAfterPreproces
15          = typename SublayerPreRes::Ordered;
16      using UnorderedAfterPreprocess
17          = typename SublayerPreRes::Unordered;
18
19      using MainLoopFun
20          = MainLoop<OrderedAfterPreprocess,
21                     UnorderedAfterPreprocess,
22                     InterConnectContainer<TInterElems...>>;
23
24      using OrderedAfterMain = typename MainLoopFun::Ordered;
25      using RemainAfterMain = typename MainLoopFun::Remain;
26
27      using type
28          = typename CascadSublayers<OrderedAfterMain,
29                                     RemainAfterMain>::type;
30  };
```

It receives two template parameters. In its only specialized version, it is specified that the two template parameters must be of container types *SubLayerContainer* and *InterConnectContainer*, that is, the information previously stripped from the syntax for structural description to represent the sublayers and the connections between them. Using these two sets of information, we can implement the topological sorting algorithm.

The topological sorting algorithm for composite layers consists of three steps in total: preprocessing, main logic, and post-processing. Next, we'll analyze the three parts one by one.

### 7.3.6.1 Pre-processing of Topological Sorting

*TopologicalOrdering_* first calls the metafunction *SublayerPreprocess_* to pre-process the input sublayer—removing the layers that are not included in *InterContainerConnect*.

A composite layer can be represented as a directed acyclic graph. But we don't require that each node in the graph have edges connected to other nodes. For instance, it is entirely feasible to define a composite layer to represent the relationships of aggregation among the layers:

```
1   SubLayer<S1, SigmoidLayer>
2   SubLayer<S2, AddLayer>
3   InConnect<Input1, S1, LayerIO>
4   InConnect<Input2, S2, AddLayerIn1>
5   InConnect<Input3, S2, AddLayerIn2>
6   OutConnect<S1, LayerIO, Output1>
7   OutConnect<S2, LayerIO, Output2>
```

The composite layer defined by the discussed statements consists of two sublayers, which are used to calculate *Sigmoid* and addition. There is no predecessor-successor relationship between the two sublayers—it is simply aggregations. Corresponding to the directed acyclic graph, the two sublayers are equivalent to two isolated nodes in the graph—not connected to other nodes (sublayers).

This kind of sublayers is included in *SubLayerContainer* but not in *InterConnectContainer*. The metafunction *SublayerPreprocess_* traverses all sublayers to find sublayers with the discussed characteristics and adds them directly to the result queue of topological sorting.

```
1   using SublayerPreRes = SublayerPreprocess_<SubLayerContainer<>,
2                                               SubLayerContainer<>,
3                                               TSubLayerElems...>;
4
5   using OrderedAfterPreproces = typename SublayerPreRes::Ordered;
6   using UnorderedAfterPreprocess = typename SublayerPreRes::Unordered;
```

*SublayerPreprocess_* is a loop itself. Due to limited space, its internal logic will not be elaborated here. It produces two results: *Ordered* and *Unordered*, which are all *SubLayerContainer* containers, including the sublayers that have been sorted after pre-processing and the sublayers that need to be further sorted respectively.

### 7.3.6.2 Main Logic

The main logic of topological sorting is implemented in the metafunction *MainLoop*, which is declared as follows:

```
1   template <typename TOrderedSublayers, typename TUnorderedSublayers,
2           typename TCheckInternals>
3   struct MainLoop;
```

It receives three template parameters, which denote a queue of sublayers that have been sorted currently (*TOrderedSublayers*), a queue of sublayers to be sorted (*TUnorderedSublayers*) and the connections among sublayers (*TCheckInternals*) respectively.

If *TCheckInternals* is not empty, *MainLoop* will handle as follows:

■ Calling the metafunction *InternalLayerPrune*, traversing the elements in *TCheckInternals* to find the sublayers without any information about predecessor layers and place them in the queue *InternalLayerPrune::PostTags*. Meanwhile, if a new layer is introduced in *InternalLayerPrune::PostTags*, then *InternalLayerPrune* will remove the connections corresponding to that layer in *TCheckInternals*. Eventually, *InternalLayerPrune* will construct a new *InterConnectContainer* to be returned as *InternalLayerPrune::type*.
■ Calling *SeparateByPostTag* to add *InternalLayerPrune::PostTags* to the sorted queue.
■ Calling *MainLoop* recursively, using the newly sorted queue with the new connection as input to execute the next loop of topological sorting.

Each time *MainLoop* calls *InternalLayerPrune*, it determines whether *InternalLayerPrune::type* is a proper subset of the original connections—indicating whether the current topological sorting consumes some of the connections. If not, then there maybe cycles in the graph corresponding to the composite layer. If so, the compiler prompts an error. The code corresponding to the logic here is as follows:

```
1    template <typename...TSO, typename...TSN, typename TIC, typename...TI>
2    struct MainLoop<SubLayerContainer<TSO...>,
3                    SubLayerContainer<TSN...>,
4                    InterConnectContainer<TIC, TI...>>
5    {
6        using CurInter = InterConnectContainer<TIC, TI...>;
7
8    // get layers with empty input arcs&construct PostTags
9    //Remove these layers from the DAG&construct NewInter
10        using ILP = InternalLayerPrune<InterConnectContainer<>,
11                                       CurInter, TagContainer<>,
12                                       TIC, TI...>;
13        using NewInter = typename ILP::type;
14        using PostTags = typename ILP::PostTags;
15
```

```
16    // Assert that no cycle exists in the composite layer
17        static_assert((ArraySize<NewInter> < ArraySize<CurInter>),
18                      "Cycle exist in the compose layer");
19
20    // move PostTags' info to sorted container
21        using SeparateByTagFun
22          = SeparateByPostTag<SubLayerContainer<TSN...>,
23                              SubLayerContainer<TSO...>,
24                              SubLayerContainer<>, PostTags>;
25        using NewOrdered = typename SeparateByTagFun::Ordered;
26        using NewUnordered = typename SeparateByTagFun::Unordered;
27
28    // Recursively call MainLoop
29        using Ordered
30          = typename MainLoop<NewOrdered, NewUnordered, NewInter>::Ordered;
31        using Remain
32          = typename MainLoop<NewOrdered, NewUnordered, NewInter>::Remain;
33    };
```

Conversely, if *TCheckInternals* is empty, the loop terminates. At this point, the main logic of topological sorting is accomplished:

```
1    template <typename TOrderedSublayers, typename TUnorderedSublayers,
2              typename TCheckInternals>
3    struct MainLoop
4    {
5        using Ordered = TOrderedSublayers;
6        using Remain = TUnorderedSublayers;
7    };
```

### 7.3.6.3 Post-processing of Topological Sorting

*MainLoop* terminates when the internal connections among the input sublayers are empty. At this point, however, not all sublayer nodes have been added to the result queue of topological sorting. At the end of *MainLoop*, sublayers with no successor layers but predecessor layers are not added to the result queue. *TopologicalOrdering_* calls the metafunction *CascadSublayers* to add the remaining sublayers after the disposition of *MainLoop* to the end of the result queue for topological sorting.

The results of topological sorting are saved in *ComposeTopology::TopologicalOrdering*, which is also a container of type *SubLayerContainer* with the elements arranged in an orderly manner according to the relationships of predecessors and successors among the sublayers.

## 7.3.7 *The Metafunction to Instantiate Sublayers*

The main function of *ComposeTopology* is topological sorting. But beyond that, it also offers a metafunction to instantiate sublayers:

```
1   template <typename...TComposeKernelInfo>
2   struct ComposeTopology
3   {
4       // Results of topological sorting
5       using TopologicalOrdering = ...;
6
7       template <typename TPolicyCont>
8       using Instances
9           = typename SublayerInstantiation<TPolicyCont,
10                                            TopologicalOrdering,
11                                            InterConnects>::type;
12  };
```

The main purpose of introducing this metafunction is to deal with the logic of policy inheritance and correction discussed earlier. Assuming that a composite layer contains two sublayers, *A* and *B*, where the successor layer of *A* is *B*, it is essential to guarantee that *IsFeedbackOutput* of *B* is *true* if *A* needs to update the internal parameters. *ComposeTopology::Instances* calls *SublayerInstantiation* to adjust the relevant policy. *SublayerInstantiation* consists of four steps: calculation of policies for each sublayer; examination of the output gradient; policy correction; instantiations of sublayers.

### 7.3.7.1 *Calculation of Policies for Each Sublayer*

*SublayerInstantiation* first calls the metafunction *GetSublayerPolicy* to obtain policies for each sublayer:

```
1   template <typename TPolicyCont, typename OrderedSublayers,
2             typename InterConnects>
3   struct SublayerInstantiation
4   {
5       using SublayerWithPolicy
6           = typename GetSublayerPolicy<TPolicyCont,
7                                        OrderedSublayers>::type;
8       // ...
9   }
```

*GetSublayerPolicy* is essentially a loop in which the metafunction *SubPolicyPicker* is called for each sublayer and each sublayer's policy is derived from the policy of the composite layer.

*GetSublayerPolicy* returns a *SublayerPolicyContainer* container. Each element in the container is another container of type *SublayerPolicies*:

```
1   template <typename TLayerTag,
2              template<typename> class TLayer,
3              typename TPolicyContainer>
4   struct SublayerPolicies
5   {
6       using Tag = TLayerTag;
7       template <typename T> using Layer = TLayer<T>;
8       using Policy = TPC;
9   };
```

It records each sublayer's name (*Tag*), corresponding type (*Layer*), and contents of policy (policy). Note that the content of policy returned by *GetSublayerPolicy* is inherited only from the policy of the composite layer and does not involve policy adjustments.

## 7.3.7.2 Examination of the Output Gradient

In the discussion of the inheritance relationship of policies, it was mentioned that the policy objects set by sublayers possess higher priority. If a policy object set by a sublayer conflicts with the policy set by the composite layer that contains it, the settings of the sublayer will prevail.

It incurs a problem: if the composite layer sets *IsFeedbackOutput* as *true* but its sublayer explicitly sets *IsFeedbackOutput* as *false*, it indicates that the composite layer should calculate the output gradient and its sublayer will not calculate the output gradient according to the discussed principle.

In order to allow the composite layer to calculate the output gradient, we must obtain the output gradient calculated by its sublayer. So, the discussed configuration is therefore invalid. *SublayerInstantiation* calls the metafunction *FeedbackOutCheck* to ensure that situations like this will not happen:

```
1   template <typename TPolicyCont, typename OrderedSublayers,
2              typename InterConnects>
3   struct SublayerInstantiation
4   {
5       // ...
6
7       using PlainPolicies = PlainPolicy<TPolicyCont>;
8       constexpr static bool IsPlainPolicyFeedbackOut
9           = PolicySelect<FeedbackPolicy,
10                      PlainPolicies>::IsFeedbackOutput;
11      static_assert(FeedbackOutCheck<IsPlainPolicyFeedbackOut,
12                          SublayerWithPolicy>::value);
13
14      // ...
15  };
```

### 7.3.7.3 Policy Correction

In a composite layer, if a predecessor layer needs to calculate the output gradient[5] or the parameter gradient for parameter update,[6] it must obtain the output gradient passed in by its successor layer. *SublayerInstantiation* calls the metafunction *FeedbackOutSet* and executes policy correction on the output of *GetSublayerPolicy* based on this principle.

```
1   template <typename TPolicyCont, typename OrderedSublayers,
2               typename InterConnects>
3   struct SublayerInstantiation
4   {
5       // ...
6
7       using FBO = FeedbackOutSet<SublayerWithPolicy, InterConnects>;
8
9       using FeedbackOutUpdate
10          = typename std::conditional_t<IsPlainPolicyFeedbackOut,
11                                        Identity_<SublayerWithPolicy>,
12                                        FBO>::type;
13  };
```

*FeedbackOutSet* is declared as follows:

```
1   template <typename TInsts, typename InterConnects>
2   struct FeedbackOutSet;
```

The metafunction receives two parameters. The first is the output of *GetSublayerPolicy*, a container of type *SublayerPolicyContainer*. The second is the connection between the sublayers. It traverses each sublayer of *SublayerPolicyContainer* in turn internally. If the current sublayer needs to calculate the output gradient or parameter gradient, the successor layer's policy will be corrected according to the connection between the sublayers.

*SublayerInstantiation* does not call *FeedbackOutSet* directly but hides its call in a branch:

```
1   using FeedbackOutUpdate
2       = typename std::conditional_t<IsPlainPolicyFeedbackOut,
3                                     Identity_<SublayerWithPolicy>,
4                                     FBO>::type;
```

If *IsPlainPolicyFeedbackOut* is *true*, it denotes that the composite layer ought to calculate the output gradient. Based on the previous behavioral examination, we know that if it is *true*, it means that *IsFeedbackOutput* of each sublayer is set as *true*. It is unnecessary to call *FeedbackOutSet* to modify the policies of sublayers. Otherwise, we should call *FeedbackOutSet*.

---

[5] That is, *IsFeedbackOutput* of the layer is *true*.
[6] That is, *IsUpdate* of the layer is *true*.

*Identity_* is a quite simple metafunction here:

```
1   template <typename T>
2   struct Identity_
3   {
4       using type = T;
5   };
```

*std::conditional_t* outputs one of the two metafunctions—*Identity_* or *FeedbackOutSet*. On this basis, *type* is called again and the corrected policy will be output.

### 7.3.7.4 Instantiations of Sublayers

After correcting the policy of each sublayer, we can execute instantiations, that is, constructing the actual type with the corrected policy for each sublayer, which is also the task of the metafunction *Instantiation*:

```
1   template <typename TInsts, typename TSublayerPolicies>
2   struct Instantiation
3   {
4       using type = TInsts;
5   };
6
7   template <typename...TInsts, typename TCur, typename...TSublayers>
8   struct Instantiation<std::tuple<TInsts...>,
9                        SublayerPolicyContainer<TCur, TSublayers...>>
10  {
11      using Tag = typename TCur::Tag;
12      using Policy = typename TCur::Policy;
13
14      template <typename T>
15      using Layer = typename TCur::template Layer<T>;
16
17      using InstLayer = Layer<Policy>;
18
19      using tmpRes = std::tuple<TInsts...,
20                                InstantiatedSublayer<Tag, InstLayer>>;
21
22      using type
23          = typename Instantiation<tmpRes,
24                  SublayerPolicyContainer<TSublayers...>>::type;
25  };
```

The metafunction receives two parameters, representing the result of instantiation and the layer to be instantiated. It is a loop structure that processes one sublayer at a time. In one loop, it takes relevant information from the layer to be instantiated (lines 11–15), then instantiates the specific class (line 17) and places the results of instantiation into the container of *std::tuple* (lines 19 and 20).

Finally, the output of *Instantiation*[7] is a container of type *std::tuple*, where each element is a container of type *InstantiatedSublayer*:

```
1    template <typename TLayerTag, typename TLayer>
2    struct InstantiatedSublayer
3    {
4        using Tag = TLayerTag;
5        using Layer = TLayer;
6    };
```

*InstantiatedSublayer* contains the tag and type of the layer and it is listed in *std::tuple* according to the result of topological sorting.

Based on these, we can further construct the sublayer objects contained in the composite layer for forward and backward propagation. All of the discussed logic is encapsulated in *ComposeKernel*.

## 7.4 The Implementation of *ComposeKernel*

Depending on *ComposeTopology*, *ComposeKernel* realizes management, initialization, loading, forward and backward propagation, and other features for sublayer objects. Accordingly, classes derived from *ComposeKernel* can employ these features directly to implement the main logic of the composite layer.

This section explores the features provided by the class template one by one.

### 7.4.1 Declarations of Class Templates

*ComposeKernel* is a class template declared as follows:

```
1    template <typename TInputType,// Composite layer input Container
2             typename TOutputType,// Composite layer output Container
3             typename TPolicyCont,// Composite layer policy
4             typename TKernelTopo // Instances of ComposeTopology
5                 >
6    class ComposeKernel;
```

---

[7] It is also essentially the output of the metafunction *SublayerInstantiation*.

This class template contains more template parameters than general layers: we should specify the types of containers for input and output, information related to the policy and instances of *ComposeTopology*.

*ComposeKernel* can be regarded as a metafunction that can serve to construct a class template denoting a composite layer. For instance, a linear layer consists of two sublayers used for matrix multiplication and addition. We can adopt *ComposeKernel* to introduce the following declaration:

```
1   struct WeightSublayer;
2   struct BiasSublayer;
3
4   using Topology
5       = ComposeTopology<SubLayer<WeightSublayer, WeightLayer>,
6                         SubLayer<BiasSublayer, BiasLayer>,
7                         InConnect<LayerIO, WeightSublayer, LayerIO>,
8                         InternalConnect<WeightSublayer, LayerIO,
9                                         BiasSublayer, LayerIO>,
10                        OutConnect<BiasSublayer, LayerIO, LayerIO>>;
11
12  template <typename TPolicies>
13  using Base = ComposeKernel<LayerIO, LayerIO, TPolicies, Topology>;
```

Lines 1 and 2 define the names of the sublayers contained in the composite layer; lines 4–10 define the connections among the sublayers; lines 12 and 13 call the metafunction *ComposeKernel* to construct the template *Base*, which corresponds to a composite layer. The input and output container of this composite layer are of type *LayerIO*. Meanwhile, the template *Base* contains a template parameter that specifies the policy of the composite layer. If we introduce appropriate template parameters for it, we can instantiate a class which contains most processing logic of composite layers—including main logic such as forward and backward propagation.[8]

## 7.4.2 Management of Sublayer Objects

*ComposeKernel* maintains an object of type *SublayerArray*, which, as its name suggests, is an array that contains all the sublayer objects.

```
1   template <typename TInputType, typename TOutputType,
2             typename TPolicyCont, typename TKernelTopo>
3   class ComposeKernel
4   {
5   private:
6       using TInstContainer
7           = typename TKernelTopo::template Instances<TPolicyCont>;
8       using SublayerArray
```

---

[8] Note that the instantiated class does not include the initialization logic of sublayers. So to strictly speak, the instantiated class contains most of the logic required for composite layers, but not all of the logic.

```
9              = typename SublayerArrayMaker<TInstContainer>::SublayerArray;
10        // ...
11   private:
12        SublayerArray sublayers;
13   };
```

Lines 6 and 7 of the code snippet declare *TInstContainer*, which is actually the result of instantiating *ComposeTopology::Instance* with policy. Based on the previous discussion, it is straightforward to be aware that *TInstContainer* is a container of type *std::tuple* in fact, where each sublayer is placed according to the result of topological sorting. Each sublayer is represented by an *InstantiatedSublayer* type that contains its tag and type.

On this basis, lines 8 and 9 calls the metafunction *SublayerArrayMaker* to construct the type *SublayerArray*, which is also a container of type *std::tuple*, except that each element of it is an object of type *std::shared_ptr <Layer>*—*Layer* represents the specific type of a sublayer.

*SublayerArray* maintains pointers to sublayer objects but *ComposeKernel* does not offer interfaces for calling constructors of sublayers to accomplish construction of sublayer objects. MetaNN does not bring in restrictions on constructors of layers, which can be called in a variety of ways. Correspondingly, there are no "uniform" methods of calling constructors for *ComposeKernel*. In order to complete construction of sublayers, *ComposeKernel* also relies on other interfaces of *SublayerArrayMaker*.

In addition to constructing the type *SublayerArray*, *SublayerArrayMaker* also supplies interfaces for initializing elements in *SublayerArray*:

```
1    template <typename TSublayerTuple>
2    struct SublayerArrayMaker
3    {
4    public:
5        using SublayerArray = ...
6
7        template <typename TTag, typename...TParams>
8        auto Set(TParams&&... params);
9
10       operator SublayerArray() const { return m_tuple; }
11   private:
12        SublayerArray m_tuple;
13   };
```

The first template parameter received by the template *Set* represents the name of the sublayer to be set, while the remaining template parameters denote the parameters required to call the constructor of the corresponding sublayer. The function *Set* will return the *SubarrayArrayMaker* object, so we can call *Set* multiple times in succession to construct each sublayer in turn. After that, we can employ the conversion operator of *SubarrayArrayMaker* to acquire the *SublayerArray* objects saved at the lower level.

In addition, *ComposeKernel* introduce an auxiliary function to construct objects of type *SubarrayArrayMaker*:

```
1   template <typename TInputType, typename TOutputType,
2               typename TPolicyCont, typename TKernelTopo>
3   class ComposeKernel
4   {
5       using TInstContainer
6           = typename TKernelTopo::template Instances<TPolicyCont>;
7   public:
8       static auto CreateSubLayers()
9       {
10          return SublayerArrayMaker<TInstContainer>();
11      }
12  };
```

These auxiliary functions collaborate to accomplish the construction of sublayer objects. Take the linear layer discussed earlier for example, we can construct the sublayer objects in the composite layer as follows:

```
1   // Declare the Class Templates Base
2   template <typename TPolicies>
3   using Base = ComposeKernel<LayerIO, LayerIO, TPolicies, Topology>;
4
5   // Assume CurPolicy is composite layer policy container
6   SublayerArray sublayers =
7   Base<CurPolicy>::CreateSubLayers()
8       .template Set<WeightSublayer>(WeightLayer Parameters)
9       .template Set<BiasSublayer>(BiasLayer Parameters)
```

Furthermore, we can bring in a class derived from the class template *Base* and encapsulate the logic of constructing sublayers in the constructor of the class:

```
1   // Declare the Class Templates Base
2   template <typename TPolicies>
3   using Base = ComposeKernel<LayerIO, LayerIO, TPolicies, Topology>;
4
5   template <typename TPolicies>
6   class LinearLayer : public Base<TPolicies>
7   {
8       using TBase = Base<TPolicies>;
9
10  public:
```

```
11      LinearLayer(const std::string& p_name,
12          size_t p_inputLen, size_t p_outputLen)
13          : TBase(TBase::CreateSubLayers()
14              .template Set<WeightSublayer>(p_name + "-weight",
15                                      p_inputLen, p_outputLen)
16          .template Set<BiasSublayer>(p_name + "-bias", p_outputLen))
17      { }
18  };
```

This is also how *LinearLayer* is implemented in the code enclosed in this book.

## 7.4.3 Parameter Acquisition, Gradient Collection, and Neutrality Detection

Chapter 6 mentioned that if a layer contains a parameter matrix, then the interface *Init* should be provided for parameter initialization and loading; the interface *SaveWeights* should be provided to obtain matrix parameters; the interface *GradCollect* should be provided to collect parameter gradients; the interface *NeutralInvariant* should be provided to detect if it is neutral. Meanwhile, each layer must offer interfaces *FeedForward* and *FeedBackward* for forward and backward propagation.

Composite layers also belong to layers, so they must conform to these requirements. The implementations of these interfaces are encapsulated inside *ComposeKernel*. Next, we'll discuss the implementations of the preceding interfaces in *ComposeKernel*.

Although in MetaNN, we specify that if a layer does not contain a parameter matrix, then interfaces such as *Init* are not required. However, this provision is intended only to simplify the writing of layers and there is no mandatory requirement. In other words, if the layer does not contain a parameter matrix, interfaces such as *Init* can also be implemented, except that they should not contain any substantive operations.

Determining whether a composite layer comprises a parameter matrix is essentially a determination of whether each of its sublayers contains a parameter matrix—which is relatively cumbersome. To simplify code writing, *ComposeKernel* implements interfaces such as *Init*. Nonetheless, if sublayers of a composite layer don't contain the appropriate interfaces, then interfaces such as *Init* won't introduce any side effects inherently.

Based on the easy-to-difficult principle, this section will begin with the implementations of interfaces *SaveWeights*, *GradCollect*, and *NeutralInvariant*. The implementations of *Init*, forward and backward propagation will be discussed later in turn.

The implementations of *SaveWeights*, *GradCollect*, and *NeutralInvariant* interfaces are analogous. Here we take *SaveWeights* as an exmaple. *SaveWeights* in *ComposeKernel* is defined as follows:

```
1   template <size_t N, typename TSave, typename TSublayers>
2   void SaveWeights(TSave& saver, const TSublayers& sublayers)
3   {
4       if constexpr (N != ArraySize<TSublayers>)
5       {
6           auto& layer = std::get<N>(sublayers);
```

```
7            LayerSaveWeights(*layer, saver);
8            SaveWeights<N + 1>(saver, sublayers);
9        }
10   }
11
12   template <typename TInputType, typename TOutputType,
13            typename TPolicyCont, typename TKernelTopo>
14   class ComposeKernel
15   {
16       // ...
17       template <typename TSave>
18       void SaveWeights(TSave& saver) const
19       {
20           SaveWeights<0>(saver, sublayers);
21       }
22   private:
23       SublayerArray sublayers;
24   };
```

*ComposeKernel::SaveWeights* calls the function templates with the same name *SaveWeights<N,TSave,TSublayers>* to obtain the parameters contained in each sublayer. This function template receives two parameters, denoting the container that stores the parameter matrix (*saver*) and the sublayers contained in the composite layer (*sublayers*). *SaveWeights<N,TSave, TSublayers>* introduces loops through *constexpr if* internally. It traverses each sublayer contained in the composite layer and uses *LayerSaveWeights*, the universal interface of sublayers, to attempt to invoke the interface *SaveWeights* for sublayers. As mentioned in Chapter 6, *LayerSaveWeights* automatically determines whether the layer passed to it contains the interface *SaveWeights*—if not, it will do nothing. Therefore, the invocation here is safe.

    *ComposeKernel* also introduces the interfaces *GradCollect* and *NeutralInvariant* in a similar way. They are also essentially accessing each sublayer in the composite layer sequentially and attempting to collect parameter gradients and execute neutral assertions for each sublayer through the layer's common interfaces. Due to limited space, there will be no code listed here.

### 7.4.4 Initialization and Loading of Parameters

If a layer contains a parameter matrix, it should also introduce the interface *Init* for initialization and loading of parameters. *ComposeKernel* defines the interface *Init* for composite layers. Essentially, this interface traverses each sublayer of the composite layer in turn and attempts to invoke the *Init* interface of the sublayer—same as *SaveWeights* discussed in the previous section. *Init* is discussed separately because we may need to specify different initialization methods for different layers.

    Consider the following scenario: a composite layer contains two linear layers,[9] named *Tag1* and *Tag2* respectively. Now we hope the *BiasLayer* corresponding to *Tag1* to initialize in one way and the remaining layers to initialize in another way.

---

[9] The linear layer itself is a composite layer that contains a *WeightLayer* and a *BiasLayer*.

We ought to adopt the initialization components to complete the initialization of layers in MetaNN. In order to achieve the preceding functions, we can define the initializers as follows:

```
1   struct Uniform1; struct Uniform2;
2   MakeInitializer<float,
3                   PInitializerIs<Uniform1>,
4                   SubPolicyContainer<Tag1,
5                                      PBiasInitializerIs<Uniform2>>>()
6       .SetFiller<Uniform1>(UniformFiller{ -1.5, 1.5 })
7       .SetFiller<Uniform2>(UniformFiller{ 0, 4 });
```

Two initializers *Uniform1* and *Uniform2* are defined here. The latter serves to initialize the first linear layer of *BiasLayer* and the former acts to initialize the remaining layers. Note that we cannot directly bring in the policy object *PBiasInitializerIs<Uniform2>* in *MakeInitializer*, which will lead to the fact that the *BiasLayer* for both linear layers are initialized with *Uniform2*. Here, we introduce *SubPolicyContainer* using the technique of policy inheritance to specify the appropriate initializer for a particular sublayer (*Tag1*).

In order to employ policy inheritance in the interface *Init*, *ComposeKernel* must introduce additional logic. *ComposeKernel::Init* delegates the initialization to a global function with the same name:

```
1    template <typename TInputType, typename TOutputType,
2             typename TPolicyCont, typename TKernelTopo>
3    class ComposeKernel
4    {
5        // ...
6
7        using TInstContainer
8            = typename TKernelTopo::template Instances<TPolicyCont>;
9
10       template <typename TInitializer, typename TBuffer,
11            typename TInitPolicies = typename TInitializer::PolicyCont>
12       void Init(TInitializer& initializer, TBuffer& loadBuffer,
13           std::ostream* log = nullptr)
14       {
15           Init<0, TInitPolicies, TInstContainer>
16               (initializer, loadBuffer, log, sublayers);
17       }
18   };
```

Compared to functions such as *SaveWeights*, the global function *Init* requires an additional template parameter: *TInstContainer*. It denotes the result of instantiating *ComposeTopology:: Instance* with delivered policy, which is a container of type *std::tuple* with each sublayer placed according to the result of topological sorting. Each sublayer is represented by an *InstantiatedSublayer* type, which contains the naming tags and specific types of the sublayers. The global interface *Init* uses the information in this container to acquire the names of each sublayer, and further derives the policy used for sublayer initialization based on the contents of initialization policy of the composite layer:

```
1    template <size_t N,
2                typename TInitPolicies, typename TSublayerInfo,
3                typename TInitializer, typename TBuffer,
4                typename TSublayers>
5    void Init(TInitializer& initializer, TBuffer& loadBuffer,
6            std::ostream* log, TSublayers& sublayers)
7    {
8        if constexpr (N != ArraySize<TSublayers>)
9        {
10            auto& layer = std::get<N>(sublayers);
11
12            using LayerInfo
13                = typename std::tuple_element<N, TSublayerInfo>::type;
14            using NewInitPolicy
15                = SubPolicyPicker<TInitPolicies, typename LayerInfo::Tag>;
16
17            LayerInit<typename LayerInfo::Layer, TInitializer,
18                    TBuffer, NewInitPolicy>
19                (*layer, initializer, loadBuffer);
20            Init<N + 1, TInitPolicies, TSublayerInfo>
21                (initializer, loadBuffer, log, sublayers);
22        }
23    }
```

Lines 12 and 13 of the code snippet obtain the corresponding *InstantiatedSublayer* container based on the index of the layer currently processed. With the information, we can use *LayerInfo::Tag* to obtain the name of the current layer. On this basis, lines 14 and 15 adopt *SubPolicyPicker* to acquire the initialization policy corresponding to the current sublayer. Lines 17–19 use it to call *LayerInit* to initialize the current layer.

## 7.4.5 Forward Propagation

The most significant task of layers is forward and backward propagation. The logic of forward and backward propagation for composite layers is much more complicated than interfaces such as *Init*. The main reason for this complexity is that, in order to be able to automatically execute forward and backward propagation, *ComposeKernel* should maintain a container internally to hold intermediate results generated by sublayers; it ought to also introduce mechanisms to recombine the input and output of sublayers for subsequent use.

Consider the composite layer described in Figure 7.1, which, in addition to invoking the interface *FeedForward* for each sublayer according to the resulting order of topological sorting, it should also accomplish the following tasks:

- Taking out the corresponding elements in the input container of the composite layer to construct the input container of *S1* and calling the forward propagation function of *S1*;
- Saving the output of *S1*;
- Taking out the corresponding elements in the input container of the composite layer and the output of *S1* to construct the input container of *S2*, and calling the forward propagation function of *S2*;
- Saving the output of *S2*;
- Obtaining the corresponding elements from the output of *S1* and *S2* to fill the output container of the composite layer.

The whole process involves a lot of operations pertinent to containers, which lead to the complexity of the code in forward propagation.

### 7.4.5.1 The Interface ComposeKernel::FeedForward

The interface *ComposeKernel::FeedForward* is implemented as follows:

```
1    template <typename TInputType, typename TOutputType,
2             typename TPolicyCont, typename TKernelTopo>
3    class ComposeKernel
4    {
5        // ...
6        using TInstContainer
7            = typename TKernelTopo::template Instances<TPolicyCont>;
8
9        template <typename TIn>
10       auto FeedForward(const TIn& p_in)
11       {
12           using InternalResType = InternalResult<TInstContainer>;
13           return FeedForwardFun<0,
14                                 typename TKernelTopo::InputConnects,
15                                 typename TKernelTopo::OutputConnects,
16                                 typename TKernelTopo::InterConnects,
17                                 TInstContainer>
18               (sublayers, p_in,
19                InternalResType::Create(), OutputType::Create());
20       }
21   };
```

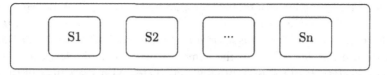

**Figure 7.2    Containers that store the results of sublayer calculations**

It first calls the metafunction *InternalResult* to construct a container (line 12) that holds the results of the sublayer calculation. On this basis, the auxiliary function *FeedForwardFun* is called to complete forward propagation.

Next, we'll start by constructing a container that holds the intermediate results of each sublayer, and on that basis, we'll discuss the implementation details of forward propagation.

### 7.4.5.2 Saving the Calculation Results of Sublayers

During forward and backward propagation of each sublayer, the input and output are stored in the associated containers. A composite layer ought to construct a new container to hold the calculation results for each sublayer. The relationships between the container for a composite layer to hold intermediate results and the sublayer containers are shown in Figure 7.2.

The outer frame represents the container constructed by the composite layer, which is used to store the calculation results of its sublayers. The output of a sublayer is also a container comprised in the container constructed by the composite layer.

The containers of different sublayers are distinct. We adopt the "heterogeneous dictionary" discussed in Chapter 2 as containers for the intermediate results of sublayers:

```
1   template <typename TProcessedRes, typename TContainer>
2   struct InternalResult_
3   {
4       using type = TProcessedRes;
5   };
6
7   template <typename...TProcessed, typename TCur, typename...TRemain>
8   struct InternalResult_<VarTypeDict<TProcessed...>,
9                   std::tuple<TCur, TRemain...>>
10  {
11      using type
12          = typename InternalResult_<VarTypeDict<TProcessed...,
13                                  typename TCur::Tag>,
14                                  std::tuple<TRemain...>>::type;
15  };
16
17  template <typename TContainer>
18  using InternalResult = typename InternalResult_<VarTypeDict<>,
19                                  TContainer>::type;
```

*InternalResult* is a metafunction that receives the output of *ComposeTopology::Instances* as its input. That is, the input of *InternalResult* is a sequence of *InstantiatedSublayers*, each *InstantiatedSublayer* represents the result of a sublayer instantiation. *InternalResult* traverses each sublayer of the sequence in turn, using *Tag* to obtain the names of sublayers and add them to the container *VarTypeDict*. A *VarTypeDict* type is eventually constructed with the names of each sublayer as the keys.

### 7.4.5.3 FeedForwardFun

*FeedForwardFun* encapsulates the implementation details of forward propagation, which is declared as follows:

```
1   template <size_t N,            // Index of the sublayer being processed
2       typename TInputConnects,      // Clauses of structural description
3       typename TOutputConnects,
4       typename TInnerConnects,
5       typename TSublayerMap,  // Instantiation information of sublayers
6       typename SublayerTuple, typename TInput,
7       typename TInternal, typename TOutput>
8   auto FeedForwardFun(SublayerTuple& sublayers,    // Sublayer objects
9           const TInput& input,  // Input container of composite layer
10          TInternal&& internal,  // Container for intermediate results
11          TOutput&& output);  // Output container of composite layer
```

The complexity of forward propagation logic is evident in the declaration of this function template. *FeedForwardFun* receives four function parameters that represent the sublayer objects saved by the composite layer (i.e., the *SublayerArray* object created previously), the input container and output container of the composite layer, and the container constructed in the previous section to save the intermediate results.

In addition to the preceding information, *FeedForwardFun* should also acquire the connections among sublayers within the composite layer, which are given through clauses of structural description to ensure that forward propagation works properly. In the section on *ComposeTopology*, we discussed that this class classifies statements of structural description into four containers, of which each includes the corresponding clauses. These clauses are supplied for *FeedForwardFun* and the corresponding functions of backward propagation. The second, third, and fourth template parameters received by *FeedForwardFun* correspond to the clause containers that represent the information of input, output, and inter-layer connections.

*FeedForwardFun* processes each sublayer in turn internally, which is also essentially a loop with its first template parameter representing the index of the sublayer currently being processed. Similar to functions such as *Init*, *FeedForwardFun* adopts the information to determine whether the loop terminates.

### 7.4.5.4 Constructing Input Containers of Sublayers

*FeedForwardFun* calls the interfaces for forward propagation of each sublayer. In order to implement this, it first constructs the input containers of sublayers. The input information of sublayers may come from two sources: the composite layer or the output of predecessor sublayers. *FeedForwardFun* constructs the container required to call the current layer by calling two auxiliary functions to acquire the appropriate information from each of these two sources:

```
1    auto FeedForwardFun(...)
2    {
3        // ...
4        auto input1
5            = InputFromInConnect<AimTag, TInputConnects>
6                (input, TSublayerInput::Create());
7        auto input2
8            = InputFromInternalConnect<AimTag, TInnerConnects>
9                (internal, std::move(input1));
10       // ...
11   }
```

*AimTag* corresponds to the name of the current layer, while *TInputConnects* and *TInnerConnects* are two containers for clauses *InConnect* and *InternalConnect* in statements of structural description. *FeedForwardFun* first calls *InputFromInConnect* to obtain input information from the input container of the composite layer and then calls *InputFromInternalConnect* to obtain input information from the predecessor sublyers.

Let's recall the method of constructing instances of input containers of sublayers. The following code snippet constructs *AddLayer*'s input container:

```
1    auto input = AddLayerInput::Create()
2                    .Set<AddLayerIn1>(i1)
3                    .Set<AddLayerIn2>(i2);
```

It first constructs a container object through the function *Create* and then calls *Set* to add contents for the container. A similar process is employed in *FeedForwardFun* to construct input containers for sublayers, except that the information in input containers comes from various portions. So, the original process of construction should be further decomposed.

Line 6 of *FeedForwardFun* calls the function *Create*, which constructs objects to be delivered to *InputFromInConnect*. *InputFromInConnect* essentially invokes several *Set* statements to configure elements in the containers. Correspondingly, *input1* is the result of calling *Create* and several *Set* statements.

However, the *Set* statements called in *InputFromInConnect* are not sufficient to fill the information in the input container of the sublayer—because it does not obtain the output information of its predecessor layers. On account of *input1*, *InputFromInternalConnect* is actually to further invoke *Set* statements based on the output of its predecessor layers, supplement the input information of the current sublayer and return the complemented result (*input2*).

Next, let's take *InputFromInConnect* as an example to see how to acquire input information.

## 7.4.5.5 The Implementation Logic of InputFromInConnect

The function *InputFromInConnect* is declared as follows:

```
1   template <typename TAimTag, typename TInputConnects,
2             typename TInput, typename TRes>
3   auto InputFromInConnect(const TInput& input, TRes&& res);
```

It receives four template parameters with two function parameters, among which:

1. *TAimTag* represents the name of the layer to be processed currently;
2. *TInputConnects* is a container in which each element is of type *InConnect*, which denotes the connections between the input container of the composite layer and the input containers of its sublayers;
3. *TInput* indicates the input container of the composite layer and *InputFromInConnect* receives the input container object of the composite layer *input* as its function parameter;
4. *TRes* represents the input containers of sublayers and *InputFromInConnect* receives the input container object of the sublayer *res* as its function parameter.

Each element in *TInputConnects* is of type *InConnect<InName,InLayertag,InLayerName>*, which indicates that in the input container of the composite layer, elements with *InName* as their keys should be delivered into the input container of the *InLayerTag* sublayer with *InLayerName* as the corresponding key. *InputFromInConnect* traverses each element in *TInputConnect* internally. If the corresponding element's *InLayerTag* is the same as *TAimTag*, then the instruction of current *InConnect* will be executed—obtaining the appropriate input object to store in the input container of the current sublayer:

```
1    template <typename TAimTag, typename TInputConnects,
2              typename TInput, typename TRes>
3    auto InputFromInConnect(const TInput& input, TRes&& res)
4    {
5        if constexpr (ArraySize<TInputConnects> == 0)
6        {
7            return std::forward<TRes>(res);
8        }
9        else
10       {
11           using TCur = SeqHead<TInputConnects>;
12           using TTail = SeqTail<TInputConnects>;
13           if constexpr (std::is_same<TAimTag,
14                                 typename TCur::InLayerTag>::value)
15           {
16               using InName = typename TCur::InName;
17               using InLayerName = typename TCur::InLayerName;
```

```
18              auto cur = std::forward<TRes>(res).
19                     template Set<InLayerName>
20                         (input.template Get<InName>());
21              return InputFromInConnect<TAimTag, TTail>
22                     (input, std::move(cur));
23          }
24      else
25      {
26          return InputFromInConnect<TAimTag, TTail>
27                 (input, std::forward<TRes>(res));
28      }
29  }
30 }
```

*ArraySize* is a metafunction that returns the number of elements in an input container. If *TInputConnects* contain no elements, the process terminates, or otherwise *InputFromInConnect* calls *SeqHead* to acquire the first element in the container *TInputConnects* to be compared with *TAimTag*. If the result of the comparison indicates that they are the same, then the input container of the sublayer will be configured (lines 18–20).

*InputFromInConnect* will call the metafunction *TTail* to remove the first element from *TInputConnects* no matter whether the elements in the input container of the sublayer are configured in the current loop. The results of *TTail* will be utilized in the next loop (lines 21 and 22 and 26 and 27).

## 7.4.5.6 *The Implementation Logic of* InputFromInternalConnect

*InputFromInternalConnect* is similar to *InputFromInConnect*, except that it obtains the corresponding input from the result of forward propagation in the predecessor layers. The function is declared as follows:

```
1  template <typename TAimTag, typename TInternalConnects,
2          typename TInternal, typename TRes>
3  auto InputFromInternalConnect(const TInternal& input, TRes&& res);
```

Among them:

- *TInternalConnects* is a container in which each element is of type *InternalConnect* and represents the connections among the sublayers of the composite layer;
- *TInternal* denotes a container that stores the intermediate results of the sublayers and Figure 7.2 shows its structure;
- The remaining parameters are the same as *InputFromInConnect*.

The implementation framework within *InputFromInternalConnect* is analogous to that of *InputFromInConnect*. Due to limited space, only how to obtain input from the intermediate result container of sublayers is listed:

```
1    auto InputFromInternalConnect(const TInternal& input, TRes&& res)
2    {
3        // ...
4        using TCur = SeqHead<TInternalConnects>;
5        if constexpr (std::is_same<TAimTag, typename TCur::InTag>::value)
6        {
7            using OutTag = typename TCur::OutTag;
8            using OutName = typename TCur::OutName;
9            using InName = typename TCur::InName;
10           auto preLayer = input.template Get<OutTag>();
11
12           auto cur = std::forward<TRes>(res).
13                     template Set<InName>
14                         (preLayer.template Get<OutName>());
15       }
16       // ...
17   }
```

*FeedForwardFun* calls the function of forward propagation for each sublayer according to the resulting order of topological sorting. Therefore, when dealing with the current sublayer, we can affirm that all of its predecessor layers have accomplished forward propagation and preserved the results in the intermediate result container of the sublayer. On this basis, if we call *InputFromInternalConnect*, it will traverse the items of type *InternalConnect* contained in *TInternalConnects*. The type *InternalConnect* is defined as follows:

```
template <typename TOutLayerTag, typename TOutName,
          typename TInLayerTag, typename TInName>
struct InternalConnect {
    using OutTag = TOutLayerTag;   // Name of the output sublayer
    using OutName = TOutName;      // Key of the output sublayer
    using InTag = TInLayerTag;     // Name of the input sublayer
    using InName = TInName;        // Key of the input sublayer
};
```

In line 5 of *InputFromInternalConnect* code snippet, if the requirements are satisfied, then the current statement describes that the result of forward propagation in a predecessor layer will be entered into the current layer. At this point, line 10 obtains the output of the sublayer corresponding to *OutTag* from the container described in Figure 7.2. Line 14 acquires the element corresponding to *OutName* from the output and adds the element to the input container of the current sublayer.

## 7.4.5.7 *Forward Propagation and Filling in Results of Output*

Once the input information is constructed, *FeedForwardFun* will call the function of forward propagation in the layer and obtain the results of the output to fill the intermediate result container and the output container of the composite layer:

```
1    auto FeedForwardFun(...)
2    {
3        // ...
4        auto res = curLayer.FeedForward(std::move(input2));
5        auto new_output = FillOutput<AimTag, TOutputConnects>
6                         (res, std::forward<TOutput>(output));
7        auto new_internal = std::forward<TInternal>(internal).
8                         template Set<AimTag>(std::move(res));
9        // ...
10   }
```

Line 4 calls the function *FeedForward* of the current layer and delivers the previously constructed input container to it, where the results are preserved in *res*. Lines 5 and 6 adopt *res* to fill the output container of the composite layer, while lines 7 and 8 use *res* to fill the intermediate result containers of sublayers for successor layers to obtain their inputs.

The only point that needs discussing in this code snippet is the call of *FillOutput* in lines 5 and 6. *FillOutput*'s declaration is as follows:

```
1    template <typename TAimTag, typename TOutputConnects,
2             typename TRes, typename TO>
3    auto FillOutput(const TRes& curLayerRes, TO&& output);
```

Among them:

- *TAimTag* represents the name of the current layer;
- *TOutputConnects* is a container in which each element is of type *OutConnect*. It denotes the connections between the output container of the composite layer and the output containers of the sublayers;
- *TRes* represents the output container of the current sublayer and *FillOutput* receives the output container object of the sublayer *curLayerRes* as its function parameter;
- *TO* denotes the output container of the composite layer and *FillOutput* receives the output container object of the composite layer *output* as its function parameter.

The output of sublayers may serve to fill in the output container of the composite layer. The method of filling is preserved in *TOutputConnects*, a container where each element is of type *OutConnect* and indicates that the output of a certain sublayer should be stored in the output container of the composite layer.

*FillOutput* traverses each *OutConnect* type in turn—if a certain type specifies that the output of the current sublayer is stored in the composite layer, then the interface *Set* of *output* is called to configure the corresponding object.

So far, we have completed the analysis of *FeedForwardFun*'s call (i.e., forward propagation) for a single sublayer. *FeedForwardFun* itself is a loop that calls each sublayer in turn. When the call is completed, the output of the composite layer is formed to be returned. The result will also be treated as the result returned by *ComposeKernel::FeedForward*.

### 7.4.6 Backward Propagation

*ComposeKernel* provides the interface *FeedBackward* for backward propagation. The logic of backward propagation is analogous to that of forward propagation and we will not discuss its details any more. Here we mainly discuss the distinctions between code of backward propagation and forward propagation.

Firstly, during forward propagation, we process each sublayer in the composite layer from front to back according to the resulting order of topological sorting. Nevertheless, the order of sublayers being processed in backward propagation is exactly the opposite of the order in forward propagation. Therefore, each sublayer should be processed from back to front in backward propagation according to the reverse order of topological sorting.

Secondly, the input of backward propagation is the output container of each sublayer, where elements may have multiple data sources. Consider the example in Figure 7.1, where the output container of the layer *S1* is delivered to the output container of the composite layer and the input container of *S2* in forward propagation. Accordingly, during backward propagation, the output container of *S1* obtains data from the output container of the composite layer and the input container of *S2* respectively.[10] Here, we should add the information from multiple data sources together and adopt it as the input for backward propagation.

## 7.5 Examples of Composite Layer Implementations

So far, we have basically accomplished the discussion of *ComposeTopology* and *ComposeKernel*. With these two components, it is effortless to combine basic layers to construct complex network structures. MetaNN contains several composite layers as examples, which will be briefly discussed in this section.

It should be noted that these composite layers are just examples for application of *ComposeTopology* and *ComposeKernel*. The code is relatively simple and far less important in MetaNN than other components. Readers can fully understand the construction processes of composite layers by reading the way the two layers are defined, so as to easily implement similar composite layers.

1. ***LinearLayer:*** It is a combination of *WeightLayer* and *BiasLayer*. Its contains two parameter matrices internally, $W$ and $b$. For an input vector $x$, it performs the operation of $y = Wx + b$ and returns.
2. ***SingleLayer:*** It executes nonlinear transformations against the input vector and returns. Its specific operations depend on the policy passed in.

---

[10] Note that this situation does not occur in forward propagation because the data source for each layer input container is unique in forward propagation.

- By default, *SingleLayer* contains a bias layer. For an input vector $x$, it performs the operation of $y = fun(Wx + b)$ and returns. *fun* represents nonlinear operations. $W$ and $b$ are the internal parameter matrices. But, if we configure Policy: *PNoBiasSingleLayer*, it will only execute $y = fun(Wx)$—that is, no bias layer is introduced.
- Currently, the nonlinear transformations of *SingleLayer* support only one of *Tanh* or *Sigmoid* operations. By default, *Sigmoid* is used. We can modify nonlinear transformations to *Tanh* via *PTanhAction*.

In fact, in addition to the two composite layers mentioned earlier, MetaNN implements another composite layer, *GruStep*. The composite layer itself is a kernel component of recurrent layers. On the basis of discussing composite layers, the next section will discuss the implementation of recurrent layers with *GRU* as an example.

# 7.6 Recurrent Layers

A recurrent layer is a basic component of the Recurrent Neural Network. We discussed RNN in Chapter 3, which has the following form:

$$\overrightarrow{h_n} = F(\overrightarrow{h_{n-1}}, \overrightarrow{x_n})$$

We set the input sequence as $\overrightarrow{x_1}, ..., \overrightarrow{x_N}$ and $\overrightarrow{h_0}$ is a preset parameter. The network will then obtain a total of $N$ outputs, $\overrightarrow{h_1}, ..., \overrightarrow{h_N}$. $F$ in the formula is a core step of calculation and the output resulting from different $F$ is distinct. Typical $F$ can be *GRU* (Gated United Unit), *LSTM* (Long Short Term Memory), and more. In MetaNN, we split the implementation of a recurrent layer into two steps: first, the core step $F$ is implemented through a composite layer; then on this basis, we achieve common recurrent logic and call the core step to complete the calculation. The recurrent logic only requires implementing once and then introducing various core steps is equivalent to implementing different calculation methods of recurrent layers.

This section will discuss the implementation of a recurrent layer with *GRU* as an example. Let's first look at the implementation of *GruStep*, the kernel algorithm for *GRU* in MetaNN.

## 7.6.1 GruStep

We can find multiple mathematical definitions of GRU by searching the Internet and they are not quite distinct from each other—mainly different in whether to introduce a bias layer. For the sake of simplicity, MetaNN implements one of the many definitions without introducing a bias layer. It is not tough to modify it and introduce the corresponding bias layer if necessary.

The mathematical definition of *GRU* in MetaNN is as follows[11]:

$$z_t = Sigmoid(W_z x_t + U_z h_{t-1})$$

$$r_t = Sigmoid(W_r x_t + U_r h_{t-1})$$

---

[11] For simplicity, arrows representing vectors above the letters are omitted here and we use lowercase letters representing vectors and capital letters representing matrices.

$$\hat{h}_t = Tanh\left(Wx_t + U(r_t \circ h_{t-1})\right)$$

$$h_t = z_t \circ \hat{h}_t + (1 - z_t) \circ h_{t-1}$$

It represents the tasks required in a loop at a time. $x_t$ is the input of the current step, $h_{t-1}$ is the output of the previous recurrent layer and $\circ$ denotes the multiplication of the corresponding elements.

Based on the preceding mathematical definition, we first introduce the container used by *GruStep*:

```
1   using GruInput = VarTypeDict<RnnLayerHiddenBefore,
2                                LayerIO>;
```

*RnnLayerHiddenBefore* is adopted to preserve the contents of $h_{t-1}$, while *LayerIO* serves to store $x_t$.

Next, we introduce sublayers and define the connections in *GruStep* based on the mathematical formulas as discussed. Take the first formula:

$$z_t = Sigmoid(W_z x_t + U_z h_{t-1})$$

for example, the corresponding introduced sublayers and connections are as follows:

```
1    struct Wz; struct Uz; struct Add_z; struct Act_z;
2
3    using Topology = ComposeTopology<
4        SubLayer<Wz, WeightLayer>,
5        SubLayer<Uz, WeightLayer>,
6        SubLayer<Add_z, AddLayer>,
7        SubLayer<Act_z, SigmoidLayer>,
8
9        // Wzxt
10       InConnect<LayerIO, Wz, LayerIO>,
11
12       // Uzht-1
13       InConnect<RnnLayerHiddenBefore, Uz, LayerIO>,
14
15       // Wzxt + Uzht-1
16       InternalConnect<Wz, LayerIO, Add_z, AddLayerIn1>,
17       InternalConnect<Uz, LayerIO, Add_z, AddLayerIn2>,
18
19       // Sigmoid (Wzxt + Uzht-1)
20       InternalConnect<Add_z, LayerIO, Act_z, LayerIO>,
21       // ...
22   >
```

That is, the output of the sublayer *Act_z* is $z_t$. The rest of the composite layer is constructed similarly to the way $z_t$ is organized and the code will not be listed here due to limited space. These statements describe the structure of *GruStep*.

On this basis, we can define *ComposeKernel* to automatically generate the logic of forward and backward propagation, etc. required by *GruStep*:

```
1    template <typename TPolicies>
2    using Base = ComposeKernel<GruInput, LayerIO, TPolicies, Topology>;
```

It indicates that the input container of the composite layer is *GruInput* (storing $x_t$ and $h_{t-1}$) and the output container is *LayerIO* (storing $h_t$).

The final step in constructing *GruStep* is to derive from the template *Base*, introduce the appropriate constructor, and construct the objects of each sublayer in it:

```
1    template <typename TPolicies>
2    class GruStep : public Base<TPolicies>
3    {
4        using TBase = Base<TPolicies>;
5
6    public:
7        GruStep(const std::string& p_name, size_t p_inLen, size_t p_outLen)
8            : TBase(TBase::CreateSubLayers()
9                    .template Set<Wz>(p_name + "-Wz", p_inLen, p_outLen)
10                   .template Set<Uz>(p_name + "-Uz", p_outLen, p_outLen)
11                   .template Set<Add_z>()
12                   .template Set<Act_z>()
13                   ...) {}
14
15   public:
16       template <typename TGrad, typename THid>
17       auto FeedStepBackward(TGrad&& p_grad, THid& hiddens)
18       {
19           auto res = TBase::FeedBackward(std::forward<TGrad>(p_grad));
20           hiddens = MakeDynamic(res.template Get<RnnLayerHiddenBefore>());
21
22           auto dynamicRes = MakeDynamic(res.template Get<LayerIO>());
23           return GruInput::Create().template Set<LayerIO>(dynamicRes);
24       }
25
26       // ...
27   }
```

In this way, we construct the composite layer *GruStep*. Calling forward and backward propagation for it is equivalent to mathematical transformations according to the formula discussed at the beginning of this section. Next, we'll build the class template *RecurrentLayer*, which invokes recurrently components like *GruStep* to implement the logic of recurrent layers.

Readers must have noticed that a new function *FeedStepBackward* has been introduced into the definition of *GruStep*. The kernel of this function is to call *FeedBackward* for backward propagation (line 20) but on this basis some new logic is introduced to post-process the results of the propagation. This function was introduced to facilitate the call of *RecurrentLayer*, which will be discussed in section 7.6.2.

## 7.6.2 *Building a* RecurrentLayer *Class Template*

MetaNN splits the construction of recurrent layers into two parts: components such as *GruStep* describe the specific functions to be performed in each loop; in addition, there is a *RecurrentLayer* class template that implements the general logic of recurrent layers. With combinations of common logic and various core components, recurrent layers like *GRU* and *LSTM* can be implemented. This section discusses the implementation of *RecurrentLayer*.

### 7.6.2.1 *Main Definitions of* RecurrentLayer

The main definition of the class template *RecurrentLayer* is as follows:

```
1   template <typename TPolicies>
2   class RecurrentLayer
3   {
4       using StepPolicy = typename
5        std::conditional_t<(!IsFeedbackOutput) && IsUpdate && UseBptt,
6                           ChangePolicy_<PFeedbackOutput, TPolicies>,
7                           Identity_<TPolicies>>::type;
8
9       using StepEnum = typename
10          PolicySelect<RecurrentLayerPolicy, CurLayerPolicy>::Step;
11      using StepType = StepEnum2Type<StepEnum, StepPolicy>;
12
13  public:
14      using InputType = typename StepType::InputType;
15      using OutputType = typename StepType::OutputType;
16
17  public:
18      template <typename TInitializer, typename TBuffer,
19               typename TInitPolicies>
20      void Init(TInitializer& initializer, TBuffer& loadBuffer,
21              std::ostream* log = nullptr);
```

```
22
23      template <typename TSave>
24      void SaveWeights(TSave& saver);
25
26      template <typename TGradCollector>
27      void GradCollect(TGradCollector& col);
28
29      template <typename TIn>
30      auto FeedForward(TIn&& p_in);
31
32      template <typename TGrad>
33      auto FeedBackward(const TGrad& p_grad);
34
35      void NeutralInvariant();
36
37  private:
38      StepType m_step;
39
40      using DataType = ...
41      DataType m_hiddens;
42      bool     m_inForward;
43  };
```

On the one hand, *RecurrentLayer* is also a layer, so it must conform to the interface specifications for layers in MetaNN, that is, to provide *InputType* and *OutputType* as container types for inputs and outputs, and functions *FeedForward* and *FeedBackward* to support forward and backward propagation. *RecurrentLayer*, on the other hand, calls the core algorithms (such as *GruStep*) it contains recurrently to implement the corresponding logic. It is precisely because of the introduction of loops that there are certain particularities in *RecurrentLayer* itself.

Lines 4–7 of the preceding code snippet adjust the policy of the core components. *UseBptt* indicates the use of *BPTT (Backpropagation through time)* algorithm in backward propagation of the recurrent layer. If it is *true*, then in order to calculate the parameter gradient in a certain step of backward propagation of the recurrent layer, we should obtain the output gradient in the previous step of backward propagation of the recurrent layer, which requires *IsFeedbackOutput* of the core component to be true. Lines 4–7 lines determine that if (1) *IsFeedbackOutput* of the core component is *false*, (2) the parameter gradient needs calculating for update, and (3) *BPTT* algorithm is used, then the policy of the core component is modified so that it can calculate the output gradient and return during backward propagation.

On this basis, lines 9–11 adopt the modified policy to derive the type of the core component. *StepEnum* obtains *StepPolicy* of the recurrent layer, which is an enumeration policy, indicating the core component of the recurrent layer is *GRU, LSTM,* or so on. Based on the information, line 9 calls the metafunction *StepEnum2Type*, using the previously obtained *StepPolicy* to instantiate and acquire *StepType*, the type of the core component in the recurrent layer.

Lines 14 and 15 adopt *StepType* to obtain the types of the input and output containers of the recurrent layer. The basic formula for a recurrent layer is $\vec{h}_n = F(\vec{h}_{n-1}, \vec{x}_n)$—which indicates that the first time the recurrent layer is called, $\vec{h}_0$ and $\vec{x}_1$ should be input and subsequent calls require input $\vec{x}_t$. But it does not prevent us from extending the input to the recurrent layer: for instance, adjusting the formula for the recurrent layer to $\vec{h}_n = F(\vec{h}_{n-1}, \vec{x}_n, \vec{y}_n)$—that is, when the recurrent layer is first invoked, $\vec{h}_0$, $\vec{x}_1$, and $\vec{y}_1$ should be input and subsequently $\vec{x}_t$ and $\vec{y}_t$ ought to be entered. The exact calling method is determined by the core component of the recurrent layer, so *RecurrentLayer* also relies on its core component to determine the appropriate types for input/output containers.

Lines 18–35 define the function interfaces that a recurrent layer should support. We'll discuss their implementations later.

Line 38 declares the core component object of type *StepType*, which is called in each forward and backward propagation.

The recurrent layer needs to maintain its intermediate state $\vec{h}_t$ inside, so that callers of the recurrent layer in other cases do not need to provide information of $\vec{h}_{t-1}$, except that the first forward propagation requires $\vec{h}_0$ to be provided. *m_hiddens* declared in lines 40 and 41 serves to record the intermediate state. *DataType* is the result of instantiation of the class template *DynamicData*, where whether matrices or lists of matrices are saved in it depends on the corresponding policy configurations for the recurrent layer.

Finally, the recurrent layer introduces a variable *m_inForward* to indicate whether it is currently in a state of forward propagation. We will further analyze the use of this variable in a follow-up discussion of forward and backward propagation.

### 7.6.2.2 How to Use RecurrentLayer

*ReLayercurrent*'s use follows the following process:

1. Calling *Init* to initialize or load parameters.
2. Forward propagation is called *N* times in turn, requiring $\vec{h}_0$ and $\vec{x}_1$ for the first call and only $\vec{x}_t$ for the rest.
3. Backward propagation is called *N* times in turn. Note that the call order of backward propagation must be completely opposite to that of forward propagation and the first call of backward propagation must be executed after all forward propagation calls are completed.

If there occurs an error in the order of calls for forward and backward propagation, then *RecurrentLayer* cannot guarantee its internal logic to be correct.

### 7.6.2.3 Implementations of Functions Such as SaveWeights

A recurrent layer is essentially the encapsulation outside its core component. Therefore, most of its functions can be delegated to the corresponding core component objects, except forward and backward propagation. Take the function *SaveWeights* for example:

```
1   template <typename TSave>
2   void SaveWeights(TSave& saver)
```

```
3   {
4       m_step.SaveWeights(saver);
5   }
```

Other methods' implementations are similar and will not be elaborated here.

## 7.6.2.4 Forward Propagation

Forward propagation of recurrent layers can be divided into two situations: the first call requires the input of $\overrightarrow{h_0}$ and subsequent calls do not require $\overrightarrow{h_{t-1}}$:

```
1   template <typename TIn>
2   auto FeedForward(TIn&& p_in)
3   {
4       auto& init = p_in.template Get<RnnLayerHiddenBefore>();
5       using rawType = std::decay_t<decltype(init)>;
6       m_inForward = true;
7
8       if constexpr(std::is_same<rawType, NullParameter>::value)
9       {
10          assert(!m_hiddens.IsEmpty());
11          auto real_in = std::move(p_in)
12                         .template Set<RnnLayerHiddenBefore>(m_hiddens);
13          auto res = m_step.FeedForward(std::move(real_in));
14          m_hiddens = MakeDynamic(res.template Get<LayerIO>());
15          return res;
16      }
17      else
18      {
19          auto res = m_step.FeedForward(std::forward<TIn>(p_in));
20          m_hiddens = MakeDynamic(res.template Get<LayerIO>());
21          return res;
22      }
23  }
```

The key for $\overrightarrow{h_0}$ is *RnnLayerHiddenBefore*. If the value corresponding to this key is not empty (i.e., lines 18–22 in the code snippet), it indicates that it is the first call of the recurrent layer, at which point the interface *FeedForward* of the core component can be called directly. Otherwise, we need to take the intermediate variable saved in the recurrent layer to fill in the key corresponding to *RnnLayerHiddenBefore* in the input container. On that basis the interface *FeedForward* of the core component is called (lines 10–15).

Regardless of the call scenarios, *FeedForward* will set *m_inForward* as *true*—indicating that it is currently in a state of forward propagation. It will also preserve the contents of *LayerIO* in the output of the core component in *m_hiddens*, which will be introduced as $\overrightarrow{h_{t-1}}$ the next time the recurrent layer calls forward propagation.

### 7.6.2.5 Backward Propagation

The code of backward propagation in a recurrent layer is as follows:

```
1    template <typename TGrad>
2    auto FeedBackward(const TGrad& p_grad)
3    {
4        if constexpr(UseBptt)
5        {
6            if (!m_inForward)
7            {
8                auto gradVal = p_grad.template Get<LayerIO>();
9                auto newGradVal = gradVal + m_hiddens;
10               auto newGrad = LayerIO::Create()
11                               .template Set<LayerIO>(newGradVal);
12               return m_step.FeedStepBackward(newGrad, m_hiddens);
13           }
14           else
15           {
16               m_inForward = false;
17               return m_step.FeedStepBackward(p_grad, m_hiddens);
18           }
19       }
20       else
21       {
22           return m_step.FeedBackward(std::forward<TGrad>(p_grad));
23       }
24   }
```

It calls the function for backward propagation of the core component to implement related features.

If the recurrent layer does not adopt *BPTT*, then this call is trivial—corresponding to line 22 of the code snippet. Otherwise, the output gradient calculated by the last backward propagation should be added to the current input gradient and the newly calculated results will used to execute backward propagation.

The purpose of *m_inForward* is embodied here. If it is *true*, the currently called backward propagation is the first call of backward propagation after forward propagation. At this point, the object stored in *m_hiddens* is the intermediate results of forward propagation instead of the output gradient calculated by the last backward propagation—therefore it cannot be added to the input gradient. Conversely, if *m_inForward* is *false*, it denotes that at least one backward propagation has been performed, at which point the content of *m_hiddens* is the output gradient of the previous backward propagation and should be added to the input gradient before backward propagation (lines 8–12).

Note that the preceding logic is only valid when *BPTT* is *true*. The maintenance of *m_inForward* is only in this branch. Meanwhile, if *BPTT* is true, the function *FeedStepBackward* offered by the core component should be called instead of the function *FeedBackward*.

## 7.6.2.6 The Function FeedStepBackward

Let's take *GruStep* as an example and look at the implementation of the function *FeedStepBackward*:

```
1    template <typename TPolicies>
2    class GruStep : public Base<TPolicies>
3    {
4      template <typename TGrad, typename THid>
5      auto FeedStepBackward(TGrad&& p_grad, THid& hiddens)
6      {
7        auto res = TBase::FeedBackward(std::forward<TGrad>(p_grad));
8        hiddens = MakeDynamic(res.template Get<RnnLayerHiddenBefore>());
9
10       auto dynamicRes = MakeDynamic(res.template Get<LayerIO>());
11       return GruInput::Create().template Set<LayerIO>(dynamicRes);
12     }
13
14     // ...
15   }
```

The core components of recurrent layers are required to provide a *FeedStepBackward* interface, which calls *FeedBackward* for backward propagation (line 7). On this basis, it extracts element with *RnnLayerHiddenBefore* as key in the result of backward propagation and preserves them in *hiddens* to be added to the input gradient for the next backward propagation.

More importantly, *FeedStepBackward* will "transform" the results of backward propagation and call *MakeDynamic* on each element in the result container to remove specific information of data types. A new container is constructed and returned using the transformed object (lines 10 and 11).

Why do we do this? Let's review the implementation of *RecurrentLayer::FeedBackward*. In the branch with *UseBptt* as *true*, we might add the value in *m_hiddens* to the input gradient and then execute backward propagation, or not do this addition and directly execute backward propagation. The selection depends on the value of *m_inForward*. The value of *m_inForward* is a runtime variable, which means that the branch with *UseBptt* as *true* should introduce two sub-branches and the selection of sub-branches is made at runtime.

Addition will alter the data type of the result[12] and the type of container for *FeedStepBackward* will vary depending on whether the addition operation is performed. When *FeedBackward* is called in *FeedStepBackward*, various types of output will be produced due to different types of input.

Whether to add or not is determined at runtime. If we attempt to return directly to the *FeedBackward* result of the core component, then *RecurrentLayer::FeedBackward* will produce different types of output at runtime, which is not allowed. We must "convert" the output of the core components to be of the same type in order to allow *RecurrentLayer::FeedBackward* to return correctly. To achieve the preceding transformation, we should first call *FeedBackward* of the core component and obtain the corresponding result container, and then convert each element in the container to the corresponding dynamic type.

The container used by a recurrent layer is defined by its core component, so the conversion process is also placed inside core components. That's why we introduce the function *FeedStepBackward* into core components of recurrent layers.

### 7.6.3 *The Use of RecurrentLayer*

MetaNN provides *tes_gru.cpp* to test the recurrent layer with *GruStep* as the core component. Due to limited space, the code will not be analyzed here. Readers can refer to the relevant code and learn how to use *RecurrentLayer*.

## 7.7 Summary

We have to say that there are quite abundant contents in this chapter. Although the author tries to filter out relatively unimportant parts, there are still more contents in this chapter than previous chapters.

This chapter focused on composite layers. *ComposeTopology* and *ComposeKernel* through metaprogramming were introduced, which collaborate in the automation of forward and backward propagation. *ComposeTopology* and *ComposeKernel* are the most complicated metaprograms in this book. The results are also remarkable. If we turn to the implementation code of *LinearLayer* in MetaNN, we can find that it is quite effortless to implement a composite layer like *LinearLayer* due to the introduction of these two classes.

Based on the discussion of composite layers, recurrent layers were introduced and the *GRU* algorithm implemented. We divided recurrent layers into core components and common structures to discuss how the two parts were implemented. Depending on common structures, we can implement different recurrent logic by constructing composite layers and introducing various core components.

No matter whether a layer is a basic layer, a composite layer, or a recurrent layer, its essence is to transform the input data and construct operation templates. In Chapter 8, we'll discuss evaluation, that is, how to quickly calculate operation templates to acquire the results.

---

[12] Let's recall—addition just constructs operation templates and the types of operation templates are relevant to the types of operands. Result types vary depending on different input types.

## 7.8 Exercises

1. Read *PlainPolicy*'s implementation code.
2. When discussing the implementation of *SubPolicyPicker*, we give an example—assuming that the policy of the composite layer is as follows:

```
using oriPC =
PolicyContainer<P1,
                SubPolicyContainer<SubX, P2,
                                   SubPolicyContainer<SubY, P3>>>
```

If we call *SubPolicyPicker<oriPC, SubX>*, it will return

```
PolicyContainer<P2, SubPolicyContainer<SubY, P3>, P1>
```

Can we have this metafunction return *PolicyContainer<P2, P1>*? Why?

3. When discussing the implementation of *SubPolicyPicker*, we give an example—assuming that the policy of the composite layer is as follows:

```
using oriPC =
PolicyContainer<P1,
                SubPolicyContainer<SubX, P2,
                                   SubPolicyContainer<SubY, P3>>>
```

If we call *SubPolicyPicker<oriPC, SubZ>*, it will return *PolicyContainer <P1>*.
Can we have this metafunction return *oriPC* directly? Why?

4. Modify the implementation of *SubPolicyPicker* so that for the following Policy containers:

```
using Ori = PolicyContainer<P1,
                            SubPolicyContainer<Sub, ...>,
                            SubPolicyContainer<Sub, ...>>;
```

it can obtain the union set of specified Policies in the two *SubPolicyContainers*.

5. This chapter discusses the eight examinations introduced in MetaNN to determine the correctness of syntax for structural description. Please consider if there is something else to examine.

6. Read and understand the structural validity detection code.

7. *SublayerInstantiation* receives the results of topological sorting as input and instantiate each sublayer. Can we adopt a sublayer container before topological sorting as input? Why?

8. When instantiating sublayers, we introduce the metafunction *Identity_*. Can we modify the code discussed in this chapter as follows?

```
using FeedbackOutUpdate
    = typename std::conditional_t<IsPlainPolicyFeedbackOut,
                            SublayerWithPolicy,
                            FeedbackOutSet<SublayerWithPolicy,
                                        InterConnects>>::type;
```

Or modify it as follows?

```
using FeedbackOutUpdate
= typename std::conditional_t<IsPlainPolicyFeedbackOut,
                        SublayerWithPolicy,
                        FeedbackOutSet<SublayerWithPolicy,
                                    InterConnects>::type>;
```

Why?

9. There's still much space for improvement in the *ComposeKernel* we've constructed. For instance, in order to construct a composite layer using *ComposeKernel*, we need to derive it and call constructors of each sublayer in turn in the constructor of the derived class. For the previously constructed *GruStep*, it means that we should write as follows:

```
GruStep(const std::string& p_name, size_t p_inLen, size_t
p_outLen)
    : TBase(TBase::CreateSubLayers()
            .template Set<Wz>(p_name + "-Wz", p_inLen, p_outLen)
            .template Set<Uz>(p_name + "-Uz", p_outLen, p_outLen)
            .template Set<Add_z>()
            .template Set<Act_z>()
            .template Set<Wr>(p_name + "-Wr", p_inLen, p_outLen)
            .template Set<Ur>(p_name + "-Ur", p_outLen, p_outLen)
            .template Set<Add_r>()
            .template Set<Act_r>()
            .template Set<W>(p_name + "-W", p_inLen, p_outLen)
            .template Set<U>(p_name + "-U", p_outLen, p_outLen)
            .template Set<Elem>()
            .template Set<Add>()
            .template Set<Act_Hat>()
            .template Set<Interpolate>())
    {}
```

It explicitly calls constructors of each sublayer, which is obviously too prolix. Many of the statements call the default constructor of a sublayer. We can try to modify the logic of *ComposeKernel* so that calls of the default constructor are omitted when constructing sublayers. Take the preceding calls as an example; the modified *ComposeKernel* supports the following shorthand:

```
GruStep(const std::string& p_name, size_t p_inLen, size_t
p_outLen)
    : TBase(TBase::CreateSubLayers()
        .template Set<Wz>(p_name + "-Wz", p_inLen, p_outLen)
        .template Set<Uz>(p_name + "-Uz", p_outLen, p_outLen)
        .template Set<Wr>(p_name + "-Wr", p_inLen, p_outLen)
        .template Set<Ur>(p_name + "-Ur", p_outLen, p_outLen)
        .template Set<W>(p_name + "-W", p_inLen, p_outLen)
        .template Set<U>(p_name + "-U", p_outLen, p_outLen))
{}
```

Sublayers that are not explicitly constructed will be initialized with the default constructor. Consider how to modify the existing code to implement this feature. One point to be aware of: if a sublayer doesn't have a default constructor, the program should be smart enough to prompt an error at compile time.

10. In *ComposeKernel*, we adopt *FeedForwardFun* for forward propagation. *FeedForwardFun* processes each sublayer in turn—firstly construct the input required for sublayers; then write the output into the intermediate result container and the output container of the composite layer after forward propagation. Now modify the algorithm and divide *FeedForwardFun* into two subfunctions. The former is responsible for calculating the forward propagation results for each sublayer and placing them in the intermediate result container while the latter serves to copy the results from the intermediate result container and place them in the output container of the composite layer. Please consider: what are the pros and cons of such modifications? Write code to verify your ideas.

11. In recurrent layers, we introduce *FeedStepBackward* to deal with the inconsistency of result types in *BPTT* branches. Consider whether there is a simpler way to solve the problem without introducing the function *FeedStepBackward*.

# Chapter 8

# Evaluation and Its Optimization

This chapter discusses the evaluation in MetaNN.

Evaluation is a fairly important step in deep learning frameworks. From the point of view of programming, the essence of a deep learning system is to transform the input data and produce the output result. Transformations like this require a large amount of computing resources. Whether the framework is able to quickly and accurately complete computations (or evaluations) directly determines the availability of it—if the entire process of evaluation is relatively slow, the entire system will be unable to conform to the actual computing requirements.

A number of software libraries have been developed to improve the performance of numerical computations. Deep learning frameworks can take advantage of the appropriate libraries to achieve acceleration of speed with the supplement of specific hardware. However, most software libraries focus on how to improve the performance of a certain algorithm, such as optimizing the algorithm to boost the performance of multiplying two matrices or providing algorithms to quickly calculate the output of a recurrent neural network such as LSTM.

MetaNN can adopt these libraries to improve system performance, which is equivalent to elevating computation speed from the level of operations. How to introduce such a software library for rapid evaluation will not be discussed in this chapter. This chapter is concerned with another dimension—how to enhance computation speed from the level of the entire network. It is precisely the metaprogramming techniques introduced in the previous chapters that provide a prerequisite for optimization of evaluation at the network level.

- Chapter 4 introduces a rich-type system, which allows optimization for different types in evaluation.
- Chapter 5 introduces expression templates, which postpone the entire network's evaluation process, thus providing a prerequisite for merging similar computations and multi-operation co-optimization.
- Chapter 6 and Chapter 7 construct layers, where the interfaces for forward and backward propagation are template member functions, thus minimizing layers' impact on optimization of computations.

Due to the support of the above techniques, it can be relatively facile to introduce performance optimization at the network level for MetaNN. It is an advantage that traditional deep learning frameworks without metaprogramming does not have. This chapter discusses the related techniques for evaluating optimization.

The evaluation in MetaNN involves the interaction with data types and operation templates, forming a relatively complex subsystem—evaluation subsystem. This chapter discusses the implementation of evaluation subsystem. We will first introduce the evaluation model in MetaNN and discuss three optimization methods on this basis: avoiding repetitive computations, merging similar computations and multi-operation co-optimization.

The first few chapters of this book focus on template metaprogramming. This chapter is slightly different from the previous chapters and does not emphasize metaprogramming, which is because the primary task of evaluation is runtime computing. Metaprogramming focuses on compile-time computing. In MetaNN, compile-time computing is not a goal, but a means—the goal is to provide better support for optimization of runtime computing. It is precisely the support of compile-time computing and metaprogramming that allows the implementation of optimization discussed in this chapter.

Although it is inevitable to involve something not relevant to metaprogramming in the discussion of evaluation, we will focus on the discussion of design principles and analyze the code related to metaprogramming.

## 8.1 Evaluation Models of MetaNN

Layers of MetaNN call the corresponding functions in the process of forward and backward propagation to construct operation templates. Evaluation in MetaNN is the process of converting operation template objects to the corresponding principal type.

### 8.1.1 Hierarchy of Operations

Operations of MetaNN construct the corresponding operation templates, which actually describe the relationships among parameters and results. A parameter of a certain operation may be the result of another operation. Accordingly, operation templates form a hierarchy among parameters and results. Figure 8.1 shows a typical hierarchy of operations.

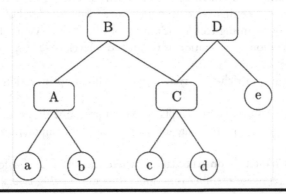

**Figure 8.1   A hierarchy of operations**

Circles represent data of principle types[1] and rounded rectangles denote operation templates in this figure. To describe them conveniently, we utilize lowercase letters to represent data of principle types and adopt uppercase letters to indicate operation templates. Here we mainly pay attention to the input structure of evaluation other than actual types of operations corresponding to operation templates, so letters are simply introduced to identify nodes in the diagram.

Comparing Figure 8.1 with Figure 5.1, it is effortless to find the differences: the input to the evaluation system is not a tree structure in the traditional sense. A single computation in a neural network may involve the evaluation of multiple objects. For example, in Figure 8.1, our goal is to complete the evaluation of the operation templates $B$ and $D$. Separately, the evaluation structure of $B$ or $D$ is a tree structure but $B$ and $D$ share some intermediate results (node $C$ in the figure). Therefore, the combination of the two constitutes the complex structure shown in Figure 8.1.

We can surely evaluate $B$ and $D$ individually. But the main advantage of MetaNN is to postpone the evaluation process to the end in the hope of increasing computation speed by combining operations. From this point of view, there is no reason for us not to combine the evaluation processes of $B$ and $D$, which would lead to more opportunities for evaluation optimization.

Based on the above structure, how to achieve evaluation? Obviously, since the evaluation of $B$ and $D$ depends on the evaluation result of $A$ and $C$, we should first evaluate $A$ and $C$ and then evaluate $B$ and $D$ on that basis in general.

From Figure 8.1, we can see that some parts can be optimized during the evaluation process. First, the evaluation processes of $B$ and $D$ are dependent on $C$. Thus, we only need to evaluate $C$ once and the result can be utilized in the evaluation processes of $B$ and $D$, which can avoid repetitive evaluation of $C$ and improve the efficiency of evaluation.

Another optimization may be relatively obscure—in the evaluation process, if computational processes of the same type can be combined, the speed of evaluation may be further enhanced. This usually requires dedicated software libraries to support. For example, some software libraries provide functions to support multiplication of multiple sets of matrices at the same time. Take Figure 8.1 as an example, assuming that both $A$ and $C$ are multiplications of matrices, it is possible to combine the evaluation processes of $A$ and $C$, which also increases the speed of evaluation.

In fact, there is another possibility of optimization. Considering Figure 8.1, one of our goals is to complete the evaluation of $D$. To complete this step, we should first evaluate $C$. In fact, if we know the input information and operation types of $C$ and $D$, we might be able to simplify the evaluation of this branch from a mathematical point of view—bypassing the process of evaluating $C$ and using $c$, $d$ and $e$ to complete the evaluation of $D$ directly.

This chapter discusses the implementation of the above three optimization methods later.

## 8.1.2 *Module Division of Evaluation Subsystems*

MetaNN introduces multiple modules to cooperate in achieving evaluation:

- *EvalPlan* serves to receive evaluation requests, organize evaluation processes, and call *EvalPool* to complete the evaluation operation;
- *EvalPool* receives the evaluation requests in *EvalPlan* and invokes the evaluation logic to complete the computations in evaluation;
- *EvalUnit* is utilized to describe specific evaluation methods;

---

[1] For instance, the principal type for matrices is the type generated by the instantiation of the template *Matrix*.

■ *EvalGroup* is used to integrate the same *EvalUnit* to combine similar computations, thus improving the efficiency of evaluation;

■ *EvalHandle* encapsulates the parameters and results of evaluation;

■ *EvalBuffer* saves the results of evaluation to avoid repetitive evaluation of a same object.

Next, we'll start with Figure 8.1 as an example to outline the evaluation processes in MetaNN. Later, we'll discuss the implementation of each module in turn.

### 8.1.2.1 Overview of an Evaluation Process

An evaluation process in MetaNN is divided into two steps: registration and computation. Data types of MetaNN must provide the function *EvalRegister* for evaluation registration. Meanwhile, MetaNN also offers the function *EvalPlan::Eval*, which triggers the actual computations in evaluation. Registration returns an *EvalHandle* object, which encapsulates the result of evaluation. A typical evaluation involves calling the function *EvalRegister* several times to obtain the corresponding *EvalHandle* objects, then calling the function *EvalPlan::Eval* once for actual computations; using the corresponding *EvalHandle* objects to acquire the result of evaluation. Take Figure 8.1 as an example, in order to complete the evaluation of *B* and *D*, we may need to write as follows:

```
1    auto handle1 = B.EvalRegister();
2    auto handle2 = D.EvalRegister();
3
4    EvalPlan::Eval()
5
6    auto resB = handle1.Data();
7    auto resD = handle2.Data();
```

*resB* and *resD* correspond to the evaluation results of *B* and *D* respectively.

Next, let's take the call of *B.EvalRegister* as an example to explain the registration process of evaluation. Typically, an object of type *EvalBuffer* will be preserved in *B*. If *B* has been evaluated before, the results of evaluation are saved in its *EvalBuffer*. At this point, *B.EvalRegister* returns the object of type *EvalHandle* directly, indicating the results of evaluation. *B.EvalRegister* will actually construct a request for evaluation and complete the entire process of evaluation only if *B* has not been evaluated before.

If we hope to construct an evaluation request in *B.EvalRegister*, *B.EvalRegister* should first call *A.EvalRegister* and obtain the corresponding *EvalHandle* object because the evaluation of *B* depends on *A*. The object represents the evaluation result of *A*. Similarly, *B.EvalRegister* also ought to call *C.EvalRegister* to acquire the appropriate handle that represents the evaluation result of *C*.

On the basis of obtaining handles that represent the evaluation results of *A* and *C*, *B.EvalRegister* can obtain a handle representing the evaluation result of *B* through its internal *EvalBuffer*. *B.EvalRegister* will call the function *DataPtr* of the three handles to obtain *const void** pointers to the parameters and the resulting data. *B. EvalRegister* then constructs an *EvalUnit* object that contains an *Eval* member function, encapsulating the specific computational logic. The *EvalUnit* object, as well as the *const void** pointers, are delivered to the interface *EvalPlan::Register* to execute registration of evaluation in *EvalPlan*.

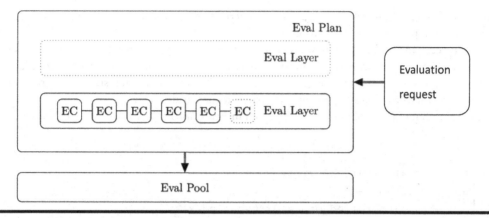

**Figure 8.2    The framework of *EvalPlan***

*EvalPlan::Register* determines the order of the current request throughout the evaluation process depending on the delivered *const void\** pointers internally. Based on this order and specific information of computations, the incoming *EvalUnit* object is placed in a certain *EvalGroup*, which encapsulates computations of the same type that can be performed simultaneously.

After all evaluation requests have been registered, *EvalPlan::Eval* can be called to trigger the actual computations. In actual computations, *EvalPlan::Eval* will call the interface *EvalGroup*, obtain the corresponding *EvalUnit* and deliver it to *EvalPool*, which calls the interface *EvalUnit::Eval* to implement the actual computations.

*EvalUnit* contains the argument handle and the result handle. When *EvalUnit::Eval* is called, we can confirm that the corresponding evaluation result has been saved in the argument handle.[2] *EvalUnit::Eval* acquires the corresponding parameter value from the argument handle, invokes the specific computational logic and saves the result in the result handle—which is utilized for subsequent evaluation or to obtain the result after the completion of evaluation (e.g., lines 6 and 7 of the discussed code snippet).

Next, we'll discuss the implementation details for each module in turn. Let's start with *EvalPlan*.

### 8.1.2.2  EvalPlan

The entire framework of *EvalPlan* is shown in Figure 8.2.

It is the kernel of the entire evaluation subsystem, which receives evaluation requests, organizes evaluation processes, and provides the interface *Eval* to trigger evaluation. We should call *EvalRegister* for each object to be evaluated to register evaluation requests in *EvalPlan* and call *EvalPlan::Eval* for the actual evaluation after the registrations are completed.

When registering, the evaluation requests will be delivered to the interface *EvalPlan::Register*. The evaluation requests contain *EvalUnit*, which represents the actual unit of computation, a pointer to the result and a vector that contains a pointer to the argument of computation.

*EvalPlan* utilizes incoming pointers to maintain the order of computations. It maintains a mapping between the computation results and the order of computations. When enter a certain

---

[2] In Figure 8.1, for instance, when *EvalUnit::Eval* relevant to *B* is called, it is guaranteed that the corresponding evaluation result is already included in the corresponding *EvalUnit* handles of *A* and *C*.

address, it can determine whether it points to a certain result of computation to be evaluated. If so, it can also return when computations should be performed.

When receiving a new computation request, *EvalPlan::Register* first traverses the pointers to the computation parameters and attempts to determine whether the corresponding computation parameter points to a registered computation. If true, then the calculation steps of the parameters are obtained and the execution time of the current request is deduced.

Computation requests of evaluation are saved in *EvalCluster* (i.e., *EC* in the figure). *EvalCluster* is defined as follows:

```
1   template <typename TDevice>
2   using EvalCluster
3       = std::unordered_map<std::type_index,
4                            std::shared_ptr<BaseEvalGroup<TDevice>>>;
```

It is a container that includes *EvalGroup* objects. Each specific *EvalGroup* is derived from the class *BaseEvalGroup<TDevice>* and serves to accumulate computations of the same type. The key in the container *EvalCluster* is *std:type_index*, which can help with distinguishing between different *EvalGroup* types. In the actual evaluation process, *EvalPlan* traverses *EvalGroup* in *EvalCluster*, obtains the corresponding evaluation request, and delivers it to *EvalPool* in order to complete the evaluation.

EvalPlan contains multiple *EvalClusters* and assigns each evaluation request to a specific *EvalCluster*. Multiple *EvalClusters* are introduced in order to describe the order of the evaluation processes. The same *EvalCluster* may contain multiple evaluation requests in an arbitrary order. However, there is a sequence among different *EvalClusters*—requests in subsequent *EvalClusters* can be executed only if all evaluation requests in earlier *EvalCultsers* have been executed.

Again, take Figure 8.1 as an example. In order to complete the evaluation of *B* in Figure 8.1, we must first evaluate *A* and *C*. To embody this point in the code, *B.EvalRegister* will first call *A.EvalRegister* and *C.EvalRegister* internally to register the corresponding evaluation requests. Later the evaluation request for *B* will be constructed and delivered to *EvalPlan*.

*EvalPlan* will first receive the execution request from *A.EvalRegister* and *C.EvalRegister* and accordingly place the computation requests in the first *EvalCluster*. After that, *EvalPlan* receives an execution request from *B*, which contains pointers to the computation parameters and points to the computation results of *A* and *C*. When *EvalPlan* traverses the parameter pointers, it will find that the computation requests for *A* and *C* are already in the first *EvalCluster* and place the computation request of *B* in the second *EvalCluster*.

In actual evaluation processes, *EvalPlan* passes the request in the first *EvalCluster* to *EvalPool*, then the request in the second *EvalCluster*, and so on, which guarantees the correctness of the evaluation sequence.

That's the kernel logic of *EvalPlan*. But readers must have found out that we have one component left to be discussed—*EvalLayer*. What does it do?

From *EvalPlan*'s point of view, the timings of evaluation requests it receives can be divided into two categories: before calling *EvalPlan::Eval* and during calling *EvalPlan::Eval*.

Most evaluation requests are registered into *EvalPlan* before *EvalPlan::Eval* is called. However, there are a few requests registered into *EvalPlan* during the call of *EvalPlan::Eval*.

For example, when evaluating *SoftmaxDerivative*, we construct an intermediate matrix and calculate the dot product of it and the input gradient. In order to calculate the dot product, we should construct a request for dot product and deliver it to *EvalPlan*. This request is constructed during the evaluation process of *SoftmaxDerivative*, which is triggered when *EvalPlan::Eval* is called. Accordingly, we obtain a new evaluation request when we call *EvalPlan::Eval*.

According to the original logic of *EvalPlan*, the parameters of the dot product request are all principal types. So, the request will be placed in the first *EvalCluster*. However, the computation request of *SoftmaxDerivative* may be in a subsequent *EvalCluster*. When calculating *SoftmaxDerivative*, the system will assume that the first *EvalCluster* request has already been processed, which will lead to the disposal of requests that should have been processed and incurs computation errors.

To deal with this problem, the concept of *EvalLayer* is introduced in *EvalPlan*. Initially, *EvalPlan* contains only one *EvalLayer* to receive the evaluation requests. Before calling *EvalPlan::Eval* to evaluate, the system will construct a new *EvalLayer* and requests entered during the evaluation process will be placed in the new *EvalLayer*. After processing each *EvalCluster*, the system will determine whether the newly constructed *EvalLayer* contains the newly introduced *EvalCluster*. If true, it denotes that a new evaluation request is introduced during processing the previous *EvalCluster*. The system will process the next EvalCluster after processing all the evaluation requests in the new *EvalLayer*.

In fact, *EvalPlan* can contain multiple *EvalLayers*—they form a stack structure. New requests may be introduced in the second *EvalLayer* when the system process requests in the first *EvalLayer*; and new requests may be introduced in the third *EvalLayer* when processing requests in the second *EvalLayer*. *EvalPlan* is designed to handle these complex situations.

### 8.1.2.3 EvalPool

*EvalPool* obtains the evaluation requests in *EvalPlan* and calls the evaluation function to complete the actual evaluation.

Objects of type *EvalUnit* are delivered to *EvalPool*, each of which contains an *Eval* interface that encapsulates the actual evaluation logic. The main task for *EvalPool* is to call this *Eval* interface to complete computations.

The implementation of *EvalPool* can be fairly simple, such as calling the function *Eval* of each *EvalUnit* object in turn. It can also be complicated, such as containing several computing threads to execute multiple computations at the same time. *EvalPool* should also supply an interface *Barrier* to wait for all evaluations in *EvalPool* to be completed. As mentioned earlier, *EvalPlan* divides the evaluation requests into *EvalCluster*. After delivering all the computation requests in a certain *EvalCluster* to *EvalPool*, it calls the interface *EvalPool::Barrier*. After the interface returns, it continues to deliver the evaluation unit in the next *EvalCluster*. Accordingly, *EvalPool* must guarantee that the computations in *EvalPool* are fully completed when its interface *Barrier* returns—in order to ensure the sequentiality of computations.

In the current version of MetaNN, only a fairly trivial *TrivalEvalPool* is implemented, which serves to evaluate incoming *EvalUnit* objects and does not involve multithreaded operations. We can also add more complex *EvalPool* to the framework if necessary, thereby promoting computational parallelism.

### 8.1.2.4 EvalUnit

*EvalUnit* contains the specific logic of evaluation. All *EvalUnit* objects are derived from *BaseEvalUnit*[3]:

```
1  template <typename TDevice>
2  class BaseEvalUnit
3  {
4  public:
5      using DeviceType = TDevice;
6      virtual ~BaseEvalUnit() = default;
7
8      virtual void Eval() = 0;
9  };
```

The derived classes ought to implement the *Eval* method to encapsulate the actual computational logic. We'll see an example of *EvalUnit*'s implementation as we discuss specific implementations of evaluation later.

### 8.1.2.5 EvalGroup

*EvalGroup* is utilized to integrate the same *EvalUnit* to combine similar computations, thus improving evaluation efficiency. Each *EvalGroup* is derived from *BaseEvalGroup*:

```
1  template <typename TDevice>
2  class BaseEvalGroup
3  {
4  public:
5      virtual ~BaseEvalGroup() = default;
6      virtual std::shared_ptr<BaseEvalUnit<TDevice>> GetEvalUnit() = 0;
7      virtual void Merge(BaseEvalUnit<TDevice>&) = 0;
8      virtual void Merge(BaseEvalUnit<TDevice>&&) = 0;
9  };
```

The derived classes should implement the interface *Merge* to add *EvalUnit* internally and the interface *GetEvalUnit* to obtain *EvalUnit*.

MetaNN currently implements only a trivial *TrivalEvalGroup*, which does not merge multiple *EvalUnits* into one, simply accumulates *EvalUnits* and returns them in turn when calling *GetEvalUnit*:

```
1  template <typename TEvalUnit>
2  class TrivalEvalGroup;
```

---

[3] *TDevice* represents the categories of computing units, such as CPU.

*TrivalEvalGroup* receives a template parameter that represents the corresponding *EvalUnit* type. Different *EvalUnits* can be instantiated to different *TivalEvalGroups*. We'll see how to use *TrivalEvalGroup* when discussing the implementation of specific evaluation logic. Meanwhile, we'll explain how to implement an *EvalGroup* that can merge *EvalUnits* based on the existing framework when talking about merging similar computations for optimization later.

### 8.1.2.6 EvalHandle

*EvalHandle* is the general term for evaluation handles in MetaNN, which can be used to obtain the corresponding results of evaluation through its interface *Data* after the completion of evaluation.

In fact, MetaNN implements three class templates that represent handles. Unlike *EvalUnit* and *EvalGroup*, these handle class templates are not derived from a base class. They are only conceptually relevant—they all provide the interface *Data* to return the corresponding results of evaluation and the interface *DataPtr* to return a pointer to the evaluation result. Distinct evaluation handles return different data types and *EvalPlan* requires a uniform representation of data to plan the order of evaluation order. Therefore, evaluation handles should provide the interface *DataPtr*, which returns a *void\** pointer to the data in the handle for *EvalPlan* to use.

These three class templates are collectively referred to as *EvalHandle*, but their specific scenarios are various.

- *EvalHandle<TData>*: It encapsulates the results of evaluation internally. In general, at the beginning of construction of this handle, the data saved in it is invalid. It provides the interface *IsEvaluated* to determine the validity of the data inside (i.e., whether evaluation has been performed). If the interface returns *false*, the system should execute evaluation and fill the handle with the results. *EvalHandle<TData>* also provides *Allocate* to allocate objects for preserving results; *MutableData* to obtain references to the result objects for the filling of results; *SetEval* to configure the validity of results after the filling of results. In addition to the above features, *EvalHandle<TData>* guarantees that the same result object is shared across multiple copies and the result are the same when multiple copies of *EvalHandle<TData>* calls *DataPtr*. It allows us to introduce multiple copies of an *EvalHandle<TData>* object in the process of evaluation, thus simplifying the writing of the evaluation code.
- *ConstEvalHandle<TData>*: MetaNN requires each of its data members to offer an interface *EvalRegister* to register evaluations and return the appropriate handle. The handle will serve to obtain the evaluation results without providing a write interface to modify the saved contents. It just needs to provide a read interface. MetaNN uses *ConstEvalHandle<TData>* to describe this read-only handle. Typically, *EvalRegister* of operation templates returns an instantiation type of *ConstEvalHandle*. In addition, MetaNN introduces the function *MakeConstEvalHandle*, which can receive data objects and construct the corresponding *ConstEvalHandle* handle.
- *DynamicsConstEvalHandle<TData>*: Chapter 6 introduces the data type *DynamicData* to preserve intermediate results of layers, which is also involved in the evaluation process. However, *DynamicData* hides specific type information, so we don't know what type of handle should be constructed when calling *EvalRegister* for this data type. To solve this problem, MetaNN introduces a data type *DynamicConstEvalHandle<TData>*. *DynamicData::EvalRegister* returns objects of this type. *DynamicConstEvalHandle<TData>* is similar to *ConstEvalHandle<TData>*—they are both read-only and we cannot modify the data inside.

### 8.1.2.7 EvalBuffer

*EvalBuffer* preserves the results of evaluation, avoiding repetitive evaluation of the same object.

In general, each object of non-principal types should contain a data field *EvalBuffer* to store the results of evaluation. An operation template is a typical non-principal type. Take *UnaryOp* as an example:

```
1   template <typename TOpTag, typename TData>
2   class UnaryOp
3   {
4       // ...
5       using Cate = OperCateCal<TOpTag, TData>;
6       using TPrincipal = PrincipalDataType<Cate, ElementType, DeviceType>;
7
8       EvalBuffer<TPrincipal> m_evalBuf;
9   };
```

*Cate* represents the category of the operation template. On this basis, the metafunction *PrincipalDataType* deduces the principal type corresponding to the current operation template instance according to the types of the computing unit and the computing device. This principal type is used to instantiate the *EvalBuffer* object *m_evalBuf*.

*EvalBuffer* is a class template that can be instantiated using different principal types (such as *Matrix*, *Scalar*, and so on). It provides three interfaces internally.

■ *IsEvaluated*: it indicates whether the data saved in it has been evaluated.
■ *Handle*: it returns a handle to modify the evaluation result.
■ *ConstHandle*: it returns a handle to obtain the results of evaluation.

The results returned by *Handle* and *ConstHandle* essentially points to the same result object of evaluation, except that the former can modify its internal data during computations and the latter is read-only to read the computation results.

### 8.1.2.8 The Auxiliary Function Evaluate

To simplify the use of the evaluation system, MetaNN also offers an auxiliary function *Evaluate*, which receives an object to be evaluated, calls the *EvalRegister* method of the object internally and then calls the function *EvalPlan::Eval* to complete the evaluation and return the result. This function simplifies the evaluation interface but can only register one object to be evaluated at a time, thus losing some opportunities for evaluation optimization.

That's all the moduls in the evaluation subsystem of MetaNN. These modules do not contain the actual computational logic but provide maintenance of computation results, scheduling of computation processes and other functions. We don't delve into the details of these modules because the implementations of these modules are relatively trivial. Even though many modules are implemented as templates, not many of them involve metaprogramming techniques. The following contents of this chapter will focus on how to introduce appropriate evaluation logic into MetaNN and further optimize evaluation processes depending on these components. Next, we'll discuss these contents with some specific code snippets.

## 8.2 Basic Evaluation Logic

This section discusses the basic evaluation logic in MetaNN through several examples.

Each data type in MetaNN requires interfaces such as *EvalRegister* to support evaluation. Distinct data types can implement the interface in different ways. Let's first look at how principal types implement this interface.

### 8.2.1 Evaluation Interface of Principal Types

MetaNN is rich-type and we can introduce a variety of types for it, which will be divided into categories. Meanwhile, we introduce a principal type for each category. Typically, the class template *Matrix<TElement,TDevice>* is the principal type of the matrix category.

Evaluation is essentially the process of converting a specific data type to the corresponding principal type. Although it does not require the introduction of substantive transformations for principal types, the principal type should also implement evaluation-related interfaces in order to ensure consistency across the framework, particularly the interface *EvalRegister*. Let's take the class template *Matrix<TElement,TDevice>* as an example to consider how this interface is implemented in the principal type:

```
1   template <typename TElem>
2   class Matrix<TElem, DeviceTags::CPU>
3   {
4       // ...
5       auto EvalRegister() const
6       {
7           return MakeConstEvalHandle(*this);
8       }
9   };
```

*EvalRegister* ought to return a handle, and therefore the rest of the framework and end users can adopt it to obtain the results of evaluation. For the principal type, it does not need to be evaluated, so its *EvalRegister* implementation is trivial and only needs to construct a *ConstEvalHandle* handle on its own and return it.

Similar to the implementation in *Matrix*, the two principal types *Scalar* and *Batch* simply construct a *ConstEvalHandle* handle in their *EvalRegister* interface and return it.

### 8.2.2 Evaluation of Non-principal Basic Data Types

In Chapter 4, in addition to principal types, several basic data types are also mentioned, like *TrivalMatrix*. These data types should also implement evaluation interfaces that translates them to the appropriate principal types. This section takes the example of *TrivalMatrix* to illustrate how to write the evaluation logic of such data types:

```
1   template<typename TElem, typename TDevice, typename TScalar>
2   class TrivalMatrix
3   {
4       // ...
5       auto EvalRegister() const
6       {
7           using TEvalUnit
8               = NSTrivalMatrix::EvalUnit<ElementType, DeviceType>;
9           using TEvalGroup = TrivalEvalGroup<TEvalUnit>;
10          if (!m_evalBuf.IsEvaluated())
11          {
12              auto evalHandle = m_evalBuf.Handle();
13              const void* outputPtr = evalHandle.DataPtr();
14
15              TEvalUnit unit(std::move(evalHandle),
16                             m_rowNum, m_colNum, m_val);
17
18              EvalPlan<DeviceType>::template Register<TEvalGroup>
19                             (std::move(unit), outputPtr, {});
20          }
21          return m_evalBuf.ConstHandle();
22      }
23
24  private:
25      EvalBuffer<Matrix<ElementType, DeviceType>> m_evalBuf;
26  };
```

Lines 7 and 8 of the code snippet specify the computing unit required to calculate *TrivalMatrix*. The kernel logic of the computation is encapsulated in *NSTrivalMatrix::EvalUnit*. On this basis, line 9 specifies the relevant *EvalGroup*. *TrivalEvalGroup*, which is discussed previously, stores *EvalUnit* objects internally and provides them to *EvalPlan* in turn for evaluation.

On this basis, line 10 of the code snippet determines whether the data contained in *m_evalBuf* has been evaluated before. *m_evalBuf* is a data member of *TrivalMatrix* and its type is an instance of the template *EvalBuffer*, which holds the evaluation results. If the current object has been evaluated before, then *m_evalBuf.IsEvaluated()* will be *true* and there is no need for a secondary evaluation. It can return the result handle directly. Otherwise, it should call the function *EvalPlan::Register* for evaluation registration.

In order to register evaluation, we should first construct the *EvalUnit* object (lines 15 and 16). When calling *EvalPlan::Register* for registration, we need to explicitly provide four kinds of information:

1. The type of *EvalGroup*: *EvalPlan* will use it to classify incoming evaluation objects.
2. The constructed *EvalUnit* object.
3. A pointer that represents the result, which *EvalPlan* uses to maintain the order of computations during evaluation. This pointer is obtained by the interface *DataPtr* that calls the result handle in line 13.
4. An array of pointers that represent evaluation parameters. For most basic data types, their evaluation does not need to depend on the values of other data. So the array is empty and is represented as *{}*.

Whether or not *EvalPlan::Register* is called, *EvalRegister* calls *m_evalBuf.ConstHandle()* to return a handle to indicate the evaluation result. If *m_evalBuf.IsEvaluated()* is *true*, the corresponding evaluation result can be obtained directly from the handle; otherwise, the corresponding evaluation result can be acquired after the call of *EvalPlan::Eval*.

*NSTrivalMatrix::EvalUnit* encapsulates specific computational logic[4]:

```
1    template <typename TElem, typename TDevice>
2    class EvalUnit;
3
4    template <typename TElem>
5    class EvalUnit<TElem, DeviceTags::CPU>
6        : public BaseEvalUnit<DeviceTags::CPU>
7    {
8    public:
9        template <typename TScaleElemType>
10       EvalUnit(EvalHandle<Matrix<TElem, DeviceTags::CPU>> resBuf,
11               size_t rowNum, size_t colNum,
12               const Scalar<TScaleElemType, DeviceTags::CPU>& val)
13           : BaseEvalUnit<DeviceTags::CPU>({})
14           , m_resHandle(std::move(resBuf))
15           , m_rowNum(rowNum)
16           , m_colNum(colNum)
17           , m_val(val.Value()) {}
18
19       void Eval() override
20       {
21           m_resHandle.Allocate(m_rowNum, m_colNum);
22           auto& mutableData = m_resHandle.MutableData();
23           auto lowLayer = LowerAccess(mutableData);
24           const size_t rowLen = lowLayer.RowLen();
25           auto mem = lowLayer.MutableRawMemory();
26           for (size_t i = 0; i < m_rowNum; ++i)
27           {
```

---

[4] The following code snippet omits the declaration of *NSTrivalMatrix*.

```
28                  for (size_t j = 0; j < m_colNum; ++j)
29                  {
30                      mem[j] = m_val;
31                  }
32                  mem += rowLen;
33              }
34              m_resHandle.SetEval();
35          }
36
37      private:
38          EvalHandle<Matrix<TElem, DeviceTags::CPU>> m_resHandle;
39          size_t m_rowNum;
40          size_t m_colNum;
41          TElem m_val;
42      };
```

Currently, *EvalUnit* introduces specialization only for CPU. We can bring in other device types when necessary later.

*EvalUnit::Eval* encapsulates the kernel computational logic—allocating space for the matrix and filling each of its elements with incoming scalar values, which is also the behavior defined by *TrivalMatrix*. Line 21 of the code snippet calls the incoming handle's interface *Allocate* to allocate the storage space for objects, while lines 22–33 execute the filling with elements. Note that in this part of code, we adopt *LowerAccess* to obtain the underlying interface of *Matrix* and execute filling based on the interface. As discussed in Chapter 4, the underlying access interface can enhance the access speed, but it is not secure and not suitable to be exposed to end users. Nonetheless, the evaluation function inside the framework is suitable to use the underlying access interface.

After the filling of data is completed, that is, the evaluation is finished, *EvalUnit::Eval* calls the member function *SetEval* of the handle, which marks that the object contained in the current handle has been evaluated. Thus, the next time we call *TrivalMatrix::EvalRegister* of the same object, *m_evalBuf.IsEvaluated()* will return *true*, so that there is no need to execute the same evaluation again.

### 8.2.3 *Evaluation of Operation Templates*

The output of forward and backward propagation in MetaNN is the operation template object. Accordingly, the kernel of prediction and training in deep learning systems is also to evaluate the operation template object. This section takes the evaluation code of the operation template *Add* as an example and analyzes how to write the evaluation logic of operation templates.

When users call the operation *operator+* in MetaNN to add matrices or lists of matrices, MetaNN returns an operation template actually instantiated from *BinaryOp*: *BinaryOp<BinaryOpTags::Add, TData1, TData2>*. The first template parameter represents the computing type *Add*, and the second and third template parameters denote the two parameter types involved in the computation. The class template *BinaryOp* itself implements *EvalRegister*, as shown here (*TPrincipal* corresponds to the type after evaluation and *m_evalBuf* serves to preserve the results after evaluation):

```
1    template <typename TOpTag, typename TData1, typename TData2>
2    class BinaryOp
3    {
4        // ...
5        auto EvalRegister() const
6        {
7            if (!m_evalBuf.IsEvaluated())
8            {
9                using TOperSeqCont = typename OperSeq_<TOpTag>::type;
10
11               using THead = SeqHead<TOperSeqCont>;
12               using TTail = SeqTail<TOperSeqCont>;
13               THead::template EvalRegister<TTail>(m_evalBuf,
14                                                   m_data1, m_data2);
15           }
16           return m_evalBuf.ConstHandle();
17       }
18
19   private:
20       TData1 m_data1;
21       TData2 m_data2;
22
23       using TPrincipal = PrincipalDataType<Cate,
24                                            ElementType, DeviceType>;
25       EvalBuffer<TPrincipal> m_evalBuf;
26   };
```

Its implementation is analogous to the function with the same name in *TrivalMatrix*, which first determines whether evaluation has been completed before and triggers the logic of evaluation registration only if no evaluation computation has been done before. But in the evaluation of operation templates, we introduce the concept of OperSeq_ (line 9). We'll talk about the purpose of this concept in a follow-up discussion of evaluation optimization. For operation templates of addition, we introduce the following definition:

```
1    template <>
2    struct OperSeq_<BinaryOpTags::Add>
3    {
4        using type = OperSeqContainer<NSAdd::NSCaseGen::Calculator>;
5    };
```

That is: line 9 of *BinaryOp::EvalRegister* obtains an object of type *OperSeqContainer*.

*OperSeqContainer* is a container that stores various computation methods. *SeqHead* and *SeqTail* are two metafunctions used to acquire the first element in the container and the other elements respectively. *BinaryOp::EvalRegister* calls these two metafunctions in lines 11 and 12 to obtain the first element of them, *NSAdd::NSCaseGen::Calculator*, and calls its *EvalRegister* method (lines 13 and 14).

*NSAdd::NSCaseGen::Calculator* contains a static function template, *EvalRegister*, which is defined mainly as follows:

```
1    template <typename TCaseTail, typename TEvalRes,
2               typename TOperator1, typename TOperator2>
3    static void EvalRegister(TEvalRes& evalRes,
4                             const TOperator1& oper1,
5                             const TOperator2& oper2)
6    {
7        using ElementType = typename TEvalRes::DataType::ElementType;
8        using DeviceType = typename TEvalRes::DataType::DeviceType;
9        using CategoryType = DataCategory<typename TEvalRes::DataType>;
10
11       auto handle1 = oper1.EvalRegister();
12       auto handle2 = oper2.EvalRegister();
13
14       using UnitType = EvalUnit<decltype(handle1), decltype(handle2),
15                                 ElementType, DeviceType, CategoryType>;
16       using GroupType = TrivalEvalGroup<UnitType>;
17
18       auto outHandle = evalRes.Handle();
19       const void* dataPtr = outHandle.DataPtr();
20       auto depVec = { handle1.DataPtr(), handle2.DataPtr() };
21
22       UnitType unit(std::move(handle1), std::move(handle2),
23                     std::move(outHandle));
24       EvalPlan<DeviceType>::template Register<GroupType>
25           (std::move(unit), dataPtr, std::move(depVec));
26   }
```

It receives three parameters, representing the result and two operand objects. Internally, the function first calls the interface *EvalRegister* of the operand objects, registers the evaluation of them, and acquires the corresponding argument handles (lines 11 and 12). On this basis, line 18 of the code snippet obtains the result handle and delivers the argument handles and the result handle to the corresponding *EvalUnit* in lines 22 and 23—constructing the corresponding computing unit. In lines 24 and 25, the constructed computing unit, along with the pointers denoting the result and the parameters, is delivered to *EvalPlan::Register* to complete the registration of evaluation.

Compared with *TrivalMatrix::EvalRegister*, the process of evaluating the addition template is more complicated. Firstly, in order to make the operation template more versatile, we do not introduce the actual registration logic into *BinaryOp* but delegate the registration process to the registration class defined in *OperSeq_* instead. Secondly, most operation templates are based on input to execute computations. In order to calculate the output, *EvalRegister* of input operands should be called to accomplish the registration. Finally, when *EvalPlan::Register* is called to submit the current evaluation request, a pointer to the operands (the third parameter in line 25) is required at the same time.

Similar to *TrivalMatrix::EvalRegister*, we should also define the type *EvalUnit* to encapsulate the computational logic of the addition operation:

```
1    template <typename TOperHandle1, typename TOperHandle2,
2              typename TElem, typename TDevice, typename TCategory>
3    class EvalUnit;
4
5    template <typename TOperHandle1, typename TOperHandle2, typename TElem>
6    class EvalUnit<TOperHandle1, TOperHandle2,
7              TElem, DeviceTags::CPU, CategoryTags::Matrix>
8    {
9        // ...
10   };
11
12   template <typename TOperHandle1, typename TOperHandle2, typename TElem>
13   class EvalUnit<TOperHandle1, TOperHandle2,
14             TElem, DeviceTags::CPU, CategoryTags::BatchMatrix>
15   {
16       // ...
17   };
```

The corresponding *EvalUnit* is introduced here for matrices and lists of matrices. There is nothing to focus on in its internal computational logic and readers can refer to the implementation of *EvalUnit* for *TrivalMatrix* to understand the code.

As for the role of OperSeq_, it will be left to the section of evaluation optimization.

## 8.2.4 DynamicData *and Evaluation*

In Chapter 6, we introduced the class template *DynamicData* to preserve the intermediate results of forward propagation in layers. This template hides the specific information of types and provides only information of computing units, computing devices, and data categories to the outside.

As one of the many data types in MetaNN, *DynamicData* should also provide the interface *EvalRegister* to register evaluation. But *DynamicData* is special as an encapsulation of underlying specific data types. Its *EvalRegister* interface is defined as follows (in the case of the matrix category):

```
1   template <typename TElem, typename TDevice>
2   class DynamicData<TElem, TDevice, CategoryTags::Matrix>
3   {
4       // ...
5       DynamicConstEvalHandle<...>
6       EvalRegister() const
7       {
8           return m_baseData->EvalRegister();
9       }
10  private:
11      std::shared_ptr<BaseData> m_baseData;
12  };
```

*m_baseData* is a pointer to the underlying data. *DynamicData::EvalRegister* itself does not introduce any logic for evaluation registration but it delegates the logic to the underlying specific data type to complete. Meanwhile, *DynamicData::EvalRegister* returns *DynamicConstEvalHandle*, a special handle that is constructed based on the result of *m_baseData->EvalRegister()* and provides an interface to obtain the results of computations.

Until now, we have discussed the basic code writing of evaluation in MetaNN in several cases. Next, we'll discuss the optimization logic in evaluation processes.

## 8.3 Optimization of Evaluation Processes

In this section, three methods of evaluation optimization are discussed based on the principles "from simple to complex, from general to special": avoiding repetitive computations, merging similar computations and multi-operation co-optimization.

### 8.3.1 Avoiding Repetitive Computations

It is likely that a same intermediate result is used multiple times in a neural network. *C* in Figure 8.1 is a typical example. Another example comes from the *GRU* formula discussed in Chapter 7:

$$z_t = Sigmoid \ (W_z x_t + U_z h_{t-1})$$

$$r_t = Sigmoid \ (W_r x_t + U_r h_{t-1})$$

$$\hat{h}_t = Tanh \ (W x_t + U(r_t \circ h_{t-1}))$$

$$h_t = z_t \circ \hat{h}_t + (1 - z_t) \circ h_{t-1}$$

If $x_t$ is the output of a predecessor layer in the network, it will be represented as an intermediate result during the evaluation process. The dot product of the intermediate result and each of the three matrices will be calculated and obviously, we hope not to evaluate $x_t$ each time a dot product is calculated. Instead, $x_t$ is evaluated only once and the result is reused in the dot products with $W_z$, $W_r$, $W$.

It is a simple idea in evaluation optimization—to improve system performance by avoiding repetitive evaluations of the same object (i.e., $x_t$ here).

How does MetaNN support this kind of evaluation optimization? In fact, the evaluation framework discussed earlier has been able to support this type of optimization. In general, each specific type that should introduce evaluation logic includes the following code structure in its *EvalRegister*:

```
1   auto EvalRegister()
2   {
3       if (!m_evalBuf.IsEvaluated())
4       {
5           // ...
6       }
7       return m_evalBuf.ConstHandle();
8   }
```

*m_evalBuf* stores the evaluation results. Evaluation is performed only if *m_evalBuf.IsEvaluated()* is *false*; otherwise, it indicates the object has been evaluated before and does not need evaluating again. Here the previous evaluation results can be returned directly.

However, using the above structure alone is not sufficient to avoiding repetitive computations entirely. Consider the following code snippet:

```
1   auto input1 = a + b;
2   auto input2 = input1;
3   auto res1 = trans1(input1);
4   auto res2 = trans2(input2);
5
6   res1.EvalRegister();
7   res2.EvalRegister();
8   EvalPlan::Eval();
```

*input2* is a copy of *input1*, while *res1* and *res2* execute transformations using *input1* and *input2* respectively. We wish the system to be smart enough to evaluate one of *input1* and *input2* only once when evaluating *res1* and *res2*.

To support this requirement, firstly, *EvalBuffer* in MetaNN shares the underlying data objects when replicating, which means that *EvalBuffer* inside the two objects shares the same evaluation result object after *input2* is copied from *input1*. Evaluation of either of the two will update the evaluation state of the other, so that it does not need to be evaluated again.

Secondly, consider line 7 of the code snippet. When calling *res2.EvalRegister()*, the call of *input2.EvalRegister()*[5] is triggered. When calling *EvalPlan::Register*, *input1* and *input2* will pass in

---

[5] Note that both *input1* and *input2* are not evaluated at this time, so the judging method of *m_evalBuf. IsEvaluated()* discussed earlier does not prevent *input2* from registering into *EvalPlan*.

the pointers denoting output, which will point to the same address. *EvalPlan* will determine internally—if an evaluation request already registered is passed in (i.e., the output pointer is already in *EvalPlan*), the current evaluation request will be ignored—which also helps to avoid repetitive evaluations.

## 8.3.2 *Merging Similar Computations*

Avoiding repetitive computations discussed in section 8.3.1 is a common method for optimization, independent of specific computational logic. On the contrary, merging of similar computations in this section can only be applied to specific computational logic.

Unlike the scenarios discussed in section 8.3.1, certain computational logic may appear multiple times in a neural network but the parameters involved in computations may change. Take the computation of *GRU* as an example, which involves six times of dot products, such as $W_z x_t$ and $U_z h_{t-1}$, with various operands in each dot product. Here, we can't simplify computations in the way of the previous section. However, we still don't have to evaluate each dot product in turn.

For example, in the *GRU* formula, three out of six dot products are the multiplications of a matrix and $x_t$, which are entirely possible to be combined and completed. Here, the elements in $x_t$ can be shared in these three dot products, which reduces the time required for data transfer.

In addition, we typically need to depend on some third-party libraries for computational acceleration. Many third-party libraries offer interfaces for batch processing to maximize computing resources. Take dot product as an example: Intel's *Math Kernel Library* (*MKL*) provides an interface *?gemm_batch*, which can read a set of matrices at once and complete multiple matrix multiplications in one call. Nvidia's *CUDA* library offers similar functionality for batch computing on GPU. If we combine the dot products of matrices that can be calculated together, we can greatly improve computational efficiency by using the interfaces in the discussed library.

To support merging computations, MetaNN's evaluation system provides the module *EvalGroup*. We can call its *Merge* method to add computation requests of the same type to it. *EvalGroup*, on the other hand, has enough freedom to determine whether to merge several computation requests.

Currently, only a trivial *EvalGroup* template is implemented in MetaNN, which simply records the delivered computation requests and does not merge. It is because MetaNN is currently only a basic framework for deep learning and there is no deep optimization for algorithms. With the optimization of algorithms, we can consider introducing libraries such as *MKL* or *CUDA* and writing several acceleration functions of batch computing. On the basis, a new *EvalGroup* type can be introduced to merge similar computations.

Also take the dot product of matrices as an example. Assuming that we need to merge computations of dot product to speed up the system, it is entirely possible to introduce an *EvalGroup* and modify the registration logic of the dot product operation:

```
1  using GroupType = ...  // EvalGroup that supports computing consolidation
2  EvalPlan<DeviceType>::template Register<GroupType>(...);
```

In the new *EvalGroup*, we ought to adjust the logic of *Merge* to combine the computations[6] possible to merge into a new *EvalUnit* instance and return the *EvalUnit* instance when *EvalPlan* acquires it to achieve merging similar computations.

The premise of merging similar computations is that the relevant computations must conform to certain conditions, so that we can construct parallel algorithms based on it to improve the performance of the system. Therefore, not all computational logic benefits from it. Fortunately, it is common to find better implemented batch versions of time-consuming operations (such as dot product of matrices) in a deep learning system. Therefore, the use of merging computations can also elevate the performance of the entire system greatly.

## 8.3.3 Multi-operation Co-optimization

Multi-operation co-optimization means considering multiple operations at the same time and simplifying them from a mathematical point of view to achieve optimization. Compared with "avoiding repetitive computations" and "merging similar computations," multi-operation co-optimization is a more peculiar method of optimization, which can also play a great role if used well.

For a deep learning framework, the so-called system optimization should optimize not only the computing speed but also the stability and ease of use for the system. Methods such as "avoiding repetitive computations" and "merging similar computations" are mainly aimed at computing speed but multi-operation co-optimization can take the three points all into account. Next, let's take a concrete example to display how to introduce multi-operation co-optimization in MetaNN.

### 8.3.3.1 Background

In numerous well-known deep learning frameworks, there seem to be some "repetitive" constructs. For example, *Caffe* has the layer *Softmax* and the layer *SoftmaxLoss*; *Tensorflow* contains the layer *tf.nn.softmax* layer and the layer *tf.nn.softmax_cross_entropy_with_logits*. There is some repetitive logic in these layers. In *Caffe*'s case, *SoftmaxLoss* requires the input of a vector $v$ and labeling information $y$. On this basis, it:

1. Executes *Softmax* transformations on the input vector $v$, $f(v_i) = \dfrac{e^{v_i}}{\sum_j e^{v_j}}$;

2. Calculates the value of the loss function $loss = -\log(f(v_y))$, where $y$ is the labeling category for the input sample.

The first step of the entire computing process is exactly the same as the layer *Softmax* in fact, while the second step is essentially a *CrossEntropy* computation. *Caffe* contains numerous similar constructs, such as a dedicated layer to calculate the *Sigmoid* value and an additional layer that calculates *Sigmoid* first, and then *CrossEntropy*. For the above cases, why not introduce a dedicated *CrossEntropy* layer? In this way, there seems no need to introduce a structure like *SoftmaxLoss* and aligning the *Softmax* layer with the *CrossEntropy* layer can exactly achieve the goal.

There is no introduction of Lazy Evaluation in *Caffe*, where each layer performs evaluation of forward and backward propagation internally. In the discussed case, if the *CrossEntropy* layer is

---

[6] Note that even computations entered into the same *EvalGroup* are not always able to be merged. For instance, *MKL* requires the participating matrices of dot product to have the same dimensions and it is not possible to invoke its interface *?gemm_batch* if the requirement is not satisfied.

introduced and the evaluation of backward propagation is executed internally, it will incur serious problems of stability.

The input to the *CrossEntropy* layer may be the output of the *Softmax* layer. *Softmax* essentially normalizes the elements in the input vector so that they are all positive and add up to 1—using the normalized values to simulate the probability of each category. For complex problems, the normalized vector may contain tens of thousands of elements. Because these elements are positive and add up to 1, values of some elements must be quite small positive values or even result in 0 due to rounding errors.

Let's assume that the labeling information $y$ corresponds to such a small value. When *CrossEntropy* execute forward propagation, the output is $-\log(f(v_y))$; for backward propagation, the output gradient is $1/f(v_y)$. Some readers must have already found out about the problem: $1/f(v_y)$ can be very large when $f(v_y)$ is very small. At the same time, the rounding error generated by $f(v_y)$ in the computation process will be magnified a lot when $1/f(v_y)$ is calculated, thus affecting the stability of the system.

As a result, deep learning frameworks such as *Caffe* introduce layers like *SoftmaxLoss* to merge two-step computations. Furthermore, through mathematical derivation, we will find that such layers can be simplified when calculating gradients. We discussed the computing method of *Softmax*'s gradient in Chapter 5, which involves the *Jacobian* matrix and dot product of input information. However, it is somewhat cumbersome. If it is multiplied by the gradient introduced by *CrossEntropy*, the $i$-th element in the corresponding output gradient can be simplified to:

$$\frac{e^{v_i}}{\sum_j e^{v_j}} - \delta_{i=y}$$

The first part of the formula is the output of forward propagation in *Softmax*. The second part $\delta_{i=y}$ is 1 when $i = y$, or otherwise 0—compared with the formula in Chapter 5, it is effortless to realize that it's a significant simplification for computations. Meanwhile, there will not be a fairly small number as the denominator in this formula, thus eliminating the possibility of stability problems discussed earlier.

Arguably, this design takes into account both speed optimization and stability, but it can beset users of the framework: they should be clear about the above principles in order to choose the right layer—which is indeed sacrificing ease of use.

Is there any way to balance all three points? If we write code in an object-oriented way, it's challenging to balance them. But through metaprogramming and compile-time computing, we can achieve a better balance for the three points. Next, let's take a look at how MetaNN solves this problem.

### 8.3.3.2 MetaNN Solutions

MetaNN contains two layers: *SoftmaxLayer* and *NegativeLogLikeLayer*. The former receives a vector and performs a *Softmax* transformation on the vector. The latter receives two vectors, $x_1$, $x_2$, which are placed with the keys *CostLayerIn* and *CostLayerLabel* respectively in their input containers. In forward propagation, this layer calculates $y = -\sum_{i,j} x_1(i,j)\log(x_2(i,j))$ and outputs the result. We can adopt these two layers to implement the behavior of the layer *SoftmaxLoss* described earlier, as shown in Figure 8.3.

In Figure 8.3, *CostLayerLabel* and *CostLayerIn* in the input container of *NegativeLogLikelihoodLayer* are connected to a one-hot vector and the output of *SoftmaxLayer* respectively. In the one-hot

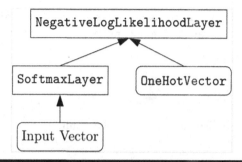

**Figure 8.3** **The structure of *SoftmaxLoss***

vector, the labeling category corresponds to a position of 1 and the other position is 0. Thus, during forward propagation, the output of *NegativeLogLikelihoodLayer* is equivalent to the output of the layer *SoftmaxLoss* in *Caffe*.

Now consider what happens to the above structure in backward propagation. Firstly, to ensure that backward propagation works properly, layers in MetaNN preserve intermediate information in forward propagation. The intermediate information saved by *SoftmaxLayer* is the *Softmax* result of the input vector, while *NegativeLogLikelihoodLayer* saves its input information.

During backward propagation, the gradient entered into the above structure will be first delivered to *NegativeLogLikelihoodLayer*. The function *NegativeLogLikelihoodDerivative* will be called and the input gradient as well as the information saved previously will be passed in as arguments, thus constructing the corresponding operation template. This operation template will be further passed to *SoftmaxLayer* as its input gradient. On the other hand, *SoftmaxLayer* calls *VecSoftmaxDerivative* and delivers the input gradient and the intermediate variable preserved in forward propagation (i.e., the *Softmax* result), thus constructing the corresponding operation template to output.

*SoftmaxLayer*'s output gradient is an operation template and its internal structure is shown in Figure 8.4.

Based on metaprogramming and compile-time computing, we can detect whether such substructures are included in the structure to be evaluated at compile time. If so, we can introduce the

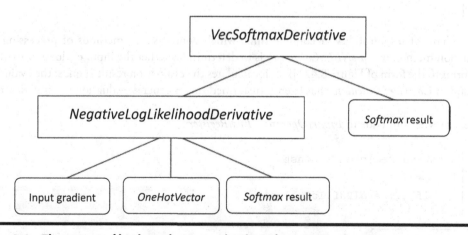

**Figure 8.4** **The output of backward propagation in *SoftmaxLayer***

appropriate optimization—obtaining the *Softmax* result ($e^{v_i} / \sum_j e^{v_j}$) and the position ($y$) of the element 1 in the one-hot vector, calculating the gradient using the following formula:

$$\frac{e^{v_i}}{\sum_j e^{v_j}} - \delta_{i=y}$$

multiplying it by the input gradient and returning the result.

### 8.3.3.3 Matching Evaluation Structures at Compile Time

MetaNN introduces *OperSeq_* to match evaluation substructures. *OperSeq_* is essentially implementing a chain of responsibility pattern. It is a classic design pattern that links objects which can handle requests of the same type as a chain and allow these objects to process requests and the submitted requests to be delivered along the chain. This pattern avoids the coupling between the sender and receiver of a request. It determines in turn whether the objects on the chain have the ability to process the request—if so, it is processed; if not, the request is delivered to the next object on the chain until an object can process it.[7]

Specifically, in our scenario, the request we are dealing with is to evaluate a structure—for example, we want to evaluate the result of *VecSoftmaxDerivative* in Figure 8.4. There are several ways to process the request, such as evaluating *NegativeLogLikelihoodDerivative* and then using the evaluation result for further computation or evaluating the above structure at once. We string different treatments into a chain structure, thus endowing each of them a chance to process it. *OperSeq_* defines such a chain structure. In order to achieve functionality similar to *SoftmaxLoss,* we bring in the following definition for the operation *VecSoftMaxDerivative*:

```
1    template <>
2    struct OperSeq_<BinaryOpTags::VecSoftmaxDerivative>
3    {
4        using type = OperSeqContainer<CaseNLL::Calculator,
5                                      CaseGen::Calculator>;
6    };
```

It is a chain of responsibility at compile time, which contains two methods of processing: the evaluation method in *CaseNLL::Calculator* is to determine whether the input evaluation structure conforms to the form of Figure 8.4—if so, it calculates the evaluation result at once; the evaluation method in *CaseGen::Calculator* has been transformed into a general evaluation method described earlier.

Let's review our code in *BinaryOperator:: EvalRegister*:

```
1    auto EvalRegister() const
2    {
3        if (!m_evalBuf.IsEvaluated())
```

---

[7] The above description comes from the Internet.

```
4          {
5              using TOperSeqCont = typename OperSeq_<TOpTag>::type;
6
7              using THead = SeqHead<TOperSeqCont>;
8              using TTail = SeqTail<TOperSeqCont>;
9              THead::template EvalRegister<TTail>(...);
10         }
11         return m_evalBuf.ConstHandle();
12     }
```

Lines 7 and 8 are equivalent to selecting the first evaluation method from the chain of responsibility, while line 9 attempts to call the function *EvalRegister* of the evaluation method to evaluate. For *VecSoftmaxDerivative*, it is equivalent to first trying the evaluation process defined by *CaseNLL::Calculator*.

*CaseNLL::Calculator*'s logical framework is as follows:

```
1    struct Calculator
2    {
3        // ...
4        template <typename TCaseRem, typename TEvalRes,
5                  typename TOperator1, typename TOperator2>
6        static void EvalRegister(TEvalRes& evalRes,
7                                 const TOperator1& oper1,
8                                 const TOperator2& oper2)
9        {
10           if constexpr (!Valid<TOperator1, TOperator2>)
11           {
12               using THead = SeqHead<TCaseRem>;
13               using TTail = SeqTail<TCaseRem>;
14               THead::template EvalRegister<TTail>(...);
15           }
16           else
17           {
18               // ...
19           }
20       }
21   };
```

Note that in line 10, we use a metafunction *Valid* here to determine whether the currently incoming structure satisfies the form of Figure 8.4. If not, it obtains the next evaluation algorithm from the evaluation chain of responsibility and calls the corresponding *EvalRegister* function. Otherwise, it goes into the *else* branch and attempts to complete the evaluation using an optimized algorithm.

*Valid* is defined as follows:

```
1   template <typename T1, typename T2>
2   constexpr bool Valid = false;
3
4   template <typename T1, typename T2, typename T3>
5   constexpr bool Valid<
6       TernaryOp<TernaryOpTags::NegativeLogLikelihoodDerivative,
7                 T1, T2, T3>,
8       T3> = true;
```

It is a quite simple branching logic and *Valid* usually returns *false*. It is *true* only if the two arguments delivered into *VecSoftmaxDerivative* satisfy the following conditions: the first argument is an operation template of *NegativeLogLikelihoodDerivative* and its third argument is of the same type as the second argument of *VecSoftmaxDerivative* (they all correspond to the *Softmax* results). At this point, the system will attempt to evaluate using the optimized algorithm.

Note that even if *Valid* is *true*, we cannot guarantee that the evaluation can be accomplished using the optimized algorithm. In order to utilize the optimized algorithm for evaluation, we must require that the two objects in Figure 8.4 marked "*Softmax* results" should be equal. It is usually satisfied for general scenarios but the framework itself cannot assume that it must be satisfied—so we must introduce the appropriate logic to judge it.

### 8.3.3.4 Equality Judgment of Objects in MetaNN

To ensure the correctness of optimization for computations, we should acquire two operands representing the results of *Softmax* computations from the operation template object of *VecSoftmaxDerivative*, so as to determine whether the two are equal. Optimization algorithms can only be executed only if the two are equal, or otherwise it should be transformed into basic evaluation logic. So how can we tell if the two objects are equal?

The optimization of numerous operations in deep learning frameworks must be carried out on the basis of ensuring that the delivered operands conform to certain conditions and the equality judgment of operands is a quite basic judgment. Data types in MetaNN are mainly matrices—the most direct way to determine whether two matrices are equal is to compare whether the corresponding elements in the two matrices are equal. However, this approach introduces a large number of comparison operations that can affect system performance. In fact, it is because a certain operand may be replicated into multiple copies with different copies participating in the operations of different parts during computations that an operation happens to adopt two "equal" operands directly or indirectly. If we can transform the task of equality judgment into the task of determining whether the two objects are copies of each other, then the corresponding amount of computations may be simplified.

Take Figure 8.4 as an example, *Softmax*'s result will be copied into two copies with one in *SoftmaxLayer* and the other in *NegativeLogLikelihoodLayer*. During backward propagation, these two copies are used as two (direct or indirect) operands of *VecSoftmaxDerivative*. We just need to make sure that the two operands of *VecSoftmaxDerivative* are copies of each other.

In MetaNN, data are copied by default using shallow copy, so it is only necessary to compare the pointers retained inside the two objects to determine whether the two objects are copies to each other. MetaNN introduces corresponding interfaces for each data type to determine whether one object is a copy of another. For example, the class *Matrix* contains the following interfaces:

```
1    template <typename TElem>
2    class Matrix<TElem, DeviceTags::CPU>
3    {
4        // ...
5        bool operator== (const Matrix& val) const
6        {
7            return (m_mem == val.m_mem) &&
8                   (m_rowNum == val.m_rowNum) &&
9                   (m_colNum == val.m_colNum) &&
10                  (m_rowLen == val.m_rowLen);
11       }
12
13       template <typename TOtherType>
14       bool operator== (const TOtherType&) const
15       {
16           return false;
17       }
18
19       template <typename TData>
20       bool operator!= (const TData& val) const
21       {
22           return !(operator==(val));
23       }
24   };
```

For the type objects *a* and *b* instantiated from the two *Matrix* templates, *a==b* is *true* only if they point to the same memory (line 7) and have the same dimensional information (lines 8–10).

MetaNN also supports comparisons of different types of object—the results of these comparisons return *false* directly. We can also write the logic of *operator!=* accordingly. Lines 13–23 of the discussed code snippet introduce the corresponding logic. Based on these interfaces, we can compare two MetaNN data objects without having to focus on their specific data types.

There is similar logic introduced in operation templates. Take *BinaryOp* as an example:

```
1    template <typename TOpTag, typename TData1, typename TData2>
2    class BinaryOp
3    {
4        // ...
5        bool operator== (const BinaryOp& val) const
6        {
```

```
7           return (m_data1 == val.m_data1) && (m_data2 == val.m_data2);
8       }
9
10      template <typename TOtherData>
11      bool operator== (const TOtherData& val) const;
12
13      template <typename TOtherData>
14      bool operator!= (const TOtherData& val) const;
15  };
```

The two *BinaryOp* objects are equal if and only if they contain equal operands.

Other templates, such as *DynamicData*, *Batch*, etc., also include the implementations of *operator==* and *operator!=*. Here we won't list them one by one.

### 8.3.3.5 Auto-trigger Optimization

After discussing the logic of equality judgment in MetaNN, let's review the evaluation implementation of *VecSoftmaxDerivative*. As mentioned earlier, *VecSoftmaxDerivative* ought to handle two situations when evaluating. *CaseNLL::Calculator* can execute optimization based on a specific data structure. If the evaluation arguments it receives does not satisfy the requirements, it calls another evaluation module *CaseGen::Calculator*. The latter adopts a general evaluation process, that is, calling the interface *EvalRegister* of the arguments and then constructing the evaluation request of *VecSoftmaxDerivative* to deliver it to *EvalPlan*.

The optimization logic described earlier is encapsulated inside MetaNN and is transparent to users of the framework, who can construct objects of *SoftmaxLayer* or *NegativeLogLikelihoodLayer* for forward and backward propagation. Once the two objects are associated—for example, using a composite layer to feed the output of *SoftmaxLayer* into the input of *NegativeLogLikelihoodLayer*— the optimization algorithm will be automatically triggered for fast computations during backward propagation.

The method of optimization discussed in this section must be utilized only if multiple operations that conform to certain structures are involved. Therefore, the author refers to this method as "multi-operation co-optimization." In this section, we have talked about the implementation of multi-operation co-optimization in the scenario of "*Softmax+CrossEntropy*" and this method can be applied in many scenarios. For instance, we might have to calculate *Log* value on the output after calculating *Softmax*, and here multi-operation co-optimization can be introduced to simplify computations; if we need to calculate *Sigmoid* first and then *CrossEntropy*, we can introduce multi-operation co-optimization to optimize computations of gradients in backward propagation.

## 8.4 Summary

This chapter discussed evaluation and optimization algorithms in MetaNN.

Compared to the previous chapters, there is not much code in this chapter and this chapter focuses more on design ideas. It is because the main topic of this book is template metaprogramming and for evaluation and optimization, there are not new metaprogramming techniques[8] involved. So, we don't spend much space here in analyzing specific code.

But this chapter is still a fairly important chapter. The author has always believed that technologies serve to solve practical problems and we should not use technologies for the purpose of using technologies. Metaprogramming is discussed because metaprogramming and compile-time computing enable us to better optimize performance at runtime. The three optimization approaches we've discussed in this chapter embody this point. In contrast, an object-oriented framework can avoid repetitive computations by some means; but only with the introduction of *Lazy Evaluation* and expression templates can we make it convenient to merge similar computations; furthermore, we can also achieve multi-operation co-optimization by using techniques of metaprogramming and compile-time computing in depth.

C++ is a programming language emphasizing execution efficiency and its standard has been developing all time with unchanged original intention of seeking efficiency. Many techniques have been introduced from C++ 03 to C++ 17, which allow us to adopt metaprogramming and compile-time computing more conveniently. We have reasons to believe that the development of standards will significantly lower the threshold for metaprogramming technology and an increasing number of people can utilize compile-time computing to build faster and more stable systems.

## 8.5 Exercises

1. In section 8.1, we describe several modules contained in the evaluation subsystem of MetaNN. Due to limited space, the section does not discuss the specific implementation code for these modules. Please read the implementation code of relevant modules and make sure to understand how they work.

2. When discussing "avoiding repetitive computations," we mentioned that *EvalPlan* ignores duplicate evaluation requests delivered, which can be further optimized. In existing logic, while *EvalPlan* can ignore duplicate requests delivered, we still have to construct evaluation requests (such as *EvalUnit*) and pass in *EvalPlan*. Please modify the interface *EvalPlan* to provide the function of query to determine whether a request has been registered. Accordingly, inside *EvalRegister* of a particular class, this interface can execute judgment as follows: if the same evaluation request already exists in *EvalPlan*, it can omit the steps to construct the evaluation request and return directly.

3. MetaNN introduces the interface *operator==* for its data classes. For ease of use, we have introduced two additional functions for each data class: *operator==* is for equality judgment among different data types and the other implements *operator!=* based on *operator==*. Their implementations are both trivial. Please simplify the code, remove the two interfaces from each data type, and use two global functions to implement the appropriate logic. Think about how to declare the corresponding global function so that it won't impact the rest of the code.[9]

---

[8] In addition to multi-computing co-optimization, some code is discussed because it involves writing the chain of responsibility pattern at compile time.

[9] For instance, we can't modify the equality behavior of two *std::vector* objects just due to the introduction of the corresponding global function.

# Postscript

## My Path to Metaprogramming Learning

My initial understanding of C++ template metaprogramming started from reading the Chinese edition of "*C++ Templates*" translated by Mr. Chen Weizhu—more than a decade ago. At that time, as a newbie of C++, I thought I couldn't fully understand the book. Later, I attempted to read the book "*C++ Template Metaprogramming*" translated by Dr. Rong Yao. Because I had obtained some experience in the design of C++ programming, I thought I could master the secrets of it. But finally I found it so challenging for me even after reading the book several times.

Meanwhile, there was a problem bothering me and lingering all the time—what is the purpose of metaprogramming?

My knowledge of C++ metaprogramming came mainly from the two books, which can indeed be regarded as classic books on C++ templates. However, the examples of metaprogramming discussed in the book "*C++ Templates*" are relatively circumscribed. The book "*C++ Template Metaprogramming*" is about *MPL*, a metaprogramming library, but I didn't know how to utilize it in my daily work. Therefore, I often read these two books and asked myself: what is the role of metaprogramming?

I believe that many developers of C++ might encounter similar questions. Nowadays, there are more and more libraries of C++ metaprogramming, from the earlier *Boost::MPL* to later *Boost::Fusion*, and *Boost::Hana*… There are numerous libraries and the techniques in each library are quite cool, but how many people can apply them to their daily work? Even if applied, most libraries might well play an auxiliary role, which is even difficult to match with the containers in the *STL*.

But I firmly believed that metaprogramming must be useful. Although I didn't know how it worked, I knew compile-time computing was Turing-complete and in theory it should be able to share some of runtime work, thus speeding up runtime computations. I didn't find it useful just because my practice wasn't enough.

So, I tried to read more documents, hoping to find an answer I was satisfied with. Maybe because my horizons were too narrow, what I found could not give me the answer. They're similar to the above two books I've read, either with examples too small or too deep to be applied to my actual projects.

Since I couldn't find the answer from books, I decided to try it myself. One of my daily tasks is to write C++ programs and I attempted to apply metaprogramming techniques in my daily work. Unfortunately, this attempt was opposed by my colleagues. The reason was also quite simple—if they could not understand my programs, then we could not collaborate with each other.

It was a quite real problem. So, I could only spend my spare time in its study on my own and the study was also in an intermittent state.

By early 2015, after another reading of "*C++ Templates*," I felt I should find a project to explore the technique in depth. At that time, I was writing and maintaining an online machine translation system based on deep learning at Baidu's Natural Language Processing Department. Naturally, I found a project—developing a deep learning framework myself.

My purpose in developing a deep learning framework was also clear: to explore the metaprogramming technology. As a result, it naturally became the protagonist of the entire framework. As metaprogramming technology adopts compile-time computing, in order to be able to explore the application of metaprogramming technology to a greater extent, I set a tone for the entire framework: what can be processed at compile time should be handled at compile and should not be placed at runtime. Meanwhile, I tried to avoid reading and using the existing deep learning frameworks because most existing frameworks were still developed in object-oriented programming and there were not many utilizing metaprogramming. I didn't want to be too much affected by existing frameworks and limited my mentality. I also avoided using existing metaprogramming libraries because I thought I could have a deeper understanding only if I wrote all the metafunctions by myself.

The development of the framework was not smooth. In addition to small modifications, I had rewritten it nine times. Each rewrite was accompanied by a further understanding of metaprogramming. Every modification and technical breakthrough brought me inexplicable joy. Now I still remember the joy of designing the heterogeneous dictionary myself; remember the joy of extending the policy in the "*C++ Templates*" to construct a policy inheritance system; remember writing the code of topological sorting at compile time to enable the whole framework to execute backward propagation automatically. Each such modification was often accompanied by a rewrite of most contents in the system and each rewrite further deepened my understanding of metaprogramming techniques.

About 2 years ago, I thought that my knowledge had accumulated to a certain level and came up with the idea of writing a book. It might come from a habit developed during college study—I was used to summing up and refining my work all the time.

There were many obstacles in the process of writing because it was also a summary and refinement of the original programs. In the process of writing, I could often find defects of the original framework, so as to adjust the framework itself and the contents of the book. In fact, even in the later period of writing, I still thought the framework was unsatisfactory. But with limited time and energy, it was nearly impossible to alter the code again and adjust the contents of the book. In theory, we can always find space for improvement for a framework. In order to ensure the book was completed on time, I transformed some ideas of adjustment into exercises for readers.

It was a challenging task to write a book and this book is about a framework created by my own, thus with inevitable mistakes. For instance, I was not good at nominating. Thus, some names of functions, variables, and types in the code might be unsuitable. Meanwhile, my literary level was not good enough—although I was trying my best, the book still contains some flaws that might affect readers' understanding. I am deeply sorry for the abovementioned problems! As a technical book, this book hopes to convey a technical system that contains a number of specific techniques to readers. I wish that readers can be able to use metaprogramming techniques in their own projects by reading this book while enduring the rough writing of me.

## About Metaprogramming

This book has been discussing metaprogramming techniques. At the end of the book, is there anything else to be talked about this technology?

In fact, there are numerous techniques worth discussing.

This book discusses some basic techniques of metaprogramming, which solve problems of "how to write metafunctions." How to write well is another topic. Metafunctions and compile-time computing can improve the performance at runtime and while a good metafunction should further improve the performance at compile time.

In general, we don't need to consider compile-time performance when coding. It is because there are relatively few parts involving compile-time computing in normal programs. However, if a large number of metafunctions are used, it can add a heavy burden on the compiler and slow the compilation speed; in extreme cases, it may cause memory over limit of the compiler and compilation failures.

When the compiler calculates at compile time, the result can be mainly classes instantiated by templates. These classes are saved in the compiler's symbol table. Next, let's take a typical example to discuss metafunctions and instantiation.

## Array Access and Metafunction Optimization

Consider a compile-time array *tuple<a0,a1,...>* and now we need to obtain the i'th element in it. With the looping code writing method, it can be written in the following form:

```
1   template <size_t N, typename Vector>
2   struct at;
3
4   template <size_t N, template<typename...> class Cont,
5            typename cur, typename...an>
6   struct at<N, Cont<cur, an...>>
7   {
8       using type = typename at<N - 1, Cont<an...>>::type;
9   };
10
11  template <template<typename...> class Cont,
12           typename cur, typename...an>
13  struct at<0, Cont<cur, an...>>
14  {
15      using type = cur;
16  };
17
18  using Check = typename at<3, tuple<int, short, long, double>>::type;
```

Although the type operated in this code can be considered as an array at compile time, the complexity of accessing a runtime array is usually $O(1)$ and at compile time, using the discussed code, the compiler should instantiate $N$ templates in order to find the $N$-th element—which is equivalent to traversing a linked list at runtime and is quite inefficient. This inefficiency is embodied at compile time, which means that we have to instantiate more types, consume more compile-time memory, and spend longer compile time.

If our program doesn't have much place to use metafunctions, the consumption of compilation resources may not be considerable. But if, as in this book, metaprogramming is used on a large scale to construct complex systems, then the problems can be quite serious.

To effectively solve such problems, we may require joint efforts at the code level and the standard level.

## Code-level Optimization

A good metaprogram should achieve its objectives with as fewer instantiations as possible. Also take the case of accessing an array as an example. The code in the previous section is just a quite basic code to access an array, which results in numerous instances during compilation. We can adopt the Big O notation in data structures and algorithms to approximately describe the complexity of algorithms at compile time. It is natural to realize that the complexity of the algorithm described earlier is $O(n)$. Further, consider the following code:

```
1  using Check1 = typename at<3, tuple<int, short, long, double>>::type;
2  using Check2 = typename at<2, tuple<int, short, long, double>>::type;
```

The complexities of *Check1* and *Check2* are both $O(n)$. Although they access the same array, the index values are different. Therefore, we cannot benefit from the Calculation of *Check1* when calculating *Check2* due to the algorithm discussed earlier.

The *Boost::MPL* contains a compile-time array construct and provides metafunctions to acquire the elements in it. Its algorithms are optimized to reduce the complexity of repeatedly obtaining the values of elements in the same array:

```
1  using Check1 = typename at<3, vector<int, short, long, double>>::type;
2  using Check2 = typename at<2, vector<int, short, long, double>>::type;
```

Suppose that the call of *Check1* is the first time to traverse the array *vector<int, short, long, double>*, where the complexity of *Check1* is also $O(n)$. When *Check2* is calculated later, it obtains the element in the same array as *Check1*. The complexity of *Check2* can therefore be reduced from $O(n)$ to $O(1)$.

The *Boost::MPL* utilizes only the techniques in the C++ 03 standard. Based on new standards such as C++ 11, we can further decrease the complexity of compile-time computing—*MPL11* on GitHub is also a metaprogramming library that uses the techniques in C++ 11 to rewrite some algorithms in *Boost::MPL*. The metafunction *at* provided has better performance at compile time. If we use this metafunction, then it can be called as follows:

```
1  using Check1 = typename at<3, vector<int, short, long, double>>::type;
2  using Check2 = typename at<2, vector<int, short, long, char>>::type;
```

Assuming that *Check1* is the first call of *at*, its complexity is $O(log(n))$. For subsequent evaluation of *Check2*, the complexity is $O(1)$ —although *Check1* calls a different array from *Check2*, the two arrays have the same length. Therefore, the compiler can also utilize the information to reduce the number of instantiations.

The implementations of these metafunctions are beyond the scope of this book and they are all open source. Interested readers can search for relevant code to analyze their implementations.

## *Standard-level Optimization*[1]

Although we can reduce the number of instances produced by compile-time operations through the optimization of metafunctions to decrease the burden on the compiler, the author argues that this solution alone is not enough. When the code is complex to a certain extent, it can cause compilation failures due to demands for too many compilation resources. To support more complex computing at compile time, we should introduce optimization at the standard level.

In fact, the problem of "resource maintenance in the computing process" also occurs at runtime. However, compared with compile-time computing, the solution for runtime is much more complete. Take resource maintenance at runtime as an example: the author believes that the most effective means of reducing resource consumption is lifetime control of objects other than algorithm optimization.

Most languages control the lifetime of objects: the corresponding resources are freed up when an object is no longer needed. C++ utilizes the concept of domains to control the use of memory—when a domain ends, objects constructed in the domain are destroyed and the resources such as memory are freed up. For instance, each runtime function corresponds to a domain. At runtime of a certain function, several intermediate variables may be generated. When it is over, the intermediate variables constructed at runtime are destroyed accordingly because the domain is over.

In contrast, there does not appear to be an effective way to control the lifetime of compile-time "objects" in the existing standards.

We can think of a type instantiated at compile time as a compile-time object. Take the following call as an example:

```
1    using Check = typename at<3, vector<int, short, long, double>>::type;
```

In order to derive the value of *Check* at compile time, the compiler may produce intermediate objects when parsing the metafunction *at*, which may be preserved in the compiler's symbol table. But there doesn't seem to be a method to explicitly inform the compiler that these intermediate variables will no longer be used and their "lifetime" can be terminated.

Therefore, the author boldly assumes here that the standard should introduce the concept of domains at compile time, so as to tell the compiler to destroy instances no longer used when the calls of corresponding metafunctions are completed—that is, to remove the corresponding entries from the symbol table maintained by the compiler.

The compiler maintains the instances it constructs in the symbol table in order to reduce unnecessary repetition of instantiations. Consider the following code:

```
1    vector<int> a; // the operation of a
2    vector<int> b; // the operation of b
```

---

[1] Note that the content of this section is just an author's point of view, used to inspire ideas. It is not a molded solution. This view may be wrong, and the author is not responsible for its correctness.

*vector<int>* and some data members are instantiated when the compiler parses related operations of *a*. The information is stored in the symbol table, so that it no longer needs to instantiate *vector<int>* when parsing *b*, thus speeding up compilation.

Some instances are resident in the compiler's symbol table, while others should be removed after the completion of metafunction calls. It raises a problem: how to tell the compiler which instances are intermediate results of metafunctions? Meanwhile, how can the compiler effectively adopt the information to optimize the compilation process? These are the directions worth studying.

The above contents are just views from the author. The author's knowledge is limited—he is not proficient in all the details of the C++ standard, know quite little about the inner operations of the compiler, and cannot modify the compiler to verify this hypothesis. This section also only serves to inspire valuable ideas—if readers have his or her own opinion on this view, please contact the author for discussion.

# About MetaNN

The main purpose of this book is to take MetaNN as an example to discuss the techniques of C++ template metaprogramming. MetaNN just plays a supporting role in this book when talking about metaprogramming. At the end of the book, the author hopes to talk over MetaNN itself.

For now, MetaNN is just a kernel that includes some concepts necessary for deep learning systems, such as data, operations, forward and backward propagation, and so on. In addition to these, a complete deep learning system contains numerous contents, such as providing a richer variety of operations, supporting different computing devices[2] and supporting concurrent training, etc. Therefore, MetaNN is only the initial implementation of a deep learning framework.

Even so, the authors argue that MetaNN has something for us to learn from. There are many distinctions between it and existing mainstream deep learning frameworks. It is these distinctions that allow us to improve such systems by comparing different implementations of similar concepts and analyzing their pros and cons.

Some features of MetaNN compared to the mainstream frameworks are listed below, including some of the author's understanding of the framework. For the design of the framework and the trade-offs of techniques, various people have different views. These contents also only serve to inspire valuable ideas. The author is willing to communicate with readers on these issues.

## Single Data Type and Rich Data Types

Currently, most deep learning frameworks introduce the concept of tensors, which represents various data types using a single data structure. MetaNN goes the other way around, introducing many data types. We can even utilize template expressions to combine data types, thus forming new types. A single data type is easier to maintain but the author believes that rich data types offer more possibilities for system optimization.

---

[2] MetaNN can be extended to support diverse computing devices. But for now, all of our algorithms are only implemented on CPU.

## Model Description and Performance Optimization

Although deep learning systems claim to divide calculations into small units in order to form complex systems by "building blocks," in many cases we have to design some of the "large building blocks" to expedite the system and reinforce the coupling among the computational logic, which will sacrifice the descriptiveness of the model to some extent.

The author was previously responsible for the development and maintenance of a machine translation online prediction system based on deep learning in Baidu. We constructed the system using C++, which calls the GPU for calculations. To optimize performance, we combined many of these functions to construct numerous "large building blocks." Tests have shown that this approach could improve its performance dozens of times compared with many deep learning frameworks at that time. Accordingly, the maintenance of these "large building blocks" is quite difficult.

For instance, we attempted to introduce a new translation model to form an ensemble model with the original one—experiments showed that this could significantly improve the quality of translation. However, in the original system, the layers that represented the deep model were already tightly coupled with each other. There were two options for introducing an additional complex construct.

1. To rewrite the entire system and continue using "large building blocks" deeply coupled at more onerous cost of maintenance than the original system.
2. To optimize the new translation model in depth—using the new model and the original model separately and merge the evaluation results in the end. This approach is less costly, but the two models are optimized separately, which can only be used in turn or using two GPUs separately. It cannot maximize computing resources.

This example explains the contradiction between model description and performance optimization. On the one hand, we hope to provide relatively basic components that allow users to use their description models more flexibly; on the other hand, we want to integrate complex calculations for better performance optimization. This contradiction cannot be easily resolved by traditional object-oriented programming. Therefore, constructs such as the *SoftmaxLoss* layer in *Caffe* have emerged.[3] But through metaprogramming and compile-time computing, we can ease the contradiction between the two to some extent: users still adopt the basic components to construct the network; with the help of compile-time computing, the computer can better understand the network structure, thus providing better optimization.

For example, we have previously encountered difficulties in the machine translation system. If we use MetaNN, upper-level users simply need to describe the structure of each model. The evaluation logic in MetaNN will automatically explore the calculations that can be merged, which can achieve multi-operation co-optimization.

## "Playground" and "One-way Road"

As a framework based on compile-time computing, metafunctions can be found everywhere in MetaNN. A lot of logic that can be achieved in object-oriented implementations at runtime are implemented using template metaprogramming. For instance, in general, a deep learning framework introduces logic for runtime to realize automatic differentiation, while MetaNN uses compile-time computing solely to implement this part.

---

[3] Chapter 8 discusses it.

There are two reasons why we choose to implement such logic at compile time rather than runtime. On the one hand, the author hopes to practice relevant techniques of C++ template metaprogramming through the implementation of such complex logic; on the other hand, some implementation is caused by the occasion that demands it.

Traditional object-oriented C++ programming pays more attention to runtime. With the introduction of metaprogramming, we should focus more on both compile time and runtime. Compile-time computations are executed before runtime computations, which impacts far more than its literal meaning. It means that once we implement some logic using runtime techniques, it will be nearly impossible for us to introduce compile-time operations next after the previous logic is executed.

The author refers to this phenomenon as "playground" and "one-way road." Compile-time computing and runtime computing are like two playgrounds where we can play around, and we have many opportunities to move from the "playground" of compile time to the "playground" of runtime. But after that, it's hard to get back to the "playground" of compile time because the connection between the two is a one-way road.

The concept is embodied in MetaNN—our ultimate goal is to introduce compile-time computing for multi-operation co-optimization when evaluating. Before that, we should choose implementation solutions at any stage warily to prevent evaluation optimization from being hindered by the premature introduction of runtime logic. For example, we should declare the interfaces between forward and backward propagation as templates and utilize compile-time computations to achieve topological sorting in automatic differentiation—all of which are affected by this limitation.

The introduction of runtime logic is subtle sometimes. For instance, this book discusses the applications of expression templates in MetaNN—plenty of related literatures introduce a base class for expression templates, which specifies interfaces that expression templates should support. Introducing a base class is not a big issue and we also introduce *DynamicData* in MetaNN, which can also be treated as a base class for expression templates. However, when we reference an expression template object, whether to use a base class reference or a derived class instance is indeed the choice of whether to introduce runtime logic.

This book does not introduce *DynamicData* when discussing operation templates or utilize objects instantiated by this class template as parameters for operation templates—which also embodies the avoidance of premature introduction of runtime logic. *DynamicData* encapsulates specific classes in a derived means, which is equivalent to hiding some information of types that can be a serious problem for optimization at compile time. Readers can consider how to implement "multi-operation co-optimization" discussed in Chapter 8, if parameters of operation templates are all instances of the class template *DynamicData*.

Although the author tries to avoid introducing runtime constructs too early, it is inevitable to deal with runtime computations in advance in some cases. Also take *DynamicData* as an example: we should declare a domain in the class to hold the intermediate results. The author chose the implementation of "introducing base classes with derivation," which can also be regarded as a solution with few other choices.

## Different Ways to Use

The advantages of MetaNN are discussed earlier but the framework also has its "disadvantages": its interface is written in C++. Currently, the mainstream deep learning frameworks are usually based on C++, using scripting languages such as Python as an interface to interact with users, but MetaNN cannot take this form. It has to be admitted that it is relatively difficult to master C++

compared with scripting languages. Therefore, if only C++ interfaces are provided, then MetaNN may not be as widely used as other deep learning frameworks.

In fact, we can also introduce scripting languages such as Python to interact with users on the basis of C++ kernel in MetaNN. But it can seriously affect the performance of MetaNN: in order to achieve such interactions, Python needs to call the compiled C++ kernel, which means that Python calls cannot benefit from the compile-time calculation of C++. Most advantages of MetaNN come from compile-time computing, so introducing scripting languages for interaction in MetaNN would deprive the framework of its advantages.

However, if we want to introduce a relatively easy-to-use interaction environment, scripting languages like Python are not the only option. In fact, it is fairly possible to develop an integrated development environment that supports "drag and drop," allowing users to organize interlayer relationships through their mouse, which can further generate and compile the corresponding C++ code. Such a system might be more intuitive than using Python. Of course, in order to achieve a similar environment, we should also pay more efforts.

## Conclusion

We have also talked enough about MetaNN itself. But it has to be acknowledged that, for the time being, much of the discussion here is not supported by sufficient arguments. The author mentioned the distinctions between MetaNN and other frameworks, as well as the advantages and problems that such distinctions may bring in. However, whether the advantages introduced by these variations can be truly embodied and whether the corresponding problems can eventually become problems can only be testified if the whole framework is implemented relatively completely.

But as discussed in this book, MetaNN is only an initial implementation of a deep learning framework for the time being. Compared to a complete framework, it still lacks quite a lot of features—after all, it was constructed by the author using spare time. To achieve a complete framework, it requires developers with different expertise to form a team and collaborate. For example, developers mastering hardware programming, such as GPU/FPGA, are required to develop hardware-accelerated code; developers proficient in network programming are needed to develop environments for parallel training; for MetaNN, developers proficient in GUI programming might be demanded to develop interactive systems. It is quite burdensome to complete the entire development for one person. So here, the author wants to apologize to readers: as far as the deep learning framework itself is concerned, currently MetaNN just offers new design ideas for reference.

Similar to MetaNN, most contents of this book are organized through the author's own explorations—in this book, the author doesn't want to cover what has been discussed in other books. But writing like this is quite risky, because most contents merely come from the author's views. Therefore, something the author considers worth discussion might be biased in reality. Again, the author sincerely apologizes for this.

# Index